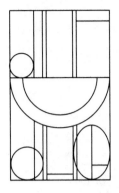

Language and Its Disturbances in Dreams

The Pioneering Work of Freud and Kraepelin Updated

Frank Heynick

A Wiley-Interscience Publication

John Wiley & Sons, Inc.

New York ■ Chichester ■ Brisbane ■ Toronto ■ Singapore

Publisher: *Tom Woll*
Editor: *Herb Reich*
Managing Editors: *Jacqueline A. Martin, Elizabeth Austin*
Editorial Supervision: *Amanda Hall and Lorraine Metcalf, Publication Services, Inc.*

This text is printed on acid-free paper.

Copyright © 1993 by John Wiley & Sons, Inc.

This publication is designed to provide accurate and
authoritative information in regard to the subject
matter covered. It is sold with the understanding that
the publisher is not engaged in rendering legal, accounting,
or other professional services. If legal advice or other
expert assistance is required, the services of a competent
professional person should be sought. *From a Declaration
of Principles jointly adopted by a Committee of the
American Bar Association and Committee of Publishers.*

Library of Congress Cataloging-in-Publication Data

Heynick, Frank
    Language and its disturbances in dreams: the pioneering work of
Freud and Kraepelin updated / Frank Heynick.
        p.   cm.
    "A Wiley-Interscience publication."
    Includes bibliographical references and index.
    ISBN 0-471-58653-6 (hard)
    1. Language and languages in dreams.   2. Language disorders in
dreams.   3. Kraepelin, Emil, 1856–1926.   4. Freud, Sigmund,
1856–1939.   5. Psycholinguistics.   I. Title.
BF1099.L35H49   1993
154.6' 3—dc20   92-34802
                                                                         CIP

Printed in the United States of America
10 9 8 7 6 5 4 3 2 1

Acknowledgments

The present work derives in large measure from my 1983 doctoral dissertation in medicine at the University of Groningen, carried out with the kind encouragement of dissertation advisers W. K. van Dijk, MD, then head of Groningen's Department of Psychiatry and Psychiatric Hospital, and Bernard Tervoort, then professor of Linguistics at the University of Amsterdam. Some of the dissertation and of the present book was written at the Department of Psychology and Language of the Eindhoven University of Technology, and I wish particularly to mention Jan B. Dijkstra of Eindhoven's Computing Sciences Department, who, along with Dr. Willem van den Burg of Groningen's Department of Neuropsychology, gave me his kind assistance in statistical matters.

The newly discovered, three-quarters-of-a-century-old dream speech specimens of Emil Kraepelin were kindly entrusted to me by the Max Planck Institute of Psychiatry in Munich. For this opportunity and their hospitality I am grateful to Detlev Ploog, MD, then head of the Institute for Clinical Research, and to Dr. Hartmut Schulz. One of my trips to Munich to research these specimens was made possible by a grant (number R30-251) from the ZWO, the Netherlands Organization for Scientific Research.

Because this book involves the interface of so many different disciplines, I am particularly grateful to the various experts in the Netherlands and abroad who looked over and commented on portions of the dissertation and present book. Let me specifically thank Dr. David Foulkes (dream research expert) of the Georgia Institute of Mental Health, Dr. Cees van den Berg (psychiatry history specialist) of Groningen's Psychiatry Department, and Dr. Norbet Corver (linguist) and Dr. Karel van Wijk (language psychologist) of the Language and Literature Department of the University of Tilburg.

The names of several other people who have helped in this project will appear in relevant parts of this book.

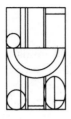

Foreword

Sigmund Freud and Emil Kraepelin, both born in 1856 and both destined to leave their mark on the psychiatry of our age, shunned each other in their own lifetimes. Although they shared a genuine interest in human language, they did so for quite different reasons.

Everybody is familiar with the Freudian slip, a *lapsus linguae* revealing a speaker's secret or unconscious thought to a listener, often producing an embarrassing or witty effect. In his publication *Jokes and Their Relation to the Unconscious,* Freud (1905/1960a) quotes Kraepelin's paper "Zur Psychologie des Komischen," in which it is concluded that not every deceived expectation has a comical effect, but only those unexpected intellectual contrasts that arouse a mainly pleasurable inner conflict of sensuous, ethical, and logical feelings. Yet despite this common interest in humor, Freud's and Kraepelin's focuses on language were very different. For Freud, his early neurolinguistic studies notwithstanding, it revolved around the neuroses and the "psychological," whereas Kraepelin was concerned with the psychoses and the organic.

So it was, too, with their interest in dreams. For Freud the content of dreaming was, as is well known, a coded "message" from the unconscious. Intentional joking, unintentional everyday slips of the tongue during daytime consciousness, and dreaming during nighttime (subsequently consciously reported in words) lay on a sort of continuum. Differences were largely matters of degree. But Kraepelin saw dreams as basically a neuronal phenomenon, devoid of "messages."

If this book were about either language only or dreams only, there would be little reason for having Freud's and Kraepelin's names together in the title. But this book concerns language (and its disturbances) *in* dreams. The literature on dreams has traditionally exhibited a systematic deafness to their verbal language, although dialogues and other utterances have abounded in dream reports since ancient times, and many works with such names "Die Sprache des Traumes," "La Langue des Rêves," and "A Grammar of Dreams" have made use of the language *metaphor.* Freud and Kraepelin are the two exceptions, albeit exceptions of quite different sorts. Their observations on the functioning of our verbal faculties in dreams deserve thorough consideration today, in light of current models of human language production that are far more sophisticated than those of their own time.

Freud directly addressed the question of the nature and genesis of verbal material in dreams, seeking to accommodate it within the overall psychoanalytic dream theory by means of his "replay hypothesis," as it is termed in this book. This maintains, in essence, that the dream itself cannot create speech. The conversations or dialogues one hears and says are basically composed of utterances heard or said recently in wakefulness, recorded in memory and "played back" at appropriate moments in the dream scenario. With this concept— reminiscent of the recurring utterances of certain types of motor aphasia, and apparently connected with his early neurolinguistic studies, although never acknowledged as such—Freud denied to dream speech that quality of verbal language that Chomsky, half a century later, would call "linguistic creativity."

In his consideration of Freud's replay hypothesis, Frank Heynick contrasts it with Kraepelin's detailed study of dream speech, which might, ironically, be seen as fitting into Freud's overall psychoanalytic model of dream generation in a far better and less ad hoc manner than the specimens Freud himself provided. Kraepelin's 1906 monograph *Über Sprachstörungen im Traume*, presented in this book for the first time in English translation, is based on 286 specimens of "dream speech," almost all of which are semantically or syntactically deviant by waking standards. Deviance was in fact Kraepelin's selection criterion for the many utterances he scrawled in a tablet at his bedside, gladly availing himself of the opportunity for the firsthand study of language processes under transient "neuropathological" conditions. Among Kraepelin's assumptions was that the biological protection of sleep demanded the "impeding of the penetration into consciousness" of external verbal stimuli. This would be brought about by a reduction in the performance of Wernicke's area, resulting in a high degree of word-deafness. In addition, larger parts of the cortical mantle would be depressed.

But for all his neuroanatomical interest, Kraepelin was also concerned with what would today be called psycholinguistics. Quite possibly under the influence of his teacher Wilhelm Wundt, who published two substantial volumes on language in 1900, Kraepelin proposed a process of sentence generation that is not very dissimilar to some quite recent models. Seeing the advantages of viewing speech production as a "series of subprocesses which are separate from one another and capable of being disturbed independently," he classified his dream speech corpus into two global categories: disturbances of thought (clarity and correct ordering of the idea in mind) and disturbances of speech proper (incorrect syntax or agrammatism). It was within this global system that Kraepelin related hallucinated sleep utterances to certain psycholinguistic as well as neuropathological characteristics of aphasias and of various forms of psychotic speech.

Dr. Heynick's translations, which also include publications by Kraepelin's con-temporaries, will—like the rest of the book—be welcomed by linguists and language psychologists, as well as psychiatrists and dream researchers. This is especially so of those for whom the German originals are inaccessible. How-ever, also included is some historical material never before published in any language, and this makes the appearance of this book all the more gratifying to us at the Max Planck Institute of Psychiatry here in Munich. Our institute was founded by Kraepelin in 1917 (then called the Deutsche Forschungsanstalt für Psychiatrie) and headed by him until his death in 1926. Kraepelin lingers on in our buildings not just in spirit but in the form of various relics. These include the approximately three hundred specimens of dream speech that he continued to scribble down on little slips of paper in the twenty years *after* the publication of his 1906 monograph, right up to his death. During one of his several visits to our institute, Dr. Heynick was, in view of his expertise in the field, entrusted with evaluating and providing English translations for these specimens. The reader will find the results in this book along with the newly discovered German originals.

Some three-quarters of a century ago, as director of our institute, Kraepelin (1920) wrote:

> It will be necessary to search for the roots and the manifestations of our inner lives everywhere—in the souls of children, of primitive men, of animals. Furthermore, it will be necessary to establish to what degree lost emotions of the individual and of the phylogenetic past are reborn in illness. (p. 29)

The Max Planck Institute of Psychiatry has indeed for several years now also been concerned with the behavior of our closest primate relatives, in-cluding the neurobiology of their vocal communication. Our observations and neuroanatomical studies have endeavored to elucidate the gap between mere vocal communication (something we share with simian species and many other vertebrates) and speech, the tandem use of voice and verbal language, which is unique to *Homo sapiens* (see Emrich & Wiegand, 1991). In recent years we have also conducted extensive research on the vocal development of in-fants, as well as on dysphonia and dysarthria. In this regard it is interesting to note from this book that both Freud and Kraepelin postulated that the peculiar neurological state of dreaming involves dramatic phylogenetic or ontogenetic regression in our language faculties, although they were far from agreement as to the form this would take.

In the final part of this book, the author sets himself the task of resolv-ing some contradictory issues. Is dream speech lacking in what we today term "linguistic creativity," as Freud maintained? Or is dream speech characterized by the kinds of ungrammaticality and "Freudian" condensations and displacements presented, ironically, by the non-Freudian Kraepelin but not by Freud himself? For this purpose, two major experiments were conducted, similar in spirit to Kraeplin's and his colleague Alfred Hoche's but with a large subject pool and following strict protocols. The first yielded several hundred utterances from "good dream recallers" adhering to specific instructions by which, after being awakened by an alarm clock, they wrote down the last utterance they had heard or said in the dream; if any. In the second experiment, volunteers were randomly awakened by telephone late at night or in the early morning, so that their dreams, which included over two hundred dream speech specimens, could be elicited and recorded.

The subsequent analysis has, for the time being at least, resolved the differences between Freud and Kraepelin, by declaring that neither of their concepts properly characterizes dream speech. The virtual absence of ungrammaticality—there is in fact also indication of a syntactic complexity comparable to that of wakeful speech—or of widespread verbal condensations and displacements, makes these corpora quite dissimilar to Kraepelin's highly selective ones. As such, these new dream speech utterances in fact more closely resemble those in Freud's *Traumdeutung*. But, unfortunately for Freud, the experiments give very little indication of their being "replayed"—a result that impinges upon some basic tenets of the psychoanalytic dream theory. In fact, the author shows that most of even very recent dream theories, whether neo-Freudian or anti-Freudian, are, each in its own way, generally quite deficient when accounting for the continued functioning of our linguistic capacities at night at a level apparently comparable to wakefulness.

In one sense, however, Dr. Heynick does take sides between Kraepelin and Freud. This book endeavors to carry on more in Kraepelin's spirit, by employing modern psycholinguistic views to understand the mental information processing that underlies our uniquely human capacity for speech. Whereas Freud has dominated the science of dreams for most of this century, the future may look upon his contemporary Kraepelin as a forerunner of a new trend in dream research that strives to contribute to the cognitive sciences, such as linguistics, as well as to psychopathology and brain science. The new trend and its old roots are captured excellently in this book.

Prof. Detlev Ploog M.D. (recent successor to Emil Kraepelin)
Director Emeritus
Institute for Clinical Research
Max Planck Institute of Psychiatry
Munich

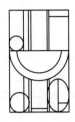

Contents

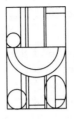

Introduction

*We psychiatrists . . . should be better at understanding
and translating the language of dreams if we knew
more about the development of language*
—Freud, "The Antithetical Meaning of Primal Words"

Find out about dreams, and you'll find out about insanity.
—John Hughlings Jackson

Almost as old as writing itself are records attesting to the fact that dreams are more than just series of images—that, to use a modern metaphor, a dream need not be a "silent movie," that it may also include a "sound track." And that, while this sound track may contain various auditory impressions, it usually abounds in verbal material. Yet from modern dream researchers back to ancient oneiromancists, we find almost no consideration of the nature of the verbal content of dreams.

Many thousands of books have been written on the subject of verbal language, three of them by Sigmund Freud. And there have certainly been many hundreds of books on dreams, two by Freud. But virtually none of these has been devoted to the *interaction* of verbal language and dreams. True, Freud and a few other authors on dreams and on language have given at least some thought to this matter in their writings. But the real exception to the deafness to verbal activity in dreams was the co-founder of modern psychiatry, Emil Kraepelin, who published a hundred-page monograph *Über Sprachstörungen im Traume* in the first decade of the twentieth century. My English translation, *On Speech Disorders in Dreams*, is, along with translations of some other relevant material from Kraepelin and his colleagues, therefore given a central place, literally and to a good extent figuratively as well, in the present work.

The rest, the main portion, of this book, now appearing in the last decade of the same century, represents, to my knowledge, the first major work since Kraepelin's devoted to the topic of verbal language in dreams. The time is,

1

I feel, particularly ripe. The theme of the interaction of psychoanalysis with linguistics has been in the air since the seventies. Evidently inspired by the Chomskyan revolution, comparisons have been made between the Freudian dream model and the transformational-generative linguistic model. But more importantly, the previous decade has witnessed an increasing trend toward collaboration between dream research and the cognitive sciences, of which linguistics and psycholinguistics are of course a part.

Part One of this book begins with a consideration of views on the (semiotic) "language" of dreams through the ages, and particularly in the years around the turn of the twentieth century, when Freud was writing his *Traumdeutung* and Kraepelin his *Über Sprachstörungen im Traume*. The various views on dreams are compared and contrasted with views held on speech.

It was Freud who—with some very new twists—revived the ancient diagnostic-medical use of dreams. The folds and convolutions gradually laid down in the hominid cortex in the last few million years of evolution have, especially when confronted with the rapid development of culture and modern civilization, resulted in a multilayered labyrinth of psychological complexes unknown to our simian ancestors and other relatives on the phylogenetic tree. Interference in the process of verbal language, the apex of this cerebral evolution, could yield signs of the inner nature of these complexes. But it was particularly by the events of dreams that symptoms were supposedly revealed that, when interpreted by the skillful medical specialist, could pinpoint specific forms of neurosis. In opposition to the prevailing scientific zeitgeist, Freud thus maintained that dreams do indeed carry information. But he just as strongly opposed the ancient and still-popular belief that the semiotic language of dream events is somehow divine or otherwise above normal human understanding. The new psychoanalytic approach maintained that dream symbolization is in fact below our comprehension: The condensations and displacements that make dreams so dreamlike are an ontogenetic (and by extension, phylogenetic) retrogression in our cognitive processes.

But what of the verbal language *in* dreams? For Freud, the content of dialogue between dream personages could be a key element in the medical-diagnostic process. Here is one example (which will not be considered further in this book): After listening to a somewhat rabble-rousing speech by the Austrian premier in his "Count Thun" dream, Freud escapes from the auditorium, and, wishing to leave Vienna as well, orders a cabdriver to take him to the station. But at a certain point Freud informs him, rather cryptically, *"Of course, I can't drive with you along the railway line itself."* Freud's extensive analysis of this bit of dialogue highlighted not only his political and social sentiments towards aristocratic politicians "in the driver's seat"; it also pointed to a childish sibling rivalry with his brother, with whom he had, as a sort of punishment, recently canceled a planned vacation, and who, when travelling with Freud in a cab the evening before, had gotten out early at a suburban railway station even though he could just as easily have accompanied Freud to the main line station.

But whatever the psychological significance of its content, the form and structure of dream dialogue such as the above are generally mundane — therefore lacking in those condensations and displacements characteristic of other (visual) dream events. The fact that dream utterances are generally not anomalous by wakeful standards made them anomalous within the psychoanalytic dream theory. How could the supposedly retrogressive ("primary process") dreaming state generate evolutionarily advanced ("secondary process") speech? The former aphasiologist Freud tried to resolve this dilemma by maintaining that speech in dreams is a retrogression nevertheless, albeit of a quite special kind. Freud's remark to the cabdriver in his dream was, he claimed in the *Traumdeutung*, basically an infantlike mimicry of elements of a real conversation he had had with his brother the day before. As such the dream speech was lacking in (to use a modern, Chomskyan, term) "linguistic creativity."

For Emil Kraepelin, who dealt with psychotics rather than neurotics, and who was fundamentally part of a quite different — somatic and nosological — tradition from Freud's, dreams and dream speech were not diagnostic instruments. They were not presumed to reveal the underlying nature and etiology of afflictions affecting the dreamer's functioning in the wakeful state. They were however "pathological" for Kraepelin in the sense that they supposedly represented, even in the sanest person, a safe, nightly lapse into conditions that in the daytime would affect psychotic patients. As such, dreams — and hypnagogic dreamlets — afforded the inquisitive psychiatrist firsthand personal experience. To paraphrase Hughling Jackson's dictum: "Find out about dream speech, and you will find out about the speech of the insane."

Ironically, the "Freudian" features of condensations, displacements, and disjunctions, seldom found in the dream speech of Freud's own reports, abound in Kraepelin's. On the other hand, Kraepelin, unlike Freud, in no way suggests that his dream speech specimens are basically a form of mimicry. The vast discrepancy between the findings of these two greats of twentieth-century psychiatry is perhaps not surprising in view of their quite different objectives. Perhaps also to be expected, therefore, was that a new, systematic series of dream speech studies, using a large pool of subjects, would yield data (presented in Part Three of this book) quite at variance with both Freud's *and* Kraepelin's on many crucial points. Dream speech (at least as recalled) seems in fact not only to be lexically, morphologically, and syntactically well formed and generally in keeping with the dream context, but also to be linguistically creative.

For Freud the distinction between primary processes (such as dreaming) and secondary processes (such as language) was central to the development of his model of the psyche, with its id and ego (and later superego) components. In light of the new findings—that our language faculties can apparently function very well *within* dreaming—revised models of the psyche will be considered later in this book that are neo-Freudian, or at least in the general spirit of Freudian psychology in that they conceptualize the mind as being, in the words of the late Arthur M. Arkin (1981, p. 288) "constructed of descriptively unconscious and conscious interactive components with widely varying degrees of interdependence, interrelatedness, and hierarchical organization in which the various components have subordinate and superordinate relations to one another, in themselves subject to change over time." Although these models are not primarily models of dreaming, their descriptions of the interaction of conscious and unconscious layers of the psyche explicitly or implicitly extend to the dreaming state.

Subsequently, several models of dreaming per se—most of them non-Freudian or anti-Freudian—will likewise be considered for their ability to account for the above characteristics of dream speech. In almost all cases the verdict is the same as with Freud's theory. Dream speech remains an anomaly. It is an essential piece in the larger puzzle of our dream life which must be accommodated in an unforced and non–ad hoc manner by any model of dreaming pretending to completeness.

But the importance of the study of our linguistic activity in dreams is not limited to our nightly life. By its nature, dream speech tells us not only about the "stuff (and processes) which dreams are made of," but also about the stuff and processes that go into the production of normal waking speech and, to the extent that dream speech is deviant, of abnormal waking speech as well. While agreeing with Freud that a knowledge of psycholinguistics is a great asset to dream research, we might also offer this paraphrase of his quote: We linguists and language psychologists should be better at understanding the development and nature of language if we knew more about the nature of dream speech. This book will hopefully point to the potential mutual benefits of collaboration among dream researchers, psychiatrists, psycholinguists, and other cognitive scientists.

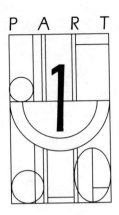

Dreams and Language
Around the Turn
of the Twentieth Century

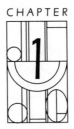

Homo Loquens
and Homo Somniens

The label *Homo loquens*, or talking man, has proven at least as appropriate as *Homo sapiens* for distinguishing our species from the other branches and twigs of the phylogenetic tree. Well over a hundred years ago, Charles Darwin (1871/1981, p. 57) wrote of the evolutionary "relation between the continued use of language and the development of the brain," stating that "the mental powers in some early progenitor of man must have been more highly developed than in any existing ape, before even the most imperfect form of speech could have come into use. . . ." This did not, however, mean that there was any shortage of "talking" animals around the turn of the twentieth century. The most famous of these was the German horse Clever Hans, supposedly capable of correctly responding to verbal questions and arithmetic problems by tapping out answers with his hooves on a special board composed of numbers and letters. However, systematic investigations by Prof. Oskar Pfungst of the Berlin Psychological Institute soon revealed that Hans was in fact responding not to the questions themselves but to unintentional subliminal cues from the questioners and spectators. (See Sebeok & Umiker-Sebeok, 1979.)

Speech and Dreaming
along the Developmental Scale

The uniquely human nature of language was taken up by, among others, Wilhelm Wundt (1900), founder of experimental psychology, indeed of the whole new science of psychology. The first volume of his work *Völkerpsychologie*, which like Freud's *Interpretation of Dreams* carries the publication date of the new century, is entitled *Die Sprache* (Language). In it, Wundt doubts whether (with the possible exception of some transitional gestures on the part of apes) animals are capable of even the most basic "naming" function of language in the form of pointing. But more important was Wundt's analysis of human

7

language on the syntactic level: His use of hierarchical tree diagrams for sentences formalized the concept that the manifest word order (*"äußere Sprachform"*) is a reflection of a more abstract structure (*"innere Sprachform"*) containing dependency relations, optional deletions, and the like. Such characteristics were believed by Wundt not only to be uniquely bound to man's cognitive capacities, but also, in turn, to influence the way humans (as a species) think, and (to the extent that morpho-syntactic structures vary from language to language) the cultures that people form—a concept later to be known as linguistic relativity. (See Heynick, 1983b.)

Let us now make an abrupt transition from verbal language to a seemingly completely different medium, but one that has often been viewed as a language of sorts. Consider the newly coined label, *Homo somniens*, or man the dreamer. Might the capacity not just to sleep, but "perchance to dream," likewise serve as a special distinguisher of our species?

It has been observed since antiquity (for example by the Roman philosopher Lucretius [1987] in 44 B.C.) that various animals, most obviously dogs and cats, make vocal noises in their sleep and show small movements in their extremities. May one then conclude that they are dreaming? The problem is obviously that, because these creatures lack the phenomenon of verbal language, they can never report to us their experiences, and we can do no more than speculate about them. As stated by Norman Malcolm (one of a long line of philosophers, extending back at least to Aristotle, to consider the array of issues raised by the phenomenology of dreams), "We say of a dog when he whines and twitches his feet in his sleep, 'He must be dreaming': [but] there is no question of what he will tell us when he wakes up" (1959, p. 62).[1]

Apart from this practical matter, however, there have been through the ages other considerations affecting the belief in whether or not dreaming is uniquely human.

The Dreaming Spirit and the Dreaming Body ───────

In the *Weltanschauung* of many primitive peoples, the idea of animals' dreaming would seem quite out of place. It was probably with the very emergence of *Homo loquens*, when humans acquired the ability to reflect on and discuss their dreams, that they began seeking explanations for their nocturnal experiences and particularly those "dreamlike" aspects that so differ from the realities of waking life. It is plausible that the phenomenology of dreams gave rise to the so very widespread notion of spirits which are only casually attached to a physical body, if at all (cf. Wundt, 1906; Jones, 1951). In any event, a common theme in societies ranging from the preagricultural to the preindustrial is that nocturnal reveries are of divine origin or, as was particularly the case in medieval Europe, demonic (cf. Van de Castle, 1973). And although some cultures believed that supernatural beings could also bring dreams to animals and even to inanimate objects, other societies considered such communication with the gods to be a prerogative of the human soul.

This, however, is not to say that the communication was intelligible. Because, apparently, the inhabitants of the other spheres do not conform to the principles of natural verbal languages, their messages transcend normal human understanding; hence the bizarreness of dreams. In primitive and ancient societies the translation of dream language into human verbal language was typically the exclusive province of the shaman-medicineman and the priest-physician. The supposed diagnostic, prognostic, and curative power of the supernatural messages accounts for this "medical" aspect (cf. Haskell, 1985).

Yet even in ancient times, this supernatural medical view began to be interwoven with a more physiological medical explanation for the dreamlike quality of dreams. Around 330 B.C., Aristotle (1987) wrote that "the movements which occur in the daytime within the body are, unless great and violent, lost sight of, in contrast with the waking movements, which are more impressive. In sleep, the opposite takes place, for even triffling [internal] movements seem considerable" (p. 130). A dream of thunder and lightning, Aristotle tells us, may be an exaggeration of ringing in the ears. A dream of fire may be a magnification of fever or the calor (heat of infection) of some organ of the body. Honey or other sweet tastes in a dream may derive from phlegm in the esophagus. Here, too, the services of a specialist are obviously required, not only to interpret the exaggerated manifestations of the symptoms, but also to sort out other physiologically caused distortions that might confound the diagnosis. Cicero (1987) writes of Plato's and the Pythagoreans' prohibition against the eating of beans before sleep. The gastric distress causes "error and confusion" and induces a "condition at war with the soul in search of truth" (p. 135).

The Age of Reason in the West had as a direct consequence the further downgrading of the supernatural explanation of the dreamlike features of dreams in favor of the physical, at least among intellectuals. (Among the common people, more primitive beliefs lingered in various guises.) The great seventeenth-century Dutch philosopher Baruch Spinoza (1677/1955, p. 326) wrote that the interpreting of dreams as oracles from heaven is as great a "childish absurdity" as the reading of the entrails of beasts. And, while providing what were perhaps the greatest pre-Freudian insights into the working of the psyche, Spinoza (1677/1951, p. 4) rebelled against his Talmudic forebears by likening dreams to deleria caused by "fevers and other bodily ailments," similar to the way in which his materialist British contemporary Thomas Hobbes attributed dreams to the "distemper of inward parts" (quoted in Van de Castle, 1973, p. 28).

Speculation continued in the same vein throughout the nineteenth century, although advances in physiology led to some increase in sophistication. In 1831 a French physician, one Dr. Pierquin of Montpellier, directly observed the sleeping brain of a woman with pathological destruction of part of the skull and the dura encephali, and is reported to have noticed engorgement in her cortical arteries at various times of the night, which imparted a reddish color, rather similar to that of wakefulness. Pierquin appears to have correctly speculated that this state went hand in hand with dreaming (Comb, 1841; Lemattre, 1870).

The theme of blood flow to the brain in dreaming, wakefulness, and nondreaming sleep was taken up a couple of decades later by the German scientist Ernst Kohlschütter (1869), who compared the first to a pathological state:

> We now know that hallucinations [of mental patients in wakefulness] owe their genesis to changes in circulation. . . . We are now justified in regarding dreams, too, as symptoms of a sporadic and partial wakeful-like modification of the brain circulation in the midst of the general slowing down of this circulation [in sleep]. The location in the brain where this occurs, and the degree to which it approaches the conditions of wakefulness, determines the nature and vividness of the dream and depends in turn on the nature and areas of the peripheral stimulus which gave rise to their genesis through the vascular-nervous center. (p. 46)

Alternatively, the supposedly meaningless hallucinations of dreams were ascribed to toxins in the bloodstream that washed the cerebrum and randomly irritated certain memory cells. Or perhaps, as one prominent hypothesis (Preyer, 1876) went, there was a metabolic need that such toxins, assumed to accumulate in wakefulness as a product of mental and physical exertion, be *oxydized* at night, with a consequent reduction of oxygen supplied by the blood to the sensitive gray matter of the cortex.

Obviously this new emphasis on physiology was not at all likely to signal a return to the ancient medical art of interpreting thunder and lightning as tinnitus. The above physiological changes supposedly led to such an increase in "entropy" (to introduce a term from the nineteenth-century physicist Ludwig Boltzmann) in the cerebral system during dreaming, that there was about as much information in a dream as in a well-shuffled deck of tarot cards. The strangeness of dreams was, in the words of Alfred Maury, a contemporary pioneer in the phenomenological description of dreams, like "the ten fingers of a man who knows nothing of music wandering over the keys of a piano" (quoted in Hobson, 1988).

Even those members of the scientific community who speculated that dream*ing* has a biological function were apt to deny any meaning to dreams. The famed late-nineteenth-century British neurologist John Hughlings Jackson (1911/1958) may have been the first to suggest a relation between dreams and *memory*: the clearing off of some mnemonic traces and the consolidation and maintenance of others. One of Jackson's contemporaries, the German physiologist W. Robert (1886), specifically emphasized the supposed waste-disposal function of dreaming, indicated by the apparent incoherence of dream content, which so often includes trivial residues from the preceding day.

Such a demoting of dreams as regards human intellectual activity, usually on physiological grounds, would naturally make the question of whether animals, too, dream a rather moot point. However, toward the end of the last century certain dissenting voices were claiming that human dreams nevertheless carry a message. Significantly enough, these were often from people somehow involved with our unique capacity for *language,* or tending to use *linguistic analogies* rather than the energy metaphors common in scientific thinking in the age of electrification. Thus the poet Ralph Waldo Emerson wrote in 1884, "Sleep . . . arms us with a terrible freedom, so that every will rushes to a deed. A skillful man reads his dreams for his self-knowledge" (quoted in Van de Castle, 1973, p. 30). The psychologist James Sully stated in 1893, "We may assure, perhaps, that in each case the dream was the expansion and complete development of a vague fugitive wish of the waking mind. . . . Like some letter in cipher, the dream inscription when scrutinized closely loses its first look of balderdash and takes on the aspect of a serious, intelligible message" (ibid, p. 30).

Nevertheless, dreams seemed well on their way to being consigned by the scientific establishment to the human mental wastebasket. Then, at the turn of the twentieth century, the medical-diagnostic view was granted a new lease on life for many decades to come by a neurophysiologist who had also made somewhat of a name for himself as a language pathologist.

Note

1. Similarly, Jean Piaget (1951/1962, pp. 176–177) states that "a dog which growls in its sleep is not necessarily evoking mental images, and its 'dream' can be interpreted in terms of mere sensory-motor automatisms." (Piaget does, however, consider it more likely that chimpanzees have images in dreams, due to their "rudimentary symbolic power.")

Freud and Regressed
Dream Speech

Whereas no one need be told that Sigmund Freud was the father of the "Freudian slip," it is far less well known, to professionals and laymen alike, that this represents but one facet of a half century of theorizing on speech disturbances and on the psychology of language in general. This theorizing not only predated Freud's work on dreams, but, more importantly, appears to have had a definite influence upon it. Much of our treatment will therefore be to compare and contrast Freud's attitide toward normal, pathological, and even poetic speech on the one hand, and his views on the semiotic "language" of dreams on the other. Ultimately, of course, our concern will be with Freud's consideration of that peculiar phenomenon of speech *in* dreams.

Speech as Opposed to Dream "Language" in Psychoanalysis

Freud's prepsychoanalytic *On Aphasia*, (1891/1953b) was an important, if unrevolutionary, contribution to neurolinguistics, and he has been described as, historically speaking, the first *Jung-Grammatiker* ("neo-grammarian") neurologist (Marshall, 1974). By bringing to the study of aphasia the "psychologization" of linguistics and neurology advocated by Chaim Steintal's school and its successors—along with their emphasis on levels of representation, formal features, and subfeatures and on the interplay with factors such as short-term memory—Freud made significant advances in the diagnostic differentiation of true organic aphasia from hysterical speech impairments. When Freud went on to develop psychoanalysis, his concern with language psychology did not cease, but rather shifted more from anatomical to topological models of the mind. Among the most notable works of Freud's psychoanalytic period that treat language disturbances and language psychology are his *Psychopathology of Everyday Life* (1901/1960b), dealing with "normal" slips of the tongue and neurotic symptom formation, and *Jokes and Their Relation to the Unconscious*

(1905/1960a), treating verbal aesthetics. An array of Freud's other writings, extending to his final works, his *Moses and Monotheism* (1939/1964a), published in the last year of his life, and *An Outline of Psychoanalysis* (1940/1964c), which appeared posthumously the following year, concern language, its role in ontogenetic and phylogenetic development, and its place in, in the words of one of Freud's first analysands, the "talking cure."

Freud has, of course, been widely criticized by recent generations of brain scientists for his use of pressure and energy concepts (the Freudian term "psychodynamics" especially conjures up images of forces and vectors), now known to be quite misleading for characterizing actual cerebral functioning. But on the other hand, Freud's lifelong linguistic interests led him, when considering our nocturnal mental abilities, to treat dreaming as a language of sorts, and he made ample use of linguistic and grammar, rather than energy, metaphors. As he states in the *Traumdeutung* (1900/1953a):

> [T]he dream-content seems like a transcript of the [underlying] dream-thoughts into another mode of expression, whose characters and *syntactic laws* [italics added] it is our business to discover by comparing the original and the translation. (p. 277)

The position on dreams that Sigmund Freud took in this book can in certain ways be seen as a remarkable synthesis of the contemporary scientific approach and the ancient and still popular dreams-have-meaning views. Let us consider here the contemporary scientific side. (The dreams-have-meaning aspect will be discussed in detail in the next section.) Drawing upon a combination of, on the one hand, inductions based on his clinical observations of his patients and on his own self-analysis and introspection, and, on the other hand, deductions derived from his physiological investigations and assumptions about the nervous system (exemplified in his hundred-page draft, *Project for a Scientific Psychology* [1966], written in 1895 and making full use of Santiago Ramón y Cajal's and Heinrich von Waldeyer's newly introduced concept of the neuron and of Hermann von Helmholtz's electrophysical biology), Freud concluded that dreaming was a *retrogressive* phenomenon. Specifically, it was a debasement of speech, a throwback to a *preverbal* mode of thinking. (See Heynick, 1985, for a detailed discussion of the influence of turn-of-the-century neurology upon the verbal aspects of the psychoanalytic dream theory.)

Speech held no less pride of place in the Freudian scheme than in the esteem of Darwin and Wundt. Freud termed it a *secondary process*, to be grouped along with intellectual operations such as mathematical calculations and critical judgment as being governed by the laws of grammar and formal logic. The secondary processes are, theoretically, characteristic of the conscious thinking of the normal adult human during wakefulness. Even when we are not talking aloud, our healthy thinking is, in a sense, an "internalized speech," a speaking in oneself. Subvocal discharges of neural energy, Freud writes in the *Project*, "put thought-processes on a level with perceptual processes, lend them reality and *make memory of them possible*" (1895/1966, p. 366). It was in fact one of Freud's neurophysiologically derived assumptions that human subvocal cognitive processes along a "train of thought" cause, by their stimulation of the neuronal complexes of the words associated with the various concepts, attention in the form of minute quantities of neuronal energy from the "ego" system of neurons to be directed to these cognitive processes as if they were actual objects. This, according to Freud's *Project*, permits higher-level "critical thought": the conscious exploring of alternative pathways within certain bounds of logic, which is characteristic of *Homo sapiens*. As Freud expressed it some years later in his important essay, "The Unconscious" (1915/1957c, p. 202), "By being linked with words, cathexes [neuronal energy] can be provided with quality even though they represent only *relations* between presentations of objects." It is such relations—the "ifs," "ands," and "buts," together with negative particles, prepositions, and the like—that help "bring about a higher psychical organization and make it possible for the primary process to be succeeded by the secondary process." (See Figure 2.1 for a graphical representation of Freud's neuroanatomical model of wakefulness.)

That internal as well as external verbal language never ceased in Freud's thinking to top the phylogenetic hierarchy as a uniquely human activity can be seen from the following passage from *Moses and Monotheism* (1939/1964a), written almost a half century after the *Project*:

> The development of speech . . . resulted in such an extraordinary advancement in intellectual activities. The new realm of intellectuality was opened up in which ideas, memories, and inferences became decisive, in contrast to the lower psychical activity which had direct perceptions by the same sense organs as its content. This was unquestionably one of the most important stages on the path to hominization [*Menschwerdung*]. (p. 113)

As for *dreaming* along the phylogenetic scale, Freud had little to say about it. Yet he seems not to have assumed that the experience is confined to humans. His statement in the *Traumdeutung*, "I do not myself know what animals dream of" (1900/1953a, p. 131), does not seem to question whether they do so in the first place. Elsewhere Freud (1920/1955b) also comments on the development of the function of dreams in the course of human evolution. That dreaming may be phylogenetically widespread, whereas speech is definitely unique to the postinfantile human, is consistent with the relative positions that Freud assigned to them on the developmental hierarchy. Dreaming is *au fond* not a secondary, but a *primary process*. It is assumed to arise in the unconscious and be largely typified by the same organization (or, rather, lack of organization) that is theoretically characteristic of the darker regions

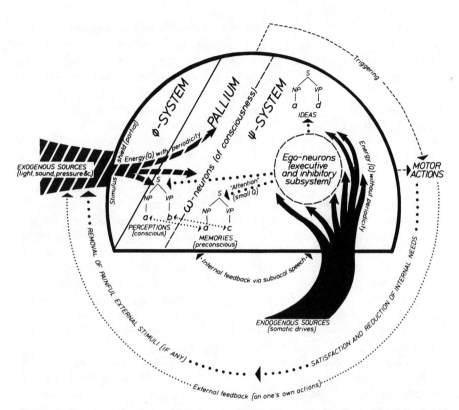

FIGURE 2.1 Schematic representation of the neuroanatomical model of the mind in *wakefulness* in Freud's (1895–96) *Project.* Increase in energy (Q) in the system is experienced as unpleasure, its reduction as pleasure. The homeostatic principle is represented by an evolved reflex arc, whose goal is to keep the overall system's Q to the minimum necessary to energize the "ego" subsystem. The strong ego, in turn, seeks to bind incoming Q from somatic sources. This permits the "secondary processes": the delay of the triggering of motoric actions (attempts at gratification) until sufficient identity is obtained between an incoming perception (with its "subject" [NP] and "predicate" [VP] components) in the neurons of consciousness and a preconscious memory of previous statisfaction. Any tendency towards hallucination of gratification by outward-flowing endogenous Q is further inhibited by the inflow of exogenous Q. "Attention" is drawn to perceptions in the form of small quantities of Q from the ego. The process of comparison, as well as higher-level, secondary-process cognitizing, is assisted by the energizing of word sound-images linked to concepts. This internal speech likewise draws attention from the ego, even when no motoric speech occurs. Actual motoric acts (including articulated speech) can be checked on through external feedback. Learning from experience involves the facilitating of synapses and the reorganization of nets on the neuronal level. (From F. Heynick, 1985, p. 328.)

of the mind: a play of condensation, displacement, and symbolization. Freud thus resolved the mystery of the dreamlike nature of dreams in a manner with more explicatory value than a simple recourse to irregular cerebral blood circulation and random irritations of brain cells by blood-borne toxins. The misconception in the primitive and popular views of a special language of dreams was in their assuming that the dreamlike features of dreams are of supernatural origin and above normal human understanding, when in fact they are *below* it. For the postinfantile human, dreaming is, in the Freudian scheme, at least a partial nightly *regression* to a preverbal form of thinking. (Figure 2.2 gives a representation of Freud's model of dreaming.)

Freud himself did not go into detail as to the developmental aspects in the infant that supposedly determine the primary-process characteristics. The task has, however, been taken up by later psychoanalytic theorists (cf. especially Noy, 1969), drawing partial, if far from unequivocal, support from the studies of Jean Piaget (1937, 1951/1962). If there is *condensation* in adult dreams—for example, a single image composed of two different faces—it is because, according to the psychoanalytic scheme of ontogenetic development, the young infant perceives as a single flux certain objects associated with a given affective state of drive satisfaction, such as feeding. If there is *displacement* and *symbolization* in adult dreams, it is because, even though the developing infant may have gone on to differentiate objects, one object can stand for another when both are associated with an affective state (for example, bottle, milk, mother), or when, at a slightly later stage, they become linked by certain superficial external attributes (for example, breast, balloon). Similar to this is symbolization *pars pro toto*, whereby one specific feature (nipple) comes to represent the whole (breast, mother). And if adult dreams take liberties in their *spacing and ordering of events*, it is because the infant, less given to linear sequencing, is rather oblivious to chronology. Thus, while the development of speech and grammatical logic results in the primary process being superseded, it is not eradicated, according to psychoanalytic theory. It remains the mode of functioning of the adult unconscious, on which dreaming provides a window.

Freud, of course, well recognized that everyday verbal language, too, can exhibit the unintended primary-process characteristics of condensation, displacement, and disjunction of elements. His *Psychopathology of Everyday Life* (1901/1960b) is replete with such instances. The Reverend Dr. William Spooner, the turn-of-the-century Oxford don immortalized in the term *spoonerism*, bequeathed us many examples of verbal condensations, as when he unintentionally stated that "Patterson... reviewed the whole situation and *emanciated* a reasoned scheme" (Potter, 1980, p. 23). It is of course well known that such primary-process slips happen more frequently under conditions of fatigue. But in dream imagery, which occurs not during sleepiness, but in sleep itself, they become the rule rather than the exception, such as the composite image in Freud's dream of "Irma's Injection" (to be considered later), in which

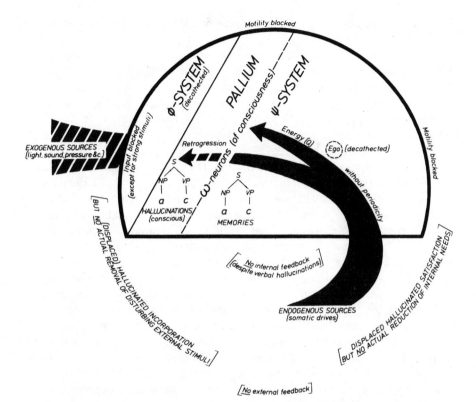

FIGURE 2.2   The neuroanatomical model of the mind during *dreaming* in Freud's *Project*. That sleep is somehow a biological necessity is taken for granted. Yet it is threatened to be disturbed by a flow of energy Q from instinctual drives, which, unlike most Q from external sources, cannot be shut out. The blocking of motor action prevents any attempt at real gratification, which would in fact endanger the sleeping organism. With the "ego" system largely decathected (de-energized), the "primary processes" dominate, with internal Q unbound and freely flowing, particularly along the well-facilitated paths of the memories of previous satisfaction. Saturation of the system is temporarily alleviated by the outward flow of internal Q to the neurons of consciousness, which, in the absence of Q from incoming perceptions, is unopposed. This is experienced phenomenologically as hallucination (with possible displacements and condensations) of previous experiences of gratification. Reality-testing and higher-level, "secondary-process" thought is prevented, partly because of the inability to the decathected ego to direct attention and cognitize the experiences. (From F. Heynick, 1985, p. 330.)

the lower part of his colleague Dr. M.'s normally bearded face resembled that of Freud's clean-shaven brother.

Similarly, when Reverend Spooner said in regard to a canoe trip to central Africa, "The *Indians* seemed quite skillful at their work" (Potter, 1980, p. 27), this substitution of one word by another on the basis of some common attribute has its everynight analogue in dreams in the primary-process displacement or symbolization of pictorial elements: for example, a box for a womb in one of the dreams ("Dead Daughter in a Case") analyzed by Freud in the *Traumdeutung*.

Substitutions may, however, be based on the opposition of the two elements rather than on some similarity. In *The Psychopathology of Everyday Life* Freud (1901/1960b, p. 59) cites the president of the Austrian Parliament, who opened the session with the words "Gentlemen, I take notice that a full quorum of members is present and herewith declare the sitting *closed*!" As Freud points out in his article, "The Antithetical Meaning of Primal Words" (1910/1957a), such switching may become standardized in the language, as for example in French, in which a word such as "plus" can mean "more" or "no more." This has, according to psychoanalytic theory, abundant analogues in our nightly life. For example, the "Diving into a Lake" dream is interpreted by Freud in the *Traumdeutung* as the patient's coming *out of* the water. Or when, visually paralleling the Austrian president's slip of the tongue, one of Freud's patients dreamt of a closed meat shop (in the "Market" dream) that supposedly symbolized an open meat shop. "There is no way of deciding at first glance whether any element [appearing in the manifest dream] that admits of a contrary is present in the dream thoughts as a positive or negative," Freud (1900/1953a, p. 318) tells us.

Somewhat related to such contraries is the matter of negation. One of the greatest typographic errors in publishing history is said to be found in the original edition of the King James Bible, where the seventh commandment reads "Thou shalt commit adultery." This omitting of negation in verbal language represents but a sporadic manifestation of something that in the psychoanalytic theory of dreams is, once more, the rule rather than the exception. " 'No' seems not to exist as far as dreams are concerned," writes Freud (1900/1953a, p. 318).

The most striking difference between verbal language production and dream generation is, however, to be found on a higher syntactic level. The ability to convert complex underlying thought into compound and coordinated verbal sentences is indisputably an exclusive capacity of postinfantile humans, barring neurological impairment. In the *Traumdeutung* Freud introduces his concept of the *dreamwork*, which converts the latent dream thoughts into the manifest dream. He allows that this dreamwork *might* map onto the perceived dream an underlying "since so-and-so, thus such-and-such was bound to happen" relationship by such means as having a shorter dream introduce a longer one. An "either-or" relationship in the dream thoughts, Freud tells us, might be mapped onto the manifest dream by the insertion of both alternatives into the dream scenario. But he clearly states (1900/1953a, p. 312) that "for the most part, dreams disregard all these logical conjunctions and it is only the substantive content of the dream thoughts that they take over and manipulate."

That primary-process features are the rule rather than the exception in our nightly life renders the dream scenarios exceedingly more ambiguous and difficult to comprehend and interpret than sentences in natural verbal languages. Of course, part of the problem is, as Freud well recognized, inherent in the very nature of plastic representation in the visual dream medium, especially with regard to negatives. Furthermore the linear, word-for-word, sequencing in verbal language need not apply in dreams, in which object-symbols may be presented simultaneously. Nevertheless, the difference between verbal language and dream language appears to have been for Freud one of principle rather than practicality. It would evidently still apply when dream event sequences are compared to sign-language sentences produced by the deaf, with their extra freedom of simultaneous presentation of signs and their relaxation of the rules for the linear sequencing of speech. If dreams are to be considered as messages in some sense—albeit of an intrapersonal rather than interpersonal sort—then the huge amounts of noise inherent in encoding into perceptual form greatly obstructs effective decoding.

The Psychoanalytic Meaning of Dreams ─────────────

As mentioned, Freud's dream theory represented, in a way, a curious synthesis of late nineteenth-century scientific views on the one hand and of ancient and still popular views on the other. Thus far, we have seen only the former: the large measure of haphazardness of the dreaming process, based partly on fin de siècle neurological principles. But Freud as a medical doctor saw no less importance in the interpretation of dreams than did the ancient physicians and primitive medicinemen.

In Freud's scheme of things, dreams are compromise formations: somewhat of a pathological phenomenon (albeit an "everynight" one) and as such to be placed in the same category as neurotic symptoms. The nocturnal regression is, it seems, not just a throwback to infantile thought processes, characterized by condensations, displacements, symbolization, and the like; it is also a throwback to infantile thought content. This content is in large measure made up of desires that are taboo to the adult mind and suppressed into the unconscious in wakefulness. They include sexual and aggressive wishes, all ultimately stemming from earliest childhood and all capable of having a deleterious effect on day-to-day functioning. Thus Freud's theory was in a sense an extension of Aristotle's view of the dream as symptom. But with Freud dreams were seldom considered to be stimulated by such mundane afflictions as ringing in the ears, calor of organs, or phlegm in the esophagus. Nor did they usually result from a painful boil "the size of an apple" at the base of Freud's scrotum as a consequence of his indulgence in some overly spicy Viennese cuisine. Freud presents such a dream ("Riding a Horse") in the *Traumdeutung* more as an exception that proves the rule. The cause of dreams is indeed strongly associated with the groin and reproductive system, according to Freud, but the input is more of a psychodynamic-biochemical than gross anatomical nature.

As a principle, Freud shared with the late nineteenth-century scientific community the commonsense notion that sleep is a biological necessity (although its exact function remains even today obscure; cf. Horne, 1988). But, in that dreams were widely viewed by his colleagues as the meaningless product of a dysfunctional, ischemic, toxin-stimulated, deoxygenated, or waste-clearing brain, Freud's next principle represented a revolutionary departure. Certain desires—kept awake by continued release into the bloodstream of biochemical substances that continue to affect the brain—threaten to disturb our indispensible sleep, according to Freud. Consequently, they are given hallucinatory gratification in the form of dreams (the psychological concomitant of the discharge of these biochemical substances into perceptual areas of the brain). As Freud (1900/1953a, p. 534), again in keeping with his fondness for linguistic metaphors, expresses it, "The dream repressed the optative [mood] and replaced it by a straightforward present [tense] . . . the first of the transformations which is brought about in the dream thoughts." For intuitive support for this hypothesis that "night dreams are just as much a wish fulfilment as daydreams" (quoted in Jones, 1953-57/1963, p. 266), Freud could point to expressions such as "the girl of my dreams," which are commonplace in so many diverse languages and are invariably positive in their connotations.

Freud thus agreed with the likes of Hughlings Jackson and Robert that there is a biological function of dreaming. But he rejected their housecleaning hypothesis, maintaining that it could not account for the appearance of childhood memories, and that the seemingly trivial elements in dreams, including apparently meaningless residues of the previous day, are only superficially trivial and in fact latently significant. One of Freud's principles was that, unlike in the case of daydreams, subsequent transformations usually make the underlying wish unrecognizable at night. This distortion is the natural consequence of retrogression to primary processes. But this entropy also eminently serves to bypass the "censor," which although more relaxed during sleep, is never completely dormant. Too blatant a representation of the repressed wish would lead to awakening by an anxiety dream and thus defeat the very purpose of sleep protection for which dreams, according to Freud, developed in the course of human evolution.

The same unconscious desires are supposedly the cause of other so-called compromise formations: neurotic symptoms, including Freudian slips and the like. Spooner's statement that Patterson *emanciated* a reasoned scheme was an apparent contamination of the target word "enunciated" with "emancipated" or "emaciated," and would no doubt have been interpreted by Freud as revealing Spooner's hidden feelings towards his colleague, perhaps ultimately extending back to sibling or Oedipal rivalry. As for the Austrian president's declaring the session closed instead of open, this was interpreted in *The Psychopathology of Everyday Life* as his half-conscious wish that the sitting be over with before it even began. And one need not inquire too closely into the conscious or unconscious desires of the typesetter who inadvertently printed "Thou shalt commit adultery."

But whereas slips in verbal language are usually minor and sporadic, dreams manifest the primary processes as the rule. Alfred Hoche, whose work will be presented later on, uses a mechanistic metaphor in comparing cognitive processes in dreams to "an idling mill, i.e., rattling without content." Freud, for his part, would sooner have maintained that listening to this apparently random internal noise in the right way could reveal previously unsuspected aspects of the motor's inner workings, aspects whose signs are largely drowned out by day, but which nevertheless affect the motor's efficiency. Or, to use a medical metaphor: a boil on the psyche, as revealed by dreams, can be as much in need of diagnosis and treatment as a boil on the scrotum. It is through free association (supposedly a sort of reversal of the dreamwork process), that the manifest dream can be mapped back onto the latent dream thoughts, thereby allowing the underlying pathology to be exposed.

Thus Freud's previously mentioned composite image (condensation) of his brother's face with that of his colleague Dr. M. showed itself upon analysis to be psychodynamically "overdetermined." Freud was consciously or unconsciously angry at both men for having recently rejected certain of his proposals. (Here, again, sibling rivalry appears to be the motivating force.) The representation of the womb by a box (displacement) in the previously mentioned dream of Freud's lady patient was not only an example of a sexual reference made innocent (a disguise facilitated by the fact that the German word for "box" [Büchse] is a vulgar term for the female genitals); the resemblance of a case to a coffin also revealed ambivalent feelings about maternity that the woman had during her pregnancy. Similarly with displacement-symbolization by reversal: The jumping *into* the water, with the meaning of coming *out of* the water, represented birth (or rebirth), the coming out of the amniotic fluid. As for the previously mentioned dream of the *closed* meat shop symbolizing an *open* meat shop, this too ultimately had a sexual meaning, as revealed by the Viennese slang expression, familiar to the female patient, "Du hast deine Fleischbank offen" ("your fly is undone"; literally, "your meat shop is open").

So, while clearly placing the origin of dreams within the dreamer, Freud in a sense also took sides in the ancient question of the divine versus the demonic origin of dreams, and opted for the netherworld.

Dream Speech and Non-Freudian Authors ──────────

The supernatural message concept and Freud's neurophysiologically based ret-rogression/degeneration approach were, each in its own way, attempts to explain the strangeness of dream semiotics. But regardless of whether dreams are con-sidered to be above or below human understanding, it would seem inherent in both these views that there are verbal languages used in daytime and semiotic languages used in nighttime, and that these are categorically different. But is it in fact the case that "ne'er the twain shall meet?"

An endless number of dream books, from antiquity through Freud to those of recent pop-psychologists, tell of visual symbols that often involve puns or plays on words in the dreamer's native language, or sometimes even in a foreign language of his or her acquaintance. Freud, too, assumed this, as when, in one of his dreams ("Clock Man") in his *Introductory Lectures* (1916–17/1961b, pp. 234–235), he interpreted the concept clock (German: Uhr) plus person (Men-sch), as meaning "primitive man" (U[h]rmensch). In contrast to supposedly uni-versal symbols (as, for example, elevation signifying grandeur), which are inde-pendent of language, or at least of any specific verbal language, such behavior is based, as Freud notes in the *Traumdeutung*, "on similarity of sounds and resem-blances between words" in particular languages, which "inevitably disappear in translation" (1900/1953a, p. 99n.). This is indeed attested to by the extensive footnoting and bracketing required in certain sections of the *Traumdeutung* dealing with language-mediated symbolism, even though English and German (unlike English and the original languages of the "oriental dream books" to which Freud was referring) are historically rather closely related. While such supposedly word-associated behavior in dreams is quite interesting in its own right, it seldom (with the rare exception of purportedly rebuslike sentences) goes beyond the primitive "naming" function of language which we mentioned in connection with primates at the beginning of this book. It therefore involves no grammatical ability. There is, however, another kind of interaction between verbal language and dreaming which is far more relevant and ubiquitous.

Consider again the belief in the divine origin of dreams. A text incribed on a stone slab near the Sphinx of Giza around 1400 B.C. has the god Armakhis-Khépri-Râ-Toum saying, from his own mouth, to Prince Thutmosis IV in a dream, *"Thine will be the country, in its length and its breadth, as well as everything that is lightened by the universal lord; thou shalt receive food from both lands . . ."* (quoted in Almansi and Béguin, 1987, p. 231). (In the present book all quotations of verbal content in dreams have been italicized by the author.) This monologue, which goes on to become rather lengthy, was presumably the inspiration for Thutmosis to begin the unification of the two kingdoms of Egypt.

A not dissimilar theme is found in one of the first dreams of the Bible, that of Jacob's ladder, in which we observe that Jehovah, when so choosing, had no difficulty at all in communicating with the dreamer in clear, concise Hebrew. In the King James translation:

> And he [Jacob] dreamed, and behold a ladder set up on the earth, and the top of it reached to heaven.... And behold the Lord stood above it, and said, "*I am the Lord, God of Abraham thy father and the God of Isaac: the land whereon thou liest, to thee will I give it and to thy seed....*" (Genesis 28: 12–13)

And the monologue continues in this vein for another two full verses.

In the *Odyssey*, the goddess Athena comes to the dreaming princess Nausicaa in the form of a mortal and admonishes her, in matter-of-fact Greek, to take her dirty linen to the washing pool (where she would later meet Odysseus). According to the "Father of History," Herodotus, the Persian King Xerxes the Great was cajoled into his ill-fated invasion of Greece by a figure purportedly sent by the gods who spoke to him at length in his dreams in Xerxes' own tongue:

> "*Son of Darius, hast thou then plainly renounced thine army's march before the Persians, and made my words of no account, as though thou hadst not heard them? Know then this for a surety: if thou leadest not thine army forthwith, this shall be the outcome of it, that as a little while made the great and mighty, so in a moment shalt thou be brought low again.*" (Quoted in Almansi and Béguin, 1987, p. 126)

The dreaming Mohammed received his messages from the Angel Gabriel in Arabic. Although some passages of the Koran may be ambiguous or obscure, the book is quite readable (cf. Dawood, 1968). Reports from such diverse groups as the Ojibwa Indians of the northeastern United States and the Senoi of Malaysia, for whom great religious importance attaches to their dreams, refer to verbal conversations between the dreamer and his or her "spirit guardian" (Garfield, 1974, pp. 63–64, 88–89). The report of a dream of a Menomini Indian youth has the Morning Star, in the form of a giant from the east, saying, "*You shall never be in danger if you make a war club such as I have and always carry it with you wherever you go. When you are in trouble, pray to me and offer me tobacco*" (Van de Castle, 1973, p. 25).

A rather special position in this regard is taken up by Freud's erstwhile disciple, Carl Gustav Jung. Up to their dramatic break in 1913, Jung appears to have shared not only Freud's general interest in language psychology, but also his conception of the relationship between verbal language and the structure of the psyche. Their first exchange of correspondence, in 1906, concerned Jung's studies on word association and his paper "Psychoanalysis and Association Experiments" (see Jung, 1919). In his research, derived from the work of the English scientist Francis Galton, Jung studied the subject's reaction time and physiological response (galvanic skin changes and pulse rate variations) to stimulus words, as well as the nature of his response words. Strong deviations from the norm in one or more of the indices signaled for Jung the presence of a "complex." This is an emotional driving force with a will and law of its own which seeks conscious expression, as when it "influences speech and action," and which can in fact dominate the personality when the ego is sufficiently weakened, as manifested by "the voices heard by the insane [when the complexes] even take on a personal ego-character" (Jung, 1967, pp. 411–412).

For Jung, the complexes that were revealed in the association experiments were at the root of hysterical symptoms and dreams. The interferences that the complexes caused, and the mechanisms of repression they evoked in response, were virtually identical to the dynamic processes Freud described for dreaming and the course of psychoanalytic therapy. Jung's reference to the voices heard by the insane clearly reflects Freud's view that "auditory hallucinations... overstep the mark of hysteria and obsessional neurosis" in that they indicate a usurping of the rational (verbal) seat of consciousness (Freud and Abraham, 1965, p. 15; the full quote will come in for more discussion in the next chapter). In a 1910 letter to Freud, we find Jung stating the following.

> The first thing about your conception of the ucs. [unconscious] is that it is in striking agreement with what I said in my... lecture on symbolism... that "logical thinking" is thinking *in words*, which like discourse is directed outwards. "Analogical" or fantasy thinking is emotionally toned, pictorial and wordless, not discourse, but an inner-directed rumination on materials belonging to the past. Logical thinking is "verbal thinking." Analogical thinking is archaic, unconscious, not put into words, and hardly formulable in words.... (Freud & Jung, 1974, pp. 298–299)

But Jung's tendency to treat split-off portions of the psyche as alternative personalities, and to reify them and give them names, would soon take him beyond the limits that Freud had set for his fledgling discipline. While complexes of the more-or-less Freudian variety, such as the Shadow, would remain part and parcel of the Jungian "personal unconscious," Jung went on to postulate a so-called racial and collective unconscious and to populate it with "archetypes" bearing names like the Wise Old Man, the Anima, and the Trickster. In a way these universal archetypes can today be seen as constraints in the Chomskyan sense (to be discussed in Part Three) in that they, within a certain leeway afforded by the specific cultures and personalities, provide a genetically transmitted mold for images which spontaneously present themselves to the dreaming mind (cf. Cambell, 1982). The fact that Jung considered archetypes as "empty and purely formal" structures whose "real nature... is not capable of being made conscious" (Jung, 1967, pp. 411–412) need not have led to the break with Freudian psychoanalysis. As Noam Chomsky (1980) points out, Freud himself at least vacillated on the question of whether the contents of the unconscious are in principle accessible to consciousness.

Rather, what Freud perceived to his great dismay was Jung's opening up of the floodgates of psychoanalysis to a "black tide of occultism." The collective unconscious, described by Jung as the "mighty depository of ancestoral experiences accumulated over millions of years," was beyond time, and its archetypes came to acquire in Jung's thinking a numinous, quasi-religious element and an association with paranormal phenomena and acausal synchronicity. In this respect, Jung's conceptions can be seen as forming a modern extension of the traditional supernatural explanation of dreams.

Be this as it may, one has only to read through a selection of Jung's dreams to see that the archetypes, in their various forms, are quite capable of conversing with the dreamer in everyday German. A curious phenomenon in Jungian dreams is the frequent appearance of a disembodied voice, often communicating a message with oracular quality. In one report, the dreamer at a solemn "House of the Gathering" is told by the voice (to the accompaniment of organ music),

> "What you are doing is dangerous. Religion is not a tax to be paid so that you can rid yourself of the woman's image, for this image cannot be got rid of. Woe unto them who use religion as a substitute for another side of the soul's life; they are in error and will be accursed. Religion is no substitute; it is to be added to the other activities of the soul as the ultimate completion. Out of the fulness of life shall you bring forth your religion; only then shall you be blessed." (Jung, 1974, p. 268)

The existence of abundant monologue in such reports need not in itself be taken as disproving the supernatural origin of dreams for those groups of people holding such beliefs. The reports do however indicate that, regardless of whatever other "languages" in which the dream may seem to be conveying a message, human verbal language is neither beyond nor below its capacities.

It appears that Jung himself, despite his original, Freud-oriented, distinguishing of the conscious and the unconscious along linguistic lines, was not very concerned about the down-to-earth verbal activities of the archetypes in his dreams, and he never addressed this apparent anomaly. In this regard he was, however, only one in a long tradition of writers on dreams with a virtual deafness to the verbal aspects of dreaming as far as their theorizing is concerned. The 1895 *Funk and Wagnalls Standard Dictionary of the English Language* defined "to dream" as "to have a train of images or fantasies pass through the mind in sleep," similar to the way a recent edition of the *Concise Oxford Dictionary of Current English* defines "dream" as a "vision, series of pictures or events presented to the sleeping person." The German psychologist K. A. Scherner in his 1861 work *Das Leben des Traumes*, quoted by Freud (1900/1953a, p. 84), states that the dreaming imagination is "without the power of conceptual speech [and therefore] obliged to paint what it says pictorially."

Any extensive bibliography of the scientific and semiscientific literature on dreams will contain titles making use of the language metaphor, such as "Die Sprache des Traumes," "La Langue des Rêves," and "The Forgotten Language." Yet typically these in fact systematically ignore language in the strict verbal sense, thereby tacitly if not explicity maintaining its nonexistence.

Such a totally "deaf" approach is all the more remarkable when one considers the literary dreams that have appeared in print through the centuries. In their book, *Theatre of Sleep: An Anthology of Literary Dreams*, Guido Almansi of the University of East Anglia's Department of English and Claude Béguin of the French Department of the University of Siena present 141 dream narratives—slightly more than half of which are fictional, and the rest purportedly genuine—from poets, storytellers, novelists, and other literati, extending from ancient times to the present but mostly predating Freud's *Traumdeutung*. Fully two-thirds of the dream narratives contain explicit dialogue (that is, with content specified) while almost another 10 percent at least make reference to conversation. (There are, in addition, a few instances of reading and writing in dreams.) Dialogues are found in the dreams of Virgil, Dante, Rabelais, Cervantes, Dickens, Dostoevsky, Ibsen, and Baudelaire, as well as a host of lesser literary greats. Some of the dialogue is elaborate, for example the following dreams in Proust's *Swann's Way* (1987/1913), written at the beginning of the century:

> The painter remarked to Swann [the dreamer] that *Napoleon III had eclipsed himself immediately after Odette.* "*They had obviously arranged it between them,*" he added; "*they must have agreed to meet at the foot of the cliff, but they wouldn't say good-bye together; it might have looked odd. She is his mistress.*" The strange young man burst into tears. Swann endeavored to console him. "*After all, she is quite right,*" he said to the young man, drying his eyes for him and taking off the fez to make him feel more at ease. "*I've advised her to do that myself a dozen times. Why be so distressed? He was obviously the man to understand her.*" (p. 82)[1]

Almansi and Béguin's "theater" metaphor thus turns out to be particularly apt. Yet Freud himself was also fond of this analogy, writing for example of dream characters playing parts in scenes (1915/1957b, p. 223). In view of Freud's conviction of the retrogressive nature of dreams, what would his position be on their verbal aspects?

Speech in Freud's Dreams: Regression, Parroting, and Secondary Revision

Before treating Freud's view's on speech generation within the dreaming process, some of his own empirical data is in order. The dream reports he presents are generally accepted by Freudians, neo-Freudians, and anti-Freudians alike as excellent descriptions of the phenomenology of dreaming, even if there is substantial disagreement about their genesis. Especially familiar is Freud's dream of "Irma's Injection," briefly referred to earlier. This is perhaps the most important in the *Traumdeutung*, since Freud credits it with having revealed to him one of the two major tenets of his dream theory: that dreams are wish fulfilments.

> I said to her Irma : *"If you still get pains, it's really your own fault."* She replied: *"If you only knew what pains I've got in my throat and stomach and abdomen— it's choking me"*.... I at once *called in* Dr. M. [who] looked quite different from usual; he was very pale, he walked with a limp and his chin was clean shaven. ... My friend Leopold was... saying, *"She has a dull area down on the left."* He also indicated that a portion of the skin of the left shoulder was infiltrated. (I noticed this, just as he did, in spite of her dress.)... M. said: *"There's no doubt it's an infection, but no matter; dysentery will supervene and the toxin will be eliminated."* (1900/1953a, p.107)

The composite images, incongruous appearances, and abrupt shifts—the primary process features—are part of the common experiences of all attentive dreamers. But once again, the report also confirms that the phenomenology of dreaming involves, literally, more than meets the eye, or the visual cortex. The underlying wish—which formed a cornerstone of the psychoanalytic theory—is expressed here not so much in visual form, but by means of verbal dialogue. Without this, Freud's dream would in fact have been as devoid of meaning as all the other historically important dreams we have considered up to now would have been without their spoken words. Irma's implied accusation that her physician, Freud, was not conscientious in performing his medical duties is in verbal form, as is Freud's self-justification, and Dr. M.'s wish-fulfilling consolation.

Consider also the characteristics of the above utterances. As in the dreams of non-Freudian authors, the sentences are fully grammatical. Furthermore, most of them go beyond the simple sentence level of complexity and contain embedded and conjoined clauses. The future tense is represented. Most striking of all are the two utterances with conditional phrases and the sentence with two negatives. As we have noted, such "ifs" and "nos" represent features that Freud explicitly states to be beyond the usual capacities of the dreamwork. Furthermore, on the semantic level, most of the dialogue seems appropriate to the overall dream scenario. Only the last utterance is manifestly absurd, at least to the medical mind. (Freud interpreted this not only as a consolation offered by Dr. M. but, on the other side of the overdetermined coin, as gratifying evidence of M.'s own incompetence, thus allowing the dreamer to have it both ways.)

All this must obviously have presented Freud with a theoretical dilemma, in view of the special position he accorded to speech as a secondary process and as representing the apex of human evolution. How could this apparently logico-grammatical process be operating effectively within the supposedly primary-process framework of dream retrogression? It seems that Freud himself, whether by a process of repression or innocent obliviousness, came close to publishing the *Traumdeutung* without addressing this question, and thereby joining the long ranks of dream psychologists who are deaf to the verbal aspects of dreaming. In a letter to his friend Wilhelm Fliess, he indicates that his section on speeches in dreams was added more or less as an afterthought (Freud, 1954, p. 288). Yet, confront the theoretical dilemma Freud did, and in a way that although logically consistent appears somewhat ad hoc.

Certainly dreams may be loaded with conversations, Freud explains in the *Traumdeutung*, but these are not generated during sleep itself. The dialogue one hears and says is in fact composed of utterances heard recently in wakefulness, recorded in memory, and (to use a modern metaphor) "played back" at appropriate moments during the dream scenario:

> The dreamwork cannot actually create speeches. However much speeches and conversations, whether reasonable or unreasonable in themselves, may figure in dreams, analysis invariably proves that all that the dream has done is to extract from the dream-thoughts fragments of speeches which have really been made or heard. (1900/1953a, p. 418)

That such a regressed linguistic process was operating in dreams was, according to Freud, noted previously (and then rather indirectly) by only one author, J. R. L. Delboeuf, who in his book *Le Sommeil et les Rêves* (1885) compared dream speech to clichés. However, a far more prominent figure, namely the aforementioned founder of experimental psychology, Wilhelm Wundt (1892/1896, p. 326), made similar, if only passing, reference to this phenomenon, stating a few years before Freud that in dreams "sometimes there is an almost normal capacity of connected expression, though when we analyze we find that the dream-speech consisted entirely of familiar expressions and current turns of language." Somewhat similar, but more restricted, ideas had been expressed in the seventeenth century by the German philosopher Gottfried Leibniz (1666–67/1969).[2]

Whatever the historical antecedents, it seems that, in coming up with this "replay hypothesis," Freud drew upon his own prepsychoanalytic (and pre-dream theory) book *On Aphasia*. In that monograph, his description of hierarchical language organization and associative processes allows that, even in the case of virtually total loss of speech due to physical trauma, certain phrases heard or said by the patient prior to his or her accident "may prove highly resistant [to loss] if they have acquired great force by being associated with great intensity" (Freud, 1891/1953b, p. 88). Such "phrases of special significance" said by the patient would, in Freud's words, "*otherwise* [italics added] represent a complex activity of language" (p. 61), but in fact are nothing more than a sort of parroting. This was in line with the concept of functional dis-involution due to John Hughlings Jackson. Regression from consciously willed to automatic functioning can result in the utilization of elementary units that are already highly organized (in this case, certain whole phrases trapped in a loop), rather than those less complex units (words and morphemes) that would normally first have to be combined into proper sequences. (See Heynick, 1985, for a more extensive treatment.)

As an example, Freud offers a quite verbal dream of a patient (the afore-mentioned "Market" dream), all the more noteworthy for its negations. The dreamer went to the butcher and was told of the item she wanted, "*That's not obtainable any longer.*" She was later offered something else and replied, "*I don't recognize that; I won't take it.*" During analysis, Freud was able to trace the first line of conversation to an utterance he had previously made to the patient, to the effect that the earliest experiences of childhood were "not obtainable any longer as such"; and the second line to part of an utterance the patient had made the previous day during a dispute with her cook: "I don't recognize that; behave yourself properly!"

In the same section where Freud discusses speeches in dreams, he also treats another exclusively human, secondary process: mathematical calcula-tions. Although far less frequent, these, too, may appear in dreaming (as they indeed do, in written form, in one of the dreams of Freud's contemporaries, Ernst Meumann, whose work will be considered later). Showing a certain con-sistency, Freud implies that nocturnal mathematical judgments, especially if accurate, are only copies of calculations already present in the latent dream thoughts, and are therefore not actually carried out by the dreamwork itself. But a comparison of the dialogue in the "Market" dream and the original from waking life serves to illustrate that in the case of verbal material the replay hypothesis involves more than just a verbatim "playback." There is, to extend the modern metaphor, "splicing" and "editing." Freud writes:

> Not only does it [the dream] drag them [the "recordings"] out of context and cut them up in pieces, incorporating some portions and rejecting others, but it often puts them together in a new order, so that a speech which appears in the dream to be a connected whole turns out in analysis to be composed of three or four detached fragments. (1900/1953a, p. 418)

Freud attributes these operations to the process of "secondary revision," which might (he vacillated on this issue) be considered "a contribution on the part of *waking thought* [italics added] to the construction of dreams"

(1900/1953a, p. 505). As such it would be separate from the dreamwork proper, to which, therefore, all the less linguistic competence need be credited:

> If we look closely into a speech that occurs in a dream, we shall find that it consists on the one hand of relatively clear and compact portions and on the other hand of portions which serve as connecting matter and have probably been filled in at a later stage, just as, in reading, we fill in any letters or syllables that may have been accidently omitted. (1900/1953a, pp. 418–419)

In his subsequent writings Freud vigorously maintained his replay hypothesis, believing it "confirmed beyond all doubt" (1915/1957b, p. 228). Furthermore, he became increasingly more restrictive as to the time period within which the original recordings are made, stating (1909/1955a, p. 21) that replays are drawn from the wakeful utterances of "previous days."

Dream psychologists have long recognized the contribution of the day's residues—the events of the *Traumtag* (the day before the dream)—to the formation of the dream. In Chapter 1 we briefly noted how these play a central role in the hypothesis of the memory house cleaning function of dreaming proposed by Robert. Perhaps the most curious variation on the role of day residues is J. W. Dunne's book on clairvoyant dreaming, *An Experiment With Time*, (1927) in which he speculates that dreams are combinations of events of the day before with events of the day to come, mixed up and distorted in such a way that the latter are not readily recognizable. Freud, for his part, saw day residues as instigators of dreams. As he wrote in his essay "An Evidential Dream," these recent and often seemingly indifferent pieces of material may "have the most numerous and varied meanings: they may be wishes or fears that have not been disposed of, or intentions, reflections, warnings, attempts at adaptations to current task . . . [but] of themselves they are unable to construct a dream" (Freud 1913/1958a, p. 274). The motivating force is provided by retrogression to more ancient material: infantile wishes and fears, and scenes and characters that may date from years, or decades past. But although therefore the images, feelings and plastic events in dreams were thus not considered by Freud necessarily to be day residues, by the time he delivered his 1916 *Introductory Lectures on Psychoanalysis*, he was convinced that as a rule such *is* the case with the verbal material of dreams:

> With a few assignable exceptions, speeches in dreams are copies and combinations of speeches which one has heard or spoken oneself *on the day before the dream*, [italics added] and which have been included in the latent thoughts either as material or as instigator of the dream. (Freud, 1916–17/1961b, p. 182)

The replay hypothesis is curious for several reasons. The dreamwork apparently has the option of resynthesizing the vocal qualities of the original recording and can play back the "soundtrack" divorced from the "video tape" of the original speaker, as in the above "Market" dream in which an utterance made by Freud in waking life is heard by his patient issuing from the mouth of a butcher. The mechanisms by which the original tapes are retrieved from memory, spliced and edited, and inserted into select points of the dream scenario, where they are generally appropriate to the context, are nowhere explained by Freud. Even if secondary revision of the end product were admitted, these fundamental operations would still require that the dreamwork proper be endowed with substantial linguistic competence. One can imagine the fate of a hapless audio editor who had to manipulate the soundtrack dialogue of a film in a language he did not understand. (For a detailed consideration of Freud's replay hypothesis and its ramifications, see Heynick, 1981a.)

Furthermore, although Freud ushered in the modern science of dreaming, he was, as we have clearly seen, by no means the first attentive dream transcriber. It would be remarkable indeed if such a relatively straightforward phenomenon as the replayed dialogue could for so long have gone unmentioned—except for the few passing references by Wundt, Leibniz, and Delboeuf—in a literature which covers some three thousand years. In fact, one historical author, the eighteenth-century Cambridge Platonist Ralph Cudworth, wrote explicitly of the well-formedness of dream dialogue in the *absence* of any replay mechanism:

> [T]hat dreams are many times thus begotten or excited by the Phantasical Power of the Soul it self, is Evident from the Orderly Connexion and Coherence of Imaginations, which many times are continued in a long Chain or Series; with the Fiction of Interlocutory Discourses and Dialogues, consisting of *apt* Answers and Replies made interchangeably to one another, and contain such things as *never were before printed upon the Brain in such a Series or Order* [italics added]; which therefore could *not* [in view of the aptness] *proceed wither from the fortuitous Dancings or Subsultations of the Spirits, or* [in view of the originality] *by antecedent Prints or Traces made by former Sensations in the Substance of the Brain* [italics added]. (Cudworth, 1731, pp.113–114)

Poetic and Literary Novelty

It appears in fact that dream reports not only show the novel use of language in the linguistic sense, but also in the literary and poetic sense. Traditionally, Coleridge's "Kubla Khan" has headed the list of poetic creations supposedly produced in sleep (in his case, opium-induced). Voltaire is quoted (Delaney, 1979, p. 132) as stating "I have known advocates who have pleaded in dreams . . . and poets who have composed verses. I have made some myself which are very passable." More recently, whole issues of the (now defunct) journal

Dreamworks have been dedicated to the dream-and-poetry theme, containing works purported to have been literally dreamt up by the poet-contributors.

Freud himself seems to have been somewhat ambiguous about creativity in dreams, apparently subscribing to the poet Schiller's remark that poetic creations demand a loosening of the "constraint imposed by your reason upon your imagination" (Freud 1900/1953a, p. 103). In fact, Freud's own description of the dreamwork mechanism involves what some consider to be a typical variety of creative work: fragmentation, rearrangement, and a new synthesis of elements (see Arkin, 1981, p. 246).

But any claim on the part of the product to literary creativity may in fact depend on whether the processes in question are random and nonmotivated or systematic and motivated. For Freud, of course, to say that behavior is "accidental" usually means that it is "consciously unintended," rather than occurring "by chance." Referring to wakeful parapraxes in *The Psychopathology of Everyday Life*, he maintains that most slips of the tongue in organically normal people can in principle be "traced to interferences by a half-suppressed idea that lies outside the intended context" (1901/1960b, p. 40). Elsewhere, Freud refers glibly to his model as a "poetic exaltation of parapraxes" in that they require explanation in terms of conflict between conscious intention and unconscious motivation (1916–17/1961b, p. 170).

In *Jokes and Their Relation to the Unconscious* (1905/1960a), Freud delimits the bounds between good wit and poor wit. He suggests how primary-process mechanisms can be placed at the deliberate disposal of consciousness when for the construction of absurd displacement shifts and double-entendre condensations: "The thought . . . with the intention of constructing a joke, plunges into the unconscious . . . seeking there for the ancient dwelling-place of its former [infantile] play with words" (p. 170).

The regressed mechanisms of Freud's (consciously unintentional) dreamwork are essentially the same as those of his (intentional) jokework and his model of (unintentional) parapraxes. The differences between nighttime dreaming and daytime joking and everyday slips of the tongue are largely matters of degree, not to be explained as "disintegrations of the apparatus or by the production of fresh splits in its interior," as one would in discussing the functioning of aphasics, but on a "dynamic basis—by the strengthening and weakening of the various components in the interplay of forces" (Freud 1900/1953a, p.608). This difference in degree, however, seems to be great enough to render wit in dreams unsuccessful by wakeful standards, according to Freud. In order for consciously produced material to qualify as a genuine joke, rather than a mere jest, it must link diverse ideas and also—on the receiving end—require a certain amount of thinking to "get it." But the deliberate jokemaker must also ensure that he operates within specific constraints, if the essence of his witticism is to be understood. Thus, to take a simple example from Freud's *Jokes and Their Relation to the Unconscious*: A lottery agent and corn-remover boasted to the poet Heinrich Heine, "And, as true as God shall grant me all good things, Doctor, I sat beside Solomon Rothschild and he treated me quite as his equal—quite *famillionairely.*" The pun can be appreciated only because the two elements in the condensation, "familiarly" and "millionaire," are easily derived by the listener. Dream displacements (presumably, whether visual or verbal) are like certain *bad* jokes, writes Freud, because they are "connected with the elements they replace by the most external and remote relations, and are therefore unintelligible" (1916–17/1961b, p. 174). In short, they flop because they require not too little tracing to get them, but too much.

These issues will be taken up in more detail in Part Three. Suffice it to restate here that the anecdotal literature on dreams, to the extent that it considers the verbal aspect at all, indicates the existence not only of "linguistic creativity," but even of literary creativity, which would seem to go a step further. This, and the other factors mentioned in this section, may explain why almost no psychoanalytic dream theorist other than Freud himself seems to have considered his replay hypothesis, while the few who have believe it to be implausible on the basis of their own anecdotal and introspective observations (cf. Baudry, 1974; Arkin, 1981).[3] In a rather ad hoc attempt to redeem the (in itself rather ad hoc) replay hypothesis, psychoanalyst Charles Fisher (1976) suggests that Freud may have been gifted with a unique "phonographic memory," enabling him, and him alone, to track down the original utterances—that is, that the hypermnesia Freud attributed to dreams in general was also part of his own specific waking endowment.

Yet, as we shall see in the next chapter, data that appears to offer a far more viable alternative for reconciling the existence of dream speech with Freud's primary-process model of dream generation was potentially available to Freud from one of his contemporaries—who, ironically, entirely distanced himself from psychoanalysis.

Notes

1. It is interesting to note that, based on the selection in Almansi and Béguin's anthology, the percentage of dreams lacking speech varies little according to whether the dreams were fiction created by the authors (23 percent of these are without dialogue or reference of conversation) or supposedly genuine (27 percent); or whether the dreams are from previous centuries (24 percent lacking speech) or after the 1899–1900 publication of Freud's *Traumdeutung* (26 percent). With some admitted arbitrariness, Almansi and Béguin divide their dream collection roughly equally into four categories, and it is here that some variation in the presence of dialogue may be detected: "instinctive dreams" (10 percent lacking speech), "realistic dreams" (24 percent), "symbolic dreams" (30 percent), and "fantastic dreams" (33 percent).

2. In one of his essays, "A fragment on dreams," Leibniz (1666–67/1967) writes the following:

> But, you say, surely we often experience judgment or reflection in dreams, or at least a knowledge of the past which involves judgment, for we both deliberate and remember. But I reply that in dreams we do not do this anew, about the appearances as they are presented, but that a judgment presents itself in a dream only if it is a judgment about the presented appearance which comes from an earlier thought and now recurs as a whole, even though we do not know that it contains the earlier thought. For entire conversations occur to us which are certainly not without judgment, and even dialogues and arguments, not because we are making judgments about them, but because judgments already made recur with the experiences themselves. (pp. 176–77)

This passage seems at first reading to be a rather stunning precursor of Freud's replay hypothesis. But Leibniz then goes on to talk about "marvelous discourses," "books and letters," "poems beautiful beyond all doubt," and "skillfully fashioned songs," all of which were created in the dreams themselves and presented spontaneously to his dreaming mind.

What therefore seems to be beyond the capacities of the dreaming mind, according to Leibniz's essay taken as a whole, is not linguistic ability and novelty, but critical judgement and reflection (even, theoretically, when not in verbal form). This was affirmed by Friederich Hacker (whose work appears in translation later in this book), and Freud himself had exactly the same view, stating in the *Traumdeutung* that "everything that appears in dreams as the ostensible activity of the function of judgement is to be regarded not as an intellectual achievement of the dreamwork, but as belonging to the material of the dream-thoughts and as having been lifted from them into the content of the dream as a ready-made structure" (1900/1953a, p. 445). But Freud clearly extended the secondary process to include sentential output of all kinds, whether involving judgements or not. (I am grateful to Rosemarie Sand for supplying me with this reference and the one to Wundt, as well as the Cudworth passage appearing later.)

3. And even in Freud's own exposition a certain inconsistency and circular reasoning has been detected, as in the "Burning Child" dream, in which he takes the presence of dialogue as proof in itself that this must have been heard previously in wakefulness by the dreamer.

Kraepelin and Nightly
Psychotic Speech

If Freud was an exception to the tradition of deafness to the verbal aspects of dreams, his contemporary, the German psychiatrist Emil Kraepelin, was all the more so. For those familiar with Kraepelin's reputation, this may seem on the face of it quite surprising. Kraepelin is known for his far-reaching innovations, and shares with Freud the title "founder of modern psychiatry." But he always remained quite removed from Freudian psychodynamics.

Before discussing Kraepelin's detailed study on speech in dreams in particular, and the way in which it compares and contrasts with Freud's, we shall consider the reasons for his interest in speech in general, and how this related to the tradition of classification of physical and mental disorders along organic lines, which began some centuries earlier.

The Nosology of Psychoses

It was the seventeenth-century English physician, Thomas Sydenham, who pioneered the modern scientific classification of disease by compiling thorough clinical descriptions of individual conditions. Like dreams, diseases had been considered in prescientific thinking to be of supernatural origin. This belief was all the more persistent regarding mental afflictions, especially in the Middle Ages, when their origins were viewed as being clearly demonic. As scientific knowledge advanced, other maladies were being classed as physical and the idea of influence from the Netherworld was rejected, but the place of diseases of the mind in the medical scheme of things remained problematic. Sydenham is credited with establishing the category of hysteria, describing it as a malady that "cannot be accounted for on the common principle of investigating disease" (that is, did not fit into established disease categories) and typically presented in patients with histories of "disturbances of mind, which are the usual causes of this disease" (quoted in Hunter & Macalpine, 1963, p. 221).

Sydenham diagnosed about one-sixth of his patients as hysteric, noting that the syndrome often included depression. Because the affliction was not deemed to be organic, the womb, to which hysteria owes its name (Greek "hysterion"), was in fact dismissed as the source, thus also allowing male patients to be so diagnosed. Sydenham thereby established a category roughly encompassing present-day (psycho)neuroses. On the other hand, of course he recognized a brain disorder such as epilepsy as being organic in nature. But what to make of the varieties of outright alienation, the psychoses? Were they to be classified as primarily organic or nonorganic ("psychological")? It was here that Sydenham had the least to contribute.

The publication in 1735 of *Systema Natura* by the Swedish botanist and onetime physician Carl Linnaeus, with its binominal (genus plus species) system for grouping plants and animals, was to reinforce the Sydenham tradition of disease classification. One overly ambitious attempt failed when, in the late eighteenth century, the famous French alienist and humanitarian Philippe Pinel endeavored to group over twenty-five hundred physical afflictions into "species, orders and families." The great reformer had more success, however, when focusing on mental diseases. In a scheme not dissimilar to that of the main genera of insanity earlier proposed by Linnaeus himself, Pinel separated psychotic illnesses into melancholias, manias with delirium, manias without delirium, and dementia. He also described the phenomena of hallucinations, flights of ideas of manic patients, unpredictable mood swings, and withdrawal of interest from the environment. Pinel's descriptions were systematic in that they distinguished between disturbances of attention, memory and judgment and recognized the significance of affects. It was Pinel's conviction that the physician should live among the mentally ill in order to observe day and night the habits and personalities of his patients and to trace the course of their disease (Alexander & Selesnick, 1968).

The field of medicine as a whole saw in the early nineteenth century the further development of nosology, the systematization of diseases according to their signs. Experimental techniques contributed to this, as when in 1832 the French physician Philippe Ricord demonstrated through a series of innoculations the distinctness of syphilis and gonorrhea, previously thought to be stages of the same disease (a misinterpretation due largely to many patients having been infected by more than one of the venereal diseases). Still, the story of medicine up to this point was by and large one of appalling ignorance, especially as to the underlying cause of those most remorseless killers of men and women, the infectious diseases. The existence of specific pathogenic "germs" had been speculated upon at least as early as the fifteen hundreds, and various "animalcules" had been described by the famed Dutch microscope maker Anton van Leeuwenhoek in the seventeenth century. However, it was not until the publication in 1858 of *Die Cellular-Pathologie* by the great Prussian physician Rudolf Virchow, and the pioneering classification of bacteria by the Breslau botanist Ferdinand Cohn, that medical science became focused on the microscopic level.

One of Cohn's protégés, Robert Koch, developed the concept of "specific etiology": that for each and every distinct infectious disease, there corresponds one and only one genus of microorganism. With the aid of the microscope, researchers can attempt to isolate the suspect microorganism, cultivate it purely, and innoculate it into another animal. Its identity as the causitive agent is considered established if the new host develops the same disease and if the process is repeatable for a chain of host animals. Subsequently, the antibody reaction test, first developed for syphilis by the Belgian Jules Bordet and the German August von Wassermann early in the twentieth century, was added to the diagnostic techniques of microscopic detection of bacteria and blood culturing. (Only with the development of the electron microscope later in the century could viruses—often hundreds of times more minute than a typical bacterium—actually be viewed, in conformity with Koch's postulates for establishing specific etiology. Their existence had, however, already been demonstrated deductively by the great Louis Pasteur.)

What of insanity and its physical concomitants? In the early nineteenth century descriptions of accumulations of ether or neural fluids in the head, the intoxication of various organs presumed to exert excitative influence on the brain, and the imbalance of Galenic humors in the body as a whole, had been interspersed with concepts such as "vegetative power," and "animal magnetism," plus the softening of brain tissue and ideas derived from the German physician Franz Joseph Gall's pseudoscience of phrenology (cf. Kraepelin, 1918/1962). With the dramatic increase in sophistication in the field of physiology in the latter half of the nineteenth century, animal magnetism gave way to Helmholz's and Waldeyer's more valid concepts of galvanism and electricity underlying the functioning of neurons. Advances in bacteriology would show some forms of insanity (paralytic dementia) to be manifestations of tertiary syphilis; on the "humoral" level some cretinism in children and adult myxedema (which manifests itself in slow speech, mental apathy, and drowsiness) were traced to inactivity of the thyroid gland. Further progress would later come with Alois Alzheimer's combining of microscopy with techniques for the staining of neural tissue. On the gross neuroanatomical level, adherents of phrenology and the concept of brain-tissue softening had to accept the mounting evidence supplied by Theodor Meynert and others of the overlap and interpenetration of cerebral functions. In a limited number of case histories, however, insanity could be demonstrated to be caused by localized cerebrovascular damage or tumors, and the general appeal of the localization concept is said to have lasted longer in Bismarckian Germany due to its theoretical "tidiness" and "order," which were so in step with the prevailing zeitgeist (Berrios & Hauser, 1988).

For the vast majority of psychiatric cases, however, no "specific etiologies" comparable to those for infectious diseases could be found. Classification continued in the older medical tradition of observation of symptoms and signs. In the 1870s, the German psychiatrist Karl Kahlbaum and his follower Ewald Hecker introduced, respectively, the category catatonia, typified by unresponsive stupor with fixed posture, and the category hebephrenia, characterized by bizarre, illogical, and senseless thought processes and actions, as well as delusions and hallucinations. It was against this background that Emil Kraepelin would make his indelible mark on psychiatry in the decades spanning the turn of the century.

Kraepelin was born in 1856, within three months of Sigmund Freud. After qualifying as a medical doctor in Würzburg in 1879, he went on to carry out research in Leipzig at the laboratory of the first scientific psychologist, the aforementioned Wilhelm Wundt. It was Wundt, a meticulous observer and classifier as well as prolific writer, who stimulated Kraepelin to write and publish, in 1883, the first version of his *Lehrbuch der Psychiatrie*, which would go through eight more editions, the last of which, in 1927, encompassing two volumes and 2500 pages.

Kraepelin was hardly less adamant than the most somatist of his predecessors that organic factors underly the various forms of insanity. But in view of the limitations of the state of the art in neuropathology, the first great task he set for himself was the reorganization of the psychiatric nosological system on the basis of clinical observations. While acknowledging the contributions of Pinel, Kahlbaum, and Hecker, Kraepelin (1918/1962) decried the generally weak methodological basis on which a wide variety of classification schemes for insanity had been drawn up in the previous hundred years: the use of invalidly small population samples or isolated (anecdotal) case histories, the ignoring of selection effects, the observational shortcomings, and the general arbitrariness.

A long-term analysis of a large patient cohort formed the basis of Kraepelin's meticulous research program. The disease courses of thousands of cases (not just ones considered "interesting") were actively followed, including outpatients as well as inpatients. Central to the study was the distinguishing of those symptoms manifest only in some forms of psychoses but heralding long-term deterioration. These Kraepelin opposed to symptoms common to all psychoses but with no prognostic importance, and to other, "accidental" symptoms likewise with no predictive value. In so doing, he developed a nosological system that would still be very much in use more than a half century after his death in 1926.

Although Kraepelin initially (and, at times, later) expressed caution regarding any concept of a unitary entity "psychosis" (Berrios & Hauser, 1988), his longitudinal studies led him to subsume Kahlbaum's catatonia and Hecker's hebephrenia as manifestations of a single disease, dementia praecox, carrying with it a somber prognosis (Alexander & Selesnick, 1968). Subsequently, paranoia (most marked by fixed and systematized delusions of persecution, often accompanied by megalomania) would be brought under the same general heading, thereby giving the present-day delimitation to the disease called, since being rechristened by Eugen Bleuler around 1911, "schizophrenia." To Kraepelin is also credited the definitive recognition that the alternating affective states of depression and elation are variations of a single morbid process, termed manic-depressive psychosis. Among the "mixed types" of this process, Kraepelin distinguished agitated depression, manic stupor, depressive mania, and several others.

What were the implications of this new classification when it came to treatment? Kraepelin was clearly a humanitarian who wished to improve the lot of his patients. He wrote approvingly of deinstitutionalization and outpatient care, and, if institutionalization was unavoidable, of the importance of communal, non-prisonlike architectural arrangements and of occupational therapy. Kraepelin deplored not just the general inhumane conditions of asylums—the product of the "Great Confinement" of the insane, which had begun in the latter part of the seventeenth century. He also pointed in particular to the barbaric medical treatments that were (to a greater or lesser extent) the product of the half-baked physical theories of insanity, and that would have been comical if not for their exacerbation of human suffering: bloodletting, emetics, and sweat chambers to purge the body of an excess of black bile or supposed poisons; rotation in whirling chairs to redistribute blood and body fluids; shock treatment by repeated dunking in icewater or extreme heat applied to head and feet in order to energize the body; and an array of other inquisitorial techniques lacking even the pretense of a theoretical basis.

Kraepelin maintained that metabolic disturbances and autointoxication lay at the root of many of the psychiatric syndromes he so diligently classified and subclassified. He also insisted that every physical treatment aimed at counteracting these disorders be humane. Partially thanks to Wundt's pioneering work in psychopharmacology, Kraepelin maintained a lifelong interest in psychophysiology and toxicology, including the problems of alcoholism. Whereas previous chemotherapy treatment had been limited to the haphazard use of a few drugs such as belladonna and opium for the stimulation of melancholics and the sedation of maniacs, Kraepelin placed cautious hope in the development of new and more effective compounds, such as chloral hydrate. The fact that such developments were—like many later psychotropic drugs such as lithium (and, for that matter, the malarial fever treatment for syphilitic paresis and insulin shock therapy for severe depression)—more often the products of accident rather than of logical biomedical deduction in no way invalidated their use for Kraepelin, as long as they could empirically be shown to do significantly more good and less harm to the patient than did the bloodletting or whirling chairs of ages past. However, he realized the limitations of what could be achieved within his own lifetime. While maintaining, in line with his humane principles, that patients should be grouped according to their needs rather than the prospect of their recovery, he was forced into a fatalistic attitude, especially concerning dementia praecox: "We must openly admit that the vast majority of the patients placed in our institutions are, according to what we know, forever lost; that even the best of care can never restore them to perfect health. Our treatment probably makes life endurable for a vast number of mental cripples whose plight would otherwise be intolerable, but only rarely does it effect a cure" (Kraepelin, 1918/1962, pp. 150–151).

The decades following the First World War, when Kraepelin wrote this, would see, along with the dramatic rise of Freud's psychoanalysis, a shifting of the border between what was considered neurotic and psychological on the one hand and psychotic and organic on the other. This was perhaps stimulated by the war itself. Shell shock, whose very name implies a physical brain trauma, had—in the national interest, especially in the German-speaking heartland of modern psychiatry—to be differentiated as psychogenic in origin and therefore not an illness in the "real," organic sense (cf. Fischer-Homberger, 1975). Even Kraepelin (1918/1962) clearly classified combat neurosis as being of psychic origin. (In the Communist East, however, where psychological complaints would represent a socially less acceptable form of self-indulgence, a physical diagnosis of "neurasthenia" or fatigue would retain more widespread validity [Porter, 1987]). Regardless of such shifting of delimitations, Kraepelin's contributions would widely be acknowledged as crucial in systematizing the chaos of clinical data. A. A. Brill (1946), a devoted follower and translator of Freud, describes the transition in psychiatry in New York in the first decade of the century from simple custodial care and neglect to—with the introduction of Kraepelin's methods—thorough descriptions, case histories, physical and neurological examinations, and the establishing of diagnoses and prognoses. Other psychiatrists, however, would criticize Kraepelin for having contributed little to, and perhaps even having retarded, an understanding of the patient's psychological processes, and for inducing a particular fatalism.[1]

The Nature of Psychotic Speech

Kraepelin's somatic outlook is reflected in his treatment of verbal behavior. The German neuroanatomist Carl Wernicke had recently situated some human linguistic functions in the upper temporal lobe of the left cortical hemisphere (for right-handers), by showing that physical trauma to this area manifested itself in various forms of aphasia. (More will be said about Wernicke's area in the next chapter.) Since Kraepelin generally viewed psychotic disorders as being no less physical in their etiology than aphasia, albeit on a subtle neurochemical rather than gross neuroanatomical level, he attributed as little "psychological" meaning to the speech of such patients as Wernicke did to the speech of aphasics. The content was, as Macbeth puts it, "a tale told by an idiot, full of sound and fury, signifying nothing." It has been suggested that Kraepelin was reinforced in his outlook by linguistic barriers. While director of the University Clinic in Dorpat (now Tartu) in Estonia, he could hardly communicate with his patients, the vast majority of whom were non–German speaking, except through an interpreter (Berrios & Hauser, 1988; Kraepelin, 1983/1987).

All this did not, of course, imply (any more than in the case of aphasics) that there was no diagnostic information to be gained from the speech of psychotics on a level other than the "message" level. For the classification of mental disorders into various types, verbal behavior was a crucial indicator to Kraepelin and his colleagues: the speech incoherence and neologisms of hebephrenis; the flights of ideas often seen when catatonics burst into an excitement phase; the inappropriate speech and occasional accusatory auditory hallucinations that accompany paranoia. And, of course, mutism itself was a powerful diagnostic signal. As Kraepelin described what was apparently an autistic phase of catatonia: "The patients become monosyllabic, sparing of their words, speak hesitatingly, suddenly mute, never relate anything on their own initiative. . . . They enter into no relations with other people" (quoted in Porter, 1987, p. 34).

Critics of Kraepelin such as psychiatrist-poet R. D. Laing would later suggest that it was Kraepelin who failed to communicate and that the schizophrenic patients' reluctance to speak reflected a knowledge that anything they said would—contentwise—be deemed meaningless. (The index cards Kraepelin used in his follow-up studies contained not only the patient's diagnostic label but also, somewhat fatalistically, and with a view toward systematizing the early indicators of the degerative process, the expected prognosis. One of Kraepelin's own dream speech specimens—to be considered later [number 265]—seems, in fact, to symbolize this all too well.) Yet, very similar criticism has reasonably been leveled at Freud's own attitude toward psychotics, first and foremost by Carl Jung (1961/1967). The repeated utterances of one of Jung's patients, whom Freud dismissed rather disparagingly, included the phrase "I am the Lorelei." Jung claimed that there was sense in this verbal behavior in that so many doctors had supposedly said about her condition "Ich weiss nicht, was soll es bedeuten" (I know not what it is supposed to mean), the first line from Heinrich Heine's classic poem "Die Lorelei." Freud, indeed, in accordance with the great importance he had attached, since his early neurolinguistic studies to the uniquely human capacity for language, considered its adequate functioning as a sine qua non for his "talking cure." As he wrote to his colleague Karl Abraham in 1908:

> Re: the Görlitz patient. His parents, good souls that they are, persuaded me to make the journey to the institution only by concealing something from me. There I found out that he also had auditory hallucinations, and thus oversteps the mark of hysteria and obsessional neurosis. (Freud & Abraham, 1965, p. 15)

In *An Outline of Psychoanalysis,* published in 1940, a year after his death, Freud's last word on the treatment of psychoses reads:

> It [the psychotic's fragmented ego] will very soon have tossed us away and the help we offer it, and sent us to join the portions of the external world which no longer mean anything to it. Thus we discover that we must renounce the idea of trying our plan of cure upon psychotics—renounce it perhaps for ever or perhaps only for the time being, till we have found some other plan better adapted for them. (Freud, 1940/1964c, p. 173)

The differences between Freud and Kraepelin were therefore mostly a matter of the division between the groups of patients to whom they had chosen to dedicate their life's work: On the one hand there were the various neurotics, treatable in principle by the "talking cure," and on the other hand the psychotics, inaccessible to verbal psychotherapy but hopefully treatable with psychopharmacology and other somatic intervention. This differentiation was such that in Kraepelin's history of psychiatry (1918/1962) as well as in his recently published autobiography (1983/1987)—both of which include the period up to the end of the First World War, when Freud's psychoanalysis was rapidly gaining ground—he expresses no disagreement with Freud; he simply never mentions him.

This is not to say that Freud deemed the etiology of schizophrenia and paranoia to be totally beyond the bounds of psychoanalytic description, even though the insight afforded did not make it amenable to psychoanalytic therapy. Most notably, the case of the chief justice of the Dresden Court of Appeal, Dr. Daniel Schreber, with his extensive memoirs of his long institutionalization for psychotic paranoia, was analyzed in depth by Freud (1911/1958).[2] Nor did Freud's pessimism about the treatment of psychotics deter him from the description and analysis of the nature of their speech, based on the principles developed in his earlier neurolinguistic studies. In his 1915 paper "The Unconscious," Freud characterizes the verbal behavior of schizophrenics as "precious" and "stilted" and as making use of "organ speech," whereby the patient's verbal description of the condition of a body part comes to represent the whole content of his thoughts. More importantly, apparently drawing upon his schema for the word-concept from his prepsychoanalytic book *On Aphasia* (which will be discussed in detail in the next chapter), Freud speculated that in schizophrenia the "word-presentation" is invested with psychic energy and therefore with consciousness, to the exclusion of the thing with which the word is associated. This would cause the patient to manipulate some words as if they were objects. Freud explictly compares this phenomenon to the operation of the dreamwork, stating that "in schizophrenia, words are subjected to the same process as that which makes dream *images* [italics added] out of latent dream-thoughts" (1915/1957c, p. 199). Yet, when it came to *dream words,* Freud stood pat with his replay hypothesis. In all his writing he hardly supplies any instances where words in dreams undergo condensations and displacements, the manipulations to which the schizophrenic psyche supposedly subjects them in wakefulness.

Such instances from dreams, as well as stilted and precious language and nocturnal "organ speech," *were* however supplied in abundance by non-psychoanalyst Kraepelin.

Kraepelin and Dream Speech: His Motivation, Methods, and Analysis

In view of Kraepelin's hardheadedness, one might be surprised to see among his more than 175 publications a hundred-page monograph entitled *Über Sprachstörungen im Traume* (On Speech Disorders in Dreams). Yet even the pioneering experimentalist Wundt did much research on the basis of introspection. And from Kraepelin's autobiography (1983/1987) it appears that he had a long-standing interest in dreams, and that this may even have been a factor in his choosing psychiatry as his specialization in the early 1870s. Furthermore, Kraepelin's interests showed a certain variety, as attested to by his article "Zur Psychologie des Komischen," which Freud would later reference in his *Jokes and Their Relation to the Unconscious*. While there can hardly be any doubt that Kraepelin was resistant to attempts to elucidate (let alone treat) schizophrenic behavior on a depth-psychology basis, the common description of him as viewing his patients as a "collection of symptoms" without a "psyche" or "inner life" (Kolb, 1977, p. 8) may be less justified. In their recent reassessment of Kraepelin, Cambridge psychiatrists G. E. Berrios and R. Hauser point to passages from Kraepelin's writings (for example the following from Kraepelin, 1920) indicating at least an awareness on his part of "psychological" factors in the formation of the patient's symptomatology:

> To what extent and by what clinical methods can we more clearly *understand* the manifestations of madness? The symptoms and signs that correspond to the underlying disease are extraordinarily varied. This implies that the antecedent conditions must have been complex. Even where clear-cut external agents are involved (e.g. a head injury or poisoning)... there is an interplay of forces at work: the nervous system of the affected individual, the deficits inherited from past generations and *his own personal history.* . . . These preconditions are specially important when considering forms of the illness which do not arise from external injury, but from circumstances of the individual concerned. . . . It seems absurd to propose that syphilis causes patients to believe that they are the proud possessors of cars . . . rather *the general desires of such people are reflected in these delusions.* . . . If these observations approximate the truth we will have to look for the key to the understanding of the clinical picture *primarily in characteristics of the individual patient. . . . His expectations play a decisive role.* (quoted in Berrios & Hauser, 1988, p. 814, their italics throughout)

Kraepelin further held views very similar to Freud's as to the importance of verbal language as a uniquely human activity. As he wrote in *On Speech Disorders in Dreams*, speech (inner or outer) is "the most important aid by means of which our experiences can be subjected to will and placed at our disposal. It is chiefly by its mediation that we succeed in raising any given ideas into consciousness, holding them there, and replacing them by others at the opportune moment, that is, as our train of thought requires." Such manipulation could not be accomplished via images, according to Kraepelin: When images are vivid (hallucinatory), they are beyond our will; when voluntarily called to mind, they are too vague.

What might cause this essential process—whether internal or external—to be disrupted? The *Jung-Grammatiker* ("neo-grammarians," already referred to briefly in Chapter 2) of late nineteenth-century Germany had a special interest in certain linguistic aberrations, substitutions, and analogies for the insights that these might offer into the mechanisms of the change in language from generation to generation, such as (to give some English, rather than German, examples), the child's natural tendency to say "tooths" for "teeth," or "eated" for "ate." It was the force of such analogy that was causing the gradual transition around the turn of the century from some older "strong" verb forms such as "dove" and "shone" to the regular forms "dived" and "shined." Similarly, an aberration such as the misdivision of the historically correct article-plus-noun form, "a napron"; has produced the now standard "an apron," while, conversely, in some dialects there has evolved the form "a nother" instead of "another." It was in this period that Rudolf Meringer and Karl Mayer (1895) of the University of Vienna published their pioneering analysis, entitled *Versprechen und Verlesen, eine psychologische-linguistische Studie* (Slips of Speech and Reading, A Psychological-Linguistic Study). This work, which contains a corpus of over eight thousand specimens of linguistic errors from "normal" people, is cited in Kraepelin's monograph, as it is in Freud's *Psychopathology of Everyday Life*.

Such everyday slips are, of course, also made by psychiatrists and psychologists themselves and may be amenable to personal introspection. But this, as well as the external observation of the speech of aphasics or psychotics, affords the researcher little insight into severely pathological language disturbances. This limitation may, however, be transcended by the observation of one's own sleep speech. As Kraepelin writes,

> Since the speech disturbances of normal waking life, especially as far as they concern inner speech, have only narrow latitude, while in the case of pathological phenomena in our area we are incapable of observing their internal genesis, the language disturbances of dreams, which in their extent and multifacetedness are by no means surpassed by those of patients, offer an exceedingly welcome opportunity to experience for ourselves the same conditions in which the most

important instrument of our mental life fails in private, so to speak, and then regains its utility.

Kraepelin's study contains 286 sleep speech utterances collected, as he tells us on the first page of his monograph, in the course of over twenty years. He reports that the majority are from himself, with a small subset (the exact size unspecified) coming from people in his circle in the university towns of Heidelberg and Munich. Kraepelin's method involved simply "placing from time to time a tablet at my bedside in order to write down immediately upon awakening what I dreamt."

Virtually all the specimens presented by Kraepelin are deviant in one way or another. In line with his enthusiasm for nosological entities, he analyzes his corpus into three main categories and some thirty subdivisions. The model of normal sentence generation that Kraepelin implicitly adopts—probably under the influence of Wundt's language psychology, to which Kraepelin refers— incorporates the most important components found in the ancient science of rhetoric, namely *inventio-dispositio, elocutio,* and *pronuntiatio.* For obvious reasons, the last of the three plays little or no part in the generation of hallucinated speech in dreams. For the purpose of excluding it from further discussion, Kraepelin early on briefly refers to sleeptalking in the strict sense—that is, articulating aloud in one's sleep—and to the disturbances in pronunciation that often characterize it.

As for the first two components, Kraepelin points to the advantage in principle of viewing these as parts of a "whole series of sub-processes which may be disrupted independently of one another." He therefore includes in his compilation of the language errors in his corpus the following two separate global categories. "Disturbances of thought," which comprise slightly less than one-fifth of the utterances, often represent the failure to meet "the first prerequisite for the intelligible expression of thought... clarity and the *proper ordering* [italics added] of the idea in mind itself." "Disturbances of speech," which comprise slightly more than a fifth of the utterances, usually involve incorrect choices of language dependency relations (acataphasia) or the faulty construction of complex sentences (agrammatism).

Despite this compartmentalization, Kraepelin on the one hand questions whether disturbances of thought should, strictly speaking, be grouped under the overall heading of language disorders in the first place. On the other hand he repeatedly points to the difficulty of distinguishing between thought disturbances and speech disturbances proper in the case of the most severely deviant utterances.

A third, and by far the largest, global category in Kraepelin's compilations is formed by "disturbances in word selection," which encompasses the remaining three-fifths of the corpus. The independence of this category seems to reflect Kraepelin's uncertainty as to the exact place of word selection in the sentence production process. On the one hand, he indicates that lexicalization is a later procedure:

> In order to give proper linguistic expression to our thoughts, we must first of all bring the relations of individual ideas together in the corresponding grammatical forms. This requires first the correct choice of the language dependency relations, then the construction of compound sentences.

Elsewhere, Kraepelin states

> The linguistic expression of a concept is the word; that of thought, discourse. The latter does not therefore render isolated concepts, but rather strings of concepts which are placed in relation to one another. If discourse is to faithfully bring a thought to expression, first of all the correct words for the constituent concepts ought to be found. Then the linguistic coinage must be made to parallel sharply and exactly the contents of the thought string in every detail. And finally the linguistic structure has to allow the clear recognition of the interrelationship between the concepts.

Whatever the model used, and however the specimens are categorized, the fact remains that virtually the whole corpus in Kraepelin's monograph is linguistically deviant and that very many specimens show apparent condensations (often called "word-blends" in modern language psychology) and displacements ("substitutions"), including *pars pro toto* phenomena; and sometimes abrupt disruptions in grammatical structure and ordering. On the face of it, then, there is not a little irony in the fact that Kraepelin, apparently having no interest in the psychoanalytic view of dreaming, should have offered such splendidly Freudian specimens, while Freud, having little use for Kraepelin and his nosology, should himself have presented specimens of dream speech in the *Traumdeutung* that usually show no manifest primary-process influence.

   It is particularly interesting, although perhaps secondary to our morphosyntactic considerations, that also the *semantic* content of some of Kraepelin's specimens would have delighted Freud. So, for example, Kraepelin's specimen 189 runs "*In Bullrich I want to stand, like I last possessed my little mother.*" Kraepelin sees "my little mother" as simply a paralogistic displacement for "my teacher," stimulated by semantic association, while "last possessed" is an ellipsis for "whom I had before." The second half of the utterance is therefore a haphazard rendering of the harmless phrase "like my former teacher." As another example, consider specimen 200, and particularly the last three words: "*O youth, how sensuously free we of mind, spring-splendor cop. it from behind.*" Kraepelin conceives the apparent abbreviation "cop." as probably a visual (printed) presentation, but cannot suggest what it might stand for, except to say that the verse as a whole was vaguely accompanied by the feeling of "variability." He adds that the entire specimen might be dismissed as words forming a rhythmical structure that are divorced from any accompanying ideas. Clearly, for Kraepelin the meanings of the words in his specimens served only to trace deviations in structure and were never considered by him to provide an external *motivating* force in the Freudian sense.[3]

Despite the general well-formedness and appropriateness of the dream dialogue that Freud himself presents, there are, to be sure, occasional Kraepelin-like morphosyntactic disturbances to be found in his reports, such as the word-blend in the utterance *"That's the breakfast-ship!"* which Freud and his party shout in unison upon seeing a strange-looking boat in his dream of the "Castle by the Sea." Although this deviant utterance would on the face of it seem to be far more innocent than the two specimens of Kraepelin's given above, Freud, as usual, had no difficulty in uncovering all sorts of emotionally charged, latent meaning, in this case, rather gloomy. ("Breakfast" relates to "breakfast trays," which in turn is associated with ancient Etruscan "toilette" [cosmetic] trays, and then to black "toilettes" [funeral garb]. "Fasting" reinforces the idea of mourning, while "break" and "ship" relate to "ship-wreck" [German "Schiffbruch," literally "ship-break"].) True to the rather contrived logic of the replay hypothesis, Freud mentions that the utterance was derived from an exclamation once made by Frau Freud in Venice, "Here comes the English warship!" (The word "English" supposedly also influenced the course of the dreamwork mechanism; hence the above associations via the English words "break" and "fast," even though in the original dream utterance, the German word for "breakfast," "Frühstück" [literally, "early bit"], contains neither element.)[4] But if such Kraepelin-like specimens had been the rule in Freud's reports rather than very much the exception, probably no recourse to such an ad hoc replay hypothesis would ever have been necessary.

In fact, Kraepelin himself denies any parroting quality to dream speech, and thereby further undermines Freud's replay hypothesis. In comparing dream speech to various deviant forms of wakeful verbal behavior, Kraepelin briefly refers, at the beginning of Section V, to the repetitious babbling of children (though not explicitly to parroting behavior), and seems to find no reflection of this in the dreaming state. (He does, like Freud in his aphasia studies, specifically refer to the parroting of certain aphasics. Interestingly enough, Kraepelin relates this not at all to the sleeping state but to a transitional phase in the *awakening* process, when "we mechanically and incomprehendingly repeat the words striking our ear.") Having no theoretical stake in viewing dreams as retrogressive phenomena, Kraepelin in fact draws the general conclusion that the mechanisms involved in dream speech production function *least of all* like those of young children. The features of his dream speech corpus that Freud would have termed primary-process were for Kraepelin more than anything else comparable to the speech confusion of dementia praecox patients, while in normal people such verbal behavior is most likely to be encountered under conditions of anxious embarrassment, distraction by side-ideas, and fatigue. These are important observations and will be discussed in detail in Part Three of the present book.

Hypnagogic Dreamlets and Selectivity

Why is there, then, such an apparent discrepancy between the data supplied by Freud and Kraepelin, especially when Kraepelin-like specimens would have fit so much better into Freud's own theoretical framework? And which of the two may be said to have provided the more reliable and typical specimens of dream speech?

As mentioned above, at the time when Kraepelin was collecting his dream specimens, the philologists Meringer and Mayer were gathering their 8000 examples of faulty speech from waking life. These were not, of course, meant to be taken as a representative sample of speech and reading in general. That in the course of twenty years Kraepelin should have been able to assemble 286 deviant dream utterances is in and of itself not compelling evidence of a very frequently malfunctioning language faculty during dreaming (even if it may be conceded that, as Kraepelin stated, the *depth* of the malfunction often surpasses that of slips of the tongue of normal people in wakefulness). This is especially so because Kraepelin himself makes no pretense of being nonselective. As the declared intent of his study was less to supply a systematic contribution to sleep research than to afford personal insights into the mechanisms of language pathology, he gives no indication of what percentage of his observed (or observable) utterances his corpus represents. But the fact that he was indeed selective is shown by his remark that on many occasions he would write down upon awakening a specimen that " —to my disappointment—at first seemed to show no deviation at all from wakeful utterances. I therefore considered the written entry pointless." (Kraepelin goes on to refer to his specimens as having been gathered as "oddities," and states that in dreams "there are usually only scattered turns of phrase which can be branded as totally incomprehensible. Between them, words, turns of phrase and whole sentences are regularly inserted which show no disturbance at all." Such good utterances are naturally absent from his corpus.)

All this does not, of course, imply that Freud for his part was not selective in his choice of reports in support of his dream theory. But it is likely that Freud's dreams were far more often chosen on the basis of criteria other than the presence (or absence) of deviances in the dialogue they contained. Indeed, in Almansi and Béguin's anthology of literary dreams—containing some hundred narratives with explicit dialogue reported in the course of over twenty-five centuries by authors who had diverse motivations (or no apparent motivation at all)—the characteristics of the dream speech resemble far more those of Freud's examples than Kraepelin's.

To complicate matters still further, it appears that Kraepelin drew much of his corpus from hypnagogic and hypnopompic experiences. He writes

> Speech utterances in dreams are an almost daily occurrence, especially during half sleep in the morning before awakening and, less often, in the evening before falling asleep. . . . A smaller number of observations stem from afternoon naps.

A more appropriate title for Kraepelin's monograph might therefore have been *Über Sprachstörungen im hypnagogischen Traume*. The hypnagogic periods of drifting off to sleep have long been considered to differ phenomenologically from true dreaming experiences, especially since the previously mentioned descriptive work of the French alienist Alfred Maury (1848, 1857) in the mid-nineteenth century.

Meumann, Hoche, and Hacker

None of this is to deny the historic importance of Kraepelin's monograph. As a book, it remains virtually unique in the history of dream research as a study of our verbal capacity during sleep. It also inspired several articles on the topic by other German scholars early in the century.

Ernst Meumann (1862–1915) worked for three years as assistant at Wilhelm Wundt's laboratory in Leipzig not long after receiving his doctorate (phil.) from the University of Tübingen in 1887. Most of Meumann's work—as professor in Zurich, Münster, Halle, Leipzig, and Hamburg—concentrated on the psychology of learning and on intelligence and its testing. But in 1907 he published an article on dreams entitled "Über Organempfindungsträume und eine merkwürdige Traumerinnerung" ("On Dreams with Organic Sensations and a Curious Dream Recollection"). This was followed two years later by "Über Lesen und Schreiben in Traume" ("On Reading and Writing in Dreams"), which appears in English translation in Part Two of the present book. (That Meumann, too, drew at least partially from hynagogic periods is evident from his statement that "these dreams appeared at the time in a highly conspicuous way, usually immediately upon falling asleep, and in any case always in the first half of the night.")

Alfred Erich Hoche (1865–1943) received his doctorate in medicine in Heidelberg in 1888 and was certified in psychiatry in 1891. Until 1934 he held the posts of professor extraordinary and full professor in Strassburg, Freiburg, Halle, and Heidelberg. Hoche's early research was mostly physiological, with particular focus on the neurology of the spinal cord. In the years prior to World War One, however, he became known for his opposition to Kraepelin's nosological system, advocating in place of elusive and shifting disease entities the doctrine of syndromes composed of various individual clinical symptoms

(Hoff, 1991; see also note 1). Hoche's later work attests to increasing diversity, and an interest in the border areas between psychiatry and other disciplines. Among his almost one hundred fifty publications are to be found articles on Shakespeare and psychiatry, mental disease and culture, psychiatry and religion, war neuroses, psychological views of history and politics, and insurance and legal issues involved with psychiatric practice (including, in 1920, a piece, particularly unfortunate in the light of events in Germany two decades later, advocating the "euthanasia" of idiots; see Proctor, 1988). Hoche also published two volumes of poetry (under a pseudonym), and three articles evaluating Freudian psychoanalysis.

It is therefore not surprising (certainly less surprising than in the case of his theoretical opponent Kraepelin) that there should have been a period when Hoche was drawn to dreams. His first such publication, in 1920, concerned the possible goals of dream research ("Mögliche Ziele der Traumforschung"). There also appeared in the same decade the article "Haben unsere Traumbilder halluzinatorischen Charakter?" ("Do Our Dream Images Have Hallucinatory Character?"; 1923), and two books, *Das träumende Ich* (*The Dreaming Ego*; 1927) and *Schlaf und Traum* (*Sleep and Dreams*; 1928). Specifically on the subject of verbal behavior in dreams, Hoche published in 1922 an article Über Sprachbildung in Traume" ("On Language Production in Dreams") and in 1926 a textbook chapter "Der Traum," with a section on dream speech, translated into English in Part Two.

Fredrich Hacker was born in Reichenhall in 1888. He studied medicine at Würzburg, Kraepelin's alma mater, receiving in 1913 his doctorate for the dissertation *Beobachtungen an einer Hautstelle mit dissoziierter Empfindungslähmung* (*Observations of a Skin Site with Dissociated Paralysis of Feeling*). Already two years before he had obtained a doctorate in philosophy from the University of Bonn for the dissertation *Systematische Traumbeobachtungen: mit besonderer Berücksichtigung der Gedanken* (*Systematic Dream Observations: With Special Regard to Thinking*), which was published in 1911 by the Leipzig publisher of Kraepelin's 1906 monograph, Wilhelm Engelmann Verlag. The English translation of his chapter "Die Sprache im Traum" ("Language in Dreams") is given in Part Two of the present book. Among his later publications was "Die Zukunft einer Desillusion" ("The Future of a Disillusionment"), published in Vienna in 1964.

There would appear precious few other articles on verbal language in dreams, and no complete volume until the present book. (The late Arthur M. Arkin's 1981 work *Sleeptalking: Psychology and Psychophysiology*, which will be treated in more detail in Part Three, is a most valuable contribution to the field of verbal behavior in sleep, but it does not generally concern dreaming.) It is to the translations of Kraepelin, Meumann, Hoche, and Hacker that we shall turn presently. But first some consideration will be given to the seemingly peculiar turn-of-the-century concept of the "sound-image" and the possibility that the printed word may play a rather unexpected role in dreams.

Notes

1. Furthermore, the classification of the various mental disorders and symptoms continues to present problems quite different from those in the grouping of more purely physical diseases. Thus, for example, psychiatrist Herman van Praag (1974) laments the hybrid term schizophrenia and considers that hebephrenia and dementia paranoia have about as much in common as peptic ulcer and myocardial infarction. Van Praag not unreasonably suggests an approach to the psychoses and schizophrenias based not on the various syndromes, but on the symptoms that are or are not present in each of them: a reversion, in fact, to an earlier view of disease.

2. Among the manifestations of Schreber's symptomatology were verbal hallucinations of reprimands. Freud saw the psychodynamics of the affliction as an underlying feminine (passive homosexual) love fantasy that through the process of repression had been variously transformed into a hate fantasy, a persecution fantasy, and (through infantile regression to narcissism) delusions of meglomania. The etiology was, according to Freud's description, to be found in the ramifications of Schreber's childhood relations with his (since deceased) father and elder brother. Other authors have agreed with Freud on this last point, but for more straightforward reasons than latent homosexual longings: The elder Dr. Schreber was a peculiarly ingenious disciplinarian with his children, and would in the next century be praised by pro-Nazi authors. Furthermore, Schreber's delusions can be seen as partly stemming from very real practical difficulties in later life, as well as being influenced by the often apocalyptic fin de siècle zeitgeist—and compounded by his forced isolation in a psychiatric institute where the threat of castration, as a therapeutic technique, is reported to have been more than just a fantasy. (Cf. Porter, 1987.)

3. Brill (1946, p. 285) regards Kraepelin as "deliberately steering clear of anything savoring of sex." Porter (1987, p. 33) considers this attitude similar to that of Dr. Nicholas Robinson, a contemporary and follower of Isaac Newton who, when a patient revealed his dreams to him of being ridden like a horse by a gentleman friend, put it down to an overheated imagination and prescribed a purge of strong medicine.

4. The undeniable talent of psychoanalysts for associating dream elements with all manner of "meaningful" underlying ideas through various intermediate links relates to a staple criticism of the Freudian dream theory. The success of such meandering is hardly more evidence that these latent elements in fact contributed to the original dream production process than that the content read into Rorschach blots had determined how the ink drops would fall on the paper. See Heynick (1981b) for specific examples of doubtful interpretation of verbal elements.

Imagining Words
and Imaging Words

Freud's *On Aphasia* (1891/1953b) can definitely be classified as still belonging to his prepsychoanalytic period. It contains several anatomical brain diagrams as well as neurologically based schemas. Although no diagrams are provided in Kraepelin's dream speech monograph (nor in the articles of Meumann, Hacker, or Hoche), it is perhaps not surprising that the "schema for the word-concept" drawn by Freud the neurologist, rather than Freud the psychoanalyst, would serve as a particularly useful tool for orientating oneself in the neurolinguistic discussion presented by Kraepelin. Freud's schema—which, let it be said, has not necessarily lost its validity in the ensuing hundred years—is also an aid in conceptualizing various phenomenological and philosophical issues. (For example, do we really hear what we hear in dreams or just imagine that we do?) Furthermore, as will be seen in the last section of this chapter, Freud's schema lends itself to adaptation so as possibly to clarify such phenomena as the influence of printed foreign word-images in Kraepelin's dreams.

The Four Language Skills and Freud's Schema
for the Word-Concept

We have already noted, if only in passing, that verbal activity in dreams is not wholly confined to speaking and listening. Reading and even writing can form part of the dream scenario. The four language skills are represented in Freud's schema for the word-concept, shown in Figure 4.1.

In this diagram—which is best seen as lying somewhere between psychological and physiological space, with the points representing not just simplified neural complexes but also nodes in a psychological flow chart—the position of the *sound-image* (A) (the native speaker's phonetic representation of a given word) is indispensible for all four language skills in his or her native tongue. This node links the *object-presentation* (B) (the network of perceptions and

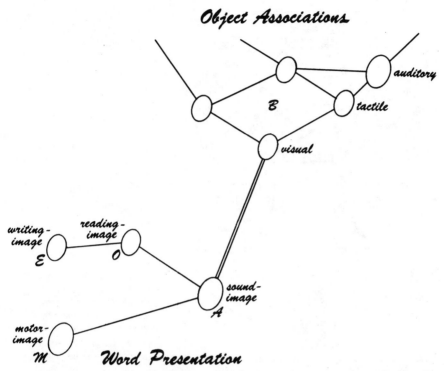

FIGURE 4.1 Freud's schema for the word-concept. From F. Heynick, 1984, p. 52; redrawn from Freud's *On Aphasia*, (1891/1953b.)

associations that form the speaker's conception of the thing referred to) to the rest of the word-presentation: on the one hand, to the *motor- (kinesthetic-) image* (M) (the feeling of the speaker's oral muscle movements of the enunciation of the word); and on the other hand, to the *reading- (print- or script-) image* (O) (the visual representation of the word for the reader) and then to the *writing- (chirokinesthetic-) image* (E) (the feeling of the writer's hand of the writing of the word). Freud's schema thus maintains a hierarchy of dependency which reflects the order in which these native-language skills are originally acquired. As such, it is more economical than previous models and avoids the proliferation of channels that characterizes the schema of one of Freud's teachers, the famed French neurologist Jean-Martin Charcot.(See Figure 4.2.)

So the normal speech production of a native-language word proceeds, according to Freud, from the concept to the sound-image to the motor-image (path $B \rightarrow A \rightarrow M$); while listening comprehension goes from the sound-image directly to the concept ($A \rightarrow B$). Writing proceeds from the concept to the sound-image to the reading-image (that is, print- or script-image) to the writing-image ($B \rightarrow A \rightarrow O \rightarrow E$); while reading comprehension flows from

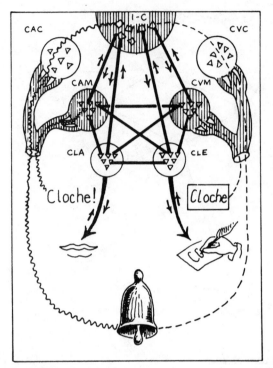

Key:
IC   ideational center
CAC   common auditory center
CLM   auditory center for words
CLA   center for articulate language
CVC   common visual center
CVM   visual center for words
CLE   center for written language

FIGURE 4.2   Charcot's schema for the word-concept, showing the proliferation of channels on which Freud greatly economized. (From Charcot, 1883.)

the reading-image (print- or script-image) to the sound-image to the concept $(O \rightarrow A \rightarrow B)$. Theoretically, the reader is thus dependent on "encoding-to-sound" (to use a more recent term from the science of reading), as he vocalizes, or subvocalizes, the printed word in order to arrive at its meaning. (Note that the rather quaint term "image" is to be taken figuratively rather than in the literal, visual sense, except in the case of the reading-image. For a more modern assessment of the role of phonological factors in reading, see Newcombe & Marshall, 1980.)

Although Freud nowhere makes reference to dreams in his aphasia monograph, the sleeping states obviously involve radical changes in our verbal behavior, and these can be approached from the neurolinguistic and phenomenological vantages of aphasia theory, as well as within the framework of Freud's subsequent psychoanalytic schema of development, and from the point of view of "continuity versus complementarity" (the extent to which dreams do or do not reflect our conscious thoughts and wakeful activities).

Consideration of the interaction in dreams of the active process of speech production and the passive process of listening comprehension brings to mind the age-old philosophical discussion of the "reality" of dream experiences. Bertrand Russell (1948, pp. 214–215) echoes the views of several other philosophers when he states that "what, in dreams, we see and hear, we do in fact see and hear," but Norman Malcolm (1959, pp. 51–52) counters that it no more follows that the sleeper "really" had such perceptions "than it follows from his having climbed a mountain in a dream that he climbed a mountain while asleep." Be this as it may, as we noted in Chapter 2 the title *Theatre of Sleep* is very appropriate for Almansi and Béguin's anthology of literary dreams. Although Freud eschewed the comparison of dreams to motion pictures ("I do not believe," he writes to Karl Abraham in 1925, that "satisfactory plastic representation of our abstractions is at all possible" [Freud and Abraham, 1965, p. 384]), this might well have been due to the fact that movies at the time were not yet "talkies." Freud in fact does occasionally use the theater metaphor, referring to characters who play parts in scenes and likening the dreamer to a "popular dramatist" who puts phrases into the mouths of his characters (1900/1953a, pp. 572–575; this is despite the obviously immense handicap under which the dreamer/dramatist must labor if Freud's replay hypothesis is to be taken at face value). A question here arises whether the perceptual rendering of the words of dialogue is not superfluous, since the audience is constituted solely of the playwright himself.

In waking life, of course, there is at the moment of enunciation feedback on one's motor-images, and the speaker hears his own speech in the form of sound-images. (In Figure 2.1, based on Freud's *Project*, the actions in the real world that are fed back to the doer of course include verbal actions.) But as for the dream theater, Freud (1900/1953a, pp. 419–420) distinguishes between dialogue that "has the sensory quality of speech" from lines that "are not . . . felt . . . as having been heard or spoken (that is, which have no acoustic or motor accompaniments in the dream)" and are perceived as being "merely thoughts." (He further points out that "it is easy as a rule to make this distinction with certainty" [p. 183].) In other words, the activation of sound-images in the case of words spoken by other players in the dream theater, and of sound-images plus motor- (kinesthetic-) images in the case of words spoken by the dreamer when he interacts with the other personages, is optional. Furthermore, Freud's replay hypothesis pertains, strictly speaking, only to the motor-acoustically perceived dream words. The "merely thought" variety is, according to Freud, sooner traceable to "our waking thought-activity . . . often carried over unmodified into our dreams," and he goes on to suggest that "another copious source of undifferentiated speeches of this kind, though one which is difficult to follow up, seems to be provided by material that has been *read*" (p. 420). The apparent assumption is that nonvocal verbal material is recorded in memory in such a way that when it is retrieved in dreams it likewise presents itself nonvocally. But here, as in so many other places, Freud was less than totally consistent when adducing evidence.[1]

Reference to such a distinction between motor-acoustically perceived words in dreams and words merely thought is also made by Kraepelin and his three contemporaries, although they appear to have differences—perhaps of a personal nature—as to which form predominates. Kraepelin states, at least regarding those lines uttered by the dreamer himself, that they had "essentially taken the form of speech motor-images, and were registered as such." Hoche suggests that the dialogue spoken by others in the dream "almost never involves genuine auditory hallucinations." Hacker writes that in "deep sleep" his own conversation "was not heard word for word such that I had a clear acoustic presentation of the individual words. Rather it was usually inner speech without reaching hallucinatory clarity of acoustic and motor presentations." However, in morning sleep or when the dialogue was laden with affect, Hacker reports that "it often came to true speech, that is, distinct acoustic and sentence presentations which frequently tended to be accompanied by clear motoric presentations of the speech organs".

The peculiar phenomenology of dreaming also allows what is in essence the opposite of knowing the meaning of a spoken message without, in fact, having heard that message: the hallucinating of speech without being able to comprehend it. This may involve a (pseudo-) foreign language, or incoherent combinations of sounds and syllables in the dreamer's own tongue—such as the specimens marked by Kraepelin as being "totally unclear," with regard not to their presentation, but to their possible meaning.

The active process of speaking and the passive process of listening have their graphemic analogues in writing and reading, respectively. These, too, do indeed occur in dreams, although proportionately far less frequently than would be expected if one assumes that daily activities are generally reflected in dreams (the continuity view). Meumann comments that his dreams featuring reading and writing are "conspicuiously few" in view of the fact that in waking life they are "my most extensive occupations, and in general my dreams often relate to the activities of the day." Hacker similarly notes the paucity of reading and writing in his dream life. (He further remarks that his only two instances involving the reading of "a whole text" occurred "curiously enough in dreams during vacation, at a time when I had read next to nothing.")

Of the forty-five specimens of Freud's own dreams presented in the *Traumdeutung*, eight make at least some reference to reading. The printed words from five of these are presented verbatim. None, however, are extensive texts of the sort Freud undoubtedly devoured in wakefulness, but rather titles, signs, and notes comprised of only a few words. (Freud makes no mention of doing any writing in his dreams.) Kraepelin for his part notes that, of the 274 dream speech specimens he discusses, there were only seventeen cases in which "I could establish with reasonable certainty that they involved not independent utterances, but rather the reading off of a printed or written text."

In the broadest sense, all this accords with the psychoanalytic concept of dreaming as a partial regression to an earlier stage of ontological development.

Reading and writing are acquired later than listening comprehension and speaking, and this is well reflected in the dependency relation in Freud's neurological-psychological schema for the word-concept. Indeed, as Meumann expresses it in quite nonpsychoanalytic terms:

> Reading and writing are very complex activities and . . . in dreams our mental life is a very reduced one. . . . How very impeding it must then be for reading and writing dreams that reading and writing are linked to certain, very precisely defined perceptual activities which have to be reactivated in their whole complex mechanism—even when only in the form of reproduced representations of this mechanism. The degree of consciousness of the dreaming state is seldom sufficient for this.

The short-circuiting in dreams of the active and passive processes of language production and comprehension, respectively, is even more intriguing in the case of reading than of listening. As Hoche puts it, when reading a "pseudohallucinated" text in dreams, "the optical images of the words were in fact not at all necessary, since the linguistic content had already been provided by the dreamer." Hacker expresses it in very similar terms: Actual reading is "not necessary, since the content of what is to be read has already been formed anyhow and it only *seems* that the content is first made known to us only upon reading it, just as we are accustomed to in waking life." However, analogously to the perception of motoric-acoustic speech sensations in dreams, the printed or written text may attain full clarity. Hoche remarks that with such "genuine hallucinatory processes . . . it also happens that one must first turn the page to find the continuation of the phrase."

On the other hand, a written text may be hallucinated in a dream without the dreamer's being able to decipher its meaning. Meumann, in particular, gives several examples of incoherent letters, syllables of existing but incorrectly conjoined words, indecipherable handwriting, chaotic shorthand lecture notes, and even confusing boldface footnotes, all of which were perfectly legible in the sense that they were seen with sharp optical clarity. This is analogous to motor-acoustically hallucinated, but incomprehensible, speech.

As with one's own speech, one's own writing in the real world allows feedback while the activity is in progress, in the form of the writing- (chirokinesthetic-) image and the reading- (script-) image of what one has just written. But as for the dream world, Meumann gives three instances in which he could not comprehend what he was writing. One case was particularly impressive in that it involved "a long letter which seemed to me extraordinarily important, and I took pains to write very 'calligraphically.' I was repeatedly pleased during the dream with the clarity and beauty of my handwriting." (The speech equivalent of this would be the dreamer's hallucinating that he himself carefully enunciates with clear sound images real words or pseudowords without his comprehending what he is saying.)

Dissociation and Foreign Print-Images in Kraepelin's Dreams

Dissociation in dreams may also have the consequence that, although reading as a manifest part of the dream scenario is relatively rare, print-images play a covert role in nocturnal language production, particularly when the sound-image, pivotal in linking the whole word-presentation to the thing-presentation, is affected.

In Kraepelin's view (Section VI) the biological protection of sleep in the "intermediate condition between deep sleep and wakefulness" demands the "impeding of the penetration into consciousness" of external verbal stimuli, since the ears—unlike the eyes—cannot be closed off at the extremities. This is brought about by a "decrease in the performance of Wernicke's area" (the seat of sound-images), resulting in the high degree of word deafness, but not total deafness, since "hearing . . . remains the important warner of approaching danger [and cannot], for reasons of safety, be completely closed off." In consequence, hallucinated speech utterances during light sleep are apt to take on characteristics of certain aphasias.

Optical areas of the brain, however, supposedly remain exceedingly active during dreaming or hypnagogic periods. When certain words have been acquired largely through reading rather than through speech, alternative strategies for language production may be resorted to in those states. As Kraepelin explains, in discussing some anomalies in his corpus specimens, there is an "immense importance attached to foreign languages in our school system, at least among the more educated classes, [and] we tend to learn foreign languages not, as in the case with the mother tongue, with our ears, but rather in the first instance preferably with the aid of visual images and motor images, so that we possibly have their elements relatively more readily at our disposal if the otherwise leading influence which the acoustic images of the mother tongue exert has been destroyed." The same would hold for bookish loan words in the native language (often of classical origin). He adds: "We can later on make up aids which, to a certain extent, are capable of standing in for the word sound-images, especially the visual images of script. . . . With their help, the mastery of the spoken means of expression can be more or less completely regained."

In a sense, such an approach would not be incompatible with the psychoanalytic model of dream generation. Although, as mentioned, Freud's conception of retrogression in dreams would—to the extent there is any verbal activity—give primacy to listening and speaking as being ontogenetically prior to reading and writing, *in general* he considered the visual to be primary to the auditory, and in so doing he agreed with virtually all other writers as to the dominance of the former in dreams. In any case, in *On Aphasia* Freud (1891/1953b) did—while having vastly economized on Charcot's schema—allow flexibility, maintaining that "the safeguards of our speech against breakdown appear to be overdetermined" (p. 74). A consequence is that in the case of language pathology "the most frequently practised associations are most likely to resist destruction," and that, as a result, "the manifestations of aphasia will be different in the highly educated from those of the illiterate" (pp. 87–88). With the former group, this could mean a shift towards visual representations. Freud points to an example in native-language pathology in which a stroke victim "lost his memory for nouns and adjectives" but was able to "draw up an alphabetical list of the most commonly used nouns [so that] when he required a word he looked it up . . . and, having recognized it by its visual image, he was able to pronounce it." In this way, "the letters of the visual word-image thus assembled elicited the sound-image, which could not be activated through the object associations alone." Freud adds that "the center which has suffered least is the one the assistance of which is sought first . . . [T]he center of the sound-images required support from the centers which are otherwise dependent on it" (pp. 40–42).

Freud provides no schema for *foreign words*, but the manner in which they would be (to use another of his terms) "superassociated" onto the native word schema would depend on the "influence of the age of acquisition and of practice" (p. 60) and, implicitly, the manner of acquisition. Figure 4.3 represents a modification of the original schema, showing virtually all the possible superassociations of a foreign word onto a native word. All things being equal, the organization of the foreign word should parallel that of the native word: paths $A_2 \rightarrow (A_1 \rightarrow)B$ and $O_2 \rightarrow A_2 \rightarrow (A_1 \rightarrow)B$ for speech comprehension and reading comprehesion respectively; paths $B \rightarrow (A_1 \rightarrow)A_2 \rightarrow M_2$ and $B \rightarrow (A_1 \rightarrow)A_2 \rightarrow O_2 \rightarrow E_2$ for speech and writing production, respectively. Any pathological disturbances (in Kraepelin's case, the partial disconnection of word sound-images) would be expected to affect the foreign language all the more strongly than the native language. This, again, is in accordance with Hughling Jackson's doctrine, subscribed to by Freud, that in the functional retrogression ("disinvolution") of a highly organized associative apparatus, what is last acquired, in this case the foreign language, is generally first to be lost.

Often, however, not all things are equal in the superassociation of the foreign nodes to the native ones. Fluent and intensive users of a foreign language acquired predominantly via silent reading might be expected, as a result of the order of acquisition plus the strength, in Freud's words, of the "most frequently practised associations" (p. 87), to have a well-facilitated channel $O_2 \rightarrow B$, whereas any similar path $O_1 \rightarrow B$ for the native language would constitute an exceptional "abbreviation," at least for the native-language reading of peoples whose words and letters "represent sounds and do not symbolize concepts" (p. 92; see for example Sasanuma, 1980, for consideration of "abbreviations" in the native language reading of Chinese and Japanese Kanji [ideographic]

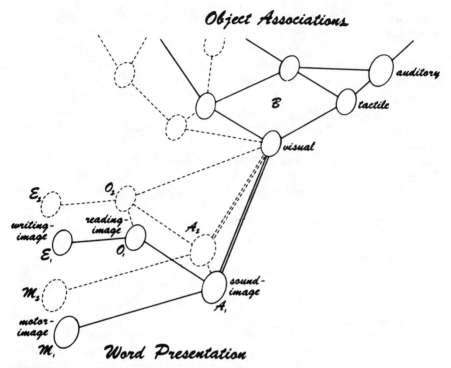

FIGURE 4.3 "Superassociations" of the foreign-language word-schema (indicated by broken lines and letters with subscript 2) onto native-language word-schema (solid lines and subscript 1). (From F. Heynick, 1984, p. 54.)

orthography). Thus, with the partial impairment of Wernicke's area, the intrusion of foreign words into hallucinated speech utterances in hypnagogic dreams of such subjects (via path $B \rightarrow O_2 \rightarrow A_2$)—perhaps accompanied, as in some of Kraepelin's descriptions, by vague images of the printed words—would not run counter to the principle of disinvolution but would be quite consistent with it. The part of the upper half of Figure 4.3 drawn in broken lines indicates that the definition (delimiting) of the object-presentation (conception) is to the speaker often less constrained for foreign words than for native words, thus affording them, according to Kraepelin, a "much larger independence and mobility, and an overall more opaque and indistinct content: properties which can only favor their appearance" when the more specific native terms cannot be retrieved. (For further consideration of the significance of printed words in dreams and their frequent co-occurence with foreign languages in the specimens of Kraepelin, Freud, Meumann, and the two experiments reported in Part Three of this book, see Heynick, 1984.)

This intrusion of foreign and classical bookish words into Kraepelin's corpus is one of several phenomena he discusses in neurolinguistic terms. The above schemas are useful in following Kraepelin's description of other phenomena as well.

Kraepelin's monograph brings up other gross neuroanatomical (cortical) considerations besides the above references to Wernicke's area. Similar considerations are found in Freud's aphasia monograph, which, as we have noted, contains several brain diagrams. But Figures 2.1 and 2.2 (pp. 15 and 17), which are based on written descriptions in Freud's unpublished, proto-psychoanalytic *Project*, drafted some five years after *On Aphasia*, are, although still anatomical in flavor, basically "psychological."[2] This attests to Freud's departure from strict neurology as he went on to develop psychoanalysis. Recent research has brought to light the fact that Freud's psychoanalytic period owes more than had previously been recognized to his earlier neurolinguistic work. The aphasia-related replay hypothesis for dream speech is an instance of this, if a relatively obscure one. A more obvious example is the important psychoanalytic concept "overdetermination" (the interpretability of a symbol or action at more than one level or aspect of the personality). This term is, as we have seen above, already present in Freud's aphasia studies, albeit in a different sense.

But on the purely physiological side of the mind-body coin, by the time he published the *Traumdeutung* Freud had explicitly abandoned organic considerations, writing, "I shall carefully avoid the temptation to determine psychical locality in any anatomical fashion" (1900/1953a, p. 536). Although never abandoning the principle that the psychoanalytic superstructure—presumably even including the most intricate and subtle processes of the Oedipus complex—would "one day have to be set upon its organic foundation" (1916–17/1961b, pp. 338–339), Freud made his disavowals only stronger in succeeding publications. In his *Introductory Lectures* he declared that "psychoanalysis must keep itself free from any hypothesis which is alien to it, whether of an anatomical, chemical or physiological kind, and must operate entirely with psychological auxilliary ideas" (1916–17/1961b, p. 21). In an obvious reference to Koch's "specific etiology," Freud (1926/1959b) went on to write, somewhat mockingly, "The ideal solution [to neuroses], which medical men no doubt still yearn for, would be to discover some bacillus which could be isolated and bred in pure culture and which, when injected into anyone, would invariably produce the same illness; or to put it less extravagantly, to demonstrate the existence of certain chemical substances the administration of which would bring about or cure particular neuroses. But the probability of a solution of this kind remains slight" (pp. 152–153).

Freud published this in 1926, the year of the death of Kraepelin, who had just completed a series of experiments with thyroid, testicular, and ovarian extracts for the treatment of schizophrenia. So it was that two greats of modern psychiatry—the one basically concerned with neurosis and psychodynamics, the other with psychosis and biochemistry—had, despite their mutual long-standing interest in dreams and language, nothing to say to one another when the new era of scientific dream research was being heralded during the first decades of the twentieth century.

Notes

1. R. Fliess (1953) points out that Freud seems to violate his own dictum when he traces the apparently motor-acoustically perceived dream utterance, "*Non vixit*," in his "Non Vixit" dream, back to a written source of the day before. For consideration of motor-acoustically versus non–motor-acoustically perceived dream utterances in terms of Freud's proto-psychoanalytic *Project*, see Heynick, 1985.

2. The brainlike shape of these figures is borrowed from a schematic diagram of Freud's *Project* in Wolheim (1971). Interestingly, as John Forrester of Cambridge University has noted (pers. commun.), a ghost of Freud's neuroanatomical sketches can be seen in the topological diagrams that he supplies in *The Ego and the Id* (1923/1961a) and the *New Introductory Lectures on Psychoanalysis* (1933/1964b) in developing his tripartite model of the psyche. The acoustic cap on the left-hand side (the usual anatomical verbal seat) of the ego in the earlier schema is replaced by the super-ego (the voice of the parent) in the later one.

PART 2

The Texts of Kraepelin and His Colleagues

Translator's Preface

"If French is the language of diplomacy, then German may be said to be the language of psychiatry, for it was in the German-speaking countries of Central Europe that most of the fundamental concepts of modern psychiatry were evolved." So began the backward-looking foreword to *Fish's Schizophrenia* (Anderson, 1962, p. xiii).

Times change. English has almost completely replaced French as the language of diplomacy and has long since become the international language of all branches of science, thus supplanting German's importance in medicine and psychiatry. A result is that very few non-Germanic psychiatrists, sleep researchers, psychologists, linguists, or other cognitive scientists have had direct access to most of the works of Kraepelin and his contemporary compatriots. This is doubly unfortunate. Not only are these pioneering texts historically important, but they are quite valuable today in their own right. This is particularly so in the case of sleep speech, in which there has been little superseding research. Even recent scientists have, therefore, drawn upon Kraepelin and his contemporaries, though often inaccurately or through inaccurate second-hand sources.

In their important book *Symbol Formation: An Organismic-Developmental Approach to Language and the Expression of Thought,*

Heinz Werner and Bernard Kaplan (1963) of Clark University relied heavily upon Kraepelin in their chapter "Handling of Linguistic Forms in Dreams." However, no mention is made of Kraepelin's admitted selectivity, nor of the fact that he seems to have drawn much of his corpus from what today would be called NREM sleep, particularly from hypnagogic and hypnopompic periods. Eighteen years later, in his classic book *Sleeptalking*, Arthur Arkin apparently took over Kraepelin's findings from Werner and Kaplan as more or less representative of verbal behavior in dreaming proper.

The problems of translating Kraepelin's *Über Sprachstörungen im Traume* rival those faced by the translators of Freud's *Psychopathology of Everyday Life* and *Jokes and Their Relation to the Unconscious*. James Strachey, the editor of the Standard Edition of Freud's works in English, cites in his introduction to *Jokes* one of the puns analyzed by Freud in that very book: "Traduttore—Traditore!" ("Translator—traitor!") But whereas Freud's jokes are often plays on words, and the slips of the tongue in his *Everyday Life* are often displacements and condensations based on phonological and semantic factors, many of the specimens in Kraepelin's monograph have degenerated much further.

However, every effort has been made to spare the reader the annoyance of extensive bracketing. Whenever possible, specimens of dream speech are given only in English translation. This often involved not a little effort with the thesaurus (and even a rhyming dictionary) and the taking of some minor liberties with the original, as one indeed must also do with poetry translation. Only in those cases in which an English equivalent would have strayed too far from the original is German bracketing provided.

As for Kraepelin's scientific prose, my translation policy is more conservative. I have endeavored, as a rule, to stick close to the original text and not take much liberty. This means that if, for example, the author used the German word *immer*, I would translate this as "always" and not (as Strachey might do in his translation of Freud) as "invariably." This is based on the assumption that Kraepelin himself could have used another German word, such as *ausnahmslos*, but chose not to. The same policy applies in general to idioms and syntactic constructions, although I have endeavored to split up some of the overly long sentences typical of the Germanic writing of Kraepelin's day.

One final note: References in the historical texts of Kraepelin and his contemporaries are to be found directly after the respective works rather than in the general reference list at the back of this book.

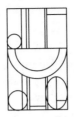

On Speech Disorders in Dreams

by Emil Kraepelin
Translated from the German by Frank Heynick[*]

I. Introduction

The peculiar changes which the whole of our mental life undergoes in dreaming have long been a favorite area of introspection, to say nothing of artificial dissection and interpretation. Particularly the relations of dreams to external and internal experiences—and furthermore the deviations in conceptual associations and personality awareness, as well as in memory and thought processes—have been endlessly described, over and over again, and have also often been compared with the findings on the mentally ill. Far less attention has been paid to the stirrings of volition in dreams, while speech utterances have been quite conspicuously neglected, although they would seem to me to offer the psychologist and alienist a series of remarkable facts. Up to now, save for some brief references, Gießler[1] has been the only one, to my knowledge, to concern himself with this question in any detail, and then without following up the connections between speech disorders in dreams and related phenomena in normal people and patients.

Through chance experiences, I have in the course of over twenty years become aware of the bizarre features which dream speech presents. Its similarity to speech confusion in particular, which I was able to point out as long ago as 1889,[2] led me to collect at my leisure in the course of years a large number of speech specimens from dreams. Part of these stem from people in my surroundings whom I asked to pay attention to such experiences. Most were supplied by myself, however, by placing from time to time a tablet at my bedside in order to write down immediately upon awakening what I dreamt. As I have found out through my trials and inquiries, anyone who dreams at

---

[*]With thanks to translation consultants Arthur van Essen and Sami Faltas.

all is able in this way to assemble a host of specimens in a short time. Speech utterances in dreams are an almost daily occurrence, especially during half sleep in the morning before awakening and, less often, in the evening before falling asleep. I hardly doubt that they are also very frequent at other times. At the given moment the conditions for their reaching into waking life simply need to be favorable, similar to the way we remember other dreams. A smaller number of observations stem from afternoon naps.

When one begins regularly to collect specimens of speech from dreams, one soon finds out two remarkable things. The first is the quite extraordinary fleetingness of one's remembrance of the actual wording of the utterances. The traces of other dream experiences also tend to be quickly lost, but it is quite common for vivid dreamers to be able to retain a series of details of their dream events. By contrast, next to nothing of the speech utterances usually persists in memory without special attention being paid to them. Indeed, it is usually not possible, despite the utmost efforts, to impress their wording into memory when one does not write them down immediately following awakening. It has often enough been the case with me of trying in vain by countless repetitions upon awakening to commit to memory a specimen which I happened not to have been able to write down. Even when I was quite certain of having memorized it, I was forced, to my annoyance, to observe a short time later that it had completely and irretrievably faded from mind. These experiences can be partly explained by the nonsensicalness of the material, which affords no connecting threads. Furthermore, it may have to do with the aftereffects of the sleeping state immediately following awakening, which wear off more slowly with vivid dreamers. Some repetition aloud following complete arousal was exceedingly more effective for retention than numerous silent attempts at memorization just before, in the intermediate condition. The dreamt experience was, to be sure, recognized as such and retained for scientific evaluation. Nevertheless, on every occasion I was impressed by the extraordinary difficulty of reporting speech from dreams even only a few minutes after awakening, whereas I find it easy in the course of the day to let long series of other experiences return and pass before me in all possible detail. The vividness and abundance of dream memories may sometimes seem not greatly surpassed by those of waking life. Yet speech presentations from dreams adhere without a doubt incomparably more weakly than those of clear consciousness.

I have furthermore often been struck by the very peculiar experience that for some time following awakening it was not possible for me to recognize the nonsensicalness of the language utterances from dreams. In a great number of instances in which I was aware of having dreamt and having experienced a speech specimen which I should try to retain, the specimen—to my disappointment—at first seemed to show no deviation at all from wakeful utterances. I therefore considered the written entry pointless. Only after longer, deeper consideration, did the complete nonsensicalness of what had been said slowly become clear to me. The spilling over of the dream disorder into awakening daytime consciousness was very noticeable in this area after the other symptoms of dreaming had already faded and been adjusted for. Such experiences remind us of that twilight condition in which the faculty for speech expression can, like speech comprehension, still be disturbed, though the delerious condition is past and general orientation has returned. In particular, the conditions of normal and pathological somnolence come into consideration.

The number of specimens I have collected totals 274. Often, unfortunately, I have nothing but the simple wording of the speech utterance, or only very short comments on the meaning and the particular attendant circumstances. The reason for this lies partly in that I initially wrote down these observations only as oddities, without intending to carry the matter any further, and partly in that a number of these come from other people, who did not know to supply more particulars. Very frequently, however, the whole of the dream proceedings was extraordinarily unclear, so that aside from the wording in question, no further distinct memory presentations could be salvaged from it in wakeful consciousness. Nevertheless, it was still possible in an adequately large number of cases to render some account of the dream thought processes which accompanied the speech utterances.

To the extent that a subsequent judgment is possible, it seems that the overwhelming majority of specimens represent words uttered by the dreamer himself. The dream utterances had therefore essentially taken the form of speech motor-images, and were registered as such. Even when the thought contents of what was spoken were very clear in my consciousness, I still very often had the feeling of speaking purely mechanically, without distinctly comprehending the actual wording of my discourse. As has already been mentioned, even when I had repeated the wordings a few times following awakening, I was at times still unable to grasp them until after a while the incorrectness or nonsensicalness of the speech expression came fully to light. In the case of seventeen specimens, I could establish with reasonable certainty that they involved not independent utterances, but rather the reading off of printed or written text. In the case of another fifteen specimens, the influence of a reading-image was probable in view of the peculiar spelling of the words, which was explicitly dreamt, too. Added to these is a small number of specimens by which, presumably, something previously read was independently recited.

If I may trust my own inner experiences, then even in all these cases, speech motor-images regularly played the main role. In the dream, I did see before me the text which I recited; however it was not actually a case of reading out, but rather more of speaking with the accompaniment of the image. What was being spoken was on the paper in front of me. In other words, the reading-images acquired no hallucinatory independence and were not decisive for the series of speech motor-images, but rather they accompanied only in vaguer outlines the whole process, similar to the case in wakefulness when we try to recite from memory something read. As a result, it was also impossible for me to determine whether in the specimen in question it was a matter of actually reading out or the independent reciting of a merely supposed text. Here, the boundaries seem to blur. I must leave undecided whether in some individual cases, and particularly with other people, it might not be otherwise. It is indeed known that there are people with very strongly impressed visual memories who are able just from memory to read out things previously read. I do not want to fail to mention here that in a half-waking state I have occasionally succeeded in simply reading out words and sentences emerging into the dark field of vision. They regularly had the same nonsensical content as those of dream utterances. In six instances, the words seen appeared as titles of visual presentations.

In only nine specimens were the speech utterances placed in the mouths of other persons. Twice this involved singing. Once, the specimens contained a question and answer. These observations are all my own, but it is still possible that some of the specimens from other people belong to these categories without having been noted as such. Here, too, the role of auditory images seemed to me not to be fundamentally greater than with the previous group, that of visual images. In so far as I am able to reconstruct the dreaming process, I do not believe myself to have actually heard the utterances in question, just as on the whole my acoustic memories, in wakefulness as in dreaming, are quite unvivid. Rather, the wording of the speech utterance appeared in my consciousness in a form of which I can give no further account other than my having simply attributed them to some other person. Perhaps one should interpret the process as inner speech accompanied by sound-images. In so doing, I think of the experiences in remembering a conversation with another person, whose utterances are, at least to me, likewise not in the form of pure auditory images, but tend rather to appear with a more or less strong admixture of speech motor-images.

In the dream itself, the content of the speech utterances is commonly taken to be completely free of mistakes. Very often, to be sure, the dreamer paid it no mind anyway, but simply tolerated what was said as the expression of often quite indistinct thought processes. In three cases, the utterances seemed to be quite successful, although soon upon awakening this feeling proved to have been deceptive. In three other cases, a word was recognized in the dream itself as being incorrect, and in one case was actually corrected. One of these instances was the single specimen which was supposedly written down in the dream. If therefore the chance correctly to judge speech errors in dreams seems to occur most seldom, there is, nevertheless, more often an indistinct feeling for the peculiarity. This is at least indicated by the experience that in nine specimens the language structure clearly appeared facetious. The divergence of thought content and speech expression was perceived as a humorous contrast, even if the nonsensicalness of the latter could not be grasped.

Ninety-six of the verbal dream recalls were more or less well-formed sentences, although five of them showed a grammatical deficiency. These sentences were mostly rather short, with only three or four specimens involving narrative language. In seventeen other cases, a number of words were strung together without recognizable coherence in content or grammar. Rhythmical structure was found in eighteen cases, nine of which were definitely verses, usually with quite imperfect rhymes. Fragments of sentences occurred forty-eight times. Here, no distinction could ever be made as to whether the speech utterance already had this incomplete form in the dream, or whether it only partly remained in memory. The same applies to the 113 instances in which isolated words or word-combinations were noted down. It seems very likely to me that in most cases they were torn from a larger context and, only because of their unusualness, better retained in memory than their less striking neighboring words. Finally, it is noteworthy that in twenty-seven cases, recalled words and phrases were clearly conceived of as translations into foreign languages. It was clear to the dreamer that the expression in question represented French, Latin, Spanish, Italian, Greek, Russian, Estonian, or Finnish designations for concepts which were in all other ways quite current in his own language. Remarkably there was no English.

If, after these preliminary remarks, we attempt to classify the observed material as a whole, the greatest of difficulties arise. Part of this is to be found in the fact that, with the unclarity of the processes which take place in individual cases, it is often quite impossible to give a closer account of the nature of the observed material. A certain arbitrariness in interpretation is therefore unavoidable. In those cases, however, the specimens are, as a rule, not simple ones; rather, multifarious disturbances link up and cross one another. Under these circumstances, we can initially only deal with a quite general survey of the manifold forms which dream language disturbances can take. The way in which the preliminary sorting of the material is to be carried further and can be adjusted will be discussed later.

As a point of departure for our study, an initial consideration is that the process of linguistic expression calls for us to distinguish a whole series of subprocesses which may be disrupted independently of one another. The first prerequisite for the intelligible expression of thought is clarity and the proper ordering of the idea in mind itself. Hence, all disturbances in the coinage of the ideas and in the logical consistency of the thought process cannot but leave their mark on the speech utterances. To be sure, we are—strictly speaking—no longer dealing with speech disorders here, but rather with thought disorders. It will be seen that a large number of specimens are to be interpreted by us in this sense, but on the other hand also that thought disturbances are very commonly tied up with true speech disturbances.

The latter constitutes what is for us by far the most important main group. In order to give proper linguistic expression to our thoughts, we must first of all bring the relations of individual ideas together in the corresponding grammatical forms. This requires first the correct choice of the language dependency relations, then the construction of compound sentences. Disorders in these processes cause in the first case alterations and unclarities in the basic idea, and in the second case, by contrast, incoherence. But it is also necessary to find the precisely appropriate language term for each idea. In dreams this process is subjected to the most frequent and radical disturbances. In particular, different sets of instances can be distinguished here according to whether, in the selecting of words, the correct expression is on the one hand just mutilated or altered, or on the other hand replaced by a completely different one, eventually perhaps by a neologism. This can result in the most diverse relations between the wrong words and the correct expression. The speech mistake is mediated by reminiscences, and conceptual analogies proximate or remote. Often, however, not the slightest link is to be traced between the intended words and the produced words. The latter, finally, may be composed of current linguistic ingredients, or have been invented completely independently.

A final form of speech disorder—one which in waking life is very familiar to us in healthy people, but especially in patients—is that of disorders of articulation. I have not observed these in dreams, apparently because we are always dealing only with inner speech, while actual innervation of the speech muscles does not take place. Only when the dreamer speaks aloud could articulation disturbances also appear. On the basis of incidental observations, I have no doubt that pronunciation is indeed often strongly impaired in such cases. These disturbances, however, completely escape self-observation. To the extent I can judge from personal experience, the dreamer never has the impression of having stuttered, hesitated, or spoken unclearly or incorrectly.

It is most appropriate to begin our detailed discussion of our observed material with the true speech disorders. Here we are in a position first of all to distinguish the fundamental disorders on the basis of particular faulty expressions—disorders which time and again creep into the more complex specimens and render understanding more difficult. For the same reason, it is recommendable to bring forth the description of word-selection disturbances and to follow it up with that of syntactic speech disturbances. Both groups are quite familiar to us from our experiences with patients. The first encompasses the field of *paraphasia*, the second that of *acataphasia* and *agrammatism*. The final part can be taken up by thought disorders, to the extent that these find expression in dream speech.

II. Disorders of Word-Selection (Paraphasia)

We may speak of disorders of word-selection when an idea is not expressed with those words which correspond to it in ordinary usage. Word errors which arise in this way are either simple alterations of the proper words, and as such easily recognized; or they are different words, in themselves meaningful but used with deviant connotations; or else they are out and out neologisms. All these cases are represented among our specimens. Of course, it would be possible to group the misbegotten word-creations in dreams under these more linguistic headings. But perhaps it is more advisable to proceed from the ideas whose expression the creations were supposed to form; this is because the nature of these ideas no doubt has considerable consequences for the generation of such mistakes.

If we are to examine our observations from this angle, we first of all have to separate a group of specimens whose accompanying ideas have remained totally *unclear and blurred*. These cases involve not so much disturbances in word-selection as the occurrence of speech presentations without clearly developed thoughts whose expression they could form. Nevertheless, it cannot be denied that it is impossible in the strict sense to separate clearly these cases from those of word-selection disturbances. The emergence of language disturbances in dreams in general is certainly most strongly dependent on the obscuring of consciousness and the consequent reduction in the clarity of ideas. The case observed here therefore corresponds to the highest degree of a condition which—to put it more mildly—also governs the disorders of word-selection. Furthermore, in particular cases the possiblity cannot be ruled out that it is only in remembering that the faulty words more clearly obtain than the accompanying object-presentation, which were perhaps originally quite vivid. For this reason, we shall incorporate in our exposition of the word-selection disturbances also those word errors without any recognizable content representation.

The specimens which remain after this delimitation seem to me to lend themselves to further division into three main groups. In the first, we are concerned with *general object-presentations*, whose content readily permits expression by means of a *short linguistic designation*. The errors here may first of all have been committed by simple mutilation of the correct word.

(1) "*Enklysma*" [idem] instead of "enema" [Klysma].

(2) "*I was on the Rhedume*" instead of "on the Rhede."

(3) "*An inclination [Hang] toward the profession [Fach]*" instead of "curtain [Vorhang] for book compartment [Bücherfach]."

(4) "*F. eats more at your place than at ours, 8–10 dumplings, 2–3 liters of semola's soup [Giesensuppe]*" instead of "semolina soup" [Griessuppe].

(5) "*Buckelor [Jankgesellen]*" instead of "bachelor" [Junggesellen].

(6) "*Princer [Dynaster]*" instead of "prince's" [Dynastes].

(7) "*Nevertheless the high-level visits experience the most unwomant [unerfrautigsten] printing errors*" instead of "most unpleasant" [unerfreulichsten].

(8) *"Harizal [Wägere] and vertical beauty,"* instead of "horizontal" [wagerechte].

(9) *"Psypes"* instead of "psychical types"; written; recognized by the dreamer himself as incorrect.

In the first two specimens, the mutilations are caused by arbitrary additions; in the third by omissions; in the fourth by a combination of admixture and omission. The next three observations contain substituted letters, with the next to the last also containing an omission. Here it was supposed to indicate the tasteful arrangement of a room in horizontal and vertical directions. The contraction "psypes" brings to mind knowledge of paralytics, similarly to "exity" for "electricity."

By and large, these specimens do not significantly differ from those which one can gather from simple slips of the tongue. Only here the influence of neighboring speech-presentations is less in evidence. The mistakes appear completely spontaneously, perhaps because in dream consciousness it is far less easy for us to trace what initiated them. There is sometimes more success in this regard with the second subgroup. In place of the correct term, other words—meaningful in themselves—appear with deviant meanings, frequently also showing mutilations and alterations. In a number of instances, the *sound kinship* proves to be the connecting link:

(10) *"Paste over stamps"* instead of "paste on stamps."

(11) *"I only want to pin on my clothes"* instead of "put on."

(12) *"Lay ack to the root"* instead of "axe."

(13) *"This is at least a vaginismus [idem]"* instead of "venture" [Wagnis].

(14) *"Aren't there on this very side some lifelong points?"* instead of "life-threatening." Refers to left side of chest.

(15) *"I always happen to [zufällig] speak the truth"* instead of "reliably" [zuverlässig].

(16) *"Café marmolata"* instead of "café with marble [Marmor] facing."

With these specimens, we are already reminded of intentional plays on words or typographic errors, although any jocular relation was far from the dreamer's mind. Clearer still is the humorous coloring of two terms from one and the same person: (17) *"piss-marrow" [Pißmark]* instead of "loin-marrow" [Lendenmark], and (18) *"nervus poculomotorius"* instead of "nervus medianus." Both were meant seriously in the dream, but it was the very fact of their ambiguity which saved them from oblivion. In the first case, the name "Bismarck" seems to have stimulated the formation of the expression, which is linguistically possible, yet newly coined, and was suggested by the relation of loin-marrow to bladder. The second specimen relates the movement of an arm to the raising of a cup, then brings about the derailment via the sound resemblance to nervus ocumotorius. To these also belongs *"frackot train" [Frackelzug]* reported by Vischer,[3] with people in burning tailcoats doing the pulling. Here too, a conceptual relation is provided first of all by the similarity of "Aufzug" (elevator lift [cf. also "Flaschenzug" (pulley)]) to "Fackelzug" (torch-lit procession; faggot-train), which is then changed by the contribution of "Frackschöße" (coattails; frocktails), into the similarly sounding "Frackelzug" (frackot train).

The last three specimens, which might just as well have been intentionally made up in waking life, indicate to us that alongside the sound kinship which plays the main role in usual slips of the tongue, other influences can determine lexical mistakes. This process is, after all, similarly observed with other slips of the tongue, if far more seldom. The following specimens belong here:

(19) *"On the other side there was a stucco of some numbers"* instead of "individual entries."

(20) *"Deportation order"* instead of "waybill."

(21) *"Where are you going? To the Pope's honoring"* instead of "welcoming."

(22) *"Secret kopeks"* instead of "secret policemen."

(23) *"Invalid clock"* instead of "old clock."

(24) *"To arrange knives"* instead of "to eliminate, to render harmless."

(25) *"Will we eat this evening so much more heavily?"* instead of "so much later" or "so much more."

(26) *"The grown hatchets [Beile] of lead [Blei]"* instead of "of one piece."

(27) *"The soldiers are in the field, now there will be forking"* instead of "impaling."

(28) *"She has already been judicially stoned"* instead of "sentenced."

(29) *"Destroyed to a year's detention by the noblest peers"* instead of "sentenced."

(30) *"J'oi seldom tam the character"* instead of "I don't have so much desire."

Conceptual relations apparently induced the word errors throughout. Just as separate patches appear in "stucco," so the "numbers" are found to be strewn about. "Waybill" and "deportation order" can both prescribe the manner for things and people not traveling of their own accord. The "welcoming" is only a form of "honoring." With "secret kopeks" the side-idea of Russian intruded, while the old inventory item was denoted by "invalid clock" due to its fragility.

The "arrangement" is the elimination of a danger in the quarrel. "More heavily" and "later" or "more"—which of the two meanings it was remained unclear upon awakening—are conceptually related comparatives. The "grown" denotes, as with rocks, the firmness of the inner continuity. Whether at the same time the "lead" would symbolize the heaviness, or was simply mediated by the sound resemblance, Beile–Blei, could no longer be made out. The similarity in the wielding of bayonettes and pitch-forks is readily evident, as is the inner relation of "being stoned" or "destroyed" to "judicial sentence."

At first sight, the last specimen, which is indeed a somewhat more complicated one, seems completely incomprehensible. It fits into the group discussed here only to the extent that the word "character" which appears instead of "desire" is still conceptually related. The desire for an act is in the final analysis a result of character. In addition, however, the expression in mind "I have" is replaced by "j'oi," thought to be Old French. Then "so" is translated into the supposedly Russian "tam" instead of the correct "tak." And finally, instead of the correct term "not . . . much," the related "seldom" appears.

In a final series of cases *no relation* at all, in either sound or concept, is discernible between the correct term and the faulty word. The associative process which led to the substitution remains completely obscure. The following are examples of this:

(31) *"Camisole"* for "launch."

(32) *"Salniter"* for "embryo."

(33) *"Scolex,"* Latin for "hunchback."

(34) *"Melos,"* French for "brother-in-law versed in business."

(35) *"Meyr,"* pronounced "may-or," Arabic for "guard."

(36) *"We sat in the allonge,"* in two corresponding groups like "complements" [Pendants].

It is indeed not without significance that the first two specimens involve words which are not current, whose relations to definite object-presentations were therefore probably only loose ones. Likewise, it is noteworthy that the next three mistakes all appear as translations into foreign languages. One could almost get the impression that the peculiarity of the newly emerging connection between object-presentation and speech-presentation forced on the dreamer the explanation that it involves a translation in which such, previously unusual, connections occur. In the last specimen however, the sound resemblance of "allonge" to "Pendant" [complement] did also play a certain part. Sometimes the faulty word is also mutilated, as in

(37) *"Constitutal position"* instead of "upright position."

(38) *"Furthermore, he will been urthered a few more times"* for "has invited a few more times."

In the first specimen, one can at most derive from the meaning of the Latin word "constituere" a certain conceptual relation to the adjective "upright," which here again was thought of as a translation. The second case is far more complicated. It looks as if the beginning "furthermore" [Im übrigen] gave rise, by means of perseverence, to a derailment in what followed. Thus came into being the nonsensical mutilated word "urthered" [erüberdernd], which the dreamer characteristically took to be a Saxon provincialism due to its remarkable form. With this malformation, which deviates totally from the thoughts in mind, the compound construction also comes to grief.

These last cases, in which on the one hand the relation between thought and false word is loosened, and on the other hand the latter takes on an unusual or quite mutilated form, supply the transition to the surprisingly large group of *neologisms*. Already with some of the observations cited above ("salniter," "scolex," "melos," "meyr"), it seems quite unimportant that the false words themselves also happen to have meanings, if remote ones. With the neologisms to be considered now, it can be clearly observed how on the one hand elements which are still meaningful frequently go into their making, with or without relation to the thought expression in mind, while on the other hand there are syllable connections which are completely arbitrarily invented and meaningless. Between the two forms there are all degrees of transition. To facilitate our survey of the great number of observations, we would like, as before, to consider first of all those with which a more or less clear sound patterning of the false word on the correct expression is recognizable. In so doing, we will make the transition by degrees from the linguistically more comprehensible forms to the completely arbitrary neologisms.

(39) *"Rind houses [Schwartenhaüser]"* for "extensive callosity of the hand" [Schwielen an der Hand].

(40) *"House calculation number"* for "double house."

(41) *"Oak queen bee [Eichweisel]"* for "squirrel" [Eichhörnchen].

(42) *"With the distinction that Italy is dragoning,"* "is power-mad," "is a dragon."

(43) *"I have grounds, spice grounds [Würzgrund],"* "grounds which are related" to Würzburg.

(44) *"Air-sid,"* more general expression for "air balloon."

(45) *"We still see the dashed-off waltz kings"* for "enrapturing."

It is difficult to give an account of how the individual mistakes came about. With "house calculation number" the concept of multiplication may have formed a connecting link, while I am inclined to accept in the case of the genesis of "oak queen bee" [Eichweisel] a phonetic sideeffect from the idea of "Schweif" (tail) suggested by "Eichhörnchen" (squirrel). The next two specimens are simple contractions of more complex expressions. In the specimens after that, the idea of "cube" played a part to which can be attributed the mutilated element "sid" instead of "side." "Dashed-off" originated from the idea of a passionately frantic dance.

(46) *"Pommerali"* for "pommes de terre," ordered in a Brussels hotel.

(47) *"An imlessized Hamlet,"* for "improvised" theater play title.

(48) *"Perpauser Siberia"* instead of "Transcaucasian."

(49) *"Parsemenie,"* Russian for "a few weeks" [a few semaines].

(50) *"Vulpiunt,"* Danish for "they want." [sie wollen].

(51) *"Duce"* for "two," *"tripap"* for "three," foreign languages; here clear recall that "pap" = times, and that also in another language a similar suffix is appended to the iterative number.

(52) *"Peince-voutes"* for "patience," pensez-vous.

(53) *"Kissioll"* for "Kissinger wine," kissell.

(54) *"The astacias of the oreomalaias"* for "national bone softening" (osteomalacia).

(55) *"Mophrodunt air"* for "damp air," saprophytes.

(56) *"Voisit, everything voisit,"* expression of surprise about a mass of termites.

(57) *"Reflise,"* wrong expression for "reflection," supposedly quoted by Sanders from an author.

(58) *"Cayphaxes,"* witty for "caymans" in the Frankfurt zoological gardens.

In the first three specimens, the false words stand in for foreign words, which we may assume to be more loosely tied to their object-presentations than are the German designations which are acquired in earliest youth and organically connected with the entire vocabulary of the mother tongue. This peculiarity makes itself felt clearly enough in the frequency and unobtrusiveness of the mixing up of these late and inadequately learned expressions.

The following three cases again bear the mark of translations into a foreign language, by which the absurdity of the emerging speech expression is to a certain extent made obvious to the dreamer. The more or less remote sound resemblances of the words actually in mind are everywhere unmistakable. In the case of "vulpiunt" the connecting link was formed by "volunt"; in the case of "duce" by the Spanish "doce," which to be sure does not mean "two," but "twelve." Very similarly, we see also in the following five specimens the word-errors brought about by the intercession of indistinct side-ideas in mind. The original thought, the card game "patience" (solitaire), links up via sound-association to "pensez-vous," and in turn calls forth the similarly-sounding, but nonsensical false words. "Kissiol" is nothing but a modification of the Russian word "kissell" (fruit-juice dessert) whose actual meaning was lost, however, and instead was brought into connection with "Kissingen" via sound-association. Here, as with many other specimens, the dreamer had the impression that the false word first originated purely as a speech motor-image and only subsequently aroused an object-association. "Astacias of the oreomalaias" is a sound paraphrase of the expression "osteomalicia," the latter having been awakened by the original thoughts. The designation "mophrodunt" suggests "saprophytes," the latter having been triggered by the idea of stuffy air. Finally, "voisit" is apparently a contraction of the two ideas in mind: "voilà" and "termites." The last two specimens, which represent drastic mutilations of the correct words and should therefore already be counted among the neologisms, were recognized by the dreamers themselves as incorrectly formed and characterized by their respective side-ideas.

Instead of sound kinship, it is also possible in the case of neologisms for a more or less remote conceptual relation to intercede in the genesis of a word-error.

(59) *"Plantar-friendship"* for "handshake."

(60) *"Here crossed gait and here finaled"* for "crossed and equilateral chair legs."

(61) *"Paris is a whole Emmaus room for stone"* for "a geological specimen collection."

(62) *"Arithmoseismic movements"* for "caressive movements" in a theater play.

(63) *"That the girl be always unpleasantly accept*[idem] *on such occasions"* for "take tips."

(64) *"E. just wrote me that Julien's skin expans* [idem] *and it died [starb] this morning"* for "burst" [barst].

(65) *"Incipiitis"* for "initial paralytic changes."

(66) *"Vendiasmen"* for "corruptibility."

(67) *"Socorzo,"* a blind beggar's sign, for "pity."

(68) *"Gli occhi cadenti,"* "blind beggar," taken to be good Italian even long after awakening.

In the first observation, the idea of "handshake" apparently aroused first that of "palm" and then that of "planta pedis," which ultimately finally came together with the side-idea "friendship" in the form of the false word. In the second specimen, the idea "gait" was presumably stimulated by that of "legs." Where the expression "finaled" stems from is unclear. Likewise, the derivation of "Emmaus room" is obscure. In any case, the specimen involves a mixing up of the idea of the geologically particularly interesting Parisian Basin with that of "specimen collection." In the last seven specimens, foreign words and translations again play their significant role, albeit often in very remote connections. With "arithmoseismic" motions the ideas in mind were of stroking and dancing, which can remind one of "seismic," whereas the first part of the word was added on senselessly. The following specimens are self-explanatory and for a part have almost a comic coloring, although the dreamer did not at all perceive them as such. The expression "socorzo" is no doubt a mutilation of "soccorso," meaning "help," but was interpreted as the semantically kindred "pity." The last observation, too, shows how a particular speech expression ("sunken eyes") can be given a new interpretation in the terms of a conceptually close idea. If one wishes, one can transfer these instances from the neologism count over to the meaningful word-errors in the previous group.

Finally, a considerable range among the neologisms is occupied by the free inventions which lack any recognizable patterning on the correct speech expression of the thought in mind.

(69) *"Girl successor to the throne"* instead of "servant girl."

(70) *"Telephonic suit"* instead of "business suit."

(71) *"Cobbler-wolfkin"* instead of "spy."

(72) *"Squeeze-gable"* instead of "cabman seat."

(73) *"Grash-botfly,"* invective for "servant girl."

(74) *"At Richter's there was a quick, an everlasting quick, a fireplace de Chimbo,"* there were grand goings-on at the festivities (a chimborasso of valuables).[4]

(75) *"A salamine with meet-others [Treffander]"* instead of "cuff [Rand] with seam."

(76) *"Formentist"* for "drawer."

(77) *"The isher of the Unterwalden Canton"* instead of "standard-bearer."

(78) *"An administratively expedited jary,"* "an official letter."

(79) *"Crapaud,"* French, "small, miserable urchin."

(80) *"Petroscapies"* for "objects of worship."

(81) *"Catibo,"* translation of "blockhead" and "pound."

(82) *"Vizge di Peru"* for "Portuguese oysters."

(83) *"Baskôlêgos"* for "keen on weapons," Greek.

(84) *"Vi ha hi mi Fors"* for "onward to Fors!", foreign cry.

(85) *"Sano orwis"* for "fruit," pronounced "soch."[5]

(86) *"La lemo oseada se arrizza,"* Spanish for "the thing is working out."

(87) *"Que se penja dé,"* Spanish, question of "whether the last five (dé) lire of the coins tossed down as price are in fact enough."

(88) *"In d.c. densh,"* witty Latin translation of "into the moon."

With "girl successor to the throne," one could still think of "nursemaid" [Kindermädchen; lit.: "children's girl"] as a connecting link, even if it did not come into the dreamer's consciousness. With the next specimens, however, it is hardly possible to trace any patterning whatsoever. The "quick" [Risch] was, according to the dreamer's recollection, presumably a more remote reminiscence of the unusual "rout" [idem], while "fireplace de Chimbo" seems to be more intelligible. The following expressions turn out to be completely free inventions. To be sure, one can in the case of "isher" think of the Greek ischo for echo, and in the case of "petroscapies" one can think of "scapular," which occurred to the dreamer. The last eight observations are here again translations—the type of language connection which affords the word-errors the easiest entry and the broadest play. The language in question was not always clear; yet the Spanish neologisms, like the Greek, allowed in a surprising way—despite their total nonsensicalness and despite the replacement of pesetas by lire—the recognition of the special quality of the speech sounds. This is not at all the case with the Latin sample. The dreamer also perceived it distinctly, striving in vain to explain to himself the details of the expression. In contrast, "Vi ha hi mi Fors" corresponds fairly well to the sounds of the Finnish language, which was probably in mind here. For the original expression was, presumably, a summons to travel "till Voss," i.e., to Vossewangen in Norway, which had been read ten years before. Yet in the dream the final syllable of Helsingfors (Helsinki) appeared, and at the same time it imprinted a Finnish stamp upon the whole. The wrong words "squeeze-gable" and "grashbotfly" are noteworthy for the evident way the dreamer is influenced by general speech attitudes in these specimens. As meaningless as they are, these words still do not lack resemblance in their linguistic construction to the mode of expression of Berlin cabmen and uneducated and crude maidservants. In the case of "grash-botfly" [Graschendassel], vague reminiscences of "quasseln" (to twaddle), "quatschen" (to talk drivel), and "Drachen" (kite, shrew) may have played a part.

A certain exceptional position in our thinking is taken up by those ideas that do not involve a combining of many similar experiences, but rather correspond to a single object: proper names in the widest sense. While as a rule close relations between kindred aggregate ideas are also reflected in speech formation so that the same word stems in various forms characterize a whole family of ideas, a proper name attaches in a far more arbitrary way to a person or object, mostly without deeper relation to the foundation of the language. The connection therefore tends to be a similarly looser one, as with foreign language designations by which, in the beginning at least, the joining of expression with idea is purely an externally learned one. Add to this that individual ideas possess far more sharply marked sensory features than general ideas. With the latter, even when they have directly evolved from sense experiences, the details of the memory-images normally become less and less distinct so that the linguistic components of the aggregate idea stand out ever more strongly compared to the perceptual traces. With individual ideas, on the other hand, the linguistic designation always plays only a side role, since here the sensory memories do not weaken but rather take on a solid shape in an ever more familiar contour. This long-known distinction is presumably also to be viewed as the cause of the everyday phenomenon that we forget proper names most readily, while those ideas which have eventually become almost pure speech forms and which express properties, activities, and grammatical relations are the longest preserved, even in the case of severely pathological speech disorders.

We therefore should not be surprised that under the heading of word-errors in dreams the individual designations take up a relatively large space.

(89) *"The recently formed Mt. Mantinea on Rügen."*

(90) *"Catalepsy,"* as a designation of origin on a pencil.

(91) *"Richard III of England and Servant,"* the latter was thought of as a small country.

(92) *"Chuzbe,"* castle of Frederick the Great in Sanssouci.

(93) *"Arktis thyeoides,"* plant name.

(94) *"Eastwurk Railway [Osterwurkbahn],"* railway in the East, reminiscence of Osterburken.

(95) *"Tophi,"* plant name, Thypha.

(96) *"Laane,"* proper name instead of Häusler (cottager).

(97) *"Apestel, Luke,"* listing of patients.

(98) *"Melms Moltke,"* instead of Helmut.

(99) *"Tomide"* for *"Toni."*

(100) *"She is like Cala,"* like a matron from the Old Testament known for her fidelity, reminiscence of "Caleb."

(101) *"Etneus,"* Latin for "Etna."

(102) *"Really, Francisca and Back, how could you stand there and watch this!?"* addressed to two young gentlemen who had an elderly person bow down.

In all these specimens there appear real, or slightly mutilated, words in the form of proper names. Where the word-errors themselves are not proper names like Laane, Franziska, Melms, and Mantinea, they usually involve foreign words: Catalepsy, Arktis, Chuzbe, Tophi, Apestel. Sometimes the connecting thread is recognizable: the sound similarity between "Tophi" and the "Typha" in mind; between the proper name "Melms" and "Helmut." The deviations involved in "Tomide" and "Etneus" are justified by their being branded as translations. In the case of "Servant" [Knecht], the dreamer had in mind the English "knight," which imposed itself in place of the expected "Wales." "Arktis" was occasioned by the obscure idea "Rubus arcticus," the plant having been thought of as a northern one occurring together with the other one.

With "Eastwurk Railway" [Osterwurkbahn], first the "east" in which the railway track was to be relocated played a role, and then the resemblance of the "Osterburken" Station. The mutilated "Apestel," whose origin remains unclear, seems to have brought about the surfacing of "Luke" which follows it. In the case of the neologism "Cala," the couple "Philemon" and "Baucis" were originally in mind and were displaced by "Joshua and Caleb." From "Caleb" came then "Cala." Also noteworthy is the use of the feminine "Francisca" for a male person, and the removal to Rügen of the newly arisen mountain, which was thought of as the "Monte Nuovo" near Naples.

From the mutilated designations we gradually arrive at the neologisms:

(103) *"Bellwing,"* girl's name.

(104) *"We used to play together, and I was Peter the Great and you of course were Parringen,"* fusion of "parricida" and "Berlichingen."

(105) *"The castle is in the Greit-Kilian area,"* in a suburb of Würzburg.

(106) *"The street recalls in its form the boire du porte."*

(107) *"Nanahatte-Nsens-Restplace,"* company sign in Estonian, Russian, and German.

(108) *"Pala suma,"* plant name.

(109) *"Lacertine wine,"* Latium?

(110) *"Esperay,"* mountain in the Alps, visible from the railway.

(111) *"Abiaco,"* steeply sloping plane on Tenerife.

(112) *"Bohuslän,"* quarter of Berlin, near the castle.

(113) *"Pente Zoo Street and Akelepřibram Street,"* on the map of Dresden.

(114) *"Rechajola,"* historic rebel, mentioned in a summons by the emperor.

(115) *"Minnisozo,"* name of a friend in Frankfurt.

(116) *"Maskio,"* first name of a Mrs. G., immediately recognized as incorrect.

Some of these specimens still allow the recognition of meaningful components. Most, however, are syllable combinations jumbled in a completely arbitrary way. Now and then the influence upon the neologism formation of ideas obscurely in mind stands out. So it is with "Parringen," which surely came into being by a fusing of parricida and Berlichingen; with "Greit-Kilian" as a suburb of Kilian's old city; and with "Lacertine" wine. "Cima della Pala" may have played a part in the case of "Pala suma," and "Cola di Rienzi" in the case of "Rechajola." The construction "Bohuslän" was accompanied by the obscure idea of a former Wendish (Bohemian) reign in Berlin ("Boguslav"), while on the map of Dresden the side-idea of neighboring Bohemia asserted itself in the name "Příbram." The remaining specimens cannot be further explained. Observations 106, 107, and 108 again bear the marks of translation and foreign languages. In the case of the last specimen (116), the incorrectness of a name uttered by another person was at once evident to the dreamer. The remaining neologisms, too, were mostly conceived, heard, or, more often, read, as foreign products. This is very evident in 107 and 113, and probably also in 108, 110, 111, 112, 114, and 115.

The third major group of word-errors comprises those cases in which, unlike up to now, the accompanying idea is not simply and concisely outlined, but rather shows a *more complicated composition*. Here, the false words do not in fact stand in for correct terms, at least not for individual words, but rather they correspond to mixtures of ideas for which our language as yet possesses no short expression. One could thus more or less imagine that it is a matter of associative neologisms for which newly formed words emerge particularly easily since correct designations are not on hand and therefore need not be repressed. The reverse is, however, also quite possible: that first the false words come into being, and only then are brought into connection with the more or less muddled ideas which are simultaneously available. In such cases, too, the linking may of course be facilitated by the lack of connections entrained by speech. Characteristically, we are dealing here almost exclusively with neologisms, whereas when it concerned ideas long ago impressed and firmly named, we encountered a larger number of word mutilations and word modifications.

(117) *"The so-called guard-parade,"* the transporting back and forth of the filled bottle from one corner of the mouth to the other; in drinking. The dreamer produced a description of the customs of buccaneer troops in South America.

(118) *"Then crown-flesh [Kronfleisch] will be just as cheap as human flesh,"* last words of Don Carlos. A female person wants to avenge Don Carlos by seducing the queen to lesbian love, so that she is venal like other people. Interference from "meat shortage" [Fleischnot, cf. also Fleischesnot, "suffering of the flesh"].

(119) *"Show sum [Schauschale],"* ("lump sum"), sum of the payment of admission to exhibitions [Schaustellungen] on a trip.

(120) *"He will find his gun-sight wagon sure enough,"* wagon which leads him directly to his goal.

(121) *"Roll cord,"* cord with which a group of convicts is held together.

(122) *"Yelp meat,"* meat cut for the dog, left behind by him in the bowl.

(123) *"Antibay,"* an island's bay which lies across from the mainland.

(124) *"Worstered antelope,"* a previously unknown animal.

(125) *"Chalkon and Charbon,"* chalcedony?; new minerals.

(126) *"Karwendel [proper name; lit.: 'bowl-helix'] dispute,"* much ado about nothing [Streit um Kaisers Bart; lit.: dispute about the emperor's beard].

(127)   "*Road mighties*," people who have the right of use to a road.

(128)   "*Your majesty hill-wood*," newspaper rack as a symbol of honor; scepter.

(129)   "*Triple sliding seat*," sled on a psychophysical machine.

(130)   "*Capriviera*," political situation in Caprivi's time.

(131)   "*Belluno-doubt*," the King of Portugal's doubt, during a visit to Italy, about bypassing the emperor of Austria, who was staying at Belluno.

(132)   "*Surrogate princesses*," those who are not related closely enough to the royal house to be able to lay claim to the appanage; reminiscence of "morganatic."

(133)   "*Substate separation*," white doctor's gown supplied by the state.

The first two specimens contain correct, meaningful words to which nevertheless a deviant meaning is attributed by the dreamer. They serve as expressions for more complex newly formed ideas; the second bears the stamp of mocking comedy due to its particular ambiguity. In the third specimen (119), we are concerned with a word-mutilation that was apparently stimulated by the side-idea "exhibition" [Schaustellung; lit.: "show-position"]. All other false words are neologisms which, to be sure, were composed of fairly meaningful elements. Some of these creations, such as "Belluno-doubt," "Capriviera," "road mighties," and "antibay," could at any rate be tolerated in the language of joke-books or in common everyday parlance. They render complex ideas in concise, comprehensible form. In contrast, the remaining specimens contain derailments and admixtures despite their linguistically correct formation. In the cases of "gun-sight wagon," "yelp meat," and "triple sliding seat," the intruding side-ideas still have at least a certain inner relationship to the dominant idea. One could concede this as well in the case of "worstered antelope" and with "surrogate princesses," in which, moreover, the suggestion of "morganatic" also played a part. But in the case of "roll cord," "Karwendel dispute," and "hill-wood," the ingredients are completely meaningless. The neologisms "chalkon" and "charbon" apparently rest upon the word "chalcedony," and would perhaps have been more appropriately listed among the paraphasic proper names considered above.

Far less clear than with these is the genesis of the following completely meaningless inventions:

(134)   "*Old Livlandic cryl-chain*," golden, antique double chain.

(135)   "*Clept space*," space which in an amphitheater is taken up by the seats themselves; "free building space," the remaining open space.

(136)   "*Ice tubulate*," Russian agency with unrestricted right of disposal over currency.

(137)   "*Chease doctor*," physician who is paid by a family foundation; half jokingly.

(138) *"Remains of ludital lions,"* fossile bones found on a North Pole expedition (diluvial?).

(139) *"R. rubs limeal poison into his eyes to be able to see better."*

(140) *"Waolow ideas,"* impractical ideas, printed.

(141) *"The old Moor and Amalia play chess, Franz and Karl corpse-chase,"* direction remark from the play *Die Räuber*.

(142) *"Eureptia,"* short summary, *"ephemeria,"* further explanation.

(143) *"Pseudointabloid,"* bogus remedy for alcoholism.

(144) *"Glossoplaties,"* inferior copies of pictures as room decoration.

(145) *"Alp tinde,"* rebus on music-note lines in a newspaper, entiende.

(146) *"Morexalrelic,"* lion's head with lush mane and a little hat.

(147) *"Certroga,"* mythical figure, dog and twins.

(148) *"Carton de Germi,"* box in which the publisher collects the receipts for review copies sent.

(149) *"Puni,"* especially clever rogue hero, in the rogue language.

(150) *"After all, we're not irreterentes,"* variety of maiden.

(151) *"Morphium and Obornium,"* new alkaloid.

(152) *"Imbetit,"* box for revolver cartridges.

(153) *"Sementier prempel,"* member of a consumer co-op.

A great many of these neologisms appear first of all as visual images: 137, 140, 141, 145, 146, and 147. This is not known for the others. The "chease doctor" was, despite its jocular ring, expressly distinguished from "cheese." The dreamer had in mind a family trust, the "Chease foundation," which, when one writes out checks for it, covers all possible expenses: for example, even losses in the game of skat. Thus arose the side-idea of "chease boys." In the case of "ludital lions," "diluvial" was presumably in mind. In the case of "limeal poison," "calomel" might have been thought of. The "waolow ideas" are connected with "wallow." They are disordered, tangled. "Ice tubulate," with its first syllable, brings to mind cold Russia, while in "clept space" a conceptual patterning is found on the Greek "klepto," space, which, so to speak, is lost, stolen. "Corpse-chase" was apparently determined in part by the preceding "chess," but obtains its especially lugubrious coloring due to the addition.

Linguistically, the next three expressions, 142, 143, and 144, bear the mark of well-formed foreign words, and, despite their meaninglessness, allow the recognition of clear reminiscence of the underlying ideas. The "glossoplaties" seem to have been influenced by "platinotype" and the expression "plated." "Alp tinde" is hardly intelligible, but was conceived of as a rebus by the dreamer; on the one hand, the Norwegian "tind" (tooth, peak) was inserted into it; on the other hand, the mutilated Spanish "entiende." Examples 146 and 147 were designations for images. In the case of "irreterentes," what was presumably in mind was "irredentists," albeit without any relation to the fundamental idea. With the remaining specimens, no links at all can be traced. "Sementier prempel" was stimulated by the names "Schrimbs" or "Preppel" in Immerman's *Münchhausen*.

From the observations imparted, we easily recognize how in the first instance close relations still exist between the trains of thought and the speech utterances, so that the latter can sometimes be looked upon as fairly successful condensations. Nevertheless, these constructions can hardly be seen as resulting from mental activity similar to that which underlies the felicitous speech creations for new or hitherto unnamed ideas. Rather, in numerous cases we face the invariable fact that of the manifold ideas emerging in dreaming consciousness, only a part struggles through to verbal expression, while other parts are forced into the background or only indirectly influence the inner speech by object or sound association. True, similar processes are no doubt the case in wakefulness as well. But in wakefulness the transformation of the contents of consiousness into speech forms is governed by main or target ideas so that the speech forms constitute a fairly complete expression of particular thought processes. In dreams, by contrast, it is a motley jumble of fragments of the contents of consciousness which achieves speech representation. Apt concise expressions can possibly be brought about in this way; but as a rule, as we have seen, significant elements get dropped in the transformation into speech, while side-ideas, and often enough completely strange chance elements intrude. The latter happens all the more frequently the more blurred and dim the thought processes are. Then namely, the appearance of pure speech formation without meaning will be ever more evident and with it the genesis of meaningless incorrect words. And indeed, in addition to specimens already presented with which accompanying ideas were still recognizable, I have collected a number of observations which represent unintelligible speech utterances for which no meaning whatsoever could be called to mind.

A first group of these show linguistically correct formations:

(154) *"Her clogged Irish stuff."*

(155) *"Connective tissue pathologists and epithelial pathologists."*

(156) *"Are they pockmarks or infusions?"* (infusion marks or injection marks).

(157) *"There is some high-school graduate dirt in it,"* in the cup.

(158) *"Crust Azores"*; reminiscence of "zonal fibres"?

(159) *"Lord string players [Lordsaitenspieler] and muscle sardines,"* persons of a festive procession; vague recollection of Mantegna's drawing at Hampton Court.

(160) *"Los angelos niños,"* meaningless composition of "Los angeles, los niños."

Meanings were either never connected with these words or were lost in awakening. In favor of the latter supposition are obscure isolated remembrances which still allowed themselves to be traced. The English flavor of "Lord string players" may be traceable to a connection with Mantegna's drawing in England, while with "muscle sardines" the reminiscence of the muting of music by "sordini" presumably played a part. The following are completely random neologisms:

(161) "*Jercuntre*," heading above the column of a cashbook.

(162) "*Famal council and torched piece square*," title above the pages of a book.

(163) "*Taguentes*," unclear recollection of a Canary Island name.

(164) "*Next year there was a peust-wus-kin.*"

(165) "*Satchpiece*," completely unclear.

These peculiar formations are presumably to be mostly interpreted as simple syllable janglings without real meaning. The first two are characteristically meaningless captions without any relation to the content. Since they find counterparts in the field of pathology, the occurrence of such a meaningless syllable patchwork in dreams is of exceptional importance.

III. Disorders of Discourse (Acataphasia and Agrammatism)

The linguistic expression of a concept is the word; that of thought, discourse. The latter does not therefore render isolated concepts, but rather strings of concepts which are placed in relation to one another. If discourse is to faithfully bring a thought to expression, first of all the correct words for the constituent concepts ought to be found. Then the linguistic coinage must be made to parallel sharply and exactly the contents of the thought string in every detail. And finally the linguistic structure has to allow the clear recognition of the interrelations between the concepts. In the previous section, we considered in detail the disturbances which word-selection in dreams can be liable to. They occupy an exceptional position in that they are already in evidence in the naming of an individual concept. To these may be contrasted the disorders of discourse in the strict sense: the mistakes in the linguistic coinage of thought and in linguistic structure. We group the former under the heading "acataphasia," the latter under "agrammatism." Of course, in individual observations the various disturbances are frequently found in combination. In particular, we quite regularly encounter mistakes in word-selection in acataphasic and agrammatical specimens.

A. Disturbances in the Linguistic Coinage of Thought

In the linguistic coinage of thought in dreams, we first of all come across mistakes which completely coincide with those of word-selection. The dreamer does not find the expression which exactly corresponds to the thought in mind, but rather he says something else, similar to a greater or lesser degree. We are dealing here with "off-the-mark" discourse, which we may designate as "paralogia," as opposed to "paraphasia," and indeed as "displacement paralogia."

(166) *"In Freiburg the inside of the plate doesn't serve for eating but for the town,"* instead of "a picture of Freiburg is found on the plate."

(167) *"Creative [schöpferische] iron mantle"* for "iron scoop vessel" [Schöpfgefäß].

(168) *"By not bringing their water horizontally, they are useless,"* for "because of the rapids, they are not useful for shipping."[6]

(169) *"Then he would view the tight, clinging pants which are connected with it as an insult, a provocation"* for "it would be embarrassing for him to have to appear in tight pants when working with the rowing machine."

(170) *"Was the pond a waterlike work?"* for "artificial."

(171) *"An attentive report"* for "thorough."[7]

(172) *"Can you do this with sympathetic remote-forming?"* for "can you see stereoscopically?"

One recognizes in these specimens that what should have been said is roughly intelligible, but that a mistake occurred in the way it was expressed. In the first observation, the thought that the inner surface of the plate is not vacant, but rather contains a picture, and that therefore the food covers this picture, is displaced so that it serves not for food but rather for the town, i.e., for the picture of the town. Moreover, the "picture of Freiburg" has become "in Freiburg." Thought and expression do not correspond; rather, the former takes on an oblique, distorted form. The second specimen does not really contain any complete thought, but only a composite concept. Nevertheless, I felt I should insert it here, since it may not have involved a disturbance simply of word-selection, but rather one of thought coinage. What was to be expressed was something like "an iron vessel which serves for scooping." The designation "mantle" intercedes for the obvious "vessel," derived from the notion of enclosing. Furthermore, instead of the simple compound "scoop vessel" [Schöpfgefäß] or "for scooping" [zum Schöpfen], "serving for, suitable for, or meant for scooping" or the like, there appears the phonetically kindred but conceptually completely different "Schöpferisch" (creative). Here, if you will, the sense of the thought in mind is still intelligibly rendered, but the mode of expression seems artificial and farfetched since what was chosen was not the obvious, natural version, but rather a newly contrived one which more-over admits of connotations. In this way, such expressions can possibly acquire the iridescent stamp of the comic, without the dreamer having intended it. Observation 168, too, which relates to rivers, shows us, besides slight displace-ments between thought and wording, a peculiar affectation in the mode of expression. First of all the idea "evenly" or "smoothly" is rendered by the con-ceptually kindred, but not exactly corresponding word "horizontally." Then the expression "flowing along," which one would expect, is replaced by the phrase "bringing their water," which to be sure is in itself intelligible, but still odd. "For shipping," a thought component essential for comprehension, has been dropped from the discourse. In specimen 169, there occurred first of all a dis-placement of thought expression in that the idea of "embarassing" changed in turn into the conceptually kindred version "insult," "provocation." Here, the dreamer seems to have searched for an apt coinage, since usually such an accu-mulation of terms is much rarer than omissions. Furthermore, the somewhat expected phrase "which are worn for it" or "are needed" is replaced by "which are connected with it," which is awkward and renders the thought obliquely. There is no talk of the rowing machine thought of, although the likelihood should not be ruled out that we are dealing with a fragment which had already been preceded by the naming of that concept.

The "waterlike work" apparently owes its origin first of all to the expression of the concept "artificial" by means of "-like," which only partially corresponds with its content. What is artificial looks natural, but is in fact only similar. Mixed in with this is the idea that the pond is of artificial "waters" so that the expression "waterlike" followed from the admixture, while the artificial origin receives further special emphasis by the designation waterlike "work." In the case of the "attentive" report, the characteristic adjective for the service is replaced by the attribute of the workers, whose attentiveness after all guaranteed the thoroughness of the work.

Finally, the last specimen is very remarkable. The expression "remote-forming" is by no means poor at characterizing the development of depth in stereoscopic vision, in which certain parts of the image recede into the back-ground so that a "remoteness" is "formed." In so doing, the interaction of both eyes is necessary, as is indicated by the adjective "sympathetic." We are there-fore dealing here with a farfetched and blurred manner of expression which nevertheless allows the outline of the underlying thought to shine through.

As already indicated, the common peculiarity of these observations rests, in my opinion, on slight displacements between thought content and linguistic expression. In part, a certain unclarity in the concepts themselves may also play a role; their hazy picture does not sharply and unequivocally determine the choice of words, but rather leaves room for the play of side influences. On the other hand, however, the disturbances observed here strongly remind one again of those of word-selection, in which we likewise saw semantically kindred designations easily stand in for one another. It is precisely the expressions which are farfetched, and brought about by the evasion of the obvious ones, that lead to the conjecture that the new creations should be viewed as replacements for the usual phrases, which could not be located.

A second form of paralogia is due not to simple displacements, but rather to gross *derailments*. The rendering of the thought in mind does not merely take an odd form through side-associations; rather it is directly prevented by diversion onto completely different paths, so that the discourse becomes contradictory, nonsensical, and incoherent. Yet, transitions are found between displacement and derailment, as will be shown in particular in the first few of the following specimens:

(173) *"The old fisherman managed to subsist sandbank-wearily;"* on a voyage of several days he so saved his strength that he was still able to escape over the sandbanks.

(174) *"The mourning-unveiling unfurled rigidity"* for "sad moods cause constraint."

(175) *"The cook, into sticks she'd run, if it were said that the fellow was undone"* instead of "her heart would break . . . was gone and done with her."

(176) *"I laugh until I'm lead"* for "I laugh until I cry."

(177) *"And the lad has to be driven on to school in a different way than through Alvarez and the brass-garden,"* totally unclear idea; recollection of awakening experiments with brass balls and the padded box in which they fell.

(178) *"The first edition is the material in short supply [Mangelstoff]; I can be short with something."* Unclear ideas; play on a proper name.

(179) *"Only because of the running of the ward did Beddle tell Kramer"* for "as the clinic is on, I have to get up at reveille."

(180) *"While with surprise [überraschend] the food, also with surprise the surplus [übrige] I viewed [hinblickte]"* for "while . . . I surveyed [überblickte]."

In the first specimen, instead of "sandbank-wearily" we would more or less have expected "freshly," which is, if you will, the very opposite of what was said. The concept of fatigue from exertion, in lieu of the conserving of strength (which was called for by the train of thought), came to be expressed at any rate in a curious fusion with the side-idea "sandbank," which here represents an isolated remnant of thoughts which did not achieve speech formation: a process which we still have to evaluate in detail in our consideration of ellipses.

In the second specimen, what was to be expressed was that the sad mood produced restraint. First of all, instead of "produced" there appeared the affected "unfurled," which in turn gave rise to the derailment "unveiling" by way of the initial sounds, as is not infrequently the case in slips of the tongue as well. A similar process seems to have taken place in observation 175. Here, the phrases in mind were "the cook came to grief," or "her heart was broken." The already emerging end of the rhythmic sentence suggested however a rhyme and thus led to the peculiar derailment, in which the concept of breaking up forced its way to expression along with that of "running to ruin." "Undone" involves an omission, of the type which we will later encounter in far more marked form. In specimen 176, too, two kindred idioms, "I laugh until I die" and "I laugh tears" seem to have emerged one next to the other. The English translation "to cry" attached to the latter, but was wrongly transformed into the phonetically similar English "to ply," which in turn stimulated the sound-association to "lead" [Blei]. It would have been impossible to disentangle these intertwined ties, had not the dreamer himself been in a position to give an account of it.

A complete suppression of already commenced trains of thought by new, abruptly emerging ideas is contained in specimen 177. The dreamer could no longer say how the final part should more or less have run, any more than he could say where the word "Alvarez" came from. In contrast, the neologism "brass-garden" was no doubt suggested by remembrance of awakening experiments by which brass balls from above hit a plank and then bounced into a padded box—an enclosure, a garden so to speak.[8] Remarkable here is the formation of a new word for a complex notion which up till then had never been given a simple name; hence the farfetched use of the word "garden" in lieu of something like "box." The next specimen appeared to the dreamer as a sentence spoken when opening a book at the bookseller's convention. The expression "Mangelstoff" (material in short supply) appeared in place of a quite similar-sounding proper name. It would denote something like the author of a book to be nominated as first-rate ("first edition"). Now, however, by way of sound association, there ensues a derailment to the otherwise completely unrelated final clause. Even less understandable is the end of specimen 179, which contains totally meaningless words, while the beginning renders the thought in mind in a displaced form. Instead of the clinic hours, there appears the semantically kindred "running of the ward." Presumably also to be interpeted as a derailment is the last specimen, in which the initial sounding of the word "surveyed" triggered the sound-related "surprising," and in so doing altered the entire further development of the discourse in this sense.

The following are closely related to the above observations, but far more complex:

(181) *"That the strokes comes through the Isis clouds like two clouds"* for "sunbeams break through the clouds."

(182) *"The wermth-sword was far from them. It served to weigh the wermth of their beards, the weight of their name"* for "the bearded Germans used their swords to tip the scales."

Here are found, first of all, two mistakes in word-selection: "strokes," actually "strokes of lightning," for the semantically kindred "beams," and then "Isis clouds" instead of "iris clouds." The dreamer thought of the messenger of the gods, Iris, and of how she soared through the clouds; at the same time he thought of the iridescent play of colors when sunbeams break through the clouds, but he made a mistake in his words. The whole sentence had the form of a lyrical poem and was sung with great feeling. Thus came about the inclination towards rhythmic structure, which presumably led to the senseless insertion of the prominent sounds "like two clouds." In the second specimen as well, we may be dealing with a derailment due to various side-ideas. First of all, as far as the incomprehensible words "wermth" and "wermth-sword" are concerned—which emerged with exactly this spelling—they seem to have resulted from a mixture of the two words "warmth" (passion) and "verve." The dreamer had in mind that the ancient Germans forcibly used their sword to tip the scales; they staked their whole personality. The linguistic expression of the thought miscarried and at the same time linked up in a senseless way with the concepts of the sword and beardedness, the latter of which in the process got to a completely wrong place. It should have run "the bearded . . . ," i.e., the dignified, Ancient Germans. In this derailment tangle, the phrase "was far from them," whose origin remains obscure, forced its way in. This probably involves the remnants of a suppressed side-idea.

As a second major form of acataphasic disorder, we can consider the contractions or ellipses, in which extensive trains of ideas are rendered only by single speech fragments. In such cases, only the explanation from the dreamer himself can shed some light on the incomprehensible gibberish:

(183) *"The eye sensations have to get up too"* for "it is not enough upon awakening to wake up, one must also open one's eyes."

(184) *"His merits now almost remained not far in the breast;"* Goethe couldn't just lock up his merits in his breast without them being felt by everyone.

(185) *"Now I can be free of this blame"* for "free to marry again," supposed quote from *Maria Stuart.*

(186) *"She sang the command-red,"* for "she sang a song loudly at dawn."

(187) *"Mainly because of weak-kneed and arrogant digestion,"* i.e., "a weak-kneed and arrogant government will not win the hearts of its subjects even if it gives them their fill to eat."

(188) *"Don't understand no discerning,"* i.e., "no one understood the dreamer when he spoke Italian with a friend in Madrid."

(189) *"In Bullrich I want to stand, like I last possessed my little mother,"* song of the Austrian troops before the battle; that they should persevere in the face of cannon thunder and gunsmoke (Bullrich) and that they want to do credit to their former teachers, the French, against whom they would now fight.

(190) *"Have you assailed him? He poeters julp. There comes the doorman too and whistles a gulp."* Couplet, sung by a Viennese comedian in honor of the dreamer, mimics the way different visitors are treated differently by the domestic servants. The girls jubulate ("poeters julp") at having turned the beggar out ("assailed"); the doorman drinks for joy.

(191) *"Here they always land the half-heads up here,"* i.e., "one can go by ship from Italy directly home in one day."

(192) *"She gave birth to Socrates' key,"* unclear statement about the conduct of Frau von Stein.

We have already met with individual shorter omissions, of the kind which also occur in common slips of the tongue. Here, however, the mutilation of the speech expression reaches degrees which are otherwise never observed in healthy people. If awakening is to lead to getting up, one has also to experience with one's eyes that one is actually awake. This is somewhat the thought which the dreamer had in mind with the first specimen, and which in its linguistic coinage was mutilated beyond comprehensibility. "His merits didn't remain far" runs the second specimen, a farfetched expression for "they didn't go unnoticed." The broader thought—that, after all, they lay in his personality and therefore revealed themselves and could not be locked in the breast, but rather had to stand out everywhere—only achieved expression in the obscure hint "in the breast," while "now almost" is to be viewed as a simple filler for rhythmically rounding out the sentence.

Mary Stuart means to say that she is now free again and could marry once more, having atoned for her past guilt. The dreamer carries, however, only the first part of the train of thought to expression, although he believed himself to have rendered it completely and in a dignified form faithful to Schiller. "Command-red" is a contraction of the concepts of singing loudly, as in commanding, and the break of day, the time of "red dawn." In the next specimen, the initial concept, a "weak-kneed and arrogant government," is only half-rendered into speech form, but then expanded by the unclear addition "mainly because of." To this is then coupled, with the dropping of all intermediate links, the concept of "digestion," which was stimulated by the end part of the idea in mind. The connecting link is formed by the obscurely emerging empirical theorem that feelings tend to be soothed during digestion. Of the whole thought content in observation 188, only the concept of "not understanding" has been turned into words, although here, as in all other instances, the dreamer believed himself to have expressed himself clearly and completely. Moreover, a hybridization of the two expressions, "don't understand no word" and "one can't discern anything" has also occurred.

Very remarkable and complex are the next two specimens, which appear in the form of rhythmic songs. "Bullrich" is a formation using the well-known proper name, which on the one hand is reminiscent of the bellowing [bullern] of cannons, and on the other hand presumably of gunsmoke as well. It would therefore mean, "I want to stand in battle." "My little mother" is a paralogism for "my teacher," stimulated by semantic association. The words in between contain the ellipses for "as my teacher did, whom I had before," the last two words having been substituted by the displaced version "last possessed." None of the remaining side-ideas which the dreamer had in mind were rendered. In specimen 190, the thought that the beggar was thrown out was expressed only by the question "Have you assailed him?" Now came to mind "the girls titter and jubulate." Instead of this, it runs, "he poeters julp." The "he" is presumably traceable to the echo of "him," which shortly preceded it, while in the case of "poeters julp" we are dealing with meaningless reminiscence of "titter and jubulate." The end is, once more, fully developed linguistically and contains a rhyme, which either was stimulated by the previous "julp," or, vice versa, helped influence this neologism by foreshadowing it phonetically. In observation 191, only a far smaller fragment of a more extensive train of ideas achieved speech expression. What preoccupied the dreamer was the thought, which seemed to him a reality, that one could of late sail by ship from Italy to Germany in one day, along a canal whose route was traced on the map. Believing himself to be explaining this new possibility, he nevertheless spoke only of "to land up here," with the unexplainable addition of "the half-heads." Everything else, by contrast, remained unexpressed. The final specimen may presumably also involve an ellipsis, although the original thought in mind was completely lost to memory. Only the unclear concept remained that the puzzling words in some way would further characterize the conduct of Frau von Stein in Weimar society.

A kind of complement to ellipses is formed by the following specimens, in which we are dealing not with concepts which struggle in vain for speech expression, but rather, conversely, with words which correspond to no ideas at all, or to very inadequate and obscure ones. They distinguish themselves from the concise, pregnant wording of ellipses by a certain abundance of euphonious, yet empty phrases, and are without exception rhythmically patterned, often also rhymed. This very peculiarity may in the first instance offer the key to understanding them. Similarly to the meaningless refrains of our songs, they involve the simple *jingle of words*, whose appeal essentially rests on the recurrence of the same sounds, the same raising and lowering in the sequence of syllables.

(193) *"Wanted to swing my plumage*
Into the sea wave,
Like the current with sea's above
into the sea's grave." —Goethe's Song to the Moon

(194) *"Oh, Palfy, poor child, do you appear suddenly again?*
Why are you there again so droll?
Oh, at the time he didn't see Diva!
You are like a dark-eyed Italian girl." —Song of the Mirza-Schaffy

(195) *"Asked about the marriage-tottering*
And even took her for teatering
As his lawful spouse."

(196) *"Was once as evangelman—*
They are two, justified still,
County Anglinghole the father does dwell."

(197) *"And with his veil the lute blows this way."*

(198) *"And love readied themselves to refresh."*

(199) *"To the diamond-writing to gritter,"* ending of a poem.

(200) *"O youth, how sensuously free we of mind, spring-splendor cop. it from behind,"* expression of changeability.

(201) *"With Manuar law, could happen so far; similarly real is Bazaar."*

The first two specimens were perceived by the dreamer as straightforward well-known quotes; and all the others, too, constitute fragments of supposed poems. Besides the rhythm, whose influence in forming expletives can be clearly discerned in various places, rhyming plays an especially prominent role in bringing about these word-jingles. The rhymes, to be sure, are not always pure. On the other hand, the need to generate them has apparently brought about the most nonsensical derailments: "with sea's above," "and even took her for teatering," "it from behind," and so on. There are several neologisms, such as "marriage-tottering" which, incidentally, was produced by the dreamer many years before the "marriage-mistake" of more recent coinage; "gritter," presumably for "glitter"; and the completely unclear "Manuar law." Furthermore, we repeatedly notice mistakes in constructions and compound sentences, which we will have to discuss later on. To this belong "with sea's above," "readied to refresh," "to the diamond-writing," and the incoherent word string "how sensuously free we of mind, spring-splendor cop. it from behind." The remarkable abbreviated "cop." points to a visual image. The last specimen reminds one of telegraphese, to be considered further on.

As a rule, no clear ideas whatever associated themselves with these effusions, which were regularly considered to be very successful poetry. Only in the case of specimen 200 did the dreamer have the thought that the verse depicted variability, although no such a meaning could be read into the words even in the remotest way. It is of course possible that we are dealing more often with ellipses—that extensive trains of ideas, perhaps of unclear coinage, find expression only in stunted and, furthermore, paraphasically and paralogically altered fragments. It is especially the last two specimens which, in their conciseness, lend support to this conjecture. On the other hand, however, the jingle with words often stands out so clearly that we may reasonably suppose that the major disturbance is not a vain struggle for words, but rather the emergence of pure words without accompanying object-representations.

B. Disorders of Language Structure

Turning now to disturbances of language structure—to *agrammatism*—we first of all have to pay attention to syntactic mistakes.

(202) *"The mollusk of the catarrh"* for "catarrh of the gastric mucus membrane."

(203) *"The processing of voluntary coal"* instead of "voluntary providing of coal."

(204) *"Sense of colorful sixth's"* for "sixth sense of plants."

In the first observation, we find a reversal of the dependency relation, along with a paraphasic derailment brought about by sound similarity: two disturbances which may also occur in ordinary slips of the tongue. The same applies for the transposition and adaptation of the adjective "voluntary" in the second specimen. Here, moreover, the "providing" has in turn become a "processing" through the intermediary of sound similarity. The last observation shows us the postposition and wrong declension of the ordinal, with, however, at the same time the insertion of an interpolation, apparently stimulated by side-association with the idea "plants," which itself achieved no expression at all. The dreamer was preoccupied with the various forms and abilities of tropical plants. In the process, there obscurely emerged the idea of animal similarity and furthermore that of the likewise-remarkable organs of balance of fish; it now became clear that the old anatomy author "Panschow"—altered from "Pansch"—had already used the designation "sense colorful of sixth's" precisely for a presumed sixth sense of plants.

(205) *"We thought, only for the castle, only from above."*

(206) *"Of course, many trace back through beggars their own prince."*

(207) *"A stettin in German house England disregarding to the Prince of Bulgaria."*

(208) *"The animals used to suffocate in growing displeasure"* for "the animals crowded together on the ship became disorderly and suffocated."

The sense of the first three observations remained totally unclear. Only the faulty speech forms "only for the castle," "their own prince," and "disregarding to the Prince" enter into our consideration here. The "stettin in the German house" is a paraphasic derailment for "prince of the German house" stimulated by the side-idea of the House of "Wettim" via sound similarity.[9] It would perhaps be somewhat possible to explain the syntactic mistakes if we had complete insight into the sense of the discourse. Nevertheless, going by the specimens of agrammatism to be cited later, it seems to me that real mistakes are involved. In the last specimen, there is first of all "displeasure" for "disorder." Then, however, the thought in mind "became disorderly" led to the expression "in growing displeasure," presumably influenced by the obscure idea of "increasing disorder." The addition "used to" may have been an attempt to render the thought that the animals "first" became disorderly and then suffocated. The syntactic transposition in this specimen apparently rests in part on elliptic speech mutilation. Finally, we should, I presume, also think of processes closely akin to ellipses as being operative in that form of language disturbance in dreams that I should like to designate as "telegraphese." It involves the more or less complete loss of all compound sentences.

(209)   *"Virgin quartz, idi–idi–bes"* for "gold discovery in Africa" — Sidi-bel-Abbes.

(210)   *"Temple at the mausoleum wholly in arithmetic proportion with as humoristic,"* pronouncement of Kaiser Wilhelm I on a planned garden kiosk.

(211)   *"The magician who becomes the stork's crooked-greed. Storm death,"* caption under a picture in the *Fliegende Blätter*, Cincinnatus at the plough, a stork in the sky.

(212)   *"Educated man, cate and house and peek en,"* satire from the magazine *Kladderadatsch.*

(213)   *"He and above, like she only fell and given notice,"* passage from a program of striking bricklayers.

(214)   *"Dainty, stinzy, violent child's mouth attacked,"* relates to the woodruff's bride, who had been reviled by a child.

(215)   *"Como everything in fragmony, everything has fracture and agony,"* description of something unpleasant.

(216)   *"The forehen represents barnpen-devil,"* obscure idea of forehell (purgatory).

(217)   *"The virgin fell long,"* completely unclear.

(218)   *"Ernst von Rieck-cocaineground,"* likewise unclear.

(219)   *"Clotzkin-Hotzkin. What is then the utmost?";* incomprehensible.

(220)   *"Drouden-load enjoyed, at that,"* unclear.

Here and there in these unstructured aggregations of words some indications of idea contents emerge. Only in the last specimens are they no longer discernible. In part this involves sound associations as in "idi-idi-bes" for "Sidi-bel-Abbes," and "forehen" instead of "forehell" (purgatory). More frequently, however, it involves conceptual ties as in "virgin quartz" ("gold quartz"?); "temple at the mausoleum"; the "given notice" in the bricklayers' program; the "violent child's mouth attacked"; the "dainty," which would presumably relate to the "bride" envisaged; the "fragmony" with the meaning of penitentiary; the "devil," who ties in with "purgatory"; the "stork," which was stimulated by the visual image. It would therefore seem as though some of the ideas which the dreamer had in mind achieved direct speech expression; others did so through the intermediary of conceptual associations; and the rest remained without logical structure and therefore could not receive syntactic expression in the language. Rather, the fragments of ideas are simply strung together, as is especially evident in specimens 209 and 214. In specimen 210, one clearly gathers from the order of the words that architectural concepts are concerned, yet without a thought being expressed. A peculiar "beating around the bush" arises here: the stimulating of ideas in a certain field without the thoughts being coined. In between, however, discourse elements that stem merely from sound similarity also repeatedly insert themselves; it comes to derailments via reminiscences. Thus the neologism "crooked-greed" in specimen 211 came into being under the influence of "magician." The first part, "crooked," tacked itself onto the picture of a bent plough handle. Between them the idea of a stork inserted itself from the visual image. The "cate" in the following specimen is also only an echo of "educated". "Fracture and agony" is an echo of "fragmony," with, to be sure, the same emotional feeling of the unpleasant. "Barnpen" is a rhyme on the derailment "forehen." Whether here the former was determined by the latter or vice versa cannot be resolved. A nonsensical rhyme appears in specimen 219, as well. The repeatedly observed neologisms are in part determined by sound effects; thus, "Hotzkin," "cate," "crooked-greed," and possibly also "forehen," "storm-death," "cocaineground" and "drouden-load" are unclear. They may involve ellipses. In the first instances, the flying stork seen by the dreamer in the picture seems to have obscurely aroused the idea of wind and then that of shooting down. The word "stinzy" [stinzig] appeared to him to be a Low German expression for "slight," and related to the "bride." This specimen is the only one of the series in which the sloppiness of the speech expression in the dream was felt to be displeasing, the other utterances having seemed completely comprehensible and linguistically correct.

In addition to these unstructured concatenations of isolated ideas and reminiscences, we could perhaps best make mention here of some specimens which appear in the form of meaningless discourse fragments, whether so produced initially, or mutilated only upon being recalled. Their thought content remained wholly unclear.

(221) *"Tom, hop, and tomfools."*
(222) *"The invention of further occupied parts."*
(223) *"First to the pants the hat-stairs,"* from a prince's address.

In the first specimen, we are dealing with a sound association. The other two defy interpretation. In the last one it is possible that the idea of "turning up" [Aufkrempeln] one's pants was in mind and on the one hand stimulated that of "hat brim" [Hutkrempe], and on the other hand the reminiscence of "stairs" [Treppe].

IV. Thought Disorders

There can be no doubt that the language disorders of dreams are quite regularly accompanied by radical thought disorders, and that a significant share in the formulation of the former should be attributed to the latter. So, on the one hand we may assume in the case of mistakes in discourse which amount to imperfections in the linguistic expression and articulation of thoughts, that also the ideas in mind are as a rule unclear and disordered. Furthermore, we have already traced word-jingles to speech concepts becoming to some extent independent because the train of thought has lost its influence upon them. Ultimately, however, thought disorders must presumably also play a role in all those derailments of word-selection, just as in those of discourse, which rest on conceptual connections, insofar as it is not the initial idea which attains the power to form language, but rather an association which has been aroused by it.

If, nevertheless, we contrast the language disorders treated up to now to another group, "thought disorders," this is done because among the collected specimens a considerable number are found in which the speech expression is relatively little disturbed, or not at all, while at the same time the mistakes of thought-work are recognizable with great clarity. Often consideration of these very observations provides sidelights which are suited for clarifying the doctrine of strict speech disorders in dreams. In the long run, however, all the various deviations are linked to one another with such great frequency that one can fairly strictly distinguish between them not by the grouping together of individual observations, but by means of conceptual dissection. The changes in mental life in dreams are, after all, not narrow, but very broadly defined. It therefore seems necessary in a description of dream speech to bring into the scope of inspection all those processes which have a share in the genesis of speech utterances.

In the discussion of neologisms, we have already pointed out that a considerable number of cases were based on completely unclear ideas, and that this very condition greatly facilitated the appearance of meaningless strings of syllables. We made similar observations later on when dealing with word-jingles which involved the arbitrary stringing together not of syllables, but rather of words and phrases. Following up these experiences, I would now like to communicate some examples in which the language often displays no essential disturbance, while nevertheless the thought content is completely incomprehensible or meaningless. Some of these are fragments, others complete, well-formed sentences:

(224) *"Among the socialists these processes contributed to bringing into oblivion their ships, their universes, their claim to fame."*

(225) *"In the contested election, had announced war."*

(226) *"To clear up the situation of schooled and stilted folk art."*

(227) *"Brother follows like beaver, seduces the other."*

(228) *"The old one had to have been acknowledged in the world's course."*

(229) *"To insignificantly leave the chicken out."*

(230) *"Lehmann's horses remain standing,"* song of students at a torchlight parade.

In these cases, it was not possible to discern any content for the language utterances, which were produced very quickly in the dream. Only in specimen 228 did the dreamer have in mind an unclear idea of some transaction in which something extra was thrown into the bargain. Possibly the accompanying thought processes were merely forgotten. However, this very circumstance also speaks for their unclarity and confusion. In the first specimen, awakening ensued before the dreamer had even finished speaking the sentence. Nevertheless, he was unable to attach any meaning whatsoever to it. In the main, this thought-free mode of discourse may involve word-jingles with the retention of linguistic form.

In some further specimens, the unclarity and vagueness of the ideas involves a snapping of the connecting threads, an incoherence which points to the lack of any leading ideas:

(231) *"No one knew that the lantern found itself against the moon in a fearfully indicated disarray. And so I convey my congratulations to the guard! Since then the little lad never again slipped through the window."*

(232) *"And little Wolf—he married just early enough for his partner Graves. He had a bent head-brim; his dreams by contrast were unhappy since when he took the tea. He died and was buried among the graves."*

(233) *"Do you know what Dr. F. here calls—Yes, steamboats, too, come now and then—twice 50 drops of opium."*

(234) *"Command your ways yourself—just build also a waterhouse in front,"* children's song of a wet nurse pushing the pram back and forth.

The first two, rather similar, specimens are from the same person. Both were conceived of as read narratives, the first as a fairy tale in the style of Andersen. Perhaps one can still recognize a certain train of thought, although the dreamer himself was unable to state anything more about it. Thus, "lantern" and "moon" were in effect said to be in a "disarray," possibly a "disproportion," while "unhappy" dreaming was linked with having tea. The proper name "Graves" seems to have triggered the ideas of dying and being buried. Otherwise, all coherence is lacking in the sentence, which, tied together, only retains the external form of a narrative. In the other two specimens, supplied by another person, the digressions are even more abrupt. The first of these had a humorous air for the dreamer. The "twice fifty drops" appeared to him as the ship's cargo. Here, a small mutilation is to be noted in the beginning. It was apparently to read "how Dr. F. here is called." In the last specimen, the digression seems to have been caused by the feeling of urinary pressure: the "waterhouse," which was to be built in front, points to this.

The incoherence we encounter here due to the absence of leading trains of thought is, of course, but a partial symptom of the general disorder which characterizes the course of our dreams as a whole. The abrupt switching of successive proceedings, the continual loss of the threads on which the events are strung, is indeed the most conspicuous peculiarity of our dream experiences. To the same fundamental disturbance can presumably also be traced those of the previously discussed derailments in which the correct expression of a thought is thwarted by the surfacing of distracting side-ideas, be they conceptual associations or reminiscences. While, therefore, in these cases the lack of target ideas and the increased distractability which it occasions are to be viewed as the essential basis of the disturbance, we continue to encounter under the thought mistakes in dreams in very marked form a process which reminds one of the displacements of language expression previously considered. Then it was a question of the occurrence of remote "farfetched" phrases in place of the simplest, most natural modes of expression. Now, by contrast, what is rendered in words is not the original thought in mind, but rather another one, ensuing via conceptual association, without the fact of this thought displacement dawning upon the dreamer. For this, the following specimens:

(235) *"If we had a greater tone and were better equipped"* for "everything more of a kind."

(236) *"The forensic ascertainment is difficult"* for "it is difficult (due to great fatigue) to ascertain what time it is."

(237) *"I have long known Pishton and Halmeade not to be accountable,"* half jokingly for "one can easily go astray there."

(238) *"The mushrooms, indeed the mushrooms, and the angels, the angels, meet"* for "the physical and the spiritual in man come together."

(239) *"The domestic policy department and the external post-office box"* for "politics and administration."

(240) *"Verse-time and human time,"* national and world history; verse thought of as "part" (of a poem).

(241) *"After all, tomorrow the fragmentary first of August can play,"* for "the preliminary celebration of the Sedan holiday can take place."

(242) *"The straightforward director, a crooked author,"* for "writes differently from what one should expect of him."

(243) *"The curl anchovies made him shudder and he fled back from just one of them,"* for "He had an aversion to everything particularly ceremonious (allonge wigs), a hint of which sufficed to frighten him off."

(244) *"If one considers, all the wild apple galleries in N.,"* for "the small, insignificant collections."

(245) *"It's quite a cocktaily individual,"* ecstatic exclamation on viewing a beautiful landscape.

(246) *"Which plays the Central Cruiser under the Great Bear,"* for "the main role"; under a vignette representing the Great Bear.

(247) *"Mr. N. was awarded the prize (for a report on dentistry), although he wasn't employed in a notary office,"* for "although he hadn't been working in a dental clinic."

(248) *"The heart need know nothing of it; the house should stay clean,"* an action which concerns one's intelligence need not be known by one's feelings. From the play *Mokobene*.

Here we are often reminded of the disturbances in word-selection, and indeed we must suppose the existence of smooth transitions. Even so, we are dealing not with simple word substitutions, but rather with the thought-expression taking a wrong turn. It therefore will not do simply to replace an isolated wrong expression with the correct one; rather the whole thought must be given a different turn of phrase. In general, the side-associations which led to the derailment are still to some extent recognizable. The "greater tone" calls to mind the fact that everything should be more in "harmony." The "forensic" ascertainment would presumably mean the "exact" ascertainment, which seemed difficult to the dreamer, since he could not bring himself to have a look at the clock.

Someone is "not accountable" who no longer knows what he is doing, just as someone who has gone astray is no longer sure where he is or where he is going. With comic intent, this condition has been transferred as an attribute to the surroundings named. Moreover, the similarity between "to account for oneself" and "to orient oneself" may also have played a part. With the aid of the side-association to low organisms, to the "primeval slime," the "mushrooms" have come to represent the bodily constituents of man; the "angels," the spiritual nature of the constituents of the soul.

In specimen 239, politics and administration were to be contrasted to one another. The former was thought of somewhat as the more internal mainspring of the affairs of state; the latter as their external formal regulation. Through obscure, no longer clarifiable, side-associations, the "post office box" [Postfach] has taken the place of "administration" and, presumably, also helped influence the language form of "domestic policy department" [innere Politikfach].

A totally different contrast is contained in "verse-time and human time." "Time" stands for that which is taking place in time: history. Just as, furthermore, a verse is only a fragment of a whole, of a poem, so is the history of a people only a part of the history of man. Thus, "verse-time" stands figuratively for "national history." Specimen 241 is very remarkable. Here, it seems, the concept of "preliminary celebration," struggling for expression, has brought about a series of similar derailments. August, which precedes September on the calendar, supersedes it here, while the first of the month supersedes the second of the month, the actual date of the Sedan Holiday. And finally, the "provisional" nature of the holiday comes into play via the conceptual side-association of "fragmentary," i.e. not entirely complete.

The "crooked author," too, is presumably not simply a word-selection mistake, but rather a thought derailment. The ambiguity of the word "straightforward" in its concrete and figurative senses brings about here also a transfer of the contrasting "crooked" from the concrete to the figurative. Observation 243 is more complex. As a symbol of the boring ceremony, the dreamer has in mind the idea of allonge wigs. The sentence was thus trimmed to this idea, giving rise to the curious phrase "he fled back from just one of them" in lieu of "from the slightest hint" of the ceremony. Only, in addition to this thought derailment via the intercession of a symbol for a concept, there also followed a remarkable disturbance in word selection. The half-conceptual, half-phonetic side-association "curl" [Locken] turned up for "allonge (full-bottom) wigs," and further on the idea of "anchovies" linked up with it, called forth by the stringy coiffure of the person in question, which is customarily called "anchovy bread" after a well-known jocular expression. Thus, idea-connections which are difficult to unravel underlie these word mistakes, too. The symbolic idea of coiffure awakened two different associations: the curls and the "anchovy rolls," which then linked up into a neologism.

In the case of the "wild apple galleries" of specimen 244, the general idea of uncultivated—not refined by art and cultivation—is replaced by the special concept of "wild apples," similar to the way in which in the previous case the idea of ceremony was replaced by the symbol of the wig. We encounter the same turn of thought from the general to the specific in observation 245, in which the peculiar adjective "cocktaily" would apparently have a meaning like "intoxicating" or "captivating." The derailment "individual" for "landscape" may have been stimulated by the former adjective. The origin of "Central Cruiser" in specimen 246 remains unclear. It is probably a matter of a side-association which was first stimulated by the "Great Bear" (Big Dipper) in the direction of the "central sun," then toward the Southern "Cross," and led to the fusion neologism. The special concept of "central sun" would appear here instead of the general idea of the "center;" or, as indicated by the expression "plays": "main role." In specimen 247, the "dental clinic" which would have been expected, was replaced by the idea of "notary office," presumably not simply as a word-selection mistake, but stimulated rather by the side-association of the "expert, duly certified person."

Finally, the last specimen gives one and the same thought first in the original mode of expression and then in a figurative one. The heart need not know what the intellect does; it should be kept clean of it, just as a house is of rubbish. The actual idea in mind was, furthermore, probably turned around: The intellect should know nothing of what the heart does. The saying was supposed to have been taken from a theater play "Mokobene"; the origin of this name is unclear.

The common feature in all these observations is the displacement of the underlying thought by the replacement of a valid link in the chain of ideas by a side-association. Here too, consequently, the result is a paralogism, a discrepancy between the content of the idea in mind and the meaning of the discourse. Only, this divergence was not brought about by language displacements, but rather by the blurring of the ideas in kindred ideational spheres. It is not the original train of thought which achieves conversion into discourse form, but rather a different yet parallel one aroused by it. It seems very noteworthy that in almost all of our specimens, the side-association which led to the thought displacement was clearly a narrower idea, richer in content, while what it suppressed was a more general, shadowy one. Perhaps therefore this disturbance may, as "metaphoric paralogism," be contrasted to the previously considered "displacement and derailment paralogisms." More than once the paralogism bore the stamp of an outright figurative mode of expression, as in the replacement of man's physical being by the "mushrooms" and his spiritual being by the "angels" in the "wild apple galleries," and in the "cocktaily" landscape. We are hardly dealing with a coincidence here; rather, in all probability it involves a common receding of the faded general ideas behind those with a more vivid sensory color and a memory content which is more accessible.

This view finds very clear confirmation when we consider a further group of specimens, in which the figurative paralogism is carried out even more consistently:

(249) *"But then she placed her feet left,"* for "she did it unwillingly."

(250) *"If he doesn't possess rolled up mental shirt sleeves,"* for "thorough knowledge and diligence."

(251) *"Take off the mental shirt collar,"* for "let oneself go, take a rest," along with "live in a boarding house."

(252) *"He announces that he has left the louse-tub of life,"* jocular obituary notice.

Indeed, these idioms could also have been used in wakefulness as humorous metaphors; the last one bore such a stamp to the dreamer, too. The colorless, residual idea is replaced by a sensory image, which renders the thought content in more lucid paraphrase. In specimen 251, the idea in mind stimulated two completely different figurative expressions, of which, to be sure, only one attained linguistic form. Therefore, an actual disturbance of thought or discourse is not at all present in these productions, but rather the expressions bear the iridescent mark of humor. The divergence of expression from thought is so slight that the true meaning is easily recognized, while the sensory vividness of the figurative paraphrase lends a certain flavor to it.

However, such specimens are rare in dreams when compared with the large number of clumsy and unintelligible thought-displacements. I will consider a few more observations, in which the sense of the paralogism is completely obscured by the remoteness of the associative connections.

(253) *"This time period is unfairly designated as grey High Court,"* for "this high plain is falsely viewed as infertile and inhospitable."

(254) *"It is a colossal force of the air, momentum, not force of the breast,"* description of a sciopticon.

(255) *"The Gingobi cannot pre-pick the G,"* for "the Giaur (foreigner) cannot profit from his advantage."

(256) *"Oracle speech in 13 words,"* for "landscape set up like a stage background."

(257) *"I throw Erwinian slags after you,"* indication of an earlier discovery of America.

In the first specimen, there first of all appears for the spatial area of the plateau the conceptually related idea of the "time period." The accompanying idea of the inhospitable then aroused the sensory image of grey, rolling fog which would allow the recognition of ghostly forms in indistinct outlines. Consequently, under the influence of the suggestion of "high" from "high plain," the association was ultimately stimulated of "high court," of gallows which emerged from the grey fog and symbolized the impression of weirdness, uneasiness. The next specimen would seem to mean that in the production of the sciopticon[10] it is a matter not of discourse, but of a figurative representation; that what is active here is not the "force of the breast" but rather a force which travels through the air in another manner. In any case, the rendering of this thought has remained very deficient, even if the attempt at a sensory coloring of the expression is unmistakable. The curious neologism "Gingobi" is on the one hand a reminiscence of "Giaur," which somewhat corresponds to the meaning. On the other hand, however, a part is played here by the association of the Japanese "gingko tree," stimulated by the idea of foreign and strange. This gave the neologism its form and presumably also influenced the expression "pre-pick," which may therefore indicate a displacement of the idea "to profit from his advantage" in the direction of the side-association of the tree. The "G," presumably to be conceived of as reverberation of "Gingobi," otherwise allows no further interpretation. Here too, the preference for the sensory means of representation is unmistakable. The origins of the next two paralogisms are obscure. That the thirteen concatenated words would correspond to the individual stage landscapes arranged one behind the other is certainly clear; however, the connecting link between the oracle language and the landscape, which, moreover, represented a very definite region, could not be traced. The last turn of phrase remains even more obscure; the dreamer had only the idea in mind that it related to the discovery of America before Columbus. Incidentally, both images are, like most of those discussed up to now, in themselves logically executed. The oracle language exists in words, the slag is just thrown in.

In individual cases, the link between the metaphoric paralogism and external impressions could be observed:

(258) "*Awakened from the little bark hut*"; the dreamer heard knocking on a faraway door.

(259) "*A monarchical coup de grâce*"; the dreamer heard the pouring of coal into a coal scuttle.

The knocking was here conceived of as one's being awakened, although the dreamer noticed at the same time that this was done not as usual on the bedroom door, but rather from a distance. The latter idea then stimulated that of the little bark hut, a familiar but remote vantage point. The noise of rolling coal produced the idea of some sudden startling event, which then took on the form reported. Whether the aftereffects of previous dreams also played a part remained unclear. Specimen 234 from the incoherent discourse could also be included in this group, since the urinary pressure produced the idea of a "waterhouse" which would be built in front. The unclear idea in mind did not achieve the intended expression, but rather one determined by side-association.

The thought disturbance underlying the metaphorical paralogism seems to come about owing to the fact that the dreamer's thought stimulates at the same time one or more kindred trains of thought which drive the original into the background. In wakefulness, too, we continually form side-associations, but they remain weak and obscure compared with that idea which lies in the direction of our train of thought, and which is therefore drawn by the dominant target idea to the focus of our consciousness. Only when such target ideas are lacking or lose their force, as in day-dreaming and in fatigue, can the side-associations displace, divert, or interrupt the train of thought. At any rate, this seems to occur, as a rule, only after the fading of the initial idea. In true dreams, by contrast, the original idea in mind can apparently already be obstructed by side-associations as it comes into being, so that it by no means achieves full clarity and in any case does not attain linguistic expression. Often the reason for this suppression may, as we have indicated, be sought in the circumstances that in dreams, in contrast to wakefulness, the faded general idea is inferior in strength to sensorially colored processes of consciousness.

However, the struggle between the ideas emerging side by side in consciousness need not always end with the complete defeat of one of them. In a series of cases, one notices that it comes to a *mixture* of various strings of ideas. Individual elements of one combine with some of another, while at the same time parts of both are suppressed. In this way, there comes about a remarkable throwing together of incompatible ideas, which, at bottom, still express a certain thought.

(260) *"A small root from the documents,"* for "a note for the museum."

(261) *"The true inner parrots,"* religious-political society.

(262) *"The cleaning of the bedroom was particularly difficult and took long because there had to be a breaking-off in the middle of the line on the page proofs."*

(263) *"In no case should one disregard the new nits of the common mouth rhagades."*

(264) *"Mrs. A. wants to tell which almonds of degeneration are strewn in the hypoglossus nucleus of life."*

(265) *"Bound hand and foot all the patients can be classified to the night-stool law,"* for "with the aid of index cards all the patients can be completely grouped."

(266) *"Just give him a tube to describe the time from 8:30 to 9 o'clock,"* for "to study the spinose proccess of the spinal marrow, the substantia gelatinosa."

(267) *"G. meant: the thunderstorm of a heavy man is entirely to be seen in the clinic,"* for "In a thunderstorm the movements of every passenger of a boat become clearly noticeable."

(268) *"That it is wished that this donkey be eaten and not dreamt away,"* for "that the tea be drunk and not get cold."

(269) *"Of late the seats of the nerves are no longer seated in the petals, but rather in speech,"* unclear ideas about plant psyche and about language being peculiarly characteristic of man.

Of the idea in mind of "note" in the first specimen, only the relation to "documents" has remained, from which the note should be removed. By contrast, digging through these documents stimulated the side-association of "root" which now links up with that of documents. The "parrots" were evidently thought of as a comical name for a society. Alongside it, however, arises the idea of higher, moral goals, true introspective life, which led to the curious hybrid designation "true inner parrots." In the next specimens, the mixing up of two trains of thought is especially evident. The cleaning up of the bedroom, being unpleasant work, was brought into connection with proofreading, while the fresh eggs of head lice were connected with syphilitic mouth disease, presumably from the aspect of neglect. The unpleasantnesses of life are, for the dreamer, like the degenerative processes in the nervous system, in particular in the hypoglossus nucleus. The idea of the latter recalls the almond kernel and thus the cakes into which the almonds have been strewn. The concise form in which the excerpts from the patients' histories appear on the index cards is compared to the "binding of arms and legs"; the classifying of this material into definite groups stimulates the curious, only partially intelligible, idea of the "night-stool law," presumably via the side-association of "binding" to a constraining chair.

The "tube" of specimen 266 is a displacement for "microscope." The time before nine o'clock, which is not filled up with any definite business, recalls the poorly differentiated structure of the substantia gelatinosa. Observation 267 shows us on the one hand an acataphasic turn of phrase in the wrong dependency relation, "the thunderstorm of a heavy man" in lieu of "in a thunderstorm one makes movements like a heavy man." Then the two thoughts—that there is something to see in the clinic, and that there is something to be perceived in the boat—are fused together in such a way that from the latter only "heavy man" is retained, whose movements draw attention. Both trains of ideas in specimen 268 somewhat allow the conception that the donkeys should not be dreamt away, and that the tea should be drunk; both are derived from the thought that the punctual tea-drinking should not be missed in a negligent, asinine way. In place of "drinking," the side-association of eating imposed itself—the sole remnant of the conceptual train the dreamer had in mind, which blended into the language expression in only an acataphasic way. The details of the last specimen unfortunately cannot be interpreted, since they were no longer clear enough to the dreamer after awakening. Globally, it involved the distinguishing features between plant and animal, and between animal and man. Plants have no nerves, and animals no speech, two trains of ideas which are inextricably intertwined. Since individual links of the thought chain are everywhere suppressed here, it is in any case a matter of ellipses as well as thought-mixing, even if the process is more complicated here than in the forms of ellipses discussed earlier.

The elliptical contraction of several simultaneous trains of thought into one conceptual mishmash is particularly marked in the following specimens:

(270) *"At it the old dogfish sat honey,"* for "Fat caterpillars, like shark eggs, sat at the flowers and sucked honey."

(271) *"With the bi-kenarrow called upon for this purpose,"* for "assembly which would distinguish among the pretenders to the Bulgarian throne according to the kilometers they covered by bicycle."

(272) *"Not clean [pure], enjoys licentious freedom, but grooms the horses well,"* relates simultaneously to Swiss honey and epileptic domestic servants.

The image which the dreamer had in mind in the first specimen was of fat caterpillars which sat at flowers and sucked honey: a side-association which was transferred from the butterflies to the caterpillars. At the same time, the linguistic rendering of sucking was suppressed. But, the idea of "caterpillars" did not achieve expression either; rather, it was repressed by the side-association of shark eggs—and specifically dogfish eggs lying like caterpillars on the ocean plants. Here the "dogfish" itself appears in place of the egg, and the adjective "old" in place of the conceptually kindred "fat." A similar combination of ellipses, side-associations, and conceptual mixing is responsible for originating the expression "bi-kenarrow," which was clearly conceived by the dreamer in the syllabification shown, even though the idea of the "bike" no doubt brought it about. Specifically, on the one hand the dreamer had in mind the idea of the bicycle track in a narrow pass. Then, however, came the word "bi-kenarrow" as a newly formed designation for an assembly which was to decide on the pretenders to the Bulgarian throne. Supposedly, the automatic wish to keep the two meanings apart was the impetus for the dreamer's deviant syllabification. It may also have been influenced by the conceptual side-association "storthing" [idem]. Nevertheless, the original meaning of the word pressed forth in the broader thought—which, to be sure, did not otherwise achieve linguistic expression—that he who would cover the most kilometers on the bicycle to the Bulgarian border would become the sovereign. Here an additional part was played by the memory of the Baden kilometer logbook which was valid only up to the border. One competitor had covered 1027 kilometers—as could be determined after awakening—the other, 967 kilometers.

In the last specimen, the dreamer had in mind first of all the idea of that which is not entirely genuine and usable; this produced on the one hand the association of Swiss honey, and on the other hand that of the epileptic domestic servant. The phrase "not clean (pure)" relates to the first; then "enjoying licentious freedom," a metaphoric paralogism for "makes diarrhea." Here we have an observation in which the paralogism goes not as usual from the general to the specific, but vice versa, if one may relate in such a way the idea of "diarrhea" to that of "licentious," unrestrained. That is why this phrase was indeed felt by the dreamer to be an especially choice one, and was accompanied by the feeling of unusualness, farfetchedness. The last part of the sentence, "groom the horses well," relates to the painstaking care with which the epileptics tend to perform their duties. This utterance was therefore also conceived of as agreeable confirmation, worth publicizing, of the previous scientific knowledge. Very noteworthy is the observation which here, as in the other specimens, clearly stands out, that the discrepancy between the trains of thought was not at all realized by the dreamer. Rather, he was convinced that his thinking was entirely consistent.

Finally, I may be allowed to communicate two observations in which two different trains of thought did not mix with one another, but rather were linked through the intermediary of sound forms, and at the same time were brought into humorous opposition. The utterances thereby get the stamp of artificial invention, as was indeed clearly felt by the dreamer, at least in the second case.

(273) *"The emperor of China as a Mandarin is sovereign; he would have to obey as a Mandrin."*

(274) *"To me passion has become a game, and game a passion—bring us a skat card,"* utterance of a well-known playwright who sat together with two colleagues in a café.

Both utterances could also have been made in wakefulness. They contain no speech disturbances and no actual thought disturbances, but rather bear the iridescent stamp of jokes. We can hardly doubt here, however, that the word-echo in the former case and the word exchange in the latter case owe their origin primarily not to any particular humorous intent, but rather to chance associations. Subsequently, to be sure, the oppositions were further developed: in the first case by the combining of the absolute power of the Mandarins with the passive role of the Mandrins controlled by a foreign hand; and in the second case by the relation to the playwright on the one hand and to the skat card on the other. To be sure, most plays on words and plays on sounds in waking life are likely to come about in a not very dissimilar way.

V. Kindred Processes

As reliably as that delicate and versatile mental instrument which we call language works, it is still inevitable that, under certain conditions in normal people and especially in the case of patients, disturbances arise in its operation; these in turn are suitable for shedding light on one or another aspect of the peculiarities of dream speech. While it may not be our task here to treat in any greater detail those symptoms which have acquired extraordinary significance for our knowledge of the relation between brain activity and mental life, we should still not fail to indicate, at least in brief, the points of contact which seem to exist between dream speech and the other deviations in the use of the linguistic means of expression. To be sure, this is not so much a matter of actually obtaining new explanations, as of indicating the directions which may lead to them.

First of all, we will have to keep in mind that speech is not an innate ability, but has to be acquired relatively slowly and late. At the individual stages which the child's language development goes through,[11] we come across imperfections and mistakes of various kinds, whose relations to dream speech appear to be worth investigating. The first large main group of children's speech disturbances, the defective expression of successive individual sounds is, to be sure, lacking in dream speech, since this disturbance belongs exclusively to external speech. In any case, the child's difficulties in expressing sounds give rise to the broadest range of "paralalisms": alterations of the words in the sense of anticipations and perseverations, of elisions, additions, and permutations. So "Nampfnopf" in place of "Tanzknopf" (toy top; lit.:"dance button"), is a double anticipation with the elision of the difficult "k"; "Ea" instead of "Wera" is a double elision; "Leva" in place of "Eva" is an addition; "schwissen" instead of "zwischen" (between) is a permutation. Such disturbances arise in children with uncommon frequency, because no stock of proper, practised words is available; the preliminary speech motor impulses are apt to mutually influence one another, while difficult sounds are supplanted or simply left out. We have quite similar experiences as adults when learning some other interdependent series of complex movements. Specimens belonging to this group are not completely lacking in dream speech, but the part they do play is most modest. True difficulties in expressing sounds of the type so prominent with children need not be taken into consideration here at all. We should probably sooner consider the influence of other, more or less clear words in mind; then we are not dealing with paralalisms, but rather with paraphrases, as was also presumed in our previous presentation.

The group of word-selection mistakes in the narrow sense, and especially neologisms, appears in children, as it does in dreams, but to a far lesser extent and in different forms. Of course, word-selection mistakes turn up in large numbers as long as the vocabulary of the child's language is still incompletely mastered. Later on, foreign words give rise to an abundance of such errors in children as they do in uneducated people. Here, unmistakable similarities to the characteristics of dream speech are present. We have seen that the dreamer, too, commits word-selection errors especially easily with foreign words, often enough prompted by phonetic or conceptual kinship. Just as a child speaks of a "participle railway" instead of a "Pacific railway," so the same thing could occur in dreams. But a distinction lies in the child's possessing the correct designation in only very indistinct outline in the first place, while the dreamer is familiar with the designation although it sometimes disappears.

A special group of word-selection errors, which is completely lacking in our dream specimens, arises in the child through linguistic analogies. The formation of the plurals, gender marks, inflections, conjugations, and comparatives is indeed not learned for every word individually; rather it is carried over from one specimen to the next on the basis of acquired general linguistic habits, which constitute a part of the "feeling for the language." The complex nature of finished speech affords the learner the opportunity for numerous derailments which the adult would "never even dream of," since the latter has absolute control over his instrument in this respect. Word-selection mistakes like those mentioned by Wundt—"Amaus" (amouse) instead of "Ameise" (ant), under the influence of "Maus–Mäuse" (mouse–mice), or; "Du bint" instead of "Du bist" (thou art), presumably under the influence of "sie sind" (you are)—seem therefore not to occur in dreams, while they are relatively frequent in the immature speech of children.

Since the child's vocabulary is first of all a very limited one, word-selection mistakes cannot but frequently arise, by applying a more readily available expression to another concept with a completely different name, on the basis of what sometimes appears to be a quite incidental similarity. Thus, a little girl, on seeing goldfish for the first time, called out, "Oh, what nice ducks!" In dreams, for obvious reasons, we observe such word substitutions very rarely, and then almost exclusively with uncommon or foreign-language terms. On the other hand, there does appear in dreams a vast range of linguistic neologisms, which in the child are greatly surpassed by the incorrect transferences and mutilations. To be sure, neologisms are not entirely lacking in speech development, especially in the initial phase. Up to the age of three, one little girl kept calling her elder sister Toni "Olte," even when the correct name would be recited to her. Wundt has pointed out that what we probably are mainly dealing with in such cases are the strongly mutilated remnants of designations which result from the child's misunderstanding. We have seen neologisms often arising in dreams when terms had to be found for complex ideas not hitherto simply named, i.e., under conditions like those of a child with an underdeveloped vocabulary. It is by no means seldom that we also recognize the influence in dreams of remote linguistic reminiscences; but the number, diversity, and independence of these creations is relatively far greater than with the child, presumably because the advanced development of the vocabulary permits a wider scope in this area. Especially foreign-language elements, which are more superficially acquired and grafted onto the development of ideas only by way of addition, lend themselves most easily to such neologisms; this is similar to the way in which we in daily life tend, with a certain predilection, to borrow word-creations for new ideas from such foreign sources.

Disturbances of discourse are quite extensive in children, since of course not only the conversion of concepts into words, but also the expression of thoughts in the shape of discourse has to be learned with effort. As far as I can tell, acataphasic errors seem to be far less important than agrammatical ones. The rhythmic monologues in the form of resounding syllables and word sequences which are sometimes observed in children, and which also play such a large part in nursery rhymes, can probably be compared to the word-jingles of dreams. On the other hand, the awkwardness in the control of word forms and grammatical dependency relationships definitely gives child speech its peculiar stamp. A nice example of syntactic transposition is offered by the utterance of a girl to her father, who had returned after a haircut: "Papa, are you hair of clean?", presumably instead of "clean of hair." In this turn of phrase, which is an apparent attempt at an appropriate expression, one may also see a displacement paralogism, in so far as the child puts a remote, self-made expression in place of the obvious, usual one.

The usual form of undeveloped child discourse seems at first sight to resemble the telegraphese observed in dreaming.[12] "Roll may more no"; "You angry be, I already eat up"; "Yet lep have?"; "You just n't car" are typical examples of it. To be sure, they are also accompanied by paralalic disturbances: "lep" for "slept"; "eat up" for "eaten up"; "n't" for "into." On closer inspection, it appears, however, that a significant distinction between the two groups is indeed to be found. In children, it involves an awkwardness in the form of expression, while the train of thought in mind is clear, and, as a rule, also distinctly recognizable. In dreams, by contrast, telegraphese always seems to appear only when the train of thought itself is unclear and confused. We have therefore also previously emphasized its kindredness with ellipses, and we could moreover adduce the frequency of meaningless neologisms in our examples as a further peculiarity by which they distinguish themselves from the agrammatical word sequences of children.

The thought disturbance group, so strongly represented in dreams, is lacking in children's speech. It is possible that, given an extensive, systematic corpus, some such specimen could be located, but presumably hardly more so than could also be established with adults in waking life. Under these circumstances, we may view the following as the essential characteristics of child speech as compared to dream language: very numerous deviations in external speech; moreover a moderate number of instances of paraphrasia, including in particular those due to false linguistic analogies; and finally marked agrammatism, and, by contrast, a scarcity of acataphasia and thought disturbances.

It is obvious that in quite a similar way the disturbances of children's speech must also appear in the learning of a foreign language. The difficulties of pronunciation lead to imperfections in the rendering of letters and syllables. Word permutations and also neologisms come about through linguistic similarities or conceptual relationships. False language analogies lead in both cases to mutilations and exchanges. Agrammatism, of course, is the form with which the beginner starts in a foreign language; those languages such as Coast Malay and Pidgin English which serve exclusively the communications requirements between peoples speaking foreign languages are, for the very reason of their complete agrammatism, far better able to fulfill this task than are languages with a more complex structure.

To a limited extent, we find the disturbances of dream speech now and then in the utterances of waking life as well. Just as in dreams, we encounter wakeful word-selection disturbances most frequently in the case of proper names and foreign words—and the more readily the less the speaker is fluent with them. The wrong use of foreign words on the basis of sound similarity or conceptual ties is indeed such an everyday phenomenon, that it has found the broadest range of witty exploitation. Here also belongs folk etymology, which by altering foreign words attempts to bring them closer to understanding. But even individual words in the mother tongue which resemble one another are readily mixed up, despite their different meanings, as for example the two words "fortunate" and "fortuitous." Many of these unintentional word substitutions distinguish themselves from those in dreams only as to the circumstances: In one case we are dealing with ignorance, in the other case with temporary incapacity. Wakeful neologisms can of course also occur, although their patterning on the word in mind is presumably closer than in dreams, in which a far greater arbitrariness prevails. But what is completely lacking in waking life are the meaningless neologisms for previously unnamed ideas, of the kind offered us by dreams. When we form new designations in wakefulness, we almost invariably do not just tie them to available words in the native or foreign language; we also allow ourselves to be guided completely by the internal conceptual relationships holding between the ideas. Only the artificial, secret languages of the developmental years sometimes show a preference for neologisms as arbitrary and meaningless as those of dream speech, and then, to be sure, not for unnamed, more complex ideas, but rather as replacements for more common and generally understood words.

The other language disturbances of dreams are likewise not entirely unknown in waking life, even if they only seldom take such odd forms. In such cases, it can, as a rule, be demonstrated that the speaker was disturbed in his mastery of speech expression by special circumstances. Anxious embarrassment, distraction by side-ideas, and fatigue are the most important causes of the genesis of disturbances of discourse. With word-jingles and telegraphese, a role can be played by certain psychomotor excitation, which discharges itself in rhythmic discourse structures with meaningless expletives and insertions, or forces sudden, abrupt utterances, without wasting time on the finishing and structuring of the individual sentence parts. Under the same conditions, thought disturbances, too, can arise which completely resemble those of dreams. Loss of coherence, metaphoric paralogisms and mixing of ideas occur occasionally in all speakers. It is from the proceedings in parliament, but especially from the lectures by "absent-minded" scholars (i.e., those who are often occupied by other thoughts), that such gleanings are likely to be drawn from time to time. The well-known comic figure "Wippchen" to a large extent owes its effect to its systematic mixing of ideas: the partial fusion of incompatible figurative forms of discourse.

As Wundt has already emphasized, a rich source of instances of absent-mindedness is offered by the decrees of Prof. Galletti.[13] Here are found, first of all, simple speech-errors and exchanges, then numerous contradictions, misunderstandings, and instances of thoughtlessness, the origin of which can now no longer be further clarified. Often, a part is played by meaning-disturbing elisions, additions, and derailments. But what especially concerns us here are the very frequent dreamlike errors of thought, chiefly in the form of metaphoric paralogisms and idea-mixing. Let me pick some examples:

"In the year 1800, Bonaparte ascended the consulate."
"Maximilian I had the hope of seeing the throne on his head."
"The battle of Leipzig cost the lives of fifteen villages in the surroundings, discounting the livestock."
"One well realized that the position of Sweden would soon have to surrender."
"In Hamburg the snow often grows."
"The Aleutian Islands live in mud huts."
"The capital Philadelphia died in 1712."
"The largest quadrupeds in the East Indies are the edible bird nests."
"The viniculture is one of the most delightful Rhine regions."
"I'm so tired that one leg doesn't see the other."

In the last examples, elisions have presumably occurred in addition to the mixing of ideas. As for the remarkable things of the East Indies—the large quadrupeds and the edible swallow-nests—supposedly something should somewhere have been stated, which was lost in the fusion. Similarly, we may assume that a special characteristic of viniculture, like the natural beauty of the Rhine regions, was intended but suppressed. The idea of fatigue stimulated the wish to sleep—that one eye not see the other—but this was suppressed by the side-idea of the legs in need of rest. Acataphasic and agrammatical turns of phrase are rare with Galletti. The following two specimens are presumably to be reckoned among them:

"In Russia they have windows of soaked oil."
"The difference between ancient and modern Persia lies mainly in the ignorance of language."

The first specimen somewhat recalls the "processing of voluntary coal" (203), and as such is a syntactic derailment for "paper windows soaked in oil"; the last sentence resembles "In Freiburg the inside of the plate doesn't serve for eating but for the town" (166). Obviously, what should have been said here was that in contrast to Modern Persian, we do not know Ancient Persian. This distinction is, however, carried over from the language as such to ancient and modern Persia; we are dealing with a displacement paralogism. So, of those disturbances with which we have become acquainted in dreams, actual thought-disturbances are first of all found in the absentminded professor, while the errors of linguistic thought expression as well as those of word-selection remain almost entirely in the background.

We thus come to the conclusion that the language disturbances in dreams indeed differ considerably in degree, but far less in kind, from those of waking life. Only the arbitrary neologisms of designations for more complex ideas are not at all found in wakefulness. It would be a rewarding task, though far beyond the scope of the present investigation, to trace in greater detail the various formation processes, such as the conditions under which errors arise in normal waking life.

In a restricted field such investigations have already been carried out with great care: slips of the tongue and slips of reading. Meringer and Mayer [14] have shown that in slips of the tongue (to which we will limit our consideration here) a most significant part is played by the permutations, anticipations, and perseverations of syllables, words, or sounds. We have often encountered these disturbances in dream speech as well, but they are far less in evidence than the neologisms, the disturbances of discourse, and those of thought. This is obviously because in inner speech the sound-images of the words, like the speech motor-images, exert far less mutual influence than in external speech. Further forms of slips of the tongue are the fusions and substitutions. The former can be somewhat grouped with the derailment paralogisms and the idea-mixings from our dream experiences, while the substitutions are more closely akin to our metaphoric paralogisms. As a rule, however, the specimens culled from wakeful slips of the tongue are far simpler and more transparent than those of dreams; they more concern individual sounds, syllables, or words, not complete phrases and thoughts. Thus, I encountered not long ago two utterances, "I still have to make experiences about this" and "How much I had to extoil!" The first case involves a fusion of two sentences: "I still have to make enquiries about this" and "I still have to experience this." Here too, the derailment via the side-idea only brought about an insignificant, immediately comprehensible alteration of the phrase. In the latter specimen, the two expressions "to toil" and "to exert oneself" were fused into one word-blend. Dream speech is sooner brought to mind by another utterance from a different person: "It will get even younger here" for "light earlier in winter." Here, apparently, the side-idea of the young day, which dawns earlier, caused the derailment, which already represents a total change of the thought. Also very similar to language disturbances in dreams, and specifically to metaphoric paralogia, is the utterance "The stomach lies south of the heart." Here, the term "south," taken from the globe, appears in place of the expression "below" the heart. To be sure, one can hardly speak of a "slip of the tongue" here; it sooner involves a "slip of the mind" in the sense of the above-mentioned howlers.

The process involved in recollection can shed a certain light on the paraphasic alterations of proper names in dreams. When we cannot hit on a certain name, we still tend to have a general idea of its sound, which, to be sure, is often deceptive. I shall give here some specimens which I happened to collect. In each case, the last name (underlined) is the one sought; the other names surfaced first, but were rejected. In between are remarks and ruminations:

Martinitz—Marcinowsky—<u>Marcinek</u>

Stahl—<u>Stadler</u>

Strelocky—Strasitzki—Strasky—Strasinoff—Stratzikoff— Stratzinoff—Stre—there has to be an o—Strekinsky—Stratizino— Strasimir—Stresomir—<u>Stratzinski</u>

Wahner—<u>Marquardt</u>

Kollasch—Matschke—Kutschke—Kallasch—Strollasch— Scholke—Scholle—Schally—Schalle—Schollasch—Schalke— Schallasch—Scholtke—Schollak—Scholok—Scholla—Scholler—it seems to me as if a letter is pronounced doubled; it is a word like in English—s doesn't occur in it—e may occur in it—Schom or Schmo—Schmollam—it isn't t—it could be r—Schmorlar—o, p, q, r, s, t, u, v, w—x, y, z—none of these—in any case not z; it is more expressive—e in any case—Schomber—Schro is no go—Schlo could come—ler as an ending, unstressed—Schmorler or Schomler—r does occur in it after all—Schlomar—<u>Schlomann</u> —I never thought of "mann."

Monosyllablic word—Pfnüer—Pfeil—Pfand—Pfeile—Wanst—a—Ma— Pfenda—Wansta—Pfandum—Bachum—Barcha—Borsta—Beiche—b, a—<u>Kohnstamm</u>.

In the first specimens, the search is always taking place in the proximity of the real name. The third specimen shows us the sudden surfacing of the name sought, after initial, rather remote, mistakes; the feeling that "there has to be an o" proves to be false. In the fifth case, the search was an extremely protracted one. In the numerous groping attempts, the correct "Sch" and "l" are mostly to be found, as is often the "o," without the right sequence being discovered and the rest of it being completed. Of the individual letters "e" and "r" which were suspected, neither of the two was correct. By contrast, the English suggestion occasioned by the reminiscence of the "Sloman Line," was correctly anticipated, although the connection itself did not become clear.

It presumably awakened the idea of an unstressed ending. Very remarkable in the last specimen is the total dissimilarity (from the target name) of the words emerging first, which are also completely different from one another; and then the sudden, virtually unmediated jump to the correct name. Only "borsta" might have given something of a link. Here too, it is evident that the presentiments (monosyllablic word—b, a) are anything but reliable guides.

This mistaking of the word sought is obviously very similar to paraphasic disturbances. Within the scope of healthy mental life, these appear only with proper names, because there in particular the tie between the linguistic symbol and the objective idea is an exceedingly loose one. Hence we may understand not only how mutilations and perversions of the correct name can readily come about in dreams, but also how quite remote names and even complete neologisms appear in place of the correct designation. This happens of course especially easily when the naming of products of the imagination is involved, as in the case of many dream specimens, when real names were therefore entirely unavailable. It is in the matter-of-factness with which the new-found names are given to such creations, that the special peculiarity of the dream lies. Quite similarly, we encounter during the process of simple recollection the emerging of drastically changed, or indeed completely arbitrarily formed names. To be sure, we know in this case that they are not correct, whereas in dreams we accept them just as unquestioningly as we do all the other contradictions to our usual experience.

An interesting experimental contribution to the knowledge of speech disorders has been supplied by Stransky,[15] in which he induced a number of subjects under the greatest possible relaxation of attention to say aloud everything which came to mind following an orally presented cue word. These discourses were recorded phonographically. The utterances of less-educated persons amounted more to the reproduction of real or fancied trivial experiences, and, to be sure, mostly in a downright incoherent way, which suggests a flight of ideas. The discourses of educated subjects, however, bore a very remarkable stamp, perhaps because the relaxation of attention had been more completely achieved. Most conspicuous of all was their extraordinary tendency to repeat the same words and phrases, which Stransky groups with the verbigeration of catatonics. Then there was often displayed, along with correctly constructed sentences, a marked agrammatism; especially frequent was the simple stringing together of words and phrases with manifold repetition and inflexions. Yet it did not come to actual telegraphese. In the latter case, we are dealing with a progressive, if quite disconnected, succession of individual ideas, which link up in a most concise version without grammatical structure. In the Stranky experiments, by contrast, we encounter—between sentences with entirely regular constructions—endless enumerations, often repetitive, whose individual members are arranged side by side, but which do not show, as telegraphese does, dissimilar parts of the sentence without grammatical connection. Furthermore, as Stransky remarks, grammatically well-constructed sentences without meaning are sometimes found; these are similar to those occurring in dreams.

A large part is played by the fusion of different words and phrases. To be sure, they mostly keep within the bounds of those which also occur in slips of the tongue, although derailment paralogisms and elliptical phrases are by no means lacking. Finally, neologisms are not at all rare, and are usually to be traced to mutilations or fusions. Nice specimens are "primodial councillor Leuban" and "yelping apparel." In the first case, the memory of a colleague was in mind, who was working on primordial deleriums. The "councillor" still lingered from a previous "provincial councillor." Further, "Lauban" and "Leubus" were fused to "Leuban." "Yelping apparel" represents a fusion with the side-idea of "wolf in sheep's clothing" stimulated by "yelping dog." These neologisms are perfect reminders of some specimens from dreams, such as "curl anchovies" (243). By contrast, completely arbitrary, senseless novel creations seem not to have occurred. Thoughtless expletives, of the kind also appearing here and there in dreams, were often pointed to by Stransky.

It is certainly very remarkable that with the greatest possible relaxation of attention, a number of disturbances of linguistic expression occur which we also find in dreams. But no less important is the fact that the composition and expression of these disturbances in no way coincide with those of dreams. Apparently, the conditions which prevail in the experiment and in dreams are essentially different, despite many similarities. A major distinction is certainly to be sought in the fact that in the one case it is a matter of inner speech, in the other case of external speech. Stransky rightly points out that in purely mechanical speaking, as was attempted in his experiments, the word motor-images must have played a very significant part in the results. To a large extent, the extraordinary tendency towards repetitions and sound alterations of the generated words can be linked to this. Just as the same sounds tend to reappear again and again in the meaningless babbling of children, so in thoughtless speaking, where, after all, no new ideas are struggling for expression, the recurrence of identical or similar sounds would seem to be the most obvious form of activity. To be sure, I would like to think that a further circumstance played a part in the experiment depicted. Most of the subjects seem to have spoken quite quickly; this indicated a certain haste in executing their task. When one speaks into the phonograph, one is, as may be concluded from my own experience, easily seized by an uncontrollable urge to take all possible advantage of the short time available and to keep on speaking without pauses. At the same time, there occurs a certain thought blocking, apparently under the influence of expectation. No doubt these phenomena gradually fade as one gets used to the experiment. But probably they still influenced one experiment or the other in that the failure of thought when there is a fervent wish to speak greatly strengthened the tendency towards repetition and expletives.

Of the pathological language disturbances, the aphasic symptoms are the most comparable to dream speech. In a certain sense, one can view the dreamer as being a sensory and motor aphasic at the same time. He is not completely deaf, in that auditory stimuli of a certain strength do affect him, but he is unable to recognize them for what they are worth. This disturbance can be very clearly traced in its various gradations during awakening. When we are awakened by words, we first perceive only that something is simply audible, without our being able to give an account of the content of what was heard. Consequently, we may also for a while take no note at all of the impressions, even though we hear them. This condition may approximately correspond to that which we are faced with in subcortical aphasia; here, as there, it verges on complete deafness. With progressive awakening, it gradually becomes clear to us that someone is speaking—that we hear words—but at first we do not yet understand their sense. In the process, we perhaps already recognize the speaker's voice, and have an idea of which language is being spoken and with what emotion, although we cannot at all comprehend the content of what is said. It may now happen that we mechanically and uncomprehendingly repeat the words striking our ear. Later on still, we presumably understand individual words, but we are not yet able to grasp the total context, until finally upon complete awakening clear language comprehension is restored. As Pick[16] already observed several years ago in the awakening of epileptics from conditions of clouded consciousness, these various gradations correspond to the behavior in cortical and especially transcortical aphasia. A more exact analysis of details cannot of course be carried out here, since we cannot subject the dreamer to any tests. Furthermore, each individual stage seems to pass over one into the next in a quite imperceptible way.

The similarity between the dream condition and sensory aphasia is shown not only in incomprehension of external impressions, but also in the behavior of inner speech. Sensory aphasia is characterized by the appearance of paraphasic disturbances which are not noticed by the speaker and therefore also not corrected by him. This very peculiarity is, however, presented by dream speech in a most marked way. We have repeatedly pointed out that the dreamer is, as a rule, completely convinced that he is correctly and intelligibly expressing his thoughts, even when producing the most meaningless combination of syllables. Sensory aphasics seem to behave in a quite similar way. Yet in both cases, absolutely well-formed utterances can insert themselves in between. The direction which the paraphasic mistakes take is frequently determined by sound similarity or the sameness of the initial letters. It often involves mutilations and distortions of the correct words, or neologisms whose sound relations are still recognizable. We observe the same thing in dreams, although then, in contrast to paraphasia, the semantic ties also play a significant part. Furthermore, in dreams we come across an extensive number of completely arbitrary inventions, whereas in paraphasia perseverance shows up more clearly than in dreams, where we could only point to isolated specimens.

Acataphasic disturbances are apparently rare in paraphasia, although the difficulty of word selection sometimes leads to peculiar, far fetched expressions, which should be classed with displacement paralogia. Thus, one patient referred to a wastepaper basket as a "straw box," and to a bird's nest as "eggs with vessel." Another one asked about visiting hours with the words, "Is future [Zukunft] today." Apparently he had in mind "herkommen" (to come here) and "zusammenkomen" (to meet). The real meaning of the word "Zukunft" (future) gradually emerged only when it was held up to him. Derailment paralogisms could also occur, especially under the influence of retention. By contrast, the conditions for the origin of elliptical idioms and pure word-jingles do not seem to be present, if one does not wish to count among the latter the insertion of recurrent expletives and expletive expressions. Very remarkable is the occasional appearance of agrammatism, especially in the case of gradual compensation in serious disturbances: a finding which Pick[17] has expressly pointed to.

As for thought disturbances, in paraphasia we should mention the insertion of words or phrases without meaning, which are mostly to be viewed as lingering expletive elements of discourse; furthermore there is a certain incoherence. Whether metaphoric paralogisms and idea-mixings occur more frequently is doubtful to me. In any case, as an instance of the former one could interpret the patients' frequent mixing up of similar tasks, such as the reciting of letters and of a series of numbers. Examples of a more complex nature, such as we meet so frequently and markedly in dreams, seem hardly to occur, however. To be sure, any judgment here is made much more difficult by the many word-selection mistakes. When a patient responds to the request to blow a kiss with "One can no longer draw billy goats up to the monuments," it cannot be decided whether there is an underlying paraphasic disturbance or thought disturbance, since we do not know what the patient wanted to express.

Unfortunately, it seems that up to now no more penetrating analysis of the mistakes encountered with sensory aphasics has been carried out on a larger scale, and it must therefore be left open whether the rules derived here from a scant number of observations may not require further broadening. It may yet well turn out that in general the paraphasic word-selection mistakes are (if we ignore the mixing-in of lingering words) far more influenced by sound similarity than by conceptual ties; that furthermore the neologisms represent mutilations and distortions more than they do free inventions; and finally that the actual thought errors are far less in evidence than those of word-selection and of discourse. In these points lie the essential differences vis-à-vis the disturbances of dream speech. Common to both is the finding that word-selection mistakes arise most readily with proper names and unusual words, notably foreign words, and the occurrence of agrammatism.

If one wishes to speak of a motor aphasia in dreams, it can in any case involve only a subcortical form. The dreamer does not encounter the least subjective difficulty in expressing his thoughts in words. He speaks with complete fluency. To be sure, if in vivid dreams his utterances go beyond the bounds of inner speech and are said aloud, they come out sometimes as real words usually ejaculated in the form of interjections; sometimes however as just poorly articulated sounds. There therefore exist impediments in the psychomotoric area which do not hinder the formation of speech motor-images, but which do make difficult or impossible their transformation into sounds.

In general, the same principles regarding the paraphasic symptoms of speech also apply to those presented in disturbances of reading ability. Here, too, we come across alterations of words in the text, or neologisms which often betray only by individual letters or by their structure the patterning on the original image, and which accumulate with the increasing difficulty of the reading matter. Because of these word deformations, the grammatical structure tends to be destroyed to a far higher degree than in simple speech, so that it sometimes comes to a meaningless concantenation of arbitrary syllable sequences with individual, only half-recognizable fragments. The specimens gathered from paralytics by Rieger[18] and his students remind us of some of our observations of dream agrammatism but also clearly distinguish themselves from them, for one thing by their patterning on the presented text, and for another by the accumulation of completely nonsensical neologisms. On the other hand, paralytics with paralexia may during reading manifest a certain delight in empty turns of phrase interspersed with neologisms, in a way similar to what we meet in dreams. The patients seem to read on in this tone when the reading matter has already been exhausted. In so doing, they have the feeling, just like the dreamer, of having acquitted themselves well. The stimulus of what is presented to them lasts yet a while and promotes paraphasic discourse in the form of empty agrammatism, even in those patients who are otherwise capable of expressing themselves completely intelligibly.

Alcohol delirium patients tend to supply paraphasic reading results quite similar to those of some paralytics. Bonhöffer[19] has reported very characteristic specimens for them. Often enough what is presented to them provides just the external impulse to the apparently hallucinatory reading off of incoherent words and phrases permeated with numerous neologisms. This is supported beyond doubt by Reichhardt's[20] observation that the patients also read off the same utterances from a blank sheet of paper. I adduce some examples:

"Long live Severs Day, since I directly it gets setumlittenly standing we can also her."
"Loden—11 after 8–7 o'clock—unauthorized [unberechtigt]—laboratory— public festival—desert [Einöde]—Eras—house—Harburg—uproar— stitch—canopic—woos and—woman—19 past 11 o'clock—Bodega—not

to the letters [Buchstaben]—mirror [Spiegel]—ages—today"; puts the page away with the words "now it's over."

"83—13—31.8.02—12—22—25—50—6/7—whisky" (from the same patient).

"Munich—mill—measure—Maximilian II of Munich—Wittelsbach—Maximillian II, King of Bavaria, begun in the year 67 with the residential capital of Munich—the small folks there, fowlers—the masculine views of the street of the idea, in the Bohemian way and again in the street of the royal capital and residency, Munich. To the little Franziska Schöllner of this place in the fowlers' employ, from here the whore has abundantly seen squares on the flower for her women; in the street of Ingolstadt about a court nurse the Second Bavarian Field Artillery Regiment into the royal court personnel to the streets. In the royal capital and residency city of Vienna the royal born in 1894 indeed the 1st, 2nd, 4th Field Artillery in gold 15579 marks to the field church to another personality of the field artillery and artillery men to the abundantly born Field Artillery Regiment in the Field Marshall Hall of Magdalena voices. One another to the understanding to matrimony. The deceased Nicholas with the respected gentlemen of the 4th Field Artillery Regiment lost to the field marshall. . . . "

Most conspicuous of all in these utterances is the complete lack of content. They obviously correspond to no train of thought at all; rather it is a matter of pure speech invention which is as good as completely dissociated from the influence of the train of thought. Yet we also know that the same delirium patients immediately before and after can narrate with fairly good coherence, and their discourse presents no trace of this incoherence devoid of thought. Very characteristic of these sequences' not being the expression of thought is the frequent mixing-in of numbers. One specimen is made up almost entirely of this. The patients read slowly, piecemeal, apparently striving to recognize the letters, which according to them were very unclear. This presumably explains the most predominant type of telegraphese: speaking in keywords. Arbitrary neologisms are found only sporadically, in contrast to the very numerous agrammatical disturbances, especially syntactic derailments, which strongly remind us of our dream specimens. Very conspicuous in the last observation is the persistence of individual words: Munich, royal capital and residency, Field Artillery Regiment with the off-shoots, field church, field marshall, Field Marshall Hall, and so on. Here, where the pseudo-reading proceeded more fluently and in sentence form, we might suppose that, in the purely mechanical course of the process, the tendency towards repetition of the same words would indeed have to be more strongly in evidence than in the case of disjointed fragments separated from one another by longer pauses.

There can hardly be any grounds for doubting that the patients really read out their utterances from the empty pages, just as they, under the influence of suggestion and with their eyes closed, have the most varied visions, among which letters and words can be found. We may recall here that, when falling asleep with eyes closed, healthy people, too, can manage to have letters surface before them, which are decipherable and which provide empty incoherent specimens quite similar to those we just mentioned. The disturbance in alcohol delirium therefore represents only one aggravation of a process, which under extremely favorable conditions can come about in normal life as well. It has already been mentioned above that in dreams, too, the peculiar utterances appear here and there as visual images and are read out. Just as we have presumed in the case of some of our specimens that the speech motor-images emerge independently in consciousness, detached from the process of conceptualization, so it also seems that the visual images are liable to break through thanks to internal stimulation. With speech auditory images it occurs for obvious reasons infinitely more frequently and strikingly. If this hallucinatory emergence of various linguistic elements is really effected without any connection to the train of thought, the result is constituted of an empty series of meaningless spoken, read, or heard words or sounds. On occasion this can also be clearly observed in the case of auditory delusions. To be sure, the word sound-images play such a decisive role in our thinking, that it is only comparatively rarely that they achieve sensory independence without remaining connected with the content of consciousness.

In this short survey of symptoms kindred to dream speech, it would take us too far afield to discuss in detail all those disturbances of word-selection and discourse which appear in the various forms of insanity. We can therefore omit treating at this point the language disturbances of mania, of epilepsy and hysteria, of senility and of idiocy, as well as some other, rarer forms of illness. This is partly because they have nothing useful to offer for the clarification of the questions occupying us, and partly because sufficient observations are not available to enable us to draw fruitful comparisons. Suffice it to briefly indicate here that in mania we often encounter—besides word-distortions via assonance and rhyme—a word-jingle which very much recalls the dream specimens we have reported. In the case of epileptics, speech disturbances arise particularly in connection with fits. This usually involves word-selection disturbances, often agrammatism as well, and, more seldom, neologisms. The senile illnesses tend on the one hand to present manifestations of perseveration, and on the other hand more or less marked paraphasic disturbances, while in the case of idiots we likewise frequently observe very clear perserveration, but it is then of course that of agrammatism peculiar to the child stage of development. Agrammatism often appears in hysterics, too, but then as an imitation of the child's mode of speaking.

If, as far as language disturbances are concerned, the kinship between all these pathological conditions and dreams is only a very remote one, there does happen to be a series of remarkable similarities regarding dementia praecox. First it can be pointed out that the tendency towards remote, farfetched turns of phrase like those we have become acquainted with in displacement paralogia forms a very widespread peculiarity in patients with dementia praecox. We commonly accept that there exists in them an outright urge to avoid the obvious natural manner of expression and to put in its place unusual, indeed self-coined turns of phrase, similarly to the way we picture the realization of affected movements. From our experience with dream speech, we know, however, that farfetched expressions can manifest themselves even without this having been intended—the finding of the obvious turn of phrase being hampered for whatever reason. The feeling of saying something unusual is completely lacking here. It remains to be seen whether similar processes can also occur in dementia praecox, but in view of the manifold disturbances of volition in this illness, the possibility may already be conceded. Here the obstacle which disturbs the natural course of the word-selection process could be something like negativism—in that it suppresses the initially emerging ideas and impulses of will. The mannerisms in speech and action would not be directly intended by the patient, as it seems to the observer, but rather would be a resort to which he is involuntarily forced as soon as the nearest path to activity is blocked by the general disturbance of negativism. In this case, as in dreams, the patient need not at all be conscious of the peculiarity of his speech. When a patient says, for example, that the "anaesthesia" he experienced was "somewhat hot-feeling," it is a displacement paralogism quite similar to our "attentive report" (171).

It is doubtful whether our explanation, which could further our understanding of many symptoms, especially in the case of hebephrenic forms, is also suited for elucidating the whole area of "speech styles." Especially the tendency frequently appearing in patients to speak with diminutive syllables with similar distortions in a particular dialect indicates that, aside from the impediment to the natural means of expression, special secondary linguistic drives may also play a part. To be sure, we will have to disinguish this form of mannerism from the simple emergence of peculiar, farfetched turns of phrase. It is noteworthy besides that in dreams, too, we now and then come across a dialectically tinged manner of expression, but then in particular when foreign languages are concerned. Not at all seldom do we hear our patients produce just such nonsensical gibberish with the pretension of its involving a foreign language. If we may judge on the basis of dream experiences, the patients need not at all be conscious of the meaninglessness of their speech.

However, by far the most surprising similarity between dreams and illness is afforded us by the study of neologisms. As is well known, they are frequent enough in dementia praecox and attain a quite amazing scope and variety in cases of language confusion, whose clinical position within the larger group has, admittedly, not yet been sufficiently clarified. If from the history of one such case, also previously observed by me,[21] we quite arbitrarily choose some expressions: "figurances," "rudderaments," "quicksilver herring," "lixivialias," "piconate," "aledartivesolo," "spear-gleam banker," "ludotorontine," "hongrive," "lavecteriments," "romblive," and so on, then the complete correspondence with neologisms supplied by dreams is immediately obvious. As with dreams, we see here many words composed of meaningful elements (quicksilver herring, spear-gleam banker), while others (ludotorontine, hongrive, lavecteriments, romblive) represent completely random accumulations of syllables. With a third group, however, suggestions of real words are still recognizable, admittedly in more or less strongly altered form (figurances, rudderaments, piconate); and finally we encounter formations which, like lixivialias and aledartivesolo, allow no meaning at all to be conjectured, but still give the impression of real words. We have seen previously that in dreams quite definite ideas, though admittedly often very unclear ones, can link up with such neologisms, and that furthermore these ideas are frequently complex, not easily named, and finally that the newly created designations very commonly bear the stamp of a foreign language.

The inventions of patients, too, appear predominantly in the unmistakable form of foreign words, as the above listing, which can easily be continued indefinitely, has already shown us. If, from the downright amazing external similarity of neologisms in dreams and illness, we may venture further conclusions about certain correspondences of inner processes, then the immediate assumption is that the patients with speech confusion similarly believe themselves to be speaking meaningfully and intelligibly, just as we in dreams—a supposition which furthermore has been expressed fairly often before, in view of the calm certainty with which they deliver their discourse. Of course this is not to say that the patient's train of thought is a completely clear and coherent one. On the contrary, there definitely exist serious disturbances, just as indeed in dreams individual meaningless discourses correspond to a certain content, while alongside them a series of radical impairments of the train of thought exists. We may perhaps merely be allowed to think of the strange discourses of patients as not simply representing "nonsense," and far less so something like the intentional product of rollicking humor, but rather as the expression of a peculiar word-selection disturbance which must be closely akin to that of dreams. It is possible that, by whatever pathological processes, the locating of the usual speech designation is rendered impossible, or else is so difficult, that the patient is forced to use neologisms as in accordance with our earlier presumptions about having to use uncommon turns of phrase. We are bound to envisage the process in dreams—and, as we may add, in sensory aphasia—as completely similar. Also to be mentioned is the possibility that our patients do not only have new words, but also new ideas. Much experience seems to support the widespread opinion that on the pathological plane there are also pathological processes of consciousness taking place for which the patient now invents new designations, like "lobster-crackings," "bomb-bursts," "de-animation," "night-overhearing," "mental dissipations," etc. For such designations which supposedly reflect definite forms of influence, the intentional invention can simply be conceded. But even then, we will still presumably have to conceive of a significant part of the neologisms as simple word-selection errors substituting for the correct designations which do not appear—something which no doubt holds true in dreams as well.

Aside from neologisms, there is also common to both speech confusion and dream speech the frequent occurrence of peculiar meaningless turns of phrase, which we may presumably conceive of as acataphasic disturbance. "To insignificantly leave the chicken out," "fearfully indicated disarray," "the fragmentary first of August," and "readied themselves to refresh" are such turns of phrase from dreams. To these we can compare from the above-mentioned diseases "happen the pencil more thickly," "abnormal stallion come of age," "unfortunate bay window of the future," "quacked Turkish red," "surgical physician taking into account swollen," etc. It is meanwhile unmistakable that such amazing word orders in language confusion are incomparably more frequent than in dreams. To be sure, the patients, too, generate individual sentences that are readily intelligible, especially as answers to questions; but they then very quickly return to their astonishing mishmash of ideas, in which only the general sentence form tends to remain fairly well preserved. In dreams, by contrast, there are usually only scattered turns of phrase which can be branded as totally incomprehensible. Between them, words, turns of phrase, and whole sentences are regularly inserted which show no disturbance at all. It must therefore remain doubtful whether the discourse of those suffering from speech confusion allows itself in principle to be deciphered similarly to the way which is successful with many dream disturbances and which yields a meaning which is to some extent intelligible. In any case, disturbances are still at play which are lacking in dreams or else have far less effect. To these belong first of all perseverations, which we observe in dreams only very occasionally, but which regularly appear strongly in speech confusion. Thus distractability seems to influence the discourse of patients far more than that of dreams. Its effect is the jumping from one idea to another, as we have encountered in derailment paralogia. It is just this virtually uninterrupted series of idea-connections— surprising us each time anew and beyond deliberate imitation—which for a good part may be traced to derailments in patients.

Add to this, however, yet a further circumstance. The patients are usually very talkative and take pleasure on given occasions in delivering running discourses with great fluency. Evidently they have as little feeling as we in dreams for the nonsensicalness of the utterances, and even consider them to be quite successful. This reminds us of word-jingles, of the generation in dreams of bombastic, usually rhythmically constructed turns of phrase with no intelligible content at all. In that case, too, we thought ourselves to be speaking quite beautifully. This seems to involve a form of satisfaction which essentially emanates from the flow of speech motor presentations and which may be akin to those which originate from other expressive movements: from singing, dancing, imitating, and the meaningless babbling of children. In waking life the joy of fine-sounding styles of discourse is kept within proper bounds by regard to the thought content, even though we not infrequently see the rhetorician himself get carried away by vacuous but euphonious turns of phrase. With patients, a particular personal mode of speaking usually tends to develop. They speak with a certain intonation, have their pet expressions and turns of phrase which return time and again, produce their most long-winded sentences in roughly the same way, and usually quickly slip into a form of rhetorical delivery. The immediate assumption is therefore that in the case of patients with marked speech confusion, there exists along with the disturbances discussed a certain relish for speaking which induces them to rattle on anything which comes to their tongue, similar to the manner of the so-called beer-discourse, which likewise comes about under the influence of psychomotor excitation with the paralysis of the higher intellectual capacities and trains of thought. Since in the patients the faculty of controlling and improving the flow of discourse has—as we might well suppose in view of their numerous paraphrasic neologisms—been lost to a greater or lesser extent, there often also disappears, in this discharging of an unbridled urge to speak, the last recognizable trace of the thought process, which we must, in accordance with our dream experiences, presumably seek behind the speech-confusion utterances, even if they are overgrown with desultory, incoherent, and empty verbiage. Indeed it is still also possible now and then to somewhat recognize in quite general outline the thoughts which move the patients.

At first sight, patients suffering from speech confusion, with their fluent semi-incomprehensible discourse, may bring sensory aphasics to mind. But the talkativeness of aphasics does not spring so much from a relish for speech activity as, far more, from the need to somehow make themselves understood to their surroundings. Thus the gibberish of aphasics is in the first place governed by word-selection disturbances, to which acataphasic and agrammatical errors join in only to a limited extent. In speech confusion, however, we also keep coming across unmistakable thought disturbances as we quite similarly do in dreams. Metaphoric paralogisms seem to be particularly frequent. I adduce some specimens from the discourse of the patients already repeatedly mentioned above:

> "I will take the liberty of doing a small concert," upon being requested to write.
>
> "I just have to do war-minister service" for "go and set the table."
>
> "I don't smoke cigars, because it is boiled somewhat thinner; I myself have the nicest eyeglasses at home," on being offered a cigar.
>
> "They can, I suppose, continue their axillaris here" for "write another newspaper here."

"I'm going inside, to set the table, it's my property" for "my special duty."

"Don't take any pleasure in it" for "Don't take the trouble."

"Saturday I have to rinse the potatoes" for "I have to bathe."

"I'd like to invite you to a small concert in puncto of the Herculesary" for "I'd like to show you this document."

"And now, I guess the traffic institute is at an end!" for "the time for entertainment."

"I wasn't allowed to immediately charge the cigar which was offered, because I delivered the contents in somewhat thicker cheese" for "I needn't have accepted the cigar."

The interpretations of the paralogisms here can of course only be inferred from the whole state of affairs, since the patient is unable to give any information about his real thoughts. Nevertheless, the specimens cited show a fair correspondence with those of dreams. In particular cases one can perhaps question whether it is not a matter of simple word-selection errors. Mostly, however, it is clear enough that we are dealing with an associatively stimulated side-idea, which achieves speech expression instead of the series of ideas originally in mind. In the third specimen, the correct answer is given first, but is then immediately paraphrased by a paralogism. The tagging on of a completely nonsensical subordinate clause to the initial paralogism is particularly noteworthy in the last specimen (to which we could easily add other, similar ones). We see from this how the patient gets carried away to a certain extent by his own verbiage. Also the addition "in puncto of the Herculesary" in the third from last specimen should presumably be viewed in this way.

In any event, on the basis of these experiences we can draw the conclusion that in the case of speech confusion there is present, along with the disturbances of word-selection and of linguistic thought-expression, also disturbances of the train of thought itself, which for a part strongly resemble those of dreams. This very extension of the disturbance across the whole range of areas that contribute to the genesis of speech indicates that, of all the pathological manifestations of language disturbances discussed, that of speech confusion in dementia praecox is closest to that of dreams. Of the processes in normal life, those most closely akin to the latter are slips of the tongue and errors of thinking in severe absentmindedness. On the other hand, in child language, as in sensory aphasia, many processes of mental life evidently operate undisturbed which under the previously discussed conditions are in some way impaired. It will be the task of further, more penetrating, analyses of linguistic processes and their disturbances to more precisely define the nature and extent of the errors made, and in so doing to clarify the inner relationships of the manifold processes which must be coordinated in the course of expressing oneself through speech.

VI. Summary

The endeavors to group the instances of speech disturbances in dreams from particular angles has shown us that they display a very great diversity. And therein lies, indeed, part of their special scientific value: They teach us just how extraordinarily complex the process of inner speech must be, when we see how in dreams the most multifarious disturbances achieve expression. In a great number of cases we were able to give an immediate account of the processes which led to the formation of faulty utterances. Since the speech disturbances of normal waking life, especially as far as they concern inner speech, have only narrow latitude, while in the case of pathological phenomena in our area we are incapable of observing their internal genesis, the language disturbances of dreams, which in their extent and multifacetedness are by no means surpassed by those of patients, offer an exceedingly welcome opportunity to experience for ourselves the same conditions in which the most important instrument of our mental life fails in private, so to speak, and then regains its utility.

Looking back at the long series of disturbances which we discussed individually, we obtain the following table, to which has been added in each case the number of instances reported.

I. Disturbances of word-selection (165)
   A. In simple general ideas (88)
       1. Mutilation and alteration (9)
       2. Replacement by other words (29)
           a. according to sound relationship (9)
           b. according to conceptual relationship (12)
           c. without relationship (8)
       3. Neologisms (50)
           a. with sound patterning (20)
           b. with conceptual patterning (10)
           c. arbitrary (20)
   B. In individual ideas (48)
       1. Mutilation (6)
       2. Replacement (8)
       3. Neologisms (34)
   C. In complex ideas (17)
   D. Senseless neologisms (12)
II. Disturbances of speech (58)
   A. Disturbances in the linguistic coinage of thoughts. Acataphasia (36)
       1. Displacement paralogisms (7)
       2. Derailment paralogisms (10)

      3. Ellipses (10)

      4. Word-jingles (9)

    B. Disturbances in linguistic structure. Agrammatism (22)

      1. Syntactic errors (7)

      2. Telegraphese (12)

      3. Agrammatical fragments (3)

III. Disturbances of thought (51)

    A. Imperfect formation of thought process (11)

      1. Thought-free speech modes (7)

      2. Incoherence (4)

    B. Slipping thought process (40)

      1. Metaphoric paralogisms (25)

      2. Ideational mixing (13)

      3. Jocular contrasts (2)

It follows from this table that the language disturbances of dreams may concern very different segments of the speech process, and that certain mistakes can be observed to occur especially often, others far more seldom. To be sure, chance may have played a large part in our collection, and it is likely that the more conspicuous disturbances, especially the lexical neologisms, more easily attracted the dreamer's attention. Nevertheless, the instances, which after all are not so small in number, may enable us to form at least an approximate judgment as to the relative frequency of the individual disturbances.

If a speech utterance is to come about, then first of all the thought in mind has to be definitely and clearly formed. If it is indistinct or muddled, there arise thought-free modes of speech or incoherence. Yet, we have reason to assume that also in the case of meaningless neologisms, of word-jingles, and of agrammatical fragments, the content of consciousness is as a rule unclear to a greater or lesser extent, as is presumably sometimes the case with some other forms as well. Under this assumption, the number of such instances would reach thirty or forty.

Subsequently, the idea in mind has to find the possibility of converting itself into linguistic form. In the case of metaphoric paralogisms, as with idea-mixing, this does not happen: What obtains linguistic expression in the former case is an associatively excited side-idea only, and in the latter case the side-idea together with the original idea. In the case of displacement paralogisms, which closely approach these forms, the thought is not rendered as it was in mind, but rather in an unclear, inappropriate, and more or less distorted form, while in the case of derailment paralogisms, the intended speech formulation is thwarted by the intrusion of extraneous elements. Finally, the ellipses are characterized as incoherent hints, in that only rudimentary fragments of the train of thought get through and attain linguistic expression.

A special task of language formation, in addition to the conversion of the individual ideas into language symbols, is their correct arrangement into compound sentences. Since there are languages which dispense with this arranging, we are dealing here with a performance which is not absolutely necessary for the expression of thought. Indeed, it is first learned by children only after they have long been able to make themselves understood, and it can also be lost independently, as is demonstrated by cases of agrammatism. In dreams, however, this happens relatively infrequently. As certain mistakes in children's speech show, drilled-in habits gradually develop which govern the declension of words and their position in the sentence. We recall here the fact, which frequently emerged from our data, that we obviously also acquire certain general linguistic attitudes later in life which permit us to choose our entire mode of expression in terms of a certain language or dialect, without having to pay particular attention to individual vocabulary words and grammatical rules. From experience, it emerges with surprising clarity that in dreams, as indeed in wakefulness, we are able to quite aptly imitate a foreign language by means of completely meaningless sequences of syllables.

Paraphasic word-selection disturbances constitute by far the most extensive group of our specimens. It would have been larger still if we had also wished to include among them the vocabulary mistakes which occasionally occur along with other forms. The nature of the faulty words generally calls to mind the experiences with paraphasia, although certain radical differences are unmistakable. The simple mutilations and alterations play only a minor part here, in contrast to paraphasia. They involve 15 specimens out of 165. To be sure, it is possible that the more conspicuous faulty words more vividly engaged the dreamer's attention and were therefore registered in greater numbers. But also the sound kindredness, which likewise plays a quite considerable part in paraphasia, led the word-selection astray in only 29 cases, and perseveration which tends to be so much in evidence there, seems here to be of hardly any significance at all. All these mistakes therefore seem to be especially favored in the case of external speech. By contrast, more faulty specimens based on conceptual patterning are found in dreams than is the case with paraphasia, where they are quite rare; we count 22 instances. The unusually numerous neologisms, however, characterize dream speech to a quite special degree: no fewer than 113 cases, whose frequency distinguishes it fundamentally from paraphasic disturbances. These very deviations approximate the symptoms of speech confusion, for there, too, neologisms so very strikingly come to the fore.

On the other hand, it is unmistakable that word-selection disturbances in dreams are subject to conditions quite similar to those of paraphasia. First of all, it is the proper names with which switching of the language designations so very easily ensues, as it does in the waking life of normal people, since they constitute a far less fundamental component of the aggregate idea and are therefore far more loosely connected with their core than is the case with other ideas. Next, unusual or foreign language designations are so readily replaced by wrong words, apparently for similar reasons. We may assume that there, too, the connection between the real and the linguistic components of the concept is less firm and therefore more easily loosened. For even when we make a conscious effort, such designations come to mind with more difficulty than do everyday words and those derived from the mother tongue. It is possible that in the case of speech confusion, too, both of the above points of view may have a bearing, even if it is difficult to find out much about them.

Very remarkable is the experience that in a certain number of cases in dreams we should resort to neologisms in order to name more complex concepts for which no standard concise designation is available. Seventeen of our specimens could be included here. This process is not, it seems, to be observed in paraphasia. But many experiences point to our having to assume something similar for speech confusion. There, it was often even thought possible to trace a large part of the neologisms back to the origin of new, pathological ideas, for which new designations had to be created. It is very doubtful to me whether this interpretation may claim a wide scope, although it presumably cannot be completely rejected within certain narrow bounds. On the contrary, I cannot convince myself that in dreams we are really dealing with newly created ideas, which would then also call for neologisms. Rather, it would seem essentially that processes are involved here which are closely related to ellipses. Of a group of ideas, only individual elements achieved linguistic expression, and then possibly in a displaced or paraphasic way, so that an incomprehensible fragment appears in speech as a representative of a complex idea. Indeed, examination shows us that the ideas which had been in mind can without difficulty be completely and intelligibly expressed in wakefulness, so that there exists in itself no need to look for new designations. The dreamer has lost his mastery over the vocabulary which would enable a linguistic rendering, and he now in a similar way resorts to imperfect expedients, as we likewise do when we are to express ourselves in a foreign and quite tongue-tying language. From this angle, the neologisms for more complex ideas seem to me to have a significance similar to that of displacement paralogisms, in that we have also accepted as their cause of origin not a deliberate search for the out-of-the-way expressions, but rather an inability to find the most obvious idiom.

Not without deeper significance is doubtlessly the fact that the overwhelming majority of neologisms bear the stamp of foreign languages. Aside from the twenty-seven instances which were clearly thought of as translations into other languages, a vast number of specimens are found which unmistakably appear in the form of foreign words. Compared to these, the neologisms belonging to the mother tongue remain very much in the background. Similar observations may be made in the case of language confusion, which likewise shows a certain predilection for foreign-sounding neologisms. We may be allowed to recall here the fact that nearly all the new words with which we have become aquainted since the acquisition of our mother tongue in earliest youth are foreign; and that in particular the immense importance attached to foreign languages in our school system, at least among the more educated classes, allows the adoption of foreign-sounding expressions and their occurrence in place of the mother tongue designations as quite an everyday process. Furthermore, it is to be taken into account that we tend to learn foreign languages not, as is the case with the mother tongue, with our ears, but rather in the first instance preferably with the aid of visual images and motor-images, and that we therefore possibly have their elements relatively more readily at our disposal if the otherwise leading influence which the acoustic images of the mother tongue exert has been destroyed. It also seems to me that such foreign-language tinges in the neologisms of patients who only know their mother tongue appear far less frequently or not at all.

Add to this, finally, that foreign-language designations appearing as representatives of whatever ideas need to overcome far less resistance than do neologisms from the mother tongue. In the latter case, after all, side-ideas turn up as a rule with greater or lesser clarity which tie in with the individual terms of the linguistic expression. And herein indeed lies the immeasurable value of language purity: that it also stimulates an abundance of accompanying ideas by which the meaning of each turn of phrase becomes evident in all its profundity. The foreign word, on the other hand—even when we are able to make its composition clear to ourselves—is only in rough outline a representation of the idea it stands for. The inner relationships holding between its linguistic content and the individual elements of the idea in mind remain more opaque, and the connection is therefore often felt to be a purely arbitrary one. In the case of the mother tongue, by contrast, where concept-formation first proceeds largely with the aid of language, it appears as an inner and indissoluable one. With abstract general ideas the linguistic designations may indeed ultimately form the main elements, to which only sparse and indistinct remnants of objective ideas attach themselves. These linguistic expressions are therefore also the very last to be lost when there is an increased impediment to word-selection. For similar reasons, common mother-tongue words, having a particularly intimate tie to the ideas they represent, can far less easily stand in for failing linguistic designations than can foreign formations, which are only loosely tied, if at all, to the objective ideas. The latter have a much greater independence and flexibility and, to be sure, also a more muddled and more indistinct content: properties which cannot but favor their occurrence in the form of error words.

Unfortunately, it has not been possible for me to investigate the question of what personal differences there exist in the production of dream speech. For this, far more extensive observations would have been necessary. The majority of the examples are due to the same person. I have at my disposal only smaller sets of observations from other persons, which does not permit a reliable comparison. One person supplied seventeen instances. It is notable that these consisted of fourteen sentences, two short phrases and only one word. It would nevertheless be mistaken to conclude from this alone a tendency toward longer utterances in dreams; for we do not know whether, with less attention being paid to the phenomenon in question, only the longer utterances were retained, while the individual peculiar words in otherwise comprehensible sentences were neglected. Also the numerous word-selection mistakes in our survey were in reality elements of utterances of which always only fragments remained in the dreamer's memory. More noteworthy is the experience that of the specimens of the above-mentioned person, four had a decidedly rhythmical form, and that five examples were rendered as supposed quotations. Two of the verselike utterances were unmistakably jingles. These facts, when compared with other observations, indicate that the person in question was especially prone to speak in elevated style in dreams. The few examples can be divided according to the kind of disturbance, so that word-selection mistakes are involved six times, acataphasic disturbances three times, and thought disturbances seven times. The last therefore took up a disproportionately large space. It is especially noteworthy that no fewer than five metaphoric paralogisms occurred: approximately three times what would have been expected on the basis of the grand total of the observations. The tendency towards figurative modes of expression in dreams was therefore especially marked here. One can, if one wishes, relate this trait to the one previously raised, and this would then do justice to the peculiar character of the person in question which is recognizable in wakefulness.

The clinical relationships, if I may put it that way, which dream speech shows towards certain pathological forms, make it desirable to give an account of the extent to which the manifold deviations which appear in our examples may be reduced to certain general basic disturbances. If we could obtain some clarity on it, not only would new light be shed on these pathologies; we would probably also be able to benefit from the approaches already derived there for the understanding of dream disturbances. We are, admittedly, still quite insufficiently prepared for deeper delving into the questions that are awaiting an answer here. What is especially lacking as well is a more thorough investigation into many of those processes whose kinship with dream speech we have briefly touched upon here. Nevertheless, we might allow ourselves at least to indicate the directions which further elucidation of dream speech can be expected to take.

In the first place, it is clear that in dreams we are dealing with a disturbance of word-selection which is extraordinarily close to that of *sensory aphasia*. In the former as in the latter, the influence of word sound-images on the kinesthetic images is heavily impaired. Consequently, the objective ideas on the one hand are converted into mutilated, wrong, or completely newly-formed words. On the other hand, we speak these words unhesitatingly in dreams, without in any way noticing their distortion, their completely different meaning, or their senselessness. Furthermore, it not infrequently happens that an extensive string of ideas finds linguistic expression in only individual, incoherent fragments. Finally, kinesthetic images can delight the dreamer, especially in rhythmic structures, as mere ringing word-jingles without any relation to a thought content. Only occasionally in any of these cases does the divergence of thought content from linguistic expression come to our consciousness in any way at all. We feel our utterance to be wrong or, far more often, comic, jocular, or, finally and most frequently, to be foreign translations that we put up with, without taking any further account of the specifics of their linguistic derivation.

It has already been repeatedly pointed out that in general we learn the native language in an essentially different way from the foreign language which comes later on. Leaving aside the unconnected, stammering sounds of earliest childhood and the fairly isolated interjections, one finds the very first linguistic presentations of any competent humans to be without exception word sound-images, to which the object-presentations then attach themselves. Only later, with the development of speech ability, which naturally lags behind language comprehension, are they followed by the speech kinesthetic images, which at first are almost always accompanied also by auditory perceptions. It is therefore completely understandable that the word sound-images supply the speech elements of the ideas in the very first place, and that they also retain in the further course of language development the controlling influence on the production of speech movements which they possessed from the start. Apparently, we should consider their relation to speaking to be very similar to that between sensations in the joints and the execution of movements. We are able to speak and move, even when the control by the word sound-images or the joint sensations has been lost; but speech, like movements, turns extraorinarily easily up the wrong path, making mistakes, losing the capacity for finer adjustments. If we can thus compare sensory aphasia to sensory ataxia, the loss of linguistic feeling in our area could in a way be likened to the loss of stereognosis.

As we know, we are able to a certain extent with the aid of our eyes to compensate for atactic disturbances which are brought about by the loss of joint sensations. Also in the field of speech, we can later on make up aids which, to a certain extent, are capable of standing in for the word sound-images, especially the visual images of script, and later on the writing motor-images which attach themselves to them. With their help, the mastery of the spoken means of expression can be more or less completely regained.

If we apply these observations, taken from aphasia theory, to language disturbances in dreams, we come to the conclusion that Wernicke's center for word sound-images more or less completely fails in its duty. Indeed we are doubtlessly word-deaf in dreams, and in this respect the experiences with speech and speech comprehension in dreams correspond well. To be sure, the word deafness in sleep may increase to almost total deafness, although we may point out that the dream conditions with which we are dealing here certainly do not correspond to any great sleep depth, and so, on the whole, we are justified in speaking of word deafness and not total deafness. Repeated experiences tell us that the dreamer perceives fairly strong auditory impressions without understanding them. We have already become acquainted with two such specimens (258 and 259). It is possible that, when he simply repeats a word called out to him, without grasping its meaning, his behavior can correspond to that of transcortical aphasia. In any case therefore, not only is the perception of auditory impressions rendered more difficult in dreams, but their mental processing as well, which penetrates into consciousness despite the perceptual impediments. In a certain connection to this may be the finding that in only nine of our 274 observations was what was spoken attributed to another person, while twenty-seven specimens are found in which reading-images apparently played a part. The word sound-images, to which we quite rightly ascribe an absolutely decisive importance for our speaking in waking life, quite obviously recede in dreams, even far behind the reading-images, which, however, in view of their later acquisition, cannot possibly claim the same importance as the former.[22] To be sure, it is possible that personal peculiarities should be taken into consideration here, since the person to whom the great majority of the specimens is due decidedly favors visual images above auditory impressions. Nevertheless, it is hardly likely that the predominance of word sound-images so solidly anchored in the acquisition of language should be fundamentally affected by this. What may also be noted is that hardly any clear auditory perceptions were present in the few specimens which in the dreams were attributed to other persons. Twice the dreamer believed himself to have heard singing on which he superimposed the words of the specimen without actually hearing them. In any event, the visual perceptions were extraordinarily more vivid, especially in the six cases of emerging pictorial representation.

If we were to summarize this discussion, the conclusion would follow that in dreams the appearance of speech motor-images is very frequent indeed, even though they cannot be converted into actual movements. But the motor-images evidently very often lack the directional influence of the word sound-images and hence present word-errors like those observed in sensory aphasia. Accordingly, word sound-images in dreams are extraordinarily rare, the more so when one considers their absolutely fundamental importance in wakefulness. By contrast, the reading-images are observed considerably more often, despite their far lesser significance for speech. The restriction in the relationship to the external world therefore does not obtain to the same degree for all connections, but rather—when we here except the cessation of actual movements—most markedly in the area of auditory sensation and especially with regard to the mental processing of the stimuli flowing along these paths. We recall here that, after all, our dreams take place essentially in visual images and motor-images, while auditory perceptions recede very much into the background—even though in wakefulness the hearing of speech provides what is pretty much the most important group of all the sensory impressions. This failure of the word sound-images may have something to do with the great transitoriness of our recall of dream utterances, since motor-images generally tend to persist more poorly than do sensory images.

If one may put it this way: The area of auditory sensation, up to its highest segments, thus appears to sleep more deeply than the area of visual sensation and, presumably, also that of motor-images, which to be sure is likewise entirely shut off from the external world. The eyes, too, are certainly protected from the outside world, and indeed by equipment which is, like our limbs, served by muscles. Hearing, by contrast, remains the important warner of approaching danger, receptive to external impressions to a certain degree. These can lead to awakening when they are very strong, but they usually do not disturb the sleeper's rest since impediments oppose their penetration into consciousness. One might be tempted to view the deeper dulling of the lower as well as the higher segments of auditory sensation as a kind of self-protection, which enables a complete rest, although, unlike with the eyes, access to this sense cannot, for reasons of safety, be completely closed off.

A certain special position among the speech disturbances is occupied by agrammatism, which at one time may appear in the form of simple concatenation of words important for the comprehension of thought, and at another time as infinitive speech. Yet, the two forms shade into one another. The essence is evidently the omitting of nonessential connecting words. Agrammatism seems to have a close relation to sensory aphasia, and often transitionally appears in the degeneration of this disturbance. It is, however, also occasionally observed after the onset of completely new brain diseases. In addition, as previously mentioned, it tends to be quite markedly inherent in the hallucinatory readings aloud by alcohol delirium patients. It seems, accordingly, that the capacity for the grammatical structuring and inflecting of words is closely linked to the emergence of word sound-images, whereas the reading-images alone do not arrange themselves into grammatical form just like that. This is completely understandable, since we indeed acquire the former capacity at a time when our disposal of the reading images is still a long way off.

On the other hand, the word-selection and the grammatical formation of discourse are to a certain extent independent of one another. In the development of children's speech, the latter lags far behind the former in time. Indeed, in some languages it fails to appear altogether, just as many idiots speak agrammatically all their lives without manifesting word-selection disturbances. Conversely, paraphasics need not exhibit any agrammatism at all, and also in the case of speech confusion the most peculiar word-selections can appear without the grammatical formation of the discourse being appreciably impaired. In dreams, agrammatism, with its 22 specimens as opposed to the 165 instances of disturbed word-selection, plays a quite minor role. We may indeed assume that the capacity for the linguistic structuring of discourse can be separately acquired and lost. It is somewhat comparable to the reciprocal adjustment of series of movements to one another from a common angle. It is a matter of higher-order coordination following definite, gradually acquired rules, which may be disturbed, although the individual members of the series are correctly formed—but which may also be well maintained when certain subprocesses proceed faultily.

Among the word-errors of dream speech, we find a group whose genesis seems to justify our marking them off from the main body of specimens. It here involves the replacement of one word by another or by a neologism on the basis of *conceptual* contiguity. In these cases, we may well imagine that the error was not first committed in the actual word-selection, but rather that, at the very beginning, instead of the original idea in mind a different though related one was correctly or faultily transposed into words. The speech impulse takes a false turn, not because the control by word sound-images was lacking, but rather because it was forced into another direction by a side-association. The disturbance therefore lies wholly or at least partly in the process preceding the speech formation, and it consists, in a way, of a derailment of the train of thought from the given idea to another one emerging next to it, with the latter then attaining speech expression.

As it seems to me, the process indicated here is but an individual case of a quite general disturbance of dream life, which furthermore is not just one of the acataphasic manifestations, but falls under the large group of thought errors. We found the essence of the displacement paralogisms to lie in the fact that instead of a turn of phrase being attained by an indistinct idea struggling for expression, it is attained by another idea, a paraphrase of the thoughts which only roughly renders their meaning. Similarly, we see in the case of metaphoric paralogia that the link-up to speech expression is attained not by the original series of ideas, but rather by one which is associatively stimulated. And in the case of idea-mixing, parts of the first chain of thought and the second chain aroused by it achieve simultaneous and jumbled conversion into speech symbols. Whereas here the displacing ideas are everywhere in a conceptual relationship to the displaced ones, we have in the case of the derailment paralogisms, and likewise in incoherence, become acquainted with processes in which the train of thought is suddenly interrupted and diverted by quite remote ideas which just happen to emerge.

It is certainly no coincidence that we again encounter these very disturbances also in those conditions of daily life which we designate "day dreams" and furthermore in absentmindedness, which in many ways is closely akin to them. Here we are in a position to trace the development of the processes in our mind. It is no doubt a matter of the absence or failure of those general ideas which, during "contemplation," determine the course of our ideas and immediately suppress all deviations from the direction which has been marked out. There arises on the one hand a certain fleetingness of the individual concepts, and on the other hand an increased distractability. If we assume, as we are fully entitled to, that both these manifestations also characterize the train of thought in dreams, then what happens is that the emerging ideas often fade back too quickly to arouse the accompanying speech presentations, while on occasion associatively stimulated side-ideas, on the already prepared groundwork, do indeed succeed in bringing themselves to bear on the speech utterances. After that, however, it is understandable that the train of thought, which is not confined to a definite pathway, is extraordinarily easily and frequently broken in on by ideas which surface from anywhere in the unconscious without any connection.

Hence, along with the failure of the word sound-images and grammatical coordination in dreams, we have to reckon with the dropping out of target ideas which ensure the steadiness and unity of the train of thought. These target ideas can be none other than the general abstracted concepts. The whole fabric of our experience takes first of all the form of sensory memory-images which have faded to a greater or lesser degree. By the very nature of their sensory tinge, our ideas may again be awakened by incidental associations, but in general they are not subject to the power of will. Johannes Müller[23] long ago pointed out that he was completely unable to call forth or alter hypnagogic visual images at will, and the hallucinations of our patients commonly show in a most marked way the same independence from will, even if clearly automatically influenced by the train of thought. The sensory memories therefore behave in these respects just like the original impressions themselves. Only with the further mental processing do they come under the dependence of will, and then not without considerable loss of their original vividness. The images which are capable of being called into consciousness at will are in general unclear shadows; and — rather unlike the hypnagogic illusions and also the dream images — they are not clearly externalized. An exception is formed by certain unique impressions, a landscape, a certain definite personage or situation, which we are sometimes able to again place before our eyes with tangible clarity. However, as soon as ideas of a more general nature are involved, the image produced at will remains blurred, unless indeed a particular unique experience happens to emerge from memory.

If, therefore, the images as they progressively become representations of general ideas fade more and more, they also increasingly become subject to the power of will. They are from minute to minute at our disposal as required, whereas we see the hypnagogic phenomena simply file past us, without our being able to control them. Hence, there evidently takes place in the formation of general ideas a linkage of sensory memories with elements of our mental life which are subject to will. Only *motor impulses* are suitable in this capacity, of which the most important by far for us are those which serve *speech*. Indeed, we see the speech designations—above all the connection of word sound-image and speech motor-image—gain greater significance in an idea as its content becomes more general. At the same time, they become completely subject to our will. We are at all times able to awaken the most general ideas, whereas often enough we cast about in vain for individual ideas. Hence, speech is, if doubtlessly not the only, at least the most important aid by means of which our experiences can be subjected to will and placed at our disposal. It is chiefly by its mediation that we succeed in raising any given ideas into consciousness, holding them there and replacing them by others at the opportune moment— that is, as our train of thought requires.

If these considerations hold true, if the material of sensory experience is mainly placed at the service of will by being linked to speech presentations, as occurs in the formation of general ideas, then it is understandable that these general ideas should have a directional power over our train of thought. In them, the role of linguistic elements is enormously increased, and we can therefore master them with the aid of speech motor-images, just as we master our actual movements. Via them, thought has become an inner speech, and therefore as subject to our will as our outer speech is. Whereas the sensory memory-images emerge and then fade away despite all efforts to retain them, we are able to turn a general idea into a guideline for our train of thought for a long time, without its slipping away from us, and we can immediately call it up afresh if it happens nevertheless to get pushed into the background.

In dreams, as everyone knows, we have lost the mastery over our train of thought. We take them as they come and go. We would have to conclude from this that there is a receding of the abstract general ideas which in wakefulness reins in our thinking. Indeed our consideration of metaphoric paralogisms has shown us that there doubtlessly exists in dreams the tendency toward a slipping of the train of thought from the general to the sensory-physical area; that the abstract way of thinking is supplanted by the graphic one. In agreement with this is the fact that the dream processes appear in the form of experiences which are independent of will—which indeed often enough distressingly thwart it. We dream in vivid sensory observations, chiefly from the domain of visual and bodily sensations, which occur with the absolute autonomy of external events. But in unconsciousness those areas in which the general ideas originate are resting. Hence the inability to recognize the contradictions; hence the aimlessness and desultoriness of the dream proceedings; hence too, what concerns us here, the slipping of thought processes into side-ideas, the derailments, the incoherence.

We may indeed presume that the general ideas, together with the mental forming of judgments and conclusions which are tied up with them, represent the highest and most complex operations of our intellect. We can see them evolve only at the higher and highest stages of ontogenetic and phylogentetic development. Also in the case of pathological impediment of mental development it is this very lack of general concepts which is most of all responsible for the inferiority of the intellectual performance. Furthermore, it is true that the highest and most difficult performances of our mental life are the ones which most urgently require the interpolation of recovery periods. We therefore need not be surprised to see the failure of abstract thought in dreams, whereas series of sensorily tinged images are played out more or less incoherently in our consciousness. Even this play probably ceases in deep sleep. The experiences of dreams show us, however, that the inner activity in the various areas of mental life peters out and restarts in a definite sequence: The most delicate instruments and hence those most in need of protection rest longest and most deeply.

Our consideration of dream speech has led us to the conclusion that essentially the *word sound-images*—along with competence for grammatical structure and *general ideas*—more or less forfeit their importance for speech expression. Since word sound-images evidently establish the links between the object-presentation and the speech motor-images in the first place, it would be conceivable that a yet deeper correlation exists between the two above-mentioned fundamental disturbances. Detailed investigations into the characteristics of mental processes in sensory aphasics, if they are possible, could perhaps show whether and to what extent abstract thinking is dependent upon the assistance of word sound-images. That in any case the thought disturbances in dreams probably have a far more general cause is demonstrated by similar deviations in areas which have nothing at all to do with language directly. Our feelings and moods in dreams are as variable and conflicting as the content of our ideas. It can therefore be assumed that the general deposits of our life experiences, and not only those which are rendered in speech form, have lost in dreams their decisive and controlling influence on our conscious processes.

If one wishes to relate anatomical concepts to the results of our study, we would on the one hand have to assume for the explanation of dream speech, as already mentioned, a decrease in the performance of Wernicke's area, which indeed is to be conceived of as at least the immediately neighboring site of agrammatical disturbances. On the other hand, we would be most correct in locating the formation of general ideas in the uppermost cortical strata, which are uniformly spread over the whole brain surface. As Nissl assumes, the cortex in man achieves a special power in the frontal sections of the brain. In any event, we will have to think of the whole shell-like dome as being in a state of unconsciousness during dreams, while a rather lively activity can still take place in the cortical terminal areas of the visual nerves.[24] Also in those areas in which speech motor-impulses come into being—which should presumably be sought in the region of Broca's coil—complete rest apparently does not reign, even if the actual conversion of these impulses into movements cannot take place.

It is noteworthy that speech confusion, the pathology which produces a picture which in many respects is strikingly similar to that of dream speech, must likewise be viewed as an extended cortical pathology with the obvious assumption that, in view of the commonly accompanying auditory delusions, there is a particular participation of the temporal lobes. Sensory aphasia, on the other hand, which encompasses only a certain part of speech disturbances in dreams, is confined to a delimited cortical region. One is free, on the basis of our experiences with brain diseases, to elaborate somewhat further on these ideas about the extent of changes in the cortex during dreaming, although the foundation for this seems to me too uncertain for the present. We would therefore wish simply to summarize once more our conclusion that in the intermediate condition between deep sleep and wakefulness represented by dreaming, there takes place—apart from a general change which embraces the whole of our higher mental life and represents the failure of the abstract deposits, and apart from the suppression of external voluntary actions—apparently no completely uniform deadening of the sensory areas. In particular, there is still found in the places where visual images originate, which are deprived of the influence of external stimuli by special mechanisms, a great vividness in the processes of consciousness, whereas in the cortical areas of hearing, to which stronger stimuli are always able to penetrate, there appear marked obstructions to interpretation and mental processing, which, with regard to language behavior, resemble to a high degree the symptoms of a definite pathology of Wernicke's coil.

It must be left undecided how far the findings collected by us, and consequently the conclusions drawn from them, will prove to be universally valid when checked against other persons. Furthermore, a more profound understanding of the hitherto only superficially grouped speech disturbances of dreams is to be expected only when the whole series of related manifestations in normal and pathological areas has been more closely investigated from similar vantage points. This has up to now been done at best for slips of the tongue and, to be sure, for children's speech, both of which, however, essentially bear other features. On the other hand, however, it is to be hoped that a more precise knowledge of dream speech can attain far-reaching significance for the explanation of many pathological disturbances. Aside from sensory aphasia, we may especially look forward to shedding light on the nature of the speech disturbances of dementia praecox and, again most of all, speech confusion. In any event, we are today already able to conclude from the dream experiences—from the internal vantages we are able to gain in dreams—that often quite specific faulty processes are evident in the nonsensical, incoherent, affected utterances of our patients. This knowledge can afford us at least a partial explanation for what at first sight is quite incomprehensible. Here, indeed, there are regularities which we may hope to uncover all the sooner if we take advantage of the self-observations which are provided in such abundance by the physiological-mental disturbances of dreams.

Postscript

In addition to the specimens already commented upon in the text, I have assembled, after completing this work, the following:

"*Alfineri*" instead of "Alfieri," simple addition of a letter.

"*Lady's struggle*," brown-red flower. "Lady's slipper" was apparently in mind along with the idea of struggle, stimulated by evening reading; word replacement with partial sound analogy; derailment by side-idea.

"*She can't undertake the role without eatment [Fression] of all her conducting objects*" for "without jeopardizing her voice." Meaningless neologism (modeling on "Pression" [pressure]?, "fraction?"); displacement paralogism, stimulated by the side-idea of sound conduction.

"*The students of the old and new Trafays have come out pretty well*" for "the photographs of the deer in two specific woods adjacent to one another." Students replaced the deer in the reserve; the two woods are designated "old" and "new," since one of them, fenced in, contains a much older tree population. Trafay, apparently a patterning on Trafoi, is an arbitrary neologism in place of the genuine, completely different names of those woods.

"*Don't you want to travel by the gavay?*" instead of "with a steam railway branch-line to Copenhagen"; arbitrary neologism.

"*Glass seeds*," chopped glass as a chain for punishment of a naughty schoolchild; neologism based on conceptual kinship for a more complex idea.

"*Avellino*," figure from a fourteenth-century bas-relief; Italian-sounding neologism for an individual idea; obscure idea in mind of "Pasquino" in Rome.

"*One wants to pit me against another Reich chancellor, a Reich chancellor of good breeding, of small intimate conversations*," obscure idea that the Reich chancellor in his personal dealings behaves differently than on official occasions, that he is very courteous; displacement paralogism.

With these, the total number of observations rises to 286.

Notes

1. Gießler, *Aus dem Tiefen des Traumlebens*, 1890, p. 184ff; "Die physiologischen Beziehungen der Traumvorgänge," 1896, *Allgemeine Zeitschrift für Psychiatrie*, *LIX*, 908, p. 28.
2. Kraepelin, *Psychiatrie*, 3. Auflage, 1889, p. 145.

3. Vischer, *Auch Einer*, II, p. 359.

4. In this way, too: *"stol-travel"* for "length of holiday" with obscure side-idea that the duration of the trip "travel" was determined by the religious authority "stole", a specimen collected later.

5. *"Pulgalcella"* = small arbor, Spanish, specimen collected later.

6. Add to this, *"One can bring the inmakers to anything"* instead of "one can induce the inventors to make any change" (they are adaptable, with a somewhat contemptuous secondary meaning), specimen collected later.

7. Similar to *"a grateful situation"* instead of "gratifying," specimen collected later.

8. Translator's note: Kraepelin is obviously referring to his student's experiments on the depth of sleep in the course of the night, as will be mentioned in Part Three of the present book (pp. 217–218).

9. The typesetter first put "rank similarity" [Rangähnlichkeit] instead of "sound similarlity" [Klangähnlichkeit], a nice example of side-associations attaching to the "princes."

10. Translater's note: A sciopticon is a magic lantern for the exhibition of photographed objects.

11. Preyer, *Die Seele des Kindes*, 1882, p. 234; Wundt, *Völkerpsychologie I. 2. Au-flage*, 1904, p. 271ff; Meumann in Wundt, *Philosophische Studien XX*, p. 152; Gutzmann, *Archiv für die gesamte Psychologie*, I, p. 67 (literature).

12. Liebmann, *Vorlesungen über Sprachstörungen, Heft 6*, 1906, p. 13.

13. Wundt, *Gallettiana*, 2. Auflage, 1876.

14. Meringer & Mayer, *Versprechen und Verlesen*, 1895.

15. Stransky, *Über Sprachverwirrtheit*, 1905.

16. Pick, *Archiv für Psychiatrie*, XXII, p. 771; *Beiträge zur Pathologie und pathologischen Anatomie des Zentralnervensystems*, 1898, p. 15ff. Cf. also Bleuler, *Neurologisches Centralblatt*, 1892, p. 562.

17. Pick, *Beiträge*, loc. cit., p. 123ff.

18. Rieger, *Sitzungsberichte der physikalisch-medizinischen Gesellschaft in Würzburg*, 13 XII, 1884; Rabbas, *Allgemeine Zeitschrift für Psychiatrie*, XLI, p. 345.

19. Bonhöffer, *Die akuten Geisteskrankheiten der Gewohnheitstrinker*, 1901, p. 23.

20. Reichhardt, *Neurologisches Centralblatt*, 1905, p. 551.

21. Otto, *Ein seltener Fall von Verwirrtheit*, diss. Munich, 1889.

22. Dodge, *Die motorischen Wortvorstellung*, 1896, p. 40.

23. Müller, *Über die phantastischen Gesichtserscheinungen*, 1826, p. 81.

24. Cf. Brodmann, *Journal für Psychologie und Neurologie*, IV, p. 194.

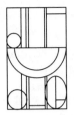

On Reading and Writing In Dreams
in Archiv für die gesamte Psychologie,
vol. 15 (1909)
by Ernst Meumann
Translated from the German by Frank Heynick

The new psychology of dreaming life has, quite rightly, increasingly envisaged investigation into particular individual dream phenomena. Kraepelin made an especially important advance in this regard with his research into language disturbances in dreams, in which he pointed to numerous interesting analogies between pathological speech changes and speaking in dreams.

Reading and writing behavior tends to show so much relation to speech behavior that one would immediately suppose that reading and writing in dreams would be altered in a similar way to speech. This indeed appears to be the case on the basis of my notes on reading and writing in dreams, although on the other hand these processes in dreams also undergo many quite peculiar changes of their own.

In the numerous dreams which I have been noting down for many years, I find much data on speech in dreams which accords closely with the phenomena described by Kraepelin. On the other hand, there are conspicuously few notes on reading and writing in dreams. It is certain to me that, to begin with, reading and writing seldom occur in my dreams, i.e., reading or writing activity seldom forms the essential or exclusive content of the dreams. One might well regard this as striking, since reading and writing are my most extensive occupations, and in general my dreams often relate to the activities of the day.

Be this as it may, I have a number of dream notes in which precise descriptions of reading and writing dreams are found, which I would like to report in the following exposition with some further elucidation.

A. Reading Dreams

The first dreams whose essential content involved reading behavior were noted down by me in the year 1894. These dreams appeared at the time in a highly conspicuous way, usually immediately upon falling asleep, and in any case always in the first half of the night. They consisted of my seeing before me with extraordinary clarity some printed or written text and my occupying myself for some time with reading it. In most cases I dreamt of reading a printed text with very clear Roman letters. The paper appeared brightly illuminated; the printed letters were to be seen very sharply. At the same time there appeared the peculiar phenomenon of the field of vision being rather small; the simultaneously seen letters were in three or four lines printed one below the other; I saw in each line some six to eight words. All around this the field of vision appeared dark or at least very obscured. What I read was always meaningful and almost invariably related to the reading material of the previous afternoon or evening. Only after many repetitions of this phenomenon, did I succeed in bringing about awakening and making some notes on this dream experience. In the great majority of cases a sound sleep followed the dreams, and I could make notes on it only the next morning. In that case I would regularly forget the details of the content of what I read and would generally be able to state only its nature; sometimes even this was impossible.

All these particulars accompanying the appearance of the dreams, and especially the content of what I read, show that the phenomenon as a whole had more the character of an aftereffect of the activities engaged in on the previous evening rather than of a usual dream. This is indicated by the following facts:

1. The occurrence of the reading dreams shortly after falling asleep, often in the very first stage of sleep, when I would otherwise seldom tend to dream.
2. The manifest connection between the text and the reading material of the previous evening, which was discernible from the optical form of the letters as well as from the content of what was read.
3. The fact that these dreams tended to occur only after those days when I had worked extraordinarily hard and had gone to bed with a certain nervous excitation.

In a similar way to such a read or written text, I have sometimes seen before me shortly after falling asleep the curve of a graphic experiment, when that evening I had been occupied with the measuring of curves. This, too, had a most remarkable and striking clarity. With the greatest sharpness I saw before me the fine white lines on a black background, and I was able to distinguish their smallest details. Strangely enough, none of the rest of the situation came to my consciousness. The whole dream consisted, as it were, exclusively of this very clearly seen optical image. I knew, by contrast, nothing of the whole surroundings in which the reading took place; not even my bodily posture or the position of the page came clearly to my consciousness.

In later years, there was no recurrence at all of these reading dreams caused by a rather immediate aftereffect of the evening's reading material. All my other reading dreams have a wholly different character. They are real dreams, which, in contrast to the above states, usually occur in the morning hours, especially with the start of daybreak, when my sleep as a rule has already become lighter. Furthermore, they sometimes show no clearly evident connection at all with the activities of the day before, although in some cases one can discern on the basis of certain indications the influence of reading material of the previous day or one of the preceding days (cf. the specimens below).

The course of these dreams is a very characteristic one. An *extraordinarily clearly seen* text suddenly emerges before me, containing in most cases printed words or, less frequently, written words; in a few cases it was composed of shorthand words, which is easily explained by the fact that I take down in shorthand almost everything I write for my personal needs. The details of the text are perceived with the greatest clarity and optical sharpness. The paper appears brightly lit; the field of vision is also very restricted, indeed usually more so than in the above mentioned dreams. In most cases I see only one line, or two lines one under the other, and with at most three words per line. The sight of this "reading field" is somewhat like the reasonably well-defined border of a very bright light when it falls through a more or less circular opening (diaphragm) onto a completely dark sheet of paper.

As for the meaning of what was read, once again two cases can be distinguished. In a hardly large number of dreams the text is completely meaningless, and the course of the dream consists mainly of my struggling in vain for a while to make some sense out of this text which in its optical respect is so clear. The meaninglessness of the text again takes a double form: Sometimes I have a totally incoherent group of letters before me, and a dim awareness that what I perceive consists of incoherent letters. Nevertheless I struggle with the text as if it contained meaningful words. In the second case, the letter combinations are the elements of meaningful words. For example, they form some syllables of known words which are, however, incorrectly put together and as wholes provide no word meanings. In such cases, the course of the dream consists once more of my struggling for some time to decipher these syllables, i.e., to discover a coherence in them; but I don't succeed.

Awakening from these dreams ensues quite probably as a consequence of these most disagreeable efforts, the aversion having risen to a certain maximum. After awakening, I could repeatedly determine from immediate memory that I had had during the dream strongly disagreeable organic sensations, whose localization was uncertain. Sometimes they were localized in the eye sockets, or displaced to the eyelids or the brow muscles, sometimes to inside the head; often they were accompanied by a general awareness of nervous excitation. These disagreeable organic sensations linger on for some time in the waking state.

I have often endeavored immediately after awakening to render as exactly as possible the text read in the dream. The experiments below give some examples of the nature and content of these texts. One observes from such attempts to jot down the dreams that it is extraordinarily difficult to retain the text in memory. Only a totally indistinct image of the read text remains immediately after awakening from by far the great majority of dreams. One almost never succeeds after awakening in rendering in writing the whole text with a feeling of completeness and correctness. Of the dreams of this type (specifically, reading dreams) I have had only eight or nine cases of which I may presume with certainty to have transcribed exactly the text read. All this is rendered especially more difficult by the meaninglessness of the text, which compels me to recite quickly the individual letters or syllables upon awakening. Even then, they sometimes get partially lost while I turn on the light and grab the pencil and paper. For years it has been my established practice always to have pencil and paper ready on hand for writing down my dreams.

The second case, which occurs more frequently in these dreams, is characterized by relatively meaningful texts. Here, again, I see before me with extraordinary clarity a text (usually printed). All other details seem to be the same as with dreams with meaningless texts, except for the fact that the text consists of individual words which are in and of themselves meaningful. During reading, I also have the feeling of understanding the sentences or sentence parts. So in this case there are none of the painful efforts at interpreting the meaning. Sometimes I even have the sense of having read something very clever, of very significant substance. Awakening often then follows due to the stimulation of my musing or due to a feeling of surprise and joy from the content of what I read. If, however, I endeavor immediately after awakening to bring this content to consciousness, it usually turns out to be of a quite insignificant nature. The sentences are sometimes meaningless phrases: Individual words, meaningful in themselves, are strung together into a meaningless sentence (cf. the specimens below). The sentences now and then also bring to mind the language disturbances in dreams reported by Kraepelin, although seldom containing distortions of individual words.

In the case of these meaningful sentences as well, their rendering after awakening is usually very difficult. The content of the sentences or sentence parts fades extraordinarily quickly. It is usually imperative that I recite the sentence several times immediately in the first phase of awakening. Even when I succeed in doing this (which isn't always so easy when struggling against the tiredness) I still sometimes forget individual words. Thus, here too, the number of entries in which I have the feeling of having rendered what I read without gaps is very modest: limited to some twenty-five percent of the dreams I have recorded with meaningful reading.

I may now proceed to report on the basis of my precise entries a number of specimens of the types of reading dreams I have described. I have numbered the individual dreams in order to be able to refer back to them.

1. Towards morning, in light sleep, I struggled with a text in Roman type, and I managed to read the meaningless words *"fire Iesu"* [idem]. There followed two groups of meaningless letter combinations, of which no recall was any longer possible after awakening. While reading, I had a vague sense of having deciphered a meaningful text. The "words" were seen very clearly, the letter type was discerned in the smallest detail.

2. I read in a newspaper an advertisement which seemed meaningful in the dream. It went, *"Children's House, 9:30 AM to 7:05."* Jotting down what I read was easy after awakening; only then did I recognize that the whole thing had no meaning. I may add that "Children's House" [Kinderhaus] is a station in the region of Münster. The recollection of a timetable published in the newspaper was probably in my mind during the dream; nevertheless, I thought I was reading an advertisement. Upon awakening, nothing definite could be determined about the cause of the dream.

3. In the newspaper I read of an English general who had received the title *"Kitchener Don Rhodes"* [idem], and this name greatly impressed me. The jotting down went easily after awakening, and with a feeling of absolute certainty. The name in the dream was evidently a fusion of the two names "Lord Kitchener" and "Cecil Rhodes," which at the time often appeared in the newspapers.[1] During the dream itself, I had the sense of hearing these names for the first time. The memory of newspaper material read shortly before probably served as the instigator of the dream, although this could not be determined with certainty. In the dream there was no awareness of the fusion of two different names.

4. I read a postcard written to me by a colleague, seeing perfectly clear before me his very characteristic handwriting. However, despite great efforts, I couldn't decipher the meaning of my colleague's message. Upon awakening, I knew nothing more of the content of this postcard, although I still clearly saw some characters before me. A certain nervous uneasiness resulting from the transacting of extensive correspondence the previous evening was quite possibly one of the causes of the dream. The dream occurred shortly after midnight.

5. I awoke from a dream shortly after midnight in which I was making an effort to read a letter from another colleague who writes with an especially unclear hand. I had received the letter the previous day and read it once again in the dream in a similar form. (With specimen 4, by contrast, I hadn't received any correspondence from the writer in a long time.) I saw before me in this case the unclear characters, completely corresponding to the original, and could also read individual words while the greater part of the letter remained illegible (as in fact tended to be the case with the original). The state of fatigued reading probably lasted very long; the awakening

ensued from the exertion. After awakening, the unpleasant stressful condition persisted quite a while. In a large number of such reading dreams there *lacked* any synthesis of the individual words into a meaningful sentence during dreaming. This was also the case in this dream. The "inner working" during the dream was directed towards this pooling of individual words into a meaningful sentence; it was, however, to no avail. This apparently has to do with the dormancy of the power of judgment in dreams.

6. The next reading dream, elaborated at length, is especially curious, also with respect to the speech phenomena which appear in it. It may be noted that the external cause of the dream could be determined with some probability. The day before, I had taken part in an exam in which Latin was tested. This experience apparently influenced the following night's dream. Specifically, I dreamt that I myself was taking the exam and being tested in Latin. A Latin text lay before me, which I was first to read out loud and then translate. Immediately upon awakening, the greater part of the dream was still securely in memory, and in writing it down I noticed that the content of the text as well as the examiner's questions and my answers were totally nonsensical. Interesting are the combinations of Latin words which appeared. The word "*Akura*" occurred in the text and I was asked what it meant. Since I felt completely at a loss, the examiner helped me: "*How is the word composed?*" I answered, "*Of 'a' and 'cura'.*" The examiner's question: "*So what does it signify?*" And I immediately gave the explanation myself: "*By this is meant, of course, the periods of stagnation in Schiller's poetic work!*" He then further elucidated this for me in what seemed in my dream to be a most clever manner, which however I could no longer make out after awakening. I then read further in the text "*conscientiae memor securus*" and racked my brains in vain for the translation, at which point awakening soon ensued. For some time after awakening, a vexed irritation remained regarding what seemed to me the degrading situation of the exam. The memory of the dream was very distinct. A check of my physical condition yielded nothing noteworthy.

7. The next dream is characteristic of the reading of a long sentence which seemed very clever in the dream, but which proved to be a pathological phrase immediately upon awakening. The previous evening I had been occupied with reading material in the form of an essay on arts and crafts which greatly interested me. The dream apparently went on from there. I saw in a newspaper (in the dream) illustrations of designs for "modern" clothes, and I read underneath the caption "*For our German dress flows with gay, amusing folds even though you're in Rome.*" In this totally nonsensical final phrase, what probably achieved expression was a vague memory of my also having read the previous evening about art in present-day Italy in particular. Quite characteristic in the disentangling of

the associations in dreams is the mixing of various groups of memories which lingered on from the reading matter of the evening before. In the dream, the feeling prevailed that the content of what was read was clearly comprehended, and especially the final phrase of the tract which I believed myself to have read seemed to me very clever.

8. The next dream is particularly curious due to the nature of the optical impressions which I had of the script in the dream. I read in the dream the headline of some daily newspaper to which I believed myself to have just subscribed. I saw before me with extraordinary clarity, printed in very large type, the letters of the headline, but with the field of vision very restricted so that only the middle letters came clearly to my awareness. Probably for this reason, the title made no sense. It contained in the upper line in very large type the letters "GTMPAPR," which I could retain so distinctly that I was able to write down their form upon awakening. The last part of the word probably embodied a reminiscence of "paper" = newspaper. Underneath in smaller type was "RNBITLENWS"; the last letters apparently meant "news." During the dream, I had a definite idea of the sense of what was printed. Despite the meaninglessness, it was easy for me to retain what I read. Upon awakening I noted down: feeling of great fatigue and a fit of dizziness localized in the head, tension in the face. (The dream occurred around six o'clock in the morning during half-sleep; this explains the relative ease of remembering it.)

The greater number of reading dreams I have recorded follow, one after the other, the pattern of the above cases. Only occasionally does a variation come about such that the reading combines with other dream situations; then, however, the recollection of the reading act after awakening is often made more difficult. This was the case with the following dream, for example, which was both a reading and a writing dream:

9. I stood in the dream at the lectern and prepared to read to my audience some literal quotation from a philosopher author. I had the quote in shorthand on a page in front of me. As soon as I began to read, the quote seemed meaningless to me. Despite fervent efforts, I couldn't find my way in the shorthand notes. On the other hand, I could read individual words in the (clearly written) text, but I couldn't find any coherence in the whole. I then grabbed a pencil and tried to write the sentence in correct form between the shorthand lines. This, too, didn't come out right. Waking ensued with a vivid feeling of displeasure, which lingered for some time. As signs of the physical condition, there arose heart palpitations and unpleasant sensations of tension localized in the head. The contrast between the purely optical conception of the words and the grasping of their meaning was particularly evident here. I even saw with full clarity

the difference in the pale pencil writing which was between the original text written in ink (both in my usual shorthand). While I did grasp the meaning of individual words, I didn't succeed in the *synthesis of the whole* into a sentence, neither when reading nor when writing it myself.

The following may be reported as examples of semi-meaningful reading:

9a. I read in the dream the table of contents of a scientific work. I saw before me with full clarity the printed table with its letters in bold type. I looked for some heading (I could no longer remember which one after awakening), and I found the following two chapter items: "*Ch. I Reason is the Power of Inner Perception.; Ch. II Intelligence is the Capacity for External Perception.*" I felt pleased with the discovery and only noted after full awakening the deficiency in what I had read.

Herein can be observed another characteristic of dream thinking. The dreamer's thoughts move in completely fluid pathways of association which are actually only fluid *linguistic* pathways. At the same time, the dreamer himself believes he has thought up something completely new and productive.

The following example is marked by the dreamer's struggling in vain to comprehend a text which is optically clearly seen:

9b. I read a printed page in a work with an unusually large format. There was a footnote underneath which for some reason particularly interested me. The letters of the footnote were in bold type and appeared before me with the greatest individual clarity. Nevertheless, I was unable to decipher the meaning of the words and struggled with them in vain for some time. After awakening, which ensued at once during these efforts, no certain recollection of what I read was possible, and even the individual letters had escaped me.

B. Writing Dreams

It is significant that dreams in which I am writing occur yet far more infrequently than the reading dreams. For years I didn't experience such dreams at all, even though I am busy writing every day, often for hours on end. This relates to the fact that clear representations of motoric activity in dreams are uncommon to begin with, and the reason for this is, in turn, likely to lie in the general relaxation of the muscular system during sleep.[2]

At the same time, it appears that these few writing dreams are under the influence of my writing activities, in that in the majority of the recorded cases I was busy with *shorthand* in the dream. I seldom write with a running hand in my dreams, and not once have I dreamt of writing with a typewriter, although

I have now been using a typewriter for about a year and a half. A gentleman of my acquaintance who has been writing with a typewriter for the last ten years, and as a rule is busy with the typewriter for six hours on the average, informed me that he can recall no dream in which he typed on the machine, whereas he recalls a dream in which he took part in a shorthand writing contest.

As for the meaning of what is written, the writing dreams, too, appear in two different forms. In the less usual cases, I write words whose meaning doesn't come clearly to consciousness. These dreams are—similarly to the reading dreams with meaningless texts—accompanied by strong feelings of displeasure, and they mostly end with the unpleasant struggling for the meaning of the text, leading to awakening. In some cases, the course of the dream was such that I had the distressing sense of having to write something (one time a letter, another time a lecture), while not being able to come up with the right thoughts, and several times I began by writing a word without any meaningful sentence coming into being. Disagreeable sensations of tension, too, probably forced their way into consciousness in this condition. The whole condition often seems to last quite a while. At least I have upon awakening the distinct recall that these distressing efforts to put a thought down on paper by first formulating it in clear words went on for a long time in the dream. Hence, these dreams are evidently analogous to the previously described reading dreams with meaningless texts. I have repeatedly endeavored, after wakening, to determine the cause of the dream. It is then observed that unclearly localized sensations of tension, which are highly disagreeable, continue after awakening and may at least be viewed as a contributory cause of such dreams. No definite external factor which would give rise in particular to this notable form of futile writing has ever become clear to me.

My second, more frequent, case of writing dreams is, on the other hand, my writing down meaningful words, which usually form a short sentence. This sentence often seems to me—similar to the case of read texts in meaningful reading dreams—to be extraordinarily important and significant or clever. Not infrequently, I have the sense in the dream of writing down a long scientific contemplation, and then there often ensues a lively stimulation of feeling which has the character of a joyful affect and leads to awakening. I have repeatedly managed to write down the last words or the last sentence after awakening. Here, too, it is very difficult to retain the memory of the written words, and only in a few cases have I succeeded in writing down the text with the conviction of having exactly rendered at least the last five or six words or the last sentence. In so doing, the sentences regularly show themselves to consist of rather meaninglessly composed words; sometimes they also have the character of a pathological phrase.

We may at this point communicate a number of specimens of writing dreams on the basis of which some more of the peculiarities of such dreams can be elucidated. As we have noted above, writing dreams are infrequent with me and in only a few cases in the course of years have I had the sense of being able to record reliable memories. I number these specimens consecutively to the above reading dreams.

10. In a dream which occurred shortly after midnight, I sat at my desk and carefully drew in calligraphic script on a sheet of paper lying before me my initials, as one tends to do in idle moments. After awakening, the cause of which was unclear to me, there remained an extraordinarily vivid image of this situation.

11. I made a written calculation on paper in my dream. I noted with great certainty: "$33 + 5 = 77$," and I thought with satisfaction of the repetition of the two same figures in 33 and 77, which seemed to me a confirmation of the correctness of the calculation. Only upon awakening was the nonsensicalness noticed. The evening before, I had been calculating for a long time. The analysis of the numerical associations in the present case is even more striking than those of word associations, being far more mechanical and totally unmistakable.

12. The same night in which I recorded dream 5 of the above reading dreams, I had a few hours later (following another intervening deep sleep) a long-elaborated writing dream. I wrote in the dream a long letter which seemed to me extraordinarily important, and I took pains to write very "calligraphically." I was repeatedly pleased during the dream with the clarity and beauty of my handwriting, which I have seldom seemed to manage. The text was before me with the greatest clarity (just like my usual longhand script). I read the writing just as surely and easily as I wrote it; yet I had no clear conception at all of how the sentences were related, and after awakening I couldn't meaningfully reconstruct any sentence; even the general sense of what was written was beyond my recall. The optical images of the words and the representation of the writing activity had dominated the dream exclusively; speech was completely inactive, hence I could no longer reproduce the words even after awakening. So here, too, there probably occurred a loosening of the associative relations. This was, to be sure, more striking than with the numerical associations in specimen 11, since for me inner speech is almost indispensible in reading (as it is for the great majority of people).

13. The next dream gives an example of the incorporation into writing dreams of memories of the day's mental work. I noted in the dream the effects of a long, rather racking, contemplation on a pedagogical question. Then I took some note paper (in the dream) and I wrote on it in *shorthand: "Cf. the paper with the heading 'where she is educated.' "* The heading was, as you see, meaningless. In the dream, I had the sense of understanding it correctly. The whole thing was a remembrance of the previous day's

work, in which I listed on sheets with various headings the findings from pedagogical literature. In this case, the shorthand was of extraordinary clarity; it corresponded to my usual (Gabelsberger) shorthand, and after awakening I still had the individual characters before me with exceptional clarity.

In the next dream the kind of handwriting once more (as in the previous cases) conformed completely to the situation dreamt.

14. I dreamt that I stood in an auditorium before the students and wrote on the board the results of a long development. They were the words, *"The result of a disposition is being announced."* This was the very vividly spoken conclusion of a long exposition by which I believed myself to have summarized everything in a most poignant manner. In the dream, the words greatly impressed me. Immediately upon awakening I still had the words clearly in memory, the sound of my own voice still rang in my ears, but the meaning was no longer clear to me. In this case I saw, in accordance with the situation, the words before me in chalk, once more with greatest clarity.

The cases reported here were the only ones for which I was able to have a truly precise recollection. To these may be added far more numerous ones which I couldn't really manage to remember after awakening, despite great efforts. It is interesting to observe here that the resolution to write down such dreams gradually induces a steady habit which facilitates awakening and recording. This passes through all stages: from the fierce struggle against falling back to sleep to which one succumbs in the beginning, to easy and sure awakening.

One must now raise the question of how it happens that the reading dreams are so rare and the writing dreams rarer still. I have made enquiries about reading and writing dreams among a number a acquaintances of mine, and it seems to me that such dreams occur just as seldom with other people. Hence we are probably dealing with a general phenomenon.

At any rate, a whole complex of very diverse causes now comes into consideration. First we should bear in mind that reading and writing are among the most common and frequent activities of educated adults. But we dream relatively infrequently of everyday things. Next comes the consideration of the fact that reading and writing are very complex activities and that in dreams our mental life is a very reduced one. Indeed, it seems that in dreams conceptualization as such takes place with a certain isolation, while judgmental activity, feeling, and volitional acts, and especially innervation of movement, are completely arrested. How very impeding it must then be for reading and writing dreams that reading and writing are linked to certain, very precisely defined perceptual activities which have to be reactivated in their whole complex mechanism—even if only in the form of reproduced representations of this mechanism. The degree of consciousness of the dreaming state is seldom sufficient for this.

The processes of remembering and forgetting in the dreams described above deserve very special consideration. I have already mentioned that as a rule forgetting supervenes extraordinarily quickly. When I couldn't note down a reading or writing dream immediately after awakening, then as a rule no reliable reconstruction of the words was possible. When falling back to sleep has taken place between awakening and the recalling of the dream, no new recall of the words I had read or written has ever been successful. I always know only that I have had such a dream. Kraepelin reports having tried to commit the words of a dream to memory by constant repetition. This is a method which I, too, have instinctively fallen into. Even this doesn't always achieve its goal. I have sometimes lost the words from memory upon awakening when, during the manipulations such as turning on the lights, I interrupted the repetition for only a few instants. This astonishingly quick supervention of forgetting is probably to be explained by the fact that the intensity of the psychophysical stimulation in sleep—including the dreaming state—is very slight. Consequently, the effect of the stimulation can also be only slight. From this follows that it is by no means the "well worn path" which determines the reproducibility of the representation (group of representations), but rather only the intensity of the psychophysical stimulation which parallels it.

We must now above all pose the question of whether this rapidity of forgetting is peculiar to speech memories and the closely related reading and writing memories, or whether it is to the same or similar extent proper to all dream representations. An easy pronouncement on this is not possible, since there can hardly be any doubt that we easily deceive ourselves as to the clarity and reliability of dream memories in general.

It must be noted that dream memories in the case of reading and writing dreams are subject after awakening to a kind of word-for-word check. There is a greater distinction between being able to report by and large correctly the vivid memory representations of some dream story, and reproducing a dreamt text. In the former case, there is lacking any check on the accuracy of the report of the presentation contents; in the latter case this is given by the words themselves. Either one remembers the words entirely, or one immediately recognizes the garbling of individual words and of verbal coherence. With all verbal memories, therefore, the reproduction is subject to a far more rigorous test. Thus it is certainly not impossible that the accuracy of the dream memories of spoken, read, or written words is not very inferior to that of other dream productions. We simply have no check on the accuracy of the other dream memories.

The phenomena described here readily invite comparisons with Kraepelin's observations on speech disturbances in dreams. They, too, show some related language behavior, for example word contamination, a dissociation of thought, and the like. But the dreams which thus far have truly been precisely described are too few in number to permit a comparison with the particular cases of speech disturbances enumerated by Kraepelin.

The *form of the wording* and the *kind of expression* of the words do, however, allow comparison with the phenomena described by Kraepelin.

There exists first of all a major distinction between the dream phenomena described above and those of Kraepelin's speech dreams, in that mine are *actually reading and writing dreams*; i.e., the reading or writing doesn't appear as an act secondary to speaking, something of a special form of inner representation of speech. Rather, it is quite the *dominant* activity, to which speech appears as the secondary act. In Kraepelin's speech dreams writing and reading acts did often occur; but it follows from the nature of Kraepelin's description that they are completely subordinated to speaking and have more the sense of rather vague accompanying phenomena than that they represent genuine writing or reading activity in dreams.

Kraepelin reports,

In the case of seventeen specimens, I could establish with reasonable certainty that they involved not independent utterances, but rather the reading off of printed or written text. In the case of another fifteen specimens, the influence of a reading-image was probable in view of the peculiar spelling of the words, which was explicitly dreamt, too.

And furthermore, Kraepelin describes the nature of the representation of the read or written words completely differently from the cases reported above. In all instances of the dreams described by him, Kraepelin seems to say that "speech presentations" played "the main role." He continues,

In the dream, I did see before me the text which I recited; however, it was not actually a case of reading out, but rather more of speaking with the accompaniment of the image. What was being spoken was on the paper in front of me. In other words, the reading-images acquired no hallucinatory independence and were not decisive for the series of speech motor-images, but rather they accompanied only in vaguer outlines the whole process, similar to the case in wakefulness when we try to recite from memory something read. As a result, it was also impossible for me to determine whether in the specimen in question it was a matter of actually reading out or the independent reciting of a merely supposed text. Here, the boundaries seem to blur. I must leave undecided whether in some individual cases, and particularly with other people, it might not be otherwise.

One sees clearly from this description that the writing and reading dreams I have described proceeded completely differently from this merely secondary participation of writing images in Kraepelin's case. With me, writing or reading activities were the main phenomenon; speaking sometimes didn't even take place at all. In all cases which I have described, the writing images achieved— what Kraepelin would call—hallucinatory independence. They lay before me with striking clarity, like an extraordinarily bright illumination; of course they were also placed in external space. Nevertheless, in the individual cases quite diverse behavior is shown in the precision and completeness of this objectiviza- tion and localization with regard to their direction and remoteness. Probably all transitions can occur from definite localizations to a downright uncertain awareness of the whole external situation. Quite definite is the hallucinatory form of the dream reading in cases such as numbers 12, 13, and 14, in which, to an extent, the entire external situation of the reading and writing is presented with the same striking definiteness as the visual images of the text itself. Un- like Kraepelin, I was never in doubt as to whether it was a matter "of actually reading out or the independent reciting of a merely supposed text." Rather, the reading and writing always exist along with a total belief in their normal course, analogous to waking life. Something approaching the phenomena described by me seems to appear only in this additional passage from Kraepelin:

> I do not want to fail to mention here that in a half-waking state I have occasionally succeeded in simply reading out words and sentences emerging into the dark field of vision. They regularly had the same nonsensical content as those of dream utterances. In six instances, the words seen appeared as titles of visual presentations.

These phenomena resemble the cases described by me. But they occur in half-wakefulness, whereas my reading and writing dreams all have the character of real dreams and not infrequently take place in deep sleep which is then followed by a longer sleep.

Apparently, however, individual peculiarities of envisioning play a part here, especially the so-called presentation-mode. This manifests itself above all in that for Kraepelin the "boundaries" between clear and unclear presentations of visually seen word-images "blur," whereas I have very rarely observed inter- mediate phenomena between actual writing or reading dreams and speech in dreams which is accompanied only secondarily by reading and writing presen- tations. Thus, my speech presentation-mode is thoroughly acoustic-motoric, with strong preponderance of acoustic elements, while Kraepelin's appears to be more visual. It is all the more certain that I must regard my reading and writing dreams as real dreams with the hallucinatory character of reading and writing processes, since talking dreams with a secondary reading or writing ac- tivity would hardly proceed in the markedly visual manner which characterizes the process described above.

Let it further be noted that in my case, as with Kraepelin and his obser- vations, talking dreams are nothing rare. At times they may come to me every evening in the very earliest hours after falling asleep and almost every morning in light sleep when this is somewhat prolonged. By contrast, as already noted above, reading and writing dreams are for me at least a relatively rare phenomenon.

Kraepelin also points to the interesting fact that the auditory presentations in dreams play a more modest role than do visual presentations, from which might be concluded that the activity of the acoustic centers in sleep are more dormant than the optical ones. I can confirm this from my talking dreams, for despite the markedly acoustic character of my inner speech, I only seldom have in my talking dreams clear auditory perceptions of a hallucinatory nature. When these do occur, however, they almost always have the character of extraordinarily *unpleasant* experiences, which not infrequently escalate in the dream to *emotions of fright and fear*. They regularly lead to awakening, and the unpleasantness persists for some time in the waking state. In this regard, the difference with the hallucinatorily clearly and distinctly objectivized visual dreams is a very striking one. I'm not, so to speak, bothered by a visual perception in dreams which entails such an "intense brightness" and such a definite objectivization as in the above cases of reading and writing in dreams. If, however, I believe myself to have a genuine auditory perception in a dream—when I dream, for example, that someone calls me by name—I arise from sleep with an emotion of alarm or fear. For me the whole auditory dream perception has the character of something abnormal, and it occurs almost only when I find myself in a condition of great exhaustion or nervous stress, whereas visual dream hallucinations are nothing at all unusual for me. On this point, I am not in agreement with one of Kraepelin's reports—if I understand it correctly. He remarks,

> Just as we have presumed in the case of some of our specimens that the speech motor-images emerge independently in consciousness, detached from the process of conceptualization, so it also seems that the visual images are liable to break through thanks to internal stimulation. With speech auditory images it occurs for obvious reasons infinitely *more frequently and strikingly*. If this *hallucinatory emergence* of various linguistic elements is really effected without any connection to the train of thought, the result is constituted of an empty series of meaningless spoken, read, or heard words or sounds. [Meumann's emphasis]

It is not clear to me from this statement that Kraepelin immediately conceives the relatively independent appearance of various components of our speech as a *hallucinatory* one. As far as the dream presentations are concerned, speech in dreams most rarely involves linguistic *auditory presentations of a hallucinatory character*. Despite my acoustic-speech nature, I believe myself almost never to hear my own voice. Rather, the auditory component when speaking in my dreams is as a rule a purely inner *conceptualization* (in the sense of reproducing conceptualization), whereas the character of real speech acts originates from motoric images, or probably even from actually executed speech movements, and for a part also from the accompanying visual images. The appearance of hallucinatory auditory images in my speaking dreams always has the character of a rare, extraordinary experience. To be sure, it stands out all the more clearly when I believe the word not to have been spoken by myself, but to have been called out to me. However, also the hearing of my own voice in dreams always has the character of a particularly intensive, emotionally exciting activity. Perhaps an individual peculiarity is manifesting itself here— only comparative observations of numerous individuals will be able to decide this.

Let it be noted in concluding, that many of the writing and reading dreams I have reported show a certain kinship with pathological writing and reading disturbances. I feel, however, that I should treat this only later, if I succeed in collecting extensive material.

Notes

1. Translator's note: This was obviously at the time of the Boer War in South Africa, 1900–1902.
2. Cf. my earlier reports on organic sensation dreams: Meumann, *Archiv für Psychologie*, 9, p. 68.

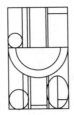

Speech in Dreams

from Systematische Traumbeobachtungen,
mit besonderer Berücksichtigung der Gedanken
(Systematic Dream Observations,
with Special Regard to Thinking), Leipzig, 1911

by Friederich Hacker

Translated from the German by Frank Heynick

Yet another phenomenon often encountered in dreams is due to the dissociation of thought processes and presentations, namely language disturbances. Verbal conceptions make up a large part of our ideas in general, and consequently we also frequently find them in our dreams. And since they can, in view of the close relation of the expression and meaning of a word, best throw light on the deviant conditions of our mental life in dreams, we should like to give some consideration here to the word- and speech-presentations.

When we think we have read something in a dream, it is usually not really a matter of reading it off as we might an unfamiliar text. We may see something written, yet already know what it says. The correct reading is not necessary, since the content of what is to be read has already been formed anyhow and it only *seems* that the content is first made known to us only upon reading it, just as we are accustomed to in waking life. If after awakening, one can still manage to visualize what he had seen before him when reading, he may often find that he saw nothing at all, or else perhaps characters, with no individual words having been read literally. Should it in fact happen that one truly reads something, then these are as a rule only letters or isolated words.

I once read on a medicine bottle *"Resorcin, strong poison for suicides"* under which was a verse and some names of suicide victims. Yet, I didn't read it all, but knew that it was there. I saw only the word "Resorcin" clearly before me and read its letters.

During a test, I missed the given topic, so I looked at my neighbor's sheet and wrote down what I could read from it. However, I had neither clear optical nor kinesthetic images, but only knew that I was writing.

I couldn't read a street name in a dream since the distance was too great. I only recognized it after strenuous looking. Of course the recognition didn't ensue from the reading, for I had already had a conception of the street name, which I now merely localized on the house in question. I then saw the street name with hallucinatory clarity.

Dreams with reading were in any case rare for me. Rarer still were dreams with writing. A few times I saw other people writing. In one case my brother wrote a message for me on a board, and I watched how he wrote. As for what he wrote, however, I can recall having had a truly clear optical conception of only the first letters of my name, while the rest was spoken inwardly with the awareness that it was being written on the board. Kraepelin was likewise often in doubt as to "whether it was a matter of actually reading out or the independent reciting of merely a supposed text." Meumann, by contrast, describes cases in which he saw before him long sentences, or observed a whole text, with "letter type discerned in the smallest detail" and read off individual words. Only twice have I observed something similar with myself, curiously enough in dreams during vacation at a time when I had read next to nothing for eight days. For the rest, what I saw with full optical clarity were usually a few words or word fragments. On the other hand, my experience was the same as Meumann's in that the individually read words seldom contained distortions.

By contrast, distortions were frequent in spoken words. The *acoustic word-presentations* in my case were in themselves far more numerous than the optical ones. But it should first of all be noted again here that usually—especially in deep sleep—when I thought I was speaking with someone, the whole conversation was not heard word for word such that I had a clear acoustic presentation of the individual words. Rather, it was usually inner speech without reaching the hallucinatory clarity of acoustic and motoric presentations.

On the other hand, in morning sleep or in cases of strong inner stimulation, or when the speech would be imparted with a special emotional force, it often came to true speech, that is, distinct acoustic word- and sentence-presentations which frequently tended to be accompanied by clear motoric presentations of the speech organs.

I wanted to climb into a coach, but because the people inside wouldn't open up, I called out, "*Damned bunch!*" But then I was embarassed by the coarse expression and because I had called it out so loudly. It was a vivid inner speech with extraordinarily clear acoustic and kinesthetic presentations.

In the following dream I spoke multiple sentences in quite correct form, one after the other:

To celebrate my stepmother's birthday, I wanted, together with my brother and friend, to roast an ox—a whole one. So that no one would see it beforehand, we hid it under a sofa. Since a leg was still showing, I tried to shove it under, but then the head stuck out. At that moment, my stepmother came in and, seeing the ox, she said, "*I'd rather have no party than have an animal killed on my account.*" The other two considered this a very noble thought, whereas I was extraordinarily vexed. I called out, "*Don't you know that we never could live in the first place if we didn't perpetually struggle? Isn't life a struggle of all against all? Let's not be taken by surprise by a tender-hearted female [Frauenzimmer]. Man would never have evolved if there were no wild beasts to fight against.*" These words made me wonder if they were quite right, and I suddenly became wide awake. I had conceived the individual words with greatest vividness and clarity, both acoustically and kinesthetically. They seemed to me to be a great oratorical feat; the expression "tender-hearted female" in particular pleased me very well.

Also notable here is the exaggerated significance which accompanies something unimportant in the dream. Kraepelin also pointed out that— similarly to what can be observed in some mentally ill people and those in a drunken state—substantial affectation underlies such dream speech, just as in dreams we also often indulge in foreign words and unusual turns of phrase or even express ourselves in foreign languages.

I sometimes used fully correct French or English idioms, but at the same time, totally wrong expressions were often used. Once I even corrected myself in the dream.

I was sitting in an English shoe store and said, "*Please, have you these boots smaller?*" Then I thought, "I should have said 'later' [sic; presumably a misprint for 'larger'—trans.], since I indeed wanted bigger shoes."

This inconsistency—the speech being fully correct one time and wrong the other—can be explained by the attention having been focused in a special way on the word. This is the point. It is just as in the case of connections in dreams: that sometimes when they are paid particular attention the correct connections come to awareness. Such a proper use of an expression or the correcting of one is of course no evidence of true language comprehension in dreams, since it often enough happens that even the simplest and most natural expressions in the native language come out completely wrong.

A train in which only women were sitting passes by us. My brother says, "*Only curtains are sitting in it.*" That "curtains" meant "women" seemed self-evident to me. I didn't at all realize that it was a peculiar and unusual expression.

It is precisely in the absence of any corresponding word that it can occasionally come to neologisms:

I had to explain an apparatus and I said, pointing to a valve, "*This part is the picbod.*" I don't know what led me to this expression.

There are, of course, great variations with such new creations. Patterning on similar-sounding words or on foreign expressions can impart to them the most varied forms. Usually, however, the dreamer understands the meaning of the words quite precisely and without being aware of the peculiarity of their manner of expression. Kraepelin, who first pointed to the multiplicity of language disturbances in dreams and showed the interesting analogies to similar conditions in mental illness, distinguished three main groups among the many instances which arise here:

1. disturbances of word-selection (paraphasia)
2. disturbances of speech (acataphasia and agrammatism)
3. disturbances of thought

It is a matter of paraphasia when the appropriate expression for a conception cannot be found, and a different word, not corresponding to normal language use, is substituted. If misapplication is made not of an individual word but of a whole or several sentences such that they do not cover the thought content, then we are dealing with acataphasia or, if it involves an incorrect linguistic structure of the syntax, agrammatism. These two main groups, which account for most cases of speech derailment, represent actual language disturbances in so far as the incorrect expressions can be attributed to a deficient language capacity. Kraepelin contrasts these to a last form, pure thought disturbances, in which the speech expression is relatively little disturbed, or not at all, while deficiency in the thought process is easily recognized. I have most seldom observed such cases in which the speech form was preserved and the underlying thought process became meaningless; it is presumably due only to chance or to special perseveration of the word contexts when the meaningless thought is connected to meaningful words.

I have been able to determine language disturbances in some seven percent of my dreams, a relatively meager number, having to do with the fact that speech is usually achieved only in dreams of superficial sleep, while in dreams of deep sleep the speech utterances, as far as I can tell, appear less often and have special difficulty in gaining access to memory. For it is only when vivid kinesthetic or acoustic word-presentations are remembered that it is possible to state whether a word or a sentence really achieved adequate linguistic expression.

It was only to be expected that the specimens I observed should be attributable not so much to actual speech disturbances but to thought disturbances, at least in so far as the dissociation in dreams between thought and presentation may be called that. I also believe that it is not so much a direct disturbance in word-selection which is to be held responsible for a presentation not being given the name it would have in current usage (what could be classified as a manifestation of paraphasia, following Kraepelin). It is rather a divorcing of meaning awareness from the word-presentation. The experience of meaning is not rendered just by the union of the thing-concept and the word-presentation.

When, for example, I said *"bromide"* instead of "Bergspitzen" (mountain peaks), a consideration of the context with the other concepts showed that it wasn't as if the word "Bergspitzen" couldn't be found, but rather that the word "bromide" happened to be more readily available and simply appeared in place of the other word. The assumption is of course that the awareness of the meaning of such a word is absent, something that often happens as it did here. The reason why a particular word and not the correct one was used is frequently evident from the circumstances. In the above specimen, it had to do with a mountain landscape and the designating of individual mountain peaks. Because just before awakening there is often the intrusion of concepts from daytime activities, and because I was much occupied at the time with chemistry and with bromide in particular, this word turned up. It cannot always be determined whether such a thing comes about due to the acoustic word-presentation surfacing and its meaning not being understood and therefore fitted into the prevailing thought, or whether a certain word was to be enunciated but that then one which was different from the immediately obvious one took its place. Either possibility can always be assumed.

I dreamt of an acquaintance and called him *"Herr Wirth,"* although he had a different name. But because he somewhat resembled the other one, whom I often associated with, this name suggested itself more readily.

Instead of four o'clock, I said *"eleven o'clock,"* without my being aware of the difference of the two time designations. The number eleven was evidently stimulated by the concept of darkness, which struck me in the dream. But I meant four o'clock, as could be seen by the further course of the dream.

It can also just as well be a completely meaningless word, merely an emerging of an acoustic presentation, which would give expression to the thought. One sees this especially in those cases where a real acoustic stimulus brings about a word-presentation.

I gave my grandfather, who wanted something to eat, a specially constructed eating instrument, which, so it seemed to me, combined the advantages of fork and spoon. But my grandfather said, "A *spoon which is a fork and a spoon in one doesn't exist,"* to which I replied very loudly, "No, *two methanes in one butane doesn't exist."* Then I realized that the alarm clock, which had just gone off, had stimulated these words in me. The words were to convey a confirmation of the assertion that no spoon exists which is a spoon and fork in one; they were not recognized as chemical names. Only when what I had said was brought home to me did I grasp its true meaning. With the sounding of the alarm, the concept of the words, which had been emphasized in the chemistry lecture of the previous day—that in the case of butane there are two isomers—was reawakened and the meaning given to the words. . . .

Frequently, however, an acoustic stimulus evokes only presentations of sounds and noise, simply because object-presentations are far more frequent than word-presentations. Thus we also see that complete mastery of speech in dreams is out of the question. When there is correct use, it is sooner due to chance and to the ready availability of linguistic expressions. We can—when linguistic expression is achieved at all (very many dreams contain no such thing and are clothed in verbal form only in the telling)—just as easily take the most innocent words in dreams for brilliant oration; or, as I believed myself to have spoken in a dream, a beautiful poem, which I soon found upon awakening to consist of a constant repetition of the words *"Halli, hallo."* Here we are truly behaving like the paranoid who believes himself to be delivering a sermon when he rolls off the names of a few animals. This very condition—that in dreams any word-presentations can be given a meaning which they would have no right to in waking life, and that often words are conferred the correct meaning, but sometimes no meaning whatsoever—takes us close to the view that what we call "thought" or "meaning" is something peculiar, independent, added onto the sign. Indeed, I could often observe in immediate memory how in a dream a content, a perception, or a presentation suddenly acquired a quite particular form after the awareness of meaning supervened. That is, the presentation itself doesn't change, but has a wholly different value for consciousness at the moment when the meaning connects with it.

This meaning is itself not simply a word, although the word is usually the carrier of meaning. In one of my dreams—which due to its unpleasant character was particularly vivid and fresh in memory—it became very clear, as in many other cases, that a meaning which doesn't coincide at all with the word-presentation is joined to the object-presentation. Or, in another dream, despite the object-presentation "toe" and despite the word-presentation "toe," the meaning for this object was not the corresponding one, but rather a chemical substance, perhaps because the reproducing tendencies still had such an orientation due to the previous concepts in the dream related to "chemistry."

Here one sees that the meaning is more than word- and object-presentation. Something has to intercede, and that is the relationship to the thing.

Observation shows us that this relationship is not itself a presentation. Whatever genetic explanation one may offer for such a psychic experience, one would still have to admit that a meaning experience, which imparts knowledge of the meaning of a thing, is psychologically quite peculiar and can, it seems to me, only with a certain forcing be traced back to simple perceptions or presentations themselves.

Titchener[1] says:

> The meaning of the printed page may now consist in the auditory-kinaesthetic accompaniment of internal speech; the word is the word's own meaning; or some verbal representation visual or auditory-kinaesthetic or visual-kinaesthetic

or what not, may give meaning to a non-verbal complex of sensations or images. These would, again, be nothing surprising—we should simply be in presence of a limiting case—in the discovery that, for minds of a certain constitution, all conscious meaning is carried either by total kinaesthetic attitude or by words. As a matter of fact, meaning is carried by all sorts of sensational and imaginal processes.

It is, however, not to be assumed that a meaningless perceptual or presentation complex gets its meaning from the addition of some kinesthetic presentations. And these kinesthetic presentations, which after all are rather undifferentiated, cannot themselves be the meaning. That would be just as unlikely as the assertion that appearance qualities are nothing more than eye movements.

Also the addition of word-presentations cannot alone ensure our comprehension of a thing. The word-presentation may be entirely present or only partially, or perhaps garbled; comprehension need not be correspondingly entirely present or only partially or garbled. Binet[2] is indeed correct when he says, "un mot en effet ne signifie rien par lui-même." I furthermore do not believe that, as Titchener[3] assumes, only the "gesture-side" need yet be added to lend significance to the word. The fact that, to be sure, we often think only in words, or that with many thoughts we can show nothing but words in consciousness, is still no proof that the words are the thoughts themselves. In the course of individual development, word and meaning have, to be sure, become so closely bound up that they seem like one and the same to us. But pathological cases and our own dream life show us that such a divorcing of word from meaning is nevertheless possible.

All in all, consideration of proceedings in dreams seems to me, for the very reason of their deviations from normal psychical behavior, to make more clearly evident many things which readily escape our observation under usual conditions. In particular, the distinction between vivid and nonvivid elements, not only due to the greater liveliness of their presentations, but above all also because of the uneven distribution of vivid and nonvivid conscious experiences.

In waking life we may be occupied for a long time with difficult matters. What comprises the content of our consciousness are a few presentations, perhaps inner speech and meaningful thought associations. In dreams, it's the other way around, since the presentations are strung together while a longer chain of reasoning is seldom achieved. The thought elements in the presentation are often lacking, or they don't connect to the pertinent presentations, so that a deeper meaning may underlie the nonsense while meaningful associations are reproduced in a truly uncomprehending fashion. I believe that in dreams in general, or at least in those of deeper sleep, much more nonsense appears than is usually supposed. This is shown especially clearly in cases where even after awakening, the meaninglessness of a verbal context is not immediately recognized. And when it is recognized, it is for the very reason that the words enable a precise checking of the exactness of the presentation content, whereas in many other cases, where word formation is not at all achieved, such isn't possible. This confusion is therefore not a peculiarity only of speech in dreams, but rather is more clearly evident there than otherwise and is the result of a general dissociation of presentation and thought which can be shown in almost every dream. Of course there also appear in dreams those phenomena, particularly contamination and perseveration, which play an especially large role in pathological cases of speech confusion, but which, as Stransky[4] has pointed out, can also be produced under experiment conditions when the subjects are given the task of free associating and, under the greatest possible relaxation of attention, of speaking about whatever happens to come to mind. In dreams we likewise have these conditions of relaxation of attention, and so we can have similar experiences. Such an example of perseveration and also of contamination is provided by the following dream:

From an Austrian comic paper there was read out to me what seemed to me to be a splendid political joke relating to an Austrian minister: "*My dear Minister Lehmanger, your nerves are more and more ajangle. Now begins your woeful wrangle. Yes, my nerves are more and more ajangle. Yes, my nerves are more and more ajangle.*"

The dream went on a short while longer, after which I awoke and only then noticed that the words had been repeated several times and that there was actually no joke at all. Lehmanger was evidently a combination of two names familiar to me, Lehmann and Angermayer.

The following is an example where the utterances in the waking state are influenced by the previous presentations:

Someone explains to me that *Fick's theory of colors explains only the circumstances but not the genesis of colors. Therefore Flick's little houses on the street couldn't remain standing, since—in contrast to Hering's houses—they are in motion.* At that moment the alarm clock sounded, and I called out to my brother—he was standing next to my bed—"*Blue, blue is too loud,*" by which I meant to say, "Shut off the alarm clock, it's ringing so loudly!"

Here, ideas of color happened to be in consciousness; and at the moment when the stimulus took affect, the words, which formed the reaction to it, were changed by the perseveration of the previous ideas.

I present this specimen also because one can at the same time see from it how totally absurd conclusions are drawn in dreams. Even a simple judgment is, like all logical functioning in dreams, often formed in a quite wrong manner. The judgment should consist not just of a series of two idea elements which have an especially close relation to one another or are distinguished by their continuous conscious associations. Rather, the two ideas should themselves be brought into relation, and this relation should not simply be conscious but also deliberate. In this way, a judgment differs from other, ordinarily reproductive connections. Whereas in waking life we almost continously pass judgments—be they ethical or aesthetic value judgments, object or conceptual judgments—we seldom act judgmentally in dreams. We have ideas, but we don't place them in relation to one another; we don't do much testing, searching or reflecting. Usually it is an extraordinarily obtrusive presentation which causes us to form judgments. Hence, since conceptual thought has so receded in dreams, most of the judgments which do appear are not abstract judgments but simple perceptual judgments. They mostly comprise relationships between thing and properties, cause and effect, means and ends, sometimes spatial but less often temporal relations. I have found in my dreams 72 percent object judgments and 20 percent conceptual judgments.

That judgments often arise which are so absurd has also to do with, among other things, the peculiarity of concepts in dreams. Whereas in waking life the concept constitutes the conscious representation of all necessary properties of a thing, in dreams any purely chance connection of any given property with a thing can function as a concept, without those very properties which are necessary being understood as part of it. Thus relations can be set up between properties of things which sometimes do not at all belong to the concept of those things, and which consequently also have nothing to do with one another. And likewise, conclusions can be drawn from judgments which have no relation to each other, as in the above case, where it was concluded from the movement of the houses that they could remain standing on the street.

In waking life, we often think in observations; it's precisely the scientist making some physical observations who distinguishes and judges with his perceptions. With our ideas in dreams we either don't think at all—as in the case in which I saw my acquaintance collapse and then immediately get up, without my noticing the impossible connection—or else we think and judge, but usually purely reproductively, as in the above case in which the previous day I had been occupied with the distinctions of the color theory and now brought these connections into relation with ideas which didn't at all pertain to them. This meaningless connecting was, however, brought forth with the sense of having reached a valid conclusion, and this sense of validity is often most strongly marked when the absurdity is greatest.

Most conclusions were reached in the dreams of the morning; in dreams of sounder sleep they were very infrequent, as were judgments. In the dreams of deep sleep, evidently, fewer relations are brought forth since we are also not endeavoring to discern and reveal things. Meaningful and meaningless conclusions occurred in 27 percent of my morning dreams and only 8 percent of my dreams of deep sleep. This higher psychical functioning begins to be reactivated only shortly before awakening, and then deficiently at first.

For normal ordered thought, far more important still than these close connections of judgmental experience is—as shown in inference procedures—another kind of connecting, in which not only are few judgments brought into relation to one another, but in which all links of a long train of ideas and thoughts are subordinated to a motive and strive toward a goal. One such connection is given us by tasks—of either a theoretical or practical kind. But there are no such things in a dream, and this follows from its nature. In a dream there is no inherent drive toward knowledge nor any practical goal to the attaining of which we subordinate our thought and action.

Notes

1. E. Bradford Titchener, *Lectures on the Experimental Psychology of the Thought Process*, New York, 1909, p. 177ff. [Titchener, one of Wundt's students, disseminated his psychology in America as professor at Cornell University.—trans.]
2. A. Binet & T. Simon, "Langage et Pensée," *Année Psychologique*, 14, 1908, p. 389.
3. Op cit., p. 288.
4. E. Stransky, *Über Sprachverwirrtheit*, Halle, 1905, p. 13ff.

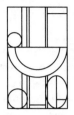

Dreams (Selection)

from Handbuch der normalen und pathologischen
Physiologie (Manual of Normal and Pathological
Physiology), A. Bethe, G. von Bergmann,
G. Embden, and E. Ellinger (eds.),
Berlin, 1927

by Alfred Hoche

Translated from the German by Frank Heynick

It is remarkable how little use has on the whole been made up to now *of statistics on the occurrence of speech in dreams*. Individual, or rather incidental, observations worthy of serious consideration are found scattered in the dream literature. The first to systematically set about the task was Kraepelin, who subjected 281 [sic] specimens from himself (and others) to a very penetrating analysis of the changes of language in dreams. His original starting point, and also partially his objective, was primarily from the vantage of speech pathology, which is of little importance to us here. The point of my extensive corpus of speech specimens from dreams was not pathology, but rather a purely psychological consideration. All the more remarkable therefore is the agreement in the formal details ascertained by two people of such differing mentality as Kraepelin and myself.

The *number* of individuals who have observed speech in dreams at all is *none too large*. What comes far more to the attention of the average dreamer are vivid images.

The *circumstances* under which speech processes take place in dreams is very varied.

To begin with, there is a special dream form of *one's own inner speech*: very vivid speech presentations, more perceptibly evident than wakeful thought, almost always with the calling up of optical word-images, seldom with abortive motoric speech sensations: images which are not transferred anywhere. These presentations are, as the case may be, either internally free-floating, or accompanied by the dreamer's realization that he is acting as speaker or reciter.

The *next most frequent form* is the *speech of others*. This almost never involves genuine auditory hallucinations. Rather, in the process by which another person speaks in the dream, someone is usually seen simultaneously with the occurrence of vivid inner speech presentations, which, thanks to the amalgamation with the image of the person seen, fuse into a whole and appear as his utterance. The participants in the dream conversations almost never show mouth movements or accompanying mimicry, yet this incompleteness of the event goes unnoticed by the dreamer.

The *third form* is the *reading* off of language elements from signs, posters, book titles, pages, documents, and the like. Here, the process is very often the same as with the speech of others; i.e., the optical images of the words were in fact not at all necessary, since the linguistic content had already been given to the dreamer. At other times, however, it involved *genuine hallucinatory processes*, by which the sensory vividness of the impressions, e.g., the illuminated white surfaces, can achieve a dazzling feeling. In the case of such hallucinatorily seen words and sentences, it also happens that one must first turn the page to find the continuation of the phrase—something that doesn't occur with optically seen words and sentences which are pseudo-hallucinated. These genuinely hallucinatory language forms comprise almost ten percent of my own cases.

The *content of speech utterances* is apparently subject to great personal diversity. Practically never do I myself have dreams from the realm of the affect-laden conscious contents of wakefulness.

The *associative genesis* of my dream speech-images is recognizable with sufficient certainty in a fifth of the cases, and then the presentation material is of an *indifferent content*, which usually the day before had been the object of interest, even if only very fleetingly (conversation, reading material, activity, etc.). It is not discernible what further circumstances elevate these or other images from the thousands of possible images and turn them into dream material. In any event, it is *not* determined by *emotional value*. An obvious part is frequently played by what in psychology has long been termed *constellation*; one specimen easily shows what is meant: A lady of my acquaintance has a predilection for idioms such as "goldenly glad" and "dearly delighted." In the evening I read the story of the lion of Androcles, which, out of gratitude for the extraction of a thorn, later spared his benefactor. In the dream this lady said to me, "*I am lionly grateful to you for your message.*"

The *intrinsic value* of the language product is on the whole downright low. 3.3 percent of my corpus specimens are witty, ironic, or sarcastic, even when reviewed from wakefulness, as when I was introduced to a court chaplain with the name "*Halo*" or when a wedding text read "*Baar and baar go well together.*" Quite frequent are the pseudo-witty remarks of dreams, i.e., those in which we take such great pleasure in dreams but which share the fate of fool's gold in turning out to be faded stuff in the morning. Those which in wakefulness still made some impression amounted in my case to one in seven.

I have encountered supposed scientific insights, discoveries, or formulations in 3 percent of the cases; when, for example, I evolve the idea of writing an "individual histology" or of announcing a lecture on "etioscopy," or when someone speaks of the "mental ataxia of stupidity" or the "metaphysical gait of the hand" in the case of a localized epileptic fit. One shouldn't forget here that it needn't at all involve independent intellectual production in the dream, but rather utterances of the *immanent reason of language*, which indeed also plays such a great role in the poetic technique of people in wakefulness.

As far as form is concerned, 20 percent of the linguistic creations in my dreams were *foreign* (Latin, Greek, French, English, Italian, Hebrew—and even Russian, of which I know next to nothing). Four-fifths of these structures had the correct *linguistic characteristics*.

10.7 percent showed rhythmic form, and 4 percent were meaningful and could just as well have been conceived in the wakeful state. 3.3 percent were senseless, and over 3 percent were a mixture of sense and nonsense. The associative influence of sounds is quite prominent here.

I found complete, *normal prose* sentences in 20.7 percent of the cases, with only 1.3 percent showing incorrect grammatical construction. Actual slips of the tongue which are recognized as such in the dream itself, and may even be corrected in it, comprised 1.7 percent—infrequent compared to the 14.7 percent of instances of motoric paraphrasia which are taken to be correct in the dream and are first recognized in waking. This involves the deforming of words by incorrect letters or syllables, appendages, garbling, etc. Rather frequent, 9.1 percent, are *nonsensical lexical combinations* of words which themselves are correct. Almost as frequent, 8.1 percent, are *neologisms* which don't draw upon old lexical residues. Neologistic *proper names of a foreign nature* but on a correct pattern—10.8 percent—call for special checking before they are acknowledged as genuine neologisms. On several occasions, material which I presented to a classical philologist and which I had taken to be novel Greek and Latin names, were shown by him to be ancient material, just like the seemingly new plant names of the botanists.

I designate the genesis of some word formations as *hybrid*, when the newly originated word shows elements from two parents. When, for example, living in St. Moritz across from the Kalonder Hotel, I dreamt the night after a conversation about Milan [Mailand] that I made the acquaintance of a certain "*Fräulein von Mailonder*"; or when "Goodfolk Lane" and "Holy Ghost Lane" became "*Holyfolk Lane*." I would like to term another sort of genesis *godfather words*: those in which a definite remote influence is recognizable, for example "moriscum" under the influence of "vobiscum," or "tenerast" under the influence of "pederast."

Innumerable further particulars will have to be reserved for more detailed publication at a later date.

Finally, as far as the relationship of content and form goes, the linguistic formations of dreams are often comparable to an *idling mill*, i.e., to a rattling without content. Here, one is aware of fleeting forms, *without being able to link them to any conceptions whatever.*

Other times, we are dealing with linguistically correct forms which, however, are nonsensical content-wise. These are downright frequent (19.5%).

The above percentages involve 700 carefully analyzed observations of language production which I have gathered for fourteen years. It therefore came on average to *one* specimen per week out of the 30 to 40 dreams which could have been registered in this period. I can say with certainty that the instances of language activity which ultimately were noted down represent only a *small fraction* of the actual occurrences. The greater part of the instances melt away, despite all systematic attentiveness training, before one gets to writing them down; or they are not grasped with sufficient certainty to permit their use. The linguistic creations show, as Kraepelin also observed, a quite exceptionally low resistance to the process of forgetting, just as they are decidedly more difficult to learn by heart than are other sentences or verses.

The distinction is so great that one is tempted to suppose some specific impediments. But it could also of course be due to the insufficiently logical or grammatical structure or to a nonsensicality of content which doesn't permit associative connections. The same difficulty is encountered, for example, in wakeful attempts to commit to long-term memory words of a language whose stock and sounds are far removed from those of German, Latin, etc. (like, for example, Hungarian or Greenlandic).

I can confirm another Kraepelin observation: the often remarkably *hesitant emerging of a critical attitude* towards the language creations of dreams, despite the subjective feeling of being completely awake. The gradations in awakening are apparently just as manifold on the side facing daylight as on the front turned towards sleep.

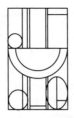

Analysis of Kraepelin's
Newly Discovered
Dream Speech Specimens

When recently at the Max-Planck-Institut für Psychiatrie (originally Kraepelin's Deutsche Forschungsanstalt) scribbled slips of paper were uncovered containing 391 variously annotated specimens of dream speech, almost all in Kraepelin's hand, these were thought at first sight to be the original corpus on which he based his 1906 monograph. However, it soon became clear from the dates that these specimens were from the two decades *after* the publication of *Über Sprachstörungen im Traume*, up to Kraepelin's death in 1926.

These slips of paper are all the more valuable because the original 286 notes of the twenty years' worth of specimens (ca. 1885–1905) that went into *Über Sprachstörungen im Traume* have never been found, and much of their supplementary information was apparently not incorporated into the published monograph.

Most important in this regard are the dates accompanying the newly discovered specimens. In Kraepelin's monograph, specimens were divided up and ordered according to their types of deviation, with no dates provided. His new corpus, by contrast, will be presented in the following pages in chronological order.

Although there are a few earlier specimens, the systematic dream recording in Kraepelin's newly discovered corpus began in the last year of World War One (1918) and extended for eight years of its aftermath. Some twenty-seven specimens or their accompanying notes make direct reference to the conflict or to military matters. For example, in March 1918 there is an utterance with, apparently, multiple lexical substitutions (displacements): *"Reels in the damimorum are earmarked for Munich,"* which referred to the Germans' being drawn into a bog (damimorum) with foot obstacles (reels).

Politics, and particularly the political turmoil, in Germany is reflected in another thirteen instances. For example, in March 1920 Kraepelin entered a specimen with a lexical condensation, *"We are 'one-despairing' [einverzweifelt] with you,"* meaning "of one mind [einverstanden] in our despair [Verzweiflung] over the political situation." A month later: *"Kohn is spiritually in misborn [mißgeborener] times,"* which apparently involved *pars pro toto* symbolization and transcendence of the usual form class of the noun "Mißgeburt" (miscarriage, literally "misbirth"). The ominous meaning: "The spirit of the times (antisemitism) is not favorable to the Jews."

The single theme most often reflected in Kraepelin's corpus is, perhaps expectedly, medical/professional activities. These appear in a total of 65 of the 391 specimens, for example the unusual conjoining of existing German words in a 1918 specimen *"Choke-hand"* [Drosselhand], meaning a "hand whose nerves have gone dead," and which can alternatively be translated as "thrush-hand." Syphilis, a subject important to Kraepelin due to its neurological complications (dementia paralytica), is referred to in three of the medical specimens or accompanying notes, e.g. the lexical substitution on semantic association made in 1919: *"She has a concubine in the lungs,"* where "concubine" is a displacement for "lues" (syphilis).

The names of Kraepelin's colleagues appear in several of these medical specimens or their annotations, including the prominent Wilhelm Wundt and Eugen Bleuler, mentioned in Part One of this book. In 1922 (two years after Wundt's death) we find the specimen, *"Here is no English lyric poetry, no interruption of information,"* to which Kraepelin adds the somewhat cryptic notes, "Wundt's birthday; description of his peculiarity." (See also the specimen of 27 October 1923.) In a 1924 dream Bleuler says to another colleague at a psychiatric convention, *"Don't take everything so explosive!"* an apparent transcending of an adjective's usual form class. A one-word proper-name specimen from 1919 reads simply *"Thiersch,"* the name of the dean of the Medical Faculty at Leipzig and pioneer in antisepsis and transplant surgery, Carl Thiersch (1822–1895). Kraepelin's comments indicate that his noting it as a deviant specimen was due to the mis-selection of the proper name due to phonetic similarity: The actual referent in the dream was Adolphe Thiers, who was president of France shortly after the Franco-Prussian War.

Some of the other names of Kraepelin's colleagues in his specimens also appear in his autobiography: Franz Tuczek was at the time (1908) professor of neurology and director of the psychiatric clinic at Marburg. Binswanger, in a 1919 specimen, probably refers to Otto Binswanger of the Jena psychiatric clinic (eponym: Binswanger's dementia). Franz Nissl, who apparently wrote to Kraepelin in a 1923 dream, had died four years earlier, soon after becoming head of the histopathology department of Kraepelin's newly formed Deutsche Forschungsanstalt für Psychiatrie in Munich. Kraepelin's former pupil Wilmanns, mentioned in a 1925 specimen, had already been professor at Heidelberg for seven years. Other colleagues appearing in the corpus can no longer be identified.

Also mentioned, in a 1924 specimen, is the architect Bottini, who built for Kraepelin a villa in Pallanza: "*Stiamo fabbricado in modo provisorio con allio ed ollio,*" where "allio" (taken by Kraepelin to mean "onion") was the construction material, and "ollio" (oil) the cement.

Botany was obviously of particular interest to Kraepelin. (His brother, Karl, was a prominent botanist, and Emil accompanied him on field trips and maintained many plant specimens at his villa in Italy.) Six new names for plants appear in the dreams, e.g. "*Euonia amptis*" (1911) and "*Rhodalia flamica*" (1923), while a few other utterances also make references to plants. A certain creativity in finding new names is likewise evident in another four specimens, such as the 1921 neologism "*Film-dispater,*" referring to a "small, peculiar, efficient tamping machine, which punches rectangular recesses of various shapes and sizes."

Other forms of creativity are found in some thirteen specimens which are marked as poetic, jocular, humorous, rhythmical, or sarcastic. For example, a 1923 utterance "*Horizon of flowerets without flowers, therefore sky without meaning on the horizon,*" taken to be the beginning of a poem; or a 1919 specimen "*There will presumably have been some small bloom-defects,*" humorously meaning that a man who for a long while was in Spain, away from his wife, would go astray (have blemishes).

Viewed according to the types of deviance, rather than theme and year, Kraepelin's newly discovered corpus breaks down in a more or less similar way to the corpus presented in his *Über Sprachstörungen im Traume*:

Approximately one fifth of the 391 specimens are in real or pseudo modern foreign languages or dialects (including, unlike the 1906 monograph, at least a couple of English or pseudo-English specimens).

The majority of the native German specimens contain anomalies on the lexical level, including neologisms and the unusual conjoining of existing words. Lexical substitutions involving existing words occur in about a fifth of all specimens. These are seldom based on apparent phonetic similarity, but often on some (perhaps remote) semantic associations. Occasional omissions are noted as well. Proper names were especially susceptible to errors; about fifteen percent of the total corpus involves the use of apparently nonexistant German or foreign names.

Only a handful of specimens involve outright syntactic errors in German. This paucity lends support to the notion that syntactic processes, once activated, may proceeed automatically in the absence of conscious attention, relatively free from disruption. Less than five percent of the corpus involves the apparent transcending of the word's usual form class (e.g. a noun taking an adjectival form).

Extensive as his corpus may be, Kraepelin's specimens do not necessarily attest to a more frequent malfunctioning of the linguistic faculty in dreams than in wakefulness. Thanks to the dates on Kraepelin's slips, we know the frequency of his reporting. Even in his most intensive year (1921), this averaged less than one specimen every four nights.

The new corpus may, however, provide further evidence that the distribution of the types of errors in dream speech and the depth of their disturbances differ from those in wakefulness, including those (whether assumed to be psychoanalytically determined or not) found in Freud's *Psychopathology of Everyday Life*. This is in line with the comparison Kraepelin makes in his 1906 monograph between his dream specimens and the utterances of various categories of somatic mental patients.

However, the errors in Kraepelin's newly discovered specimens generally appear also more deviant than those found in the *dream* dialogue reported in other dream books, including Freud's *Traumdeutung*. This suggests that, similar to the case of the specimens he assembled in the twenty years before 1906, much of Kraepelin's later corpus was drawn from hypnagogic and hypnopompic sleep, rather than what we today call REM sleep.

These are topics which will be taken up again in Part Three of this book.

Notes on the Corpus Presentation and Their Rendering in English

The form of presentation of the specimens is similar to that used in the English version of Kraepelin's 1906 *Über Sprachstörungen im Traume*, presented above.

Quotation marks, " ", are used here, first of all, to set off from Kraepelin's other notes the actual specimens of dream speech, which are furthermore italicized. Since the German originals have never been previously published, they are also provided, unitalicized between brackets [ ]. The transcriptions of Kraepelin's comments (as opposed to the actual dream speech specimens) follows the conventions used in the English version of the 1906 text. When sound-associations may be involved, the original German words are given along with the English renderings; all other parts of Kraepelin's comments are given only in English translation.

Any added clarification of Kraepelin's text by the translator is given between brackets [ ]. The sequence [. . .] indicates illegibility of Kraepelin's notes, whereas a sequence of dots without brackets . . . are Kraepelin's own. Any uncertainty in transcription is indicated by a question mark in brackets, [?]; other question marks are Kraepelin's.

The specimens are presented in chronological order. Kraepelin's dates are given in parentheses after each specimen: day/month (in Roman numerals)/year. Where the day of the month is not specified, the specimen is included at the end of the month in question, and similarly for the few instances of an unspecified month in a given year. In the cases where a slip of paper contains more specimens than dates, the specimens without a date are followed in the transcription by (←) or (→), referring, respectively, to the previous specimen having a date or the next specimen having a date.

Often included with the dates are initials or names. The letter E (or in a few instances the letters E Kr or E K) appears very frequently and apparently stands for Emil (Kraepelin), although it is usually not clear what significance this would have had. The asterisk * following the five specimens bearing the names of two of Kraepelin's four daughters, Toni or Eva, indicates that these were not in his own handwriting. (Kraepelin's grandson, Prof. Hans-Peter Dürr, informs me that his mother, Eva, was frequently asked by her father about her dreams; the ages of Toni and Eva varied from about twenty to thirty-five when they recorded their five specimens.) In a handful of instances, the names Karl (Emil's brother), Ina (his wife or youngest daughter), and Emma (his sister) appear after the date, sometimes in combination with E. From 1922 onward, there are almost fifty specimens followed by Suna, the place of Kraepelin's Italian villa. One specimen (in 1924) was evidently jotted down in Barcelona.

[Handwritten manuscript pages — specimens of Kraepelin's dream speech notes, dated April 1918, 29 July 1921, and February 1921]

Specimens of Kraepelin's dream speech notes. The translations of these specimens are given in the text accoring to their dates (April 1918, 29 July 1921, and February 1921).

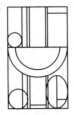

Kraepelin's Newly Discovered Dream Speech Corpus (1908–1926)

Translated from the German by Frank Heynick*

Pre-1918

"Dipseligic tipsiness" [Dipseliger Schwips]. Drunkenness from two kinds of drink. (V/1908)

"Blirr-blerr" [idem]. Mental illnesses which strike suddenly ("like lightning" [blitzschnell]). Conceived of as a specially terse and felicitous neologism. Purpose to inform the woman for that reason. (←)

"Catenaric disturbance" [Catenarische Störung]. Locomotion disturbance. Disturbance due to iron (catena), external conditions (shackling), in contrast to a specific one arising from internal causes (lues or paralysis). Prisoners with chains (remark by Tuczek). (←)

"Sotte" [idem]. Escaping prisoners in socks, without shoes. Adverbial element. (←)

"Devicit cunitere vixta" [idem]. Language confusion. Pseudo-Latin, as specimen of utterance of a patient, considered very characteristic. (5/VI/1908)

"In France, one slays the cranes with lead" [In Frankreich erschlägt man die Kraniche mit Blei]. The birds on the chalk-cliffs, with slingshots loaded with lead. Picture before my eyes. (VI/1909, E)

"Go on maiden, be smart and push back a bit tne sky cloth" [Geh Mädel, sei gescheidt und druck a weng das Himmelstuch zurück [dialect]]. (→)

"Fox and Cygane" [Fuchs und Zygäne]. (28/VII/1911)

"Euonia amptis" [idem]. Subtropical plant with blackish tendrils similar to the parsiflora, blooms half like veronica, half like euptrasia, fruit like papilionacea. "Amptis" recalls "aspis," since the bloom stems develop small petal rosettes on the stalk joint. (2/XII/1911)

*With many thanks to the translation consultants Johanna Wilde-Frenz and Sami Faltas, and to Frau Maria Frenz for transcribing and transliterating the originals.

"Barassi Carlo Palaeza, Dirimpetto dei Carieri" [idem]. (→)

"Lake feather" [Seefeder]. Long narrow property on the lake. (→)

"Dissnufling of the pastures" [Verschnuffelung der Viehweiden]. Disfiguration [Verschandelung]. (13/VI/1912).

"American Psychiatrists Meeting in Melanchston" [Amerikanische Psychiater-versammlung in Melanchston]. Agenda: Is a villa owner happy? 1915: Munich: dementia praecox. (VIII/1912).

"Plasmodium pelae" [idem]. Tricks of fate. (4/II/1914)

"A dish of sill" [Ein Gang Sims]. Serve a cup of bouillon with a jar of toothpicks. "Sill" [sims] abbreviation of "sillooz" [Simooz]. Reminiscence of "athlete soup," but imperfect. (9/VI/1914)

"Nobeme" [idem]. Such people, who really must have known. (1915, Toni)*

"Que je ne me skairiolone" [idem]. "That I not complain." (→)

"Kaegos' favorable with six privatum" [Kaegos' günstig mit sechs privatum]. Imster (town) newspaper. Actually without sufficient motivation. Situation in the trenches (side walls with apple cake). Only sporadic firing. The accusation of discontent with the situation in the war is dismissed. (13/XI/1916)

"When the workers yet get back their double rot-gut and their lell-meat" [Wenn die Arbeiter erst wieder ihren Doppelfusel und ihr Liechfleisch kriegen]. Expression for the bad times which will yet come after the war. (Meat which lies around a long time and therefore already smells.) (VI/1917, Eva)*

"Do I twist the quintchouc or do I twist the caoutchouc [rubber]?" [Dreh' ich den Quintschuk oder dreh' ich den Kautschuk?]. Expression that it remains always the same no matter how one goes about the business. The expression in mind was, "I don't twist the hand here." The last two expressions [sic] arose in conversation with a lady doctor, who thus expressed herself in a particularly educated and à propos manner. (VI/1917, Toni)*

1918

"Ceratabel" [idem]. Replacement for bicycle inner tubes. Fabric ("cera") impreg-nated with wax, similarly to the oilcloth on the table ("tabel"). (1/I/1918, E)

"Axino-plates" [Axino-Platten]. Special kind of photographic plate. (II/1918, E)

"Boelcus or the like" [Bölkus oder so ähnlich]. Deepest darkest night. And then came the B. (occurring of death). In the dream supposedly an excellent mnemonic aid to impress the word; nevertheless, hopelessly forgotten. English reminiscence to plunging with a zeppelin. (13/III/1918, E)

"Ladidvinatebes in Travisish hinterland" [Ladidvinazeben im Tavisischen Hinter-lande]. Health resort in a half-civilized African country, the only one still accessible during the war. (16/III/1918, E)

"Reels in the damimorum are earmarked for Munich" [Für München sind Spulen im Damimorum vorgesehen]. The Germans have been drawn into a bog ("damimorum"). Reels = foot obstacles. (27/III/1918, E; just upon awakening)

"I'm ready to resulate my journey" [Ich bin bereit, meinen Reise zu beschlüssigen]. *"To hasten"* [Beschleunigen]. (Karl) (28/III/1918, E)

"Choke-hand" [Drosselhand; alt.: "thrush-hand"]. Hand whose nerves have gone dead. (III/1918, E)

"He who understands the rural part residences of the Saxon nobility" [Wer die ländlichen Teilsitze des sächsischen Adel versteht]. He who classes the medium landowners (as they are to be found in Saxony) along with the great landowners, also interprets [versteht; lit: "understands"] them under this heading. (III/1918, E; very difficult to retain)

"Favionville" [idem]. Set incidentally and temporarily as with an individual pane in a larger window; it will be opened alone without greater effect. (3/IV/1918).

"Humatoric codicil" [Humatorischer Codizill]. Cacti on the street as bequest of the people, posthumous estate, remnants of an unimportant nature. (←)

"A mixture of musecic, mouseron and psychopaths" [Ein Gemisch von Musekik, mouseron und Psychopathen]. Inferior type of clinical material. (29/IV/1918, E)

"Dabbow—Daps; Schwebbow—Schweps" [idem]. Names of vases, the terms abbreviated as popular. (Reminiscence of Trabbow and Lieps [idem].) (29/IV/1918, E)

"Neoneobost" [idem]. Jocular. Naturally inclined to be malicious [boshaft], and having become so ("neo"). (IV/1918, E)

"Just dress up the fullness" [Kleide mal die Fülle auf]. Fill me up with this course (soup). (V/1918, E Kr)

"Fenille-Cornet" [idem]. Diplomatic note. (6/VIII/1918)

"The Siegrist Griess" [Der Siegrist Grieß]. Import. Name of an estate, a foundation, or the like. (28/IX/1918)

"Plum-shooting" [Pflaumenschießen]. Giving the coup de grace to someone seriously ill. (6/X/1918)

"Gradually, however, the hermiatrophia faciei of the facial order of the persons concerned started to get stretched" [Allmählich jedoch begann die Hermiatrophia faciei aus der Gesichtsordung der Betreffenden gestreckt zu werden]. For "started to get better." (6/X/1918)

"Grazaga & Orrio Titaxeorti" [idem]. Two small, uninhabited islands in Helgoland Bay. (10/X/1918)

"Bill-bill-bread" [Bill-bill-brot]. Epileptic's bread with bromine additive. Reminiscence of the involuntary urinary evacuation in an epileptic seizure. (XI/1918, E)

"The molars are bad, the liver teeth (by comparison) pitiful" [Die Stockzähne sind schlecht, die Leberzähne (daneben) erbärmlich]. (XI/1918, E)

"A child-day and a bram-day" [Ein Kindtag und ein Bramtag]. A day for children (pleasure, presents) and another one, on which there is "restraining" [gebremst]— some things are forbidden. (XI/1918, E)

"Française j'ai aimé" [idem]. "I'm a Frenchwoman, dear France." Cry of a girl at the end of a specification of the acts which she committed in favor of France as a spy during the war. (XII/1918, E)

1919

"*Un bout de aigreux*" [idem]. Sense no longer clear. (30/I/1919, E; afternoon nap)
"*The buyers don't go on strike (the) acquire!*" [(Die) Werbe streiken die Käufer
nicht!]. If someone wants to acquire something, he will have to see to it that it
doesn't get run into the ground. (1/II/1919, E)

"*Heat, bodily care on the right side*" [Hitze, Körperliche Pflege auf der rechten
Seite]. Physician's remark during one of the rounds. (27/II/1919, E)

"*Partial-sum salary*" [Teilsummenbezüge]. Monthly rate of a payment. (II/1919, E)

"*She has a concubine in the lungs*" [Sie hat in der Lunge eine Concubine]. Parasitic disease, lues. (2/III/1919, E)

"*Maiden of the soul of the deflowered souls*" [Jungfer der Seele der entjungferten
Seelen]. Solemn sermon. (9/III/1919, E)

"*Blood bananas*" [Blutbananen]. Small banana-like things in blood, found by
Binswanger. (III/1919)

"*Endure the jubilation of ? a right-table-appearance*" [Durchhallt den Jubel der ?
eine Rechttafelerscheinung]. Scene: Patriotic festival with jubilation ("hurrah").
Above right in the background of a balcony the Kaiser at a banquet table, whose
presence up to then was not known, and who has now risen and drinks to the
crowd. (28/VI/1919, E)

"*Overbeareable hat*" [Überhebebarer Hut]. "Overbearing" [überheblicher], whose el-
egance is out of keeping with the rest of the clothes. The "beare" [hebe; lit: "lever"]
was felt to be an annoying printing-error, which had been overlooked, instead of
"overbearable" [überhebbar]. (←).

"*Gumgs*" [Gumgen]. Inferior fish, living in the water of muddy rivers, disdain-
fully offered by the innkeeper. Reminiscence of "Grundeln" ("groundles"), "Rütten"
("roods"). (30/VI/1919, E)

"*Frielig—was not reelected by the Dampjes*" [Frielig—wurde von den Dampjes
nicht wiedergewählt]. "Dampjes": Dutch for smokers, nickname for the masses.
(5/VII/1919)

"*Only Mark Harmonium Hater touches me always like fresh water*" [Nur Marc Harmonium Hasser berührt mich immer wie frisches Wasser]. Utterance of a daughter concerning her perceptions of the approaching steps of various persons. M.
H. H.—name of a young man, American style. (Reminiscence of "Mark Antony"
[Marc Antonius].) (15/VII/1919, E)

"*Life-daily*" [Lebenstäglich]. For "lifelong" [lebenslönglich] ([cf.] "all' meiner Leb-
tage" [lit.: "all my (life-)days"]). (15/VII/1919, E)

"*Game contribution, his best rescuer*" [Spielbeitrag sein bester Retter]. Contribution
by Ernst Mertbär. Program number in a lecture series. (22/VII/1919, E; afternoon)

"*Thiersch*" [idem]. As president of the French Republic (Thiers). (←).

"*Apertaria*" [idem]. Popular, special diminutive for "aperta" (Italian). (←)

"*Partinger*" [Scheidecker]. Mocking nickname for a farmer who got divorced several
times. (VII/1919)

"Meuchel—Lösche—Vinvirra" [idem]. Departure and destination points of a steamship (Italian lake? Switzerland?). (VII/1919, E)

"To glafumble" [Glafummelen]. To smoothe down bread spread with butter and honey with the aid of tautly stretched cloth. (Visual image.) (→)

"A layed-out minetard" [Ein aufgelegter Meintard]. Two similar cases of paralysis for the clinic. Visual image: two dolls, swaddled and strapped into little, equally long, rounded-off planks. (12/VIII/1919, E)

"To 'ladle out' congratulations" [Glück-Wünsche "schöpfen"]. Instead of "offer" [aussprechen; lit.: "express"]. (4/IX/1919, E)

"You know yourself that you lack flower tendrils and little channel ears" [Das weißt Du doch selbst, daß es Dir an Blumenranken und Kanalöhrchen fehlt]. Gracefulness and nice hairdo, locks around the ears. (Remark to daughter, probably Ina.) (10/IX/1919, E)

"The physicians have 58 livers, and Prof. Lotz has one of them" [Die Ärzte haben 58 Lebern, und eine davon hat Prof. Lotz]. "Courage, joy of persuasion." Loud utterance by Prince Regent Leopold, leaning against the wall (he found no seat) at a Social Democratic meeting, when Prof. L. arose, went up to him, and greeted him. (IX/1919, E)

"Dover channel zone" [Kanalzone Dover]. Back on the Condi–La Chapelle–Comblizy–Marenal line. In the evening, east of the Chatillon-Euchery-Chaumizy lines. Italians and French between Ardre and Meuse. From Brunai-Tafmor east of Reims. Coraillet-Hochberg-Keilberg-Pöhlberg hill chain up to the Roman.[. . .] Northwest of Prosses, south of Suipps, between Anberion, and southeast of Tahnet. French north of Prosses-[. . .]-Peitting. (→)

"Water lamp" [Wasserlampe]. Lamp with which one can also give illumination on water. (18/X/1919, E)

"Hamster" [idem]. A low, tortoise-shaped vehicle on which the loads can be "more easily" [leichter] carried off (on a side road) similar to the "barges" [Leichtern], for the transporting away from larger vehicles [. . .]. (23/X/1919, E)

"The decrease of the guard and stage block" [Die Abnahme des Abwehr- und Bühnenblocks]. Exchange of ration cards. (25/X/1919, E; afternoon)

"Bill of lading of one such free-birth" [Frachtbrief von einer solchen Freigeburt]. Registry office certificate of one such naivity. (15/XI/1919, E)

"Creamer! Brest! Chicken! Soup!" [Rahmer! Brest! Hühnchen! Suppe!]. Call of a lady to her lady's maid. (XI/1919, E)

"To the snow-flurried villa in Eglfing" [In die schneegetriebene Villa nach Eglfing]. A young girl wants to bring her husband-to-be (warm nest, snow-covered, in the countryside). (XI/1919, E)

"There will presumably have been some small bloom-defects" [Da wird's wohl manchen kleinen Schmelzdefekt gegeben haben]. Because the man (a long time from his wife in Spain) will presumably sometimes have gone astray, have had a blemish. Humorously intended. (XI/1919, E)

"Can take the borash train" [Kann den Boraschtzug nehmen]. *"Can use the borash train."* Rieger, on the train to Vienna. Schwabian "sh" instead of "s." Orient Express—Hurricane (quick as the wind)—Boreas. (30/XII/1919, E)

"La fallantrière" [idem]. The drop cure. (1919, Toni)*

1920

"There's nothing like diabetes, which demands the whole literature" [Es gibt ja nichts wie Diabetes, was so die gesamte Literatur anmaßt]. "with which one has to take all the literature into consideration." (10/I/1920, E)

"Sur-tensed performance" [Overspänstige Leistungen]. Efforts to overcome the fearful anxiety upon entering a room which is haunted; "Ghost"[Gespenst]. (18/I/1920, E)

"Berthamy" [Berthamie]. Some ships were brought by the Germans into the Lake of Bertham (reminiscence of Cortez, conquest of Mexico), which were captured one after the other by the Russians. A Russian newspaper greeted these successes as "Berthamies." (21/I/1920, E)

"Head-pusher" [Kopfschieber]. Wide-meshed hair net, with which mesh the hair rises right up so that it wobbles when the net is moved (a kind of pleasant ventilation). (I/1920, E)

"Dichotomous and pagotomic" [Dichotomisch und pagotomisch]. Meaning unclear. (II/1920, E)

"Dream-lost energy-kinship" [Traumverlorene Energieverwandtshaft]. Transfer of indistinct ("dream-lost") analogies ("energy?") from one area to another. (2/III/1920, E Kr)

"In botan-blue thrall-paper" [In botanblauem Zirzbogen]. On elegant ("thrall") writing paper, blue (aquamarine) tinted. (6/III/1920, E)

"The answer always threatened satisfactorily" [Die Antwort drohte stets zufriedenstellend]. "The answer turned out as expected." (11/III/1920, E)

"Leaf-louse omouse" [Laublaus omaus]. Mysterious words, which have a relation to the vehme. (The previous evening, reading material on the vehme and the secret recognition signs.) (18/III/1920, E)

"Board-lollipop" [Bretterlutscher]. To slide [rutschen], smooth. Cradle-board [Wiegebrett], smooth-grained wood, as a present for Toni. (21/III/1920, E)

"We are 'one-despairing' with you" [Wir sind mit Ihnen "einverzweifelt"]. "Of one mind [einverstanden] in our despair [Verzweiflung] over the political situation in Germany." Declaration of the army to right-wing political parties. (29/III/1920, E)

"We need only accounts of falsent the dog and valence the donkey" [Wir brauchen nur Rechenschaften aus falsent den Hund und valenz den Esel]. Sense completely unclear. Statement which was given from two viewpoints. (Different writing of "falsent" and "valence" intentional.) (6/IV/1920, E)

"Kohn is spiritually in misborn times" [Kohn ist geistlich in mißgeborener Zeit]. The spirit of the times (antisemitism) is not favorable to the Jews. (13/IV/1920, E)

"Knee-joits out!" [Kniegänke vor!]. In stretching out for a test of the knee-jerk reflex. (14/IV/1920, E)

"*Ready for rearing*" [Erziehungsbereit]. Tender singing at a performance. Sentimental picture, mother and child, similar to [the song] "A rose has sprung." (IV/1920, E)

"*Gold Globicum*" [idem]. Popular humorous expression for "coliticum" [idem]. (6/V/1920, E)

"*The pens are quite good*" [Die Federn sind recht gut]. Even when one occasionally makes a writing error with them, it doesn't matter. (12/V/1920)

"*Medinopses*" [idem]. Connection of intellectual disturbances with emotional disturbances. (22/V/1920, E)

"*Verificateskimo*" [Verifikateskimo]. Transaction place for the relations between Germany and her allies, the Eskimos, in a war. This results in precise statements of payment concerning the participation of the Eskimos, the publicizing of which was not desired. (V/1920, E)

"*You'll foll one day from the scent-krind*" [Du fellst mir mal aus der Duftkrinde]. Be thunderstruck [aus allen wolken gefallen sein]; be astonished. (V/1920, E)

"*Posito ili Resto*" [idem]. Polish. Help or quiet. (1/VI/1920, E)

"*Jasili Kodscha*" [idem]. Balkan. A girl's Balkan ex-suitor. (28/VI/1920)

"*The slog farrt*" [Der Slog furtz]. English tooth powder. (15/VII/1920)

"*North of Poland and Saradiffen*" [Nördlich von Polen und Saradiffen]. Saradiffen = mountain range. (18/VII/1920, E)

"*Sémil hugue*" [idem]. Must be French. Was on a sign on an inn, and meant "meat and eggs sold here." "Semile huge" [idem], pronounced [in German] "simeil hötsche," = the same sign in England. (24/VII/1920, Toni)*

"*When someone has already mostered on the fourth day*" [Wenn jemand schon am vierten Tage schon gemostert hat]. Already four days after a severe wound (shot in the face or in the arm), can already change the bandage himself or converse or go out. "Has overcome the thing." (3/VIII/1920, E)

"*I don't shrink before the administrator*" [Ich schrumpfe nicht bei Verwalters]. I don't intend to have a trolley line which I control stop again at the administrative residence. (15/VIII/1920, E)

"*Lambiffe*" [idem]. French word for cunnilingus. (19/VIII/1920, E)

"*Awaken with licking*" [Mit geschleckten Wecken]. Cleansed (spick and span, as if licked clean) after a rail journey. (24/VIII/1920)

"*Olympionbamay*" [idem]. Name of a new North American state with a peculiar flag. (→)

"*I was surprised that not a little rest replanted those so outdaten life*" [Ich war erstaunt, daß nicht ein wenig Rast die so veraltet Leben wiederpflanzte]. (→)

"*I just didn't have for heart to make no bones around it*" [Da konnt' ich nicht ums Herz die Mördergrube bringen]. A girl betrayed by a young man appears, revolver in hand. She tries timidly to conceal herself behind her companion. She wants to tell him that she was surprised that he, on seeing her, doesn't at all think of times past, former life—has completely forgotten her. Only, she sees that he himself is a miserable, pitiful weakling, and so she cannot bring herself to shoot him. All this conceived of as an outdoor theater play. (2/IX/1920, E)

"Drive stalk" [Treibhalm]. Technical detail of a machine, which was described. (17/IX/1920)

"Snout-beard" [Maulbart]. Moustache [Schnurrbart]. (IX/1920, E)

"He was already fading" [Er war schon einmal am Vergehen]. The boy was already dying, close to death. (IX/1920, E)

"The Tigerwurst Place" [Zur Tigerwurst Lage]. Name of a hotel at the station in Bonn, read while riding past. (IX/1920, E, Z)

"Maulbert" [idem]. (IX/1920)

"Even when the axis of the handle is an enlarged at[...]*"* [Auch wenn die Achse des Stiels ein vergrößerter At[...] ist]. Sentence on an advertising sheet for an X-ray apparatus (description of the advantages). (→)

"Fairy-tale width" [Märchenbreite]. Poor maps, on which the places looked for weren't at all to be found. (3/X/1920, E)

"Ultre damacul" [Ultre Damakul]. Paraphasic utterance of a patient. (8/X/1920, E, afternoon)

"Koppy-bohn" [idem]. Falsification of memory. Name of a fat housekeeper at Wundt's. Upon awakening, the recollection that such a housekeeper was indeed there, only with a different name. Recollection of Frau Hambreiter. (27/X/1920, E)

"Do you know why you have such small hand exercises, when you always take such short walks?" [Weißt Du, warum Du so kleine Handbüngen hast, wenn Du Immer so kleine Spaziergänge machst?]. Instead of "long trips." (7/XI/1920, E)

"How many threads of cotton are in. 100 protestion or 100 allenos" [Wieviel Fäden Baumwolle darin sind. 100 protestion oder 100 allenos]. Sarcastic question from Grossier: One has to distinguish between two cotton fabrics of almost the same type: protestion and protestion allenos (a different type, but in fact the same), petty difference. (→)

"Two snakes glued together by a shot, one like sun dragons of medium size" [Zwei durch einen Schuß aneinander geklebte Schlangen, die eine wie Sonnendrachen mittlerer Größe]. (30/XI/1920)

"From an administration, which rimly, free fuel is about" [Von einer Verwaltung, die rändlig, frei Brennstoff um ist]. Lengthy decree in which the supplying of free heating was discussed. (3/XII/1920, E)

"I am goated, that in all cases feeblemindedness should be involved" [Ich bin zickiert, dasz in allen Fällen Schwachsinn dabei sein soll]. "Goated" = "rather surprised." Explanation of pathological cases, which was not approved. (3/XII/1920, E)

"A case for the twid" [Ein Fall für den Spinder]. "Twid" [Spinder] = "twit" [Spinner; lit.: "spinner"]. Disparaging remark about me by Dr. Seiff. (4/XII/1920, E)

"Cheesemaker and egger" [Käser und Eierer]. "Egg administrator." (13/XII/1920, Ina)

"For an Engelhardt" [For an Engelhardt]. "Smoked herring." As currency for certain values (as in Bolshevist Russia). (30/XII/1920)

"Underbreak pipes" [Unterbruchrohre]. Overflow or drainage pipes in the basement of a building. (30/XII/1920, E)

1921

"Breitensank" [idem; lit.: "Broad-sank"]. Name of a village on a picture. (14/I/1921, E)

"Among your herbarium one found a whole throng of strangers" [Zwischen ihrem Herbarium fand man ein ganzes Gewimmel Fremde]. Attempt, in a suspicious, dirty yard, to move along on an apparatus to the entrance door of the house, by pressing the keys which resembled a typewriter with dual, changeable keyboard for vowels and consonants. Everywhere through riffraff—that claims everything's not alright, it's improper (a whole throng of strangers) there (in the herbarium)—and so the obstructing and seizing justified. (17/I/21, E)

"I say to you, your eyes sparkled so, when I penetrated to your cubs" [Ich sage Dir, Deine Augen blitzten sehr, wie ich hier auf Deine Welfen zudrang]. Probably "took your hand" [dich anfaßte]. With Karl, who took my hand quickly, eagerly hurrying down some stairs, step by step, in step. Endeavoring to patter down as quickly and evenly as possible. (30/I/1921, E)

"Si Keverit" [idem]. *"Ceverit"* [idem]. Passage by train through a sand wave, which softly starts to crumble. If only it had been broken up, hollowed out ("excavare" [idem]). (21/I/1921, E)

"Room-thickness" [Zimmerdicke]. Thickness of a book, which could serve as support for an ancient building, upon whose walls it presses up. Reminiscence of "room–linden tree" [Zimmerlinde], in so far as the tree forms a fixed part of the house. (II/1921, E) [?]

"She died of cardiectasis and her woman was so shaken" [Sie starb an Herzerweiterung und ihre Frau war so angegriffen]. I collapsed in a cellar, from which a lift led to the ward, and my companion was likewise becoming faint. (Unclear.) (II/1921, E)

"In Heidelberg they're called an odagnio" [In Heidelberg heißen sie eine Odagnio]. (Grapefruit.) Eating a grapefruit takes up a lot of time, goes slowly (adagio) because it's so big. Furthermore, it's a hazard, because it's so sour. (Odagio remininiscent of the Russian; "a" instead of "o"). (II/1921, E)

"To be a state geologist means to be togeleogist-poor" [Landsgeologe sein heißt zogeleogelarm sein]. Rather like "bitter poverty-stricken" [bitterbettelarm; lit: "bitter beggar-poor"]. Scholarship recipients who were considered only in cases of utmost need. (2/III/1921, E)

"A pebble-proof armor" [Ein kieselsicherer Panzer]. "Bullet-proof" [kugelsicher]. "Pebble" = "firm." (4/III/1921, E)

"In the spoiled calves, come from the others" [Im verdorbenen Kälber aus anderem geworden]. "What would have become of me, then a young girl, if I had felt the urge to go out helplessly alone in the world!" (11/III/1921, E)

"Fontitis" [idem]. Throat inflammation, which Nana had when the tonsils were removed. (→)

"Cabu" [idem]. Italian vegetable plant unfamiliar to me; single specimen on a patch shown to me by Lorenzini. ("Kappus" [idem].) (29/III/1921, E, Suna)

"Of the water of the basin brook, unfortunately only a masterful part benefited the ship" [Von dem Wasser des Kesselbaches ist leider nur ein herrischer Teil dem Schiffe zu gute gekommen]. The ship lacks water, which is supplied from the basin brook, but is for a large part lost. It was, however, hoped to be able to get to the next harbor. "Masterful" [herrisch] = "precious little" [herzlich wenig]. "Basin brook" [Kesselbach; lit.: "kettle/boiler brook"] apparent reminiscence of "ship's boiler" [Schiffskessel]. (6/IV/1921, E, Suna)

"Limit myself to traveling out of Porzelt; the Mead is very pretty" [Beschränke mich, von Porzelt aus zu fahren; die Au ist sehr schön]. "Porzelt" = former assistant; should probably run "Porlezza." The whole region of Lago Maggiore (known to the locals as "the Mead") is somewhat too extensive. One need visit only a part, the prettiest (from Porlezza on). (8/IV/1921, E, Suna)

"Burnt beans, cotto" [Angebrannte Bohnen, cotto]. Someone (Anton?) declares that the beans are burnt; I translate this into the Italian "cotto." (→)

"Serre" [idem]. Animal, by appearance a heavy panther, but in fact a harmless herbivore which cannot turn over again once it is lying on its back (turtle), and is completely defenceless. Was found in the Saedberg Mental Asylum. (10/IV/1921, E, Suna)

"Troops formed of the rifle-beginners of the Army" [Truppen, gebildet aus den Schützungsbeginnern der Reichswehr]. Of personnel who resigned from the Army, became superfluous (citizen's force). Reminiscence of "colonial force" [Schutztruppe; lit.: "defence troops"]. (→)

"From his honest blue eyes, he spat out the pearls of his will all around" [Aus seinen ehrlichen blauen Augen spuckte er die Perlen seines Willens überall umher]. A straightforward, upright man with honest blue eyes, who goes his own way, carefree, and acts as he thinks. (15/IV/1921, E, Suna)

"It's better to spash you than to splash you" [Es ist besser, Dich zu bespitzen als zu bespritzen]. Emma, joking with a coffee pot, waves it as if she wanted to pour it on me. In retaliation for a preceding exchange of words. But then gives in and fills up my cup. (→)

"Jacob the servant had a 101-pound perjury on his conscience" [Den 101 pfündigen Meineid auf dem Gewissen hat der Diener Jakob]. Jacob the servant (name forgotten) had a heavy (100-pound) murder on his conscience, has now confessed to it. (→)

"Numero quattro cento due nove" [idem]. House number. (16/IV/1921, E, Suna)

"Bacterially driven ships run alongside on the whole route" [Bakteriell betriebene Schiffe laufen auf der ganze Strecke nebenher]. On the river most abounding in water, the Mississippi, there are, aside from the actual riverboat traffic on the side canals, ships conveyed by mechanical devices which move on great trestles. (→)

"De Crobite" [idem]. Name of the general who commands the French fleet. (17/IV/1921, E, Suna)

"The enemy (Russian) matériel was partly utilized again, partly brought to a large heap and there subjected to 'antelysis' " [Das feindliche (russische) Kriegsgerät wurde z.T. wieder verwendet, z.T. auf einen grossen Haufen gebracht und dort der "Antelyse" zugeführt]. (19/IV/1921)

"Yes, that would be quite right with me without the villa" [Ja, das wäre mir ganz recht ohne Villa]. A wagon fully loaded with furniture is pulled with effort by a team of horses up a sloping street. Since it constantly comes to a standstill, someone suggests unloading part of the goods to lighten the furniture wagon. I agree with the idea that in the long run only a small part of the furniture is needed. Those destined for the "villa," which are really of no concern to me, can be unloaded without further ado. (20/IV/1921, E, Suna)

"The patient couldn't be chained to his day anymore" [Der Kranke konnte nicht mehr an seinen Tag gefesselt werden]. "He couldn't go, had to be chained to his chair (wheelchair) all day." (26/IV/1921, E)

"Musculus palas & hypopalas? palas superior & inferior?" [idem]. Neurological case in which the electric reaction of the respective muscles was to be shown to me (consultation) by a young doctor (or lady doctor?); it should be demonstrable (diagnostically important), somewhere on the back of the patient. Was carried in by two male nurses, very frail had a fever over 39. I felt unneeded (patient moribund), and felt most unsure in relation to these neurological refinements; had never heard of the diagnostic symptom on the m. palas. (IV/1921, E, Suna)

"The Bavarian litter-mountain-guest" [Der Bayrische Streuberggast]. Someone who sleeps in litter in the Alpine hut]. (→)

"In any case, it indicates an appetitus generis and an appetitus theory" [Jedenfalls spricht es für einen appetitus generis und für eine appetitus theorie]. A medical case which can be interpreted one way or the other. (3/V/21, E)

"Tender connecting piece" [Empfindsames Zwischenstück]. A ring of metal was pressed through with force and a ductile connecting piece inserted in the gap. The remark was made that one could also insert a "tender" connecting piece, i.e., a piece of chocolate or cake (pleasant, delightful). (5/V/1921, E)

"Amnestia" [idem]. Botanical name of a plant, actually a peculiar galeopsis, which is found between purchased bushes instead of in the forest. I first thought it to be ruber purpura. (8/V/1921, E. Kr)

"Cajus, you announce your retreat to the four defeated by time and to the string, Dan" [Cajus, den vier von Zeit besiegten und der Saite kündigst Dan Du den Rückzug an]. Two persons, Cajus and Dan, part in the evening after string-music. A sort of performance, Roman costume. They part company with these words. Oddly enough: "four" instead of "two." (18/V/1921, E)

"Saying like 'surge puer' masfrow" [Spruch, wie "surge puer" masefruh]. (←)

"The cow passes through the communal cattle" [Gemeindevieh durchläuft die Kuh]. (←)

"Till the brow, from who she revealed the unsuspecting head" [Bis die Stirn, aus dem erschloß sie das ahnungslose Haupt]. Till she undid ("revealed") her hair. (Erotic act.) "Unsuspecting" → "surprising." (31/V/1921, E)

"For the duration of kemmelism" [Während der Dauer des Kemmelismus]. Storm on the Kemmel Mountain. (V/1921)

"Liwussa" [idem]. = "Diesday." (V/1921)

"In the latage of stages" [Im Spätstum der Stadien]. "In the late stage (of lues)." (V/1921, E)

"Country fiddler who has already learned to play with [musical] doublestops and with the half commission" [Ländlicher Geiger, der schon gelernt hatte mit Doppelgriffen und mit der halben Commission zu spielen]. Halftones, (musical) accidental. (3/VI/1921, E)

"First of all one needs to know the counter-laurel there" [Da muß man erst einmal den Gegenlorbeer kennen]. Graber. "Counter-laurel" = "repute in which the other is held." Comment that someone has made disparaging remarks about someone else. "One must first know how others judge someone in order to be able to assess the importance of the comments." (12/VI/1921, E)

"I've always in a day's work at Meyers" [Ich hab' mich bei Meyers stets bei Tagewerk]. "I have always done my duty as a worker at the Meyers plant." (→)

"Hammbull" [idem]. Name of a roughneck personage. (14/VI/1921, E)

"Finally the Englishman ventured radiating-off from the general path into the house of Venus Urania" [Schließlich wagte es der Engländer abstrahlend von dem Allgemeinen Wege in das Haus der Venus Urania]. First of all, someone had a fierce struggle with a dog, when he entered a large estate through the back gate. The dog confronted him, accompanied by a man, attacked him, and, after strong resistance, pursued him out the back gate. The victim now sought to reach the large powerhouse ("Venus Urania") before him, through a "radiating-off" side door. (21/VI/1921, E)

"That is the nicest yellow bark-slime" [Das ist der schönste gelbe Borkenschleim]. Side idea of a vessel whose liquid contents have brewed above a yellow rim. (→)

"It's as clear as gravy" [Das ist klar wie Kloßbrühe]. Something like "Kessus" [idem]. Among many other things, a symptom of an eye affliction discovered in me. (22/VI/1921, E)

"The uni- and formity of the numbers to the apologize" [Die Ein- und Förmigkeit der Zahlen zur entschuldigen]. The uniformity of the numbers and their being influenced by beer. (3/VII/1921, E)

"Schwimbzuo" [idem]. Polish. Attempt by the Poles (and Hungarians) to reshape German words in their language. (3/VII/1921, E)

"Ranemodes, racedaemonicus" [idem]. Instead of "ravemosus" [idem]. Interference of "lavedaemon" [idem]. (5/VII/1921, E)

"Film-dispater" [idem]. Small, peculiar, efficient tamping machine, which punches rectangular recesses of various shapes and sizes. (23/VII/1921, E)

"Four-nail" [Viernagel]. Old-German mercenary; of the shoe, studded with four hobnails. (26/VII/1921, E)

"The mediary stirring-word" [Das mediäre Rührwort]. An author's somewhat dubious platitude. (Disparaging remark about him.) (29/VII/1921, E. K.)

"To glance seeingly" [Schauendes Blicken]. "Soothsaying." (VII/1921)

"Cours general" [idem]. Rather similar to "Corps general" [idem]. (VII/1921, E)

"Brom-Eltenburg, Brom—?" [idem]. Enumeration of small states (Saxony, Altenburg i./m). (6/VIII/1921, E)

"Pistesses" [Pistessen]. Green and white striped Spanish flags on small boats. (Cannot be prohibited, since they are used only on the boats.) Reminiscence of "pinnaces" [Pinassen]. German merchant flag with black, white, and red. (3/IX/1921, E)

"Strimer-brad" [Streimer-Bratt]. Disapproving assessment that a building pompously decorated on the outside was erected on the inside not entirely of bricks, but rather half of a kind of substitute stone ("strimer-brad"; white, limestone-looking stone between the bricks). Thought of half-timbered constructions. Reminiscence of [the English word] "lime," "bric-à-brac" (rubbish [Schund]). (14/IX/1921, E)

"La crima di sulpezzo" [idem]. Ash cone of a volcano. (→)

"(You have indeed a) pannus medius" [(Sie haben ja einen) pannus medius]. Utterance by Hess when on the second day after an operation on the left eye, I wanted to leave the clinic. (16/IX/1921, E, Suna)

"The abscess looked predidon" [Das Geschwür sah praedidon aus]. (Greek πραεδιδῶν .) Forming *before* a certain causative event (an infection), therefore not yet connected with it. (Remembrance of a consultation the same day, at which the distinction between arteriosclerosis and lues came into consideration.) (25/IX/1921, E)

"Thou catastrophic Porcel" [Du schicksalsschwerer Porzel]. Suggestion of "porcelain" [Porzellan], precious, costly. It relates to the Nibelungs [from a twelfth Century German epic], the brave, worthy heroes. To this was also added a comparison with precious metals. (30/IX/1921, E)

"Rare bird [lit.: "white raven"], your wings yield today to our goals" [Weißer Rabe, Deine Schwingen weichen heute unseren Zielen]. Should read something like "Today he can stir his wings in order to drive at his goal." Fragment of an inscription on a wall of a decayed monastery (now an educational institution). (→)

"Ash guastness" [Aschenwächtheit]. Unclear concept of a fabric which was treated with ash lye and retained its colors. (Recollection of a conversation about the suitability of ash for washing and of a treatise on the colorfastness of aniline dyes.) (30/IX/1921, E, Suna)

"Bismark drank two rounds of beer, with the exception of the special champagneforelander" [Bismark trank zwei Lagen Bier met Ausnahme des besonderen Sektvorlander]. He joined in two rounds of beer, which were drunk in company without, however, taking champagne beforehand. Recollection of an anecdote in which, in company at his place, the replacement of champagne by beer was suggested in a humorous manner. (1/X/1921, E, Suna)

"Now there are a multitude of capes [alt.: "vomits"], which nobody can reach" [Nun sind da eine Menge von Kotzen, an die kein Mensch ran kann]. There are there a multitude of regulations which no one can obey. (Military physician with long Christ curls, probably revolutionaries.) (2/X/1921, E)

"Stoge" [Poparz]. A statesman who had retired resentfully for eight years and now is beginning to become conciliatory again. (12/X/1921)

"The ainder master, fro' soil-leaf onward and traveled finished" [Das Ainder Meister vom Bodenblatt an und fertig gefahren]. Fragment of a poem from a newspaper. (→)

"Eydros a meliaconica" [idem]. A very tender, pretty pear quince[?]. (14/X/1921, E, Suna)

"Gyption" [idem]. A billionaire wants to give so much money to Germany that she can pay her debts. She would then become a "Gyption," a second Egypt. (15/X/21, E, Suna)

"Nape-jibber" [Nackenmauschel]. Shower in the bathroom. (15/X/21)

"We should incorporate magnalies into those creations" [Wir sollten jenen Schöpfungen Magnaleen angliedern]. At private mental asylums the wards were to be incorporated in which runaway or unfaithful women would get an educational-psychiatric treatment. ("Magdalenins" [Magdaleninnen] influenced by "magnolias" [Magnolien].) (17/X/1921, E, Suna)

"Brow-skin-buzzing" [Stirnhautgesause]. Headaches, buzzing, bad sensations in the head. (18/X/1921, E, Suna)

"Glaci-wounds" [Glaciwunden]. Wounds which heal smoothly [glatt] without any complications at all. Involvement with head wounds. (22/X/1921)

"Isa [Ina?]: I'd like a place" [Isa [Ina?]: ich möchte einen Platz]. "Place" [Platz], suggestive of "Schnaps" [idem; cf. English "spot"], [i.e.,] can also mean "schnaps"). Unintentionally funny, was laughed at. (→)

"Doll-tumble-cake" [Puppensturzkuchen]. By mistake a small bundle of stuff had been sent along to Italy. It should be found again there if the things get "tumbled" and the doll's kitchen gets furnished. (25/XI/1921, E)

"Pampa de Espagne" [idem]. Child ("bambino, bimbo" [idem]). Spanish-like. (XI/1921, E)

"This is Miranda, w.l." [Das ist Miranda, w.l.]. Enumeration with unclear meaning. (2/XII/1921, E)

"Rappaport cake" [Rappaportkuchen]. Tray for the transport of corpse pieces. (→)

"Caraway-Brook Court in Kalw" [Kümmelbacher Hof in Kalw]. (Postal district of Berlin [?].) Assembly site of alienists. (→)

"'Foreigners meeting' of the region" ["Fremdentagung" des Kreises]. At which everyone is free to spend his day as he likes. No communal undertakings. (22/XII/1921)

"Theseus, the man, recedes" [Theseus als Mann tritt hier zurück]. Chorus song: Theseus had all sorts of faults, but still he was a real man. (30/XII/1921, E. Kr)

"Women's praise encountered there a pamphlet with many pictures, the john-pictures [toilet-pictures]" [Frauenlob fand dort ein Heft mit vielen Bildern, die Clo-bildern.] Extolling Rudolf von Habsburg. (31/XII/1921, E)

1922

"The nostata is coming" [Die Nostata kommt]. One had to use the back door (of a Roman camp). Obscure idea of a post with a lance ("nosta"). When there is danger, the main gate in front is not passable. (8/I/1922, E)

"Valutasis" [idem]. Word with unknown meaning. I looked up the main word in a sort of catalogue in order to know what it means, but couldn't find it. It was used

in a conversation on the railway. Reminiscence of Estonian "valutat" ("it hurts; it causes pain"). (→)

"Pea" [idem]. Head. (15/I/1922, E)

"So quickly to Sudenow" [So flott nach Sudenow]. A place to migrate to (small nest, village, situated in the distance). (16/I/1922, E)

"Brain-lying, sloodge-eyes, hand-gallop" [Hirnliegen, Schlüteraugen, Handgalopp]. At a review of the troops, a short gallop ("hand-gallop") would take place in filing by. (Reminiscence of "to have the horse in hand.") Further with automobiles ("brain-lying") and with sledges [Schlitten] ("sloodge-eyes"), particularly difficult (Estonian sledge). (24/I/1922, E)

"Hypergaeismus" [idem]. In dozing; no clear meaning. Previous dream of stalactite caverns. (2/II/1922, E)

"Which is then to be explained by the police [. . .]*"* [Daß dabei von der Polizei dann zu erklären sei [. . .]]. Everyone of a bunch of people who were visiting somewhere would be given, upon entering, a chocolate bar manufactured by the host himself. (12/II/1922, E)

"Glolling" [Glazieren]. University riding. (4/III/1922, E)

"Heavens move the eternal light" [Himmel bewegen das ewige Licht]. (Passage from a hymn.) I was invited to visit a mental asylum situated on a mountain, and hoped to be able to evacuate my bladder there. Then I had my doubts, since I did not know the institution; but I figured that I would find a toilet in a more highly situated institution, more familiar to me. (11/III/1922, Suna)

"Thier-N-H-Elyseon" [idem]. Pharmaceutical preparation. (14/III/1922, Suna)

"In the party course here, nations had their weapons struck from their hands" [Im Parteigange hier war Völkern die Waffe aus der Hand geschlagen]. (→)

"Tragelies" [Tragelien]. Peculiar, sweet, but rather tasteless fruits, reminiscent of sheep dung, which would be used for psychological experiments. The greatest possible change of the fruits was desired. (Reminiscences of a visit to upper gardens). (26/III/1922, E, Suna)

"Sluggish, slumbish" [idem]. Risqué [schlüpfrig; lit.: "slippery"]; "slumbish" was recognized as the correct word, although I considered "sluggish" to be quite appropriate, too. (III/1922, E)

"Ansiliavior" [idem]. A previously worthless waste material in the slag of the mines (suggestion of "aluminum" [idem]), which was exploited and made useful during the war through Oetra's efforts (reminiscence of Kedtberg). (→)

"Gallisch [Gallic] and Lokota have become so disturbing with their noise" [Gallisch und Lokota sind duch ihren Lärm so störend geworden]. Two female patients. (→)

"Spegat & Rut" [idem]. Two proper names. (Beginning of IV/1922, E, Suna)

"Pelium africanum" [idem]. (→)

"Iridacere" [idem]. (6/V/1922, E)

"He gave up the little cloth of the multiple sclerosis" [Das Läppchen multipler Sklerose hat er aufgegeben]. An Indian native gave up the rubbing which had been

prescribed for him for multiple sclerosis. In reality, it concerned another, unidentified ailment, so the treatment was useless. (22/V/1922, E)

"Made the complaint of the Chinamen a much earlier getaway" [Machte ein viel früheres Fortkommen der Klage der Chinamänner]. "The departure from Egypt was made easier for the Israelites by special circumstances." (V/1922, E)

"The Laucht-like, famulus-like arrangement of medical examination facilities" [Die Lauchtähnliche, famulusähnliche Einrichtung von ärtzlichen Untersuchungsstellen]. Examination for infectious diseases, which one could attend either as an independent researcher ("Laucht": reminiscence of "Nocht" [idem], the director of the Hamburg Tropical Institute) or as a beginner. (→)

"Isolin, 1442 marks" [Isolin, 1442 M]. Isolin, a substance sprayed in the air from tubes, with pleasant, refreshing, and cleansing effect, which, as it were, coats the body with a fine layer. Price of the tube, which is sprayed all at once, 1442 marks. (20/VI/1922, E)

"Godd must vid the war" [Got [sic] muß vid den Krieg]. Beginning of a long poster at a station in Flanders. Content incomprehensible (25/VI/1922, E)

"Martyrs association" [Märtyrerverein]. Dissatisfied royal neurotics. (VI/1922)

"Young-trouts" [Jungforellen]. Bag with sweets. Reminiscence of "morsels" [Morsellen], then of the "little bears" of chocolate. (9/VII/1922, E)

"A whole wagon of state of ?" [Einen ganzen Staatswagon von ?]. Reminiscence of "reason of state" [Staatsraison]. (→)

"Subito hani dano" [idem]. Italian idiom. (14/VII/1922, E)

"Yesterday he took up the annual principal of our assets" [Gestern hat er die Annualsubstanz unseres Vermögens aufgenommen]. "Struck the balance." (17/VII/1922, E)

"Basilio must become more modern" [Basilio muß moderner werden]. King Louis II, huge and slender, appeared suddenly to Ina and me; moves very nimbly, but shows a certain distrust towards me and calls out the above sentence to me. I had the impression that as a consequence of delusions he would soon become uneasy. (→)

"How many embankment-basins have already crashed down!" [Wieviele Dammschüsseln sind schon abgestürzt!]. Small dumping wagons going rather insecurely on a high embankment. (19/VII/1922, E)

"Quid menas?" [idem]. "What are you threatening?" What dangers can result from the semiconscious state of a boy? ("Menace" [idem]) (9/IX/1922, E)

"Meabis" [idem]. (→)

"Spenandy microorganism" [Spenandiger Mikroorganismus]. (→)

"Then one blows now and then" [Dann bläst man ab und zu]. When a child is disobedient, one acts as if it was exactly what one wanted of him, in order to cover up the failure. (24/IX/1922, E)

"Here is no English lyric poetry, no interruption of information" [Hier ist keine englische Lyrik, kein Abbrechen der Auskünfte]. Wundt's birthday; description of his peculiarity. (5/X/1922)

"*One pays nuki crowns for a ton*" [Für eine Tonne zahlt man nuki Kronen]. "Nuki" = 100; Greek. A Swede in Portugal, who wants to move to Germany (Hamburg) in order to do better in business there with small ships (shipping company). Doubt on the part of the trustees as to whether he wouldn't be better off going to a country with higher currency in order to earn more. (15/X/1922, E)

"*He fears change in the mental result*" [Er früchtet Veränderung des mentalen Resultates]. Feared having his mental personality influenced by someone else. (28/XI/1922, E)

"*We sing songs together of the great glass bells*" [Wir singen zusammen Lieder der großen Glasglocke]. The song of the bell [Schiller]. (30/XI/1922, E, Emma and Ina)

"*It costs innumerable little scraps*" [Das kostet eine Unzahl von Fetzchen]. Fuel. (30/XI/1922)

"*There where the brook of the earth flows*" [Dort, wo der Bach der Erde fließt]. Female urethrea. (→)

"*Zum Lanzer*" [idem; lit.: "at the Lanzer"]. Inn. (29/XII/1922, E)

1923

"*Woom*" [idem]. Designation of a scraper for " autopsy toxin." (6/I/1923, E)

"*There's a girl's name: 'Leaky' *" [Es gibt einen Mädchennamen: "Undicht"]. Association to the word "leaky" in a conversation. (13/I/1923, E)

"*When we really look over the patient's ancestral line*" [Wenn wir wirklich die Ahnenreihe der Patientin betrachten]. The case history, the series [Reihe] of medical expressions. (16/I/1923, E)

"*The one says: We still don't plant enough with this watery ledge*" [Der eine sagt: Wir planzten doch nicht genug mit diesem wässrigen Absatz]. In the garden street everything is disarranged. Says the one, there aren't enough trees, because our sewage doesn't carry enough fertilizer, is too watery. The other one sees only gardens everywhere. In the Frauenhof or Reichenbachstraße, when one looks toward town, one sees no trees; if one looks towards the Isar, one gets the impression of a park. (18/I/1923, E)

"*His supposed slaying crying-to-heaven initial murderous shouting*" [Sein angeblich meuchelndes himmelschreiendes anfängliches mörderliches Schreien]. It is crying-to-heaven. Assassination. (23/I/1923, E)

"*One could speak of L.C., only it doesn't work, because it's a higher exclamation mark*" [Man konnte von L.C. sprechen, das geht nur nicht, weil das ein höheres Ausrufungszeichen ist]. It has to do with preparations of a syphlitic affliction of female carriers. And the case couldn't be classed as L.C., since a broader extension of the disease process is proper to it. (29/I/1923, E)

"*Spritzenburg Foundation*" [Spritzenburg Stiftung]. "Hindenburg Foundation." Idea that Hindenburg lives in a villa with well-kept, sprayed lawn and fountain. (←)

"*It must be no case history*" [Das muß keine Krankengeschichte sein]. "No detailed representation of a process." The omission of "e" [sic] was wrongly conceived of as nominative. (←)

"Every power, which at present sur de land (sur de sea) brought to us" [Jeder Macht, die zur Zeit on de Land (on de Meer) zu uns brachte]. "Which attacked us on land or at sea." (17/II/1923, E)

"Gladly sustained the stain is reprieved; ready it is now to be conceived" [Bereitmal ist das Mal erlassen; Bereitmal ist es nun zu fassen]. Summons to dinner at a large party. (17/II/1923, Toni)*

"I'm traveling to Milz [lit.: "spleen"]" [Ich fahre nach Milz.] Deviation of the railroad to Rostock. Bathing resort. (White stag Bilz?) (23/II/1923, E)

"Horizon of flowerets without flowers, therefore sky without meaning on the horizon" [Horizont der Blümeln ohne Blumen deshalb am Horizont der Himmel ohne Sinn]. A poem which in its beginnings has in the first sentence no great poetic value. (→)

"Fummettes" [Fummetten]. Symbolic, the scenes of fire. Ravages which alcohol leaves behind. (24/II/1923, E)

"Slowly and lazily worly the day on" [Langsam und träge zerschlich der Tag]. (9/III/1923, E)

"The courageous way to Großhesselohe" [Der mutige Weg nach Großhesselohe]. (→)

"The hereditary book of the deceased" [Das Erbbuch des Verstorbenen]. "Book inherited from the deceased." (11/III/1923, E)

"Twacht" [idem]. "Kiss," Low German. (20/III/1923, E)

"Today Frau Grosabeit wishes a soldier (double)" [Frau Grosabeit wünscht heute einen Soldaten (doppelt)]. (→)

"View of lower Golling" [Aussicht über niederen Golling]. Saddleback hill ridge at Henlig over which one sees the lake. (23/III/1923, E)

"Burgisel" [idem]. Name of mountain. Reminiscence of Pilate. (←)

"With the prevention of the great impending war" [Mit der Verhinderung des grossen drohenden Krieges]. (30/III/1923, E)

"Raysik, Ay, Intibevo" [idem]. Three place-names. (III/1923, E)

"One had the impression like the town was a stream-demagogic masses-quarter" [Man hat den Eindruck, als sei die Stadt ein stromdemagogisches Massenquartier]. The chaos with the streaming back of the masses in the war. (3/IV/1923, E, Suna)

"Brignolervo Latriae Stazione" [idem]. Of a railway. Feeling that it had to be on the Italian Sea. (4/IV/1923, E)

"I'll pin a cluffing there afterwards" [Da steck ich hernach ein Klüfing]. "Needle." Utterance by Ina, who wanted to fasten with a needle a window curtain as protection against the penetrating morning light ("fire"). (9/IV/1923, E)

"Sort de j'en [. . .] je bève" [idem]. (11/IV/1923, E)

"Food make-believe" [Speisemache]. Hall for the feeding of students, as it seemed correct for my appropriate age. (26/IV/1923, E, Irma)

"Presential-prick" [Praesentialstich]. Physiological examinations. (4/V/1923, E, Suna)

"*According to these realizations, Tappert*" [Nach diesen Erkenntnissen, Tappert].
"Experiences" [Erfahrungen]? Etc. According to the experiences which Toni has
had up to now in her marriage. (15/V/1923, E, Suna)

"*Obtradnatar*" [idem]. Command in playing out the grog from coffee cups. Karl
gives the commands, then insertion of spoons, stirring and drinking up, similar to
students' toast. (19/V/1923, E, Suna)

"*Aneuria*" [Aneurie]. Inability to learn. (20/V/1923).

"*Twelolve*" [Zwölelf]. (22/V/1923)

"*With manga, sonetta*" [Beim Manga, Sonetta]. Dances, Italian. (31/V/1923, E,
Suna)

"*Snurtle-gurshle*" [Schnürzelgurschel] . Meaning no longer determinable. (V/1923)

"*Hole in the running-woods*" [Loch in den Laufhölzern]. (3/VI/1923, E, Suna)

"*Cimema*" [idem]. A picture from me for Mingazini. (14/VI/1923, E)

"*Coat for me again the conjugances*" [Schmiert mir die Conjuganzen wieder]. Approximately: The plants collected on a hike (cryptogames? and composites?) should
be cared for in such a way that they don't decay. (17/VI/1923, E Suna)

"*Many of his symptoms already indicate checkmate*" [Es sprechen viele seiner
Erscheinungen schon für matt]. = "Some reasons." Utterance by Graber in the
Broncke business. (19/VI/1923, E, Suna)

"*Thing-crotes*" [Dingkroten]. Hooks on the wall for the fastening of cords. (20/
VI/1923, E, Suna)

"*The crossbow, the leaden one; thirst...American size*" [Die Armbrust, das Bleierne;
Durst... Amerikanische Größe]. (26/VI/1923, E, Suna)

"*In the bifat*" [Im bifat]. Half indicator. (VI/1923, E, Suna)

"*The war broke out,* [...] *not* [...] *with bitter words*" [Der Krieg brach aus, [...]
nicht [...] mit bitteren Worten]. (→)

"*The Daspath*" [Der Daspath]. World language. (→)

"*Nissl writes to me: dat Agro-Cagro*" [Nissl schreibt mir: dat Agro-Cagro]. Perhaps a
new guinea pig. (5/VII/1923, E, Suna)

"*This is water for (to measure) the serology*" [Das ist Wasser für die Serologie (zu
messen)]. "Mouthwash" [Zahnwasser]. (6/VII/1923, E)

"*Over-garden the white hangs*" [Übergarten das weiße hängt]. (→)

"*To renew ('to tin') the glaze on the beer mugs which are brought into the morel
collection*" [Die Glasur an Bierkrügen erneuen ("verzinnen") die zum
Morchelsammeln gebraucht werden. (→)

"*Orgies*" [Orgien]. Small oil bottles of old-fashioned kind. (→)

"*Peignards*" [idem]. Small, rather bent male figures in the manner of chandelier
little women as Gothic ornamentation. (9/VII/1923, Suna)

"*In correct, nose-amazing admiration; correctly pinned, corresponding to the
first*" [In richtiger, nasenverblüffender Verwunderung; in richtiger, der ersten
entsprechenden Steckweise]. In admiration of things (a street with old-fashioned

buildings in Basel or Bern) which stick out into the nose. In correct style; in period. (←)

"And especially the name from the letter, repeated from memory" [Und besonders den Namen aus dem Brief frei wiederholte]. An especially gifted child who not only was quick of understanding but also asked intelligent questions on his own initiative. (23/VII/1923).

"Tell him then is, will he become it? Tell him then, will he become so?" [Sag es ihm dann ist, wird er es? Sag es dem dann, wird er es so?]. As if imitating. Touching story, short poem, four lines, the two last ones. A horse is brought to the surroundings of his master who's in prison. It shakes and neighs. The large crowd sympathizes. That's how an animal acts. "Dom won't act that way." (24/VII/1923, E, Suna)

"The fambrook has to be paid for immediately" [Das Erbach muß gleich bezahlt werden]. "Fambrook" [Erbach] = "family tomb" [Erbbegräbnis]. (6/VIII/1923, E, Suna)

"I had then only save with me" [Ich hatte damals nur Spar bei mir]. Only change— "brak" [idem]. (→)

"Vi tafalk!" [idem]. At a funeral ceremony in the Glawisic region. Order to the grave digger named "Vi" to bring the coffin for the body (catafalque tomb). (→)

"To whom do I grant a respite from this license? To whom do I owe this fee?" [Wem stunde ich diese Lizenz? Wem schulde ich diese Gebühr?]. Question from a somewhat foreign (Czech) gentleman (grease director type). Approx. two marks. (13/VIII/1923)

"Lucius Farfureius" [idem]. Roman name. (17/VIII/1923)

"Emergency snuffer" [Notschnupfer]. Old-fashioned petroleum lamp housed in a fold-away case, which produced a fountainlike jet of water by its burning. Present from Fanny. (18/VIII/1923, E, Suna)

"I can't understand that every child sees me, that here the glaced notes take precedence over the canisic tailed ones." [Ich kann es nicht verstehen, daß mich jedes Kind sieht, daß hier die glaciten Noten vor den canisisch Geschwänzten den Vorrang haben]. In a piece of music, deeper regularities of the thoroughbass. Completely incomprehensible to me. (25/VIII/1923, Suna)

"Hose culture and training dressage" [Schlauchkultur und -dressur]. See to it that nothing harmful and only pure water gets sprayed and the hose direction is controlled. (27/VIII/1923, Suna)

"Arskon & Agresso" [idem]. Two villages on a road. (29/VIII/1923, E, Suna)

"Your memory capacities" [Deine Gedächtnismöglichkeiten]. Grasping point for clinging in a difficult climbing tour. (5/IX/1923, E)

"Spirtentierce" [Spirtenterz]. Name of a Malay girl at the seaside. (9/IX/1923)

"North and south flora dissolve the states" [Nord- und Südflora löst die Staaten auf]. The borders of the flora in north and south do not conform to those of the states. (IX/1923, E)

"Cabinets-work" [Schranksarbeiten]. Differences in characteristics of animal embryoes in unicellular animals. (IX/1923)

"Nasiki" [idem]. With soft, suggestive repetition: "nasiki—nasiki." Tasty tidbits baked in the heating-oven. (1/X/1923, E)

"Surprise—Tilly—lucky fellow—dollar hat—Friedrich—left Leberkött—wood tussed—compartment—Entente Johannes—fancies—whimsical—Seeburg—much endured" [Überraschung—Tilly—Glückspilz—Dollarhut—Friedrich—Leberkött verlassen—Hotzgethust—Fach—Entente Johannes—Einfall—Schnörkelhaft—Seeburg—viel gelitten]. Entente Johannes not a transformation into French sounds, read in German. (→)

"Shoe-tips eyes show servants" [Schuhspitze Augen zeigen Diener]. (→)

"Weave fount nothing forgotten" [Webebrunn nichts vergessen]. (→)

"Bread-head-pot" [Brotkopftopf]. (→)

"One of them said: She, who she a heavy type—tysfies" [Einer sagte: sie, die sie ein schwerer Typus—Fridigt]. Fragment from a long document, as when some points are read off. (10/X/1923, E)

"How one now—guilty; Sanges—(AB) Cobdeon—Napoleon" [Wie man nun—schuldig; Sanges—(AB) Cobdeon—Napoleon]. Half being in full consciousness with finely written letter. Some of them emerged legibly. Later the visual images receded or else subsequently became tolerably clear only after the words came to mind. (←)

"Rhodalia flamica" [idem]. Plant name. (25/X/1923, E)

"Bystagabor" [idem]. Stork [Adebar]. (←)

"The Vistula-turners" [Die Weichseldreher]. Political proper name, Sodosto revolutionary party. (←)

"Passio note" [Passiozettel]. Customs declaration. (←)

"Pia Coscodikow; Taraetoi" [idem]. Proper names. (←)

"Dit was Bräsigen-meintik" [idem]. "Bräsig's trick." (28/X/1923)

"Bria" [idem]. Capital of Peru (Lima). (←)

"Compassion for the courageous sow pen" [Mitleid mit dem mutige Saugehege]. For a run-down political party.(←)

"And 'hotted' besides" [Und dabei "heizig"]. The foot was hot, heated up, sick. (←)

"Oh, it's all just 'onriphing'; they're 'quoripisel'" [Ach, das ist alles nur "Anriphen"; es sind "Quoripisel"]. In a conversation about unverifiable wild rumors. "Onriphing" [Anriphen], i.e., it only seems that way to the ear. "Quoripisel" [idem], i.e., confusion triggered by emotional need (patterned on "mixed pickels" [idem], or in German "Gerissel." (10/XI/1923)*

"La familles pullulcates" [idem]. Homeless family. (30/XI/1923, E)

"Rigard Mordane" [idem]. A parasite transmitting pathogenic germs. Unclear. (1/XII/1923, E, afternoon)

"Reitbolda" [idem; lit.: "Ride-bolda"]. Village in Thuringia. (18/XII/1923)

"The University of the Joy-of-Parenthood Customs House" [Die Hochschule des Zollhauses Kindersegen]. (23/XII/1923)

"Mini infra" [idem]. Inferior. (←)

1924

"Zeppelin to divert the cycling-legs" [Zeppelin, um die Radelbeine abzulenken].
A zeppelin circles over a large city (Paris?) in order to divert as many combatants
("cycling-legs"; bicyclist troop ready to march) as possible with the necessary defensive measures. (Very long vacillating over whether this specimen offers anything
particular and if noting it is worthwhile. Important for the understanding of drowsiness.) (→)

"Don't take everything so explosive!" [Nehmen Sie doch nicht alles so explosibel!].
Bleuler, who replies something to another participant at a psychiatric conference,
senses his agitation. He [B.] then suddenly recognizes him as a good friend and
they hug one another impetuously. (21/I/1924, E)

"Ein Plumy" [A plumy]. Big wood log for the fireplace. (30/I/1924, E)

"Urethra metal" [Harnröhrenmetall; Lit.: "urine-tube metal"]. Pieces of broken
catheter. (I/1924, E)

"The court sucks quagmire from a state of affairs" [Das Gericht saugt Sumpf aus
einer Sachlage]. He apparently abuses the facts [Tatsachen]. (I/1924, E)

"Middleroom Müller" [Mittelzimmer-Müller]. From a minister program. The first
part should read "smooth work," sitting in a room and producing; the second part,
"accessibility for the man in the street." (I/1924, E)

"Don't pull her right, because the . . . Your hand which feeds gets bitten" [Zieh sie
nicht recht, da die . . . Du ziehst Dir da was rechtes heran; alt.: "You rear someone
without any positive result"]. (→)

"Motive of favorable attitude towards scientific endeavors" [Motiv wohlwollendes
Verhalten gegenüber wissenschaftlichen Bestrebungen]. Clinic–research institute.
(I/1924, E)

"Cook-ill" [Kochkrank; alt.: "Koch-ill" (if referring to Robert Koch)]. Deathly ill.
(5/II/1924, E)

"A small crockil head" [Ein kleiner Krockillkopf]. (11/II/1924, Ina, evaluated)

"Gorden cup" [Gordenscher Becher]. Of papier-mâché. Especially hygienic, since it
can always be replaced. For "Susderheimer" [idem] beer (a kind of "health beer").
(II/1924, E)

"Imdenttin" [idem]. Political program; political party. (II/1924, E)

"Trechen-bielercog place" [Tretjen-Biälerkogstelle]. Bullet-holes in the corridor of
rocks. (II/1924, E)

"Hernia or Rangard (Rangall?)" [Hernia oder Rangard (Rangall?)]. Spoken unclearly. Male or female rabbit (Ramler [idem]). (→)

"We help statically electrify legs of tabicore" [Wir helfen Beine statisch elektrisieren
von Tabikern]. Static electricity; static ataxis; help them get on their feet [Beinen;
lit.: "legs"]. (II/1924, E)

"She drives your autopsello" [Sie fährt mit deinem Autopsello]. Peculiar, small,
rapid auto. (II/1924, E)

"He is better than the underwriting note; silly teenage girls have grown accustomed to it" [Er ist besser als der Unterpfandbrief; Backfische haben sich daran gewöhnt]. An elevator, whose advantages were obvious. Humorous praise. (The first two lines forgotten.) He as a business "word" is better than an inferior ("under" [unter]) mortgage bond [Unterpfandbrief]. Even the completely inexperienced ("silly teenage girls" [Backfische]) have realized that. (1/III/1924, E)

"Frivolous Milan e l'allodot" [Der frivole Mailand e l'allodot]. Poincaré complains that in Milan he was already declared politically "half dead" [halbtot] ("allodot"). (18/III/1924, E)

"Flutter message" [Flatterspruch]. Radiogram message [Funkspruch] which flutters around the world. (III/1924, E)

"Rustinoster month" [Monat Rustinoster]. "November." (III/1924, E)

"Who repeated a nervous fit in the specialist's manner" [Der in Gutachterform einen Nervenanfall wiederholte]. "Described the fit." (III/1924, E)

"Declatone-sinister" [Deklatonsinister]. Motives which are wrongly attributed to a son returned home, when his voice is heard. (IV/1924, E)

"Enkryrie" [idem]. (←)

"Always the same, who believe in the heavily defeated man" [Immer dieselben, die an den schwer Geschlagenen glauben]. Steadfast politician. (→).

"Glaciering" [Gletschern]. "Going to a summer resort" [Sommerfrische; lit.: "cool of summer"]. (IV/1924)

"Stiamo fabbricado in modo provisorio con allio ed ollio" [idem]. There is construction, temporarily and playfully, of onions ("allio") and oil (as cement). Reminiscence of "by the skin of your teeth" [Ach und Krach]. (10/VIII/1924, E; afternoon visit by Bottini, conversation in Italian)

"Domisiton Glacier" [Domisitongletscher]. Glacier in Switzerland, which was crossed. (VIII/1924, E, Suna)

"Real, loneliest annihilation" [Wirkliche einsamste Vernichtung]. Complete, such that the annihilated person is totally eliminated, lonely. (IX/1924, E, Suna)

"The vaglia" [Die Vaglia]. "Currency" [Valuta]. (IX/1924, E, Suna)

"Had chamber" [Hatte Kammer]. The brother of a dethroned prince (story from the land of sun) has the task of advising him as the lower chamber used to do. He was with him and "had chamber," i.e., duty in the manner of chamber. (IX/1924, E, Suna")

"Around Arburgna in Greece (Ionia); Socrates around Ilex" [Bei Arburgna in Griechenland (Ionia); Sokrates bei Ilex]. Socrates died near Ilex (town in Italy) and near Arbugtum in Greece. Here a disruption in the train of thought. Obscure idea that there existed a connection with Seneca. (IX/1924, E, Suna)

"Areasfrouw; care you in frow" [idem]. Address to a young Dutch fiancée. (13/XII/1924, E, Barcelona)

"Yes, for the people" [Ja, den Leuten]. Question to a young theologian: Have you already given a sermon? "Yes, for the people," i.e., people with round hats on, therefore only outdoors, at a gathering, not in the church. (XII/1924, E)

1925

"Remiservation" [idem]. "Postponement, delay." (→)

"Dregalies" [Dregalien]. "Cockchafer larvae." (6/III/1925, E)

"Moon-fracture" [Mondbruch]. Scheme of the phases of the moon for clinical use (Wilmanns). (9/IV/1925, E)

"During vorace the animals arrived with push" [Beim Gefräß kamen die Tiere mit Stoß an]. "During feeding with tripe, the pigs turned up quickly." (19/VI/1925, afternoon, E)

"Riding by foot" [Zu Fuß fahren]. Instead of "bicycle riding" [Radfahren]. In contrast to car riding. (26/VIII/1925, E, Suna)

"Infrarivals" [Niederkunft; lit.: "childbirth"]. Inscription on the oldest station in Europe (Livorno? Liverpool?). In the departure hall (counterpart of "arrivals" [Ankunft]). (VIII/1925, E, Suna)

"The statement is more reliable the more it is removed from a top judgment" [Die Aussage ist um so zuverlässiger, je mehr sie sich von einem Spitzenurteil entfernt]. "Tendentious, deliberately brutal." (23/X/1925, E)

"Two-vegetable shop" [Zwei-Gemüsegeschäft]. Vegetable shop which can ride around on a carriage with a two-horse team, therefore rather eminent. (1/XII/1925, E)

"Letter texts" [Lettertexte]. Inscription on a letter box [Briefkasten] in an indetermined country (not conceived of as French, even less as English; possibly Spanish). (1/XII/1925, E)

1926

"At these... will I rest. The sphere suffered and protection-enough..." [An diesen ... will ich ruhen. Die Sphäre litt und Schutzgenug...]. Fragment of a poem. Upon awakening. (→)

"Quibona" [idem]. Goddess with wall-crown. (→)

"Faevreizd" [idem]. Incomprehensible word in half-slumber. Somewhat analogous to the meaningless letter combinations caused by the "misprint gremlin." (25/I/1926, E)

"Badapaia" [idem]. Waiter's expression for a certain piece of meat (cutlet, surloin, tenderloin). (I/1926, E)

"Why do the legs cry out in bed like that? That's fresh! That's very fresh!" [Warum schreien die Beine im Bette so? Das ist frech! Das ist sehr frech!] Noise on turning over in bed. Fear of disturbing the wife by it—her half-joking protest. (4/IV/1926, E)

"There's no more scrambled ox" [Rührochs gibt es nicht mehr]. In an inn. "Fried eggs." ("Scrambled egg" [Rührei]; "eggs sunny-side up" [Ochsenaugen; lit.: "ox-eyes"]). (5/IV/1926, E)

"All had the same rather rage-full look" [Alle hatten das gleiche, etwas grimmhafte Aussehen]. The pictures of a number of former elementary school teachers who had come up in the world (heightened self-assurance and defensive position). (22/V/1926, Suna)

"*Agree the hand veterinary ideas*" [Dem Handveterinärgedanken zustimmen]. The establishment of scattered veterinary stations in the countryside. (25/V/1926, E, Suna)

"*Candy day*" [Candy-tag]. "Didn't you also have your candy day?" Day on which the English fear the taking of candy. (21/VII/1926, E, Suna)

"*Who's does the leathers?*" [Wer's die Leder macht]. In leafing through notes, the question arises of who sees to it that the individual volumes of notes bound in leather are opened. (29/VII/1926, E, Suna)

"*Bamboo dwarf*" [Bambuszwerg]. Small boat for transportation on tropical rivers. (1/VIII/1926, E, Suna)

"*Maskinova*" [idem]. A patient who had already been in the institution for decades. Reminiscence of the iron mask. (9/VIII/1926, E)

"*47 million self-debotsers*" [47 Millionen Selbstentbotser]. Automatic detonators which were exploded. (4/IX/1926, E, Suna)

"*Pas dove*" [idem]. A daughter who doesn't want to do an exam at the place specified for her, but wants to choose the place herself. (17/IX/1926)

PART

3

Dreams and Language Updated

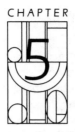

Modern Psycholinguistics
and REM Sleep

The quarter century after Kraepelin made his final entry to his dream speech corpus, and the decade after Freud penned his last notes on the "talking cure" in his uncompleted *Outline of Psychoanalysis*, were comparatively tranquil as far as both linguistics and dream research were concerned. It was just after the midpoint of the twentieth century that something of a revolution occurred in the respective fields: the transformational-generative movement in linguistics, and the discovery of clocklike REM periods as the physiological concomitants of dreaming. Although the close occurrence in time of these two developments was quite coincidental, the zeitgeist of the ensuing decades would see at least some general influence of linguistics upon dream theorization. The matter of verbal language *in* dreams—the obvious convergence of the two disciplines— would, however, remain dormant for years to come.

The TG Grammar Revolution

The transformational-generative (TG) revolution in linguistics, which got underway with the publication of Noam Chomsky's *Syntactic Structures* in 1957, has only strengthened the respect for verbal language that was already so evident in the days of Freud, Kraepelin, Wundt, and Darwin. Esoteric notions such as "recursive functions" and "structure-dependent rules" were introduced, as well as the concept of a mentally internalized grammar capable of generating from a finite set of elements (words and morphemes) the infinite set of all and only the well-formed strings (that is, the sentences) that make up a given natural human language.

Recent empirical studies of infrahuman primates have done little to disprove that such a grammatical system is unique to man—after the first few years of life—or that this uniqueness is a matter of kind rather than degree: a qualitatively new and different phenomenon which emerged in the course of human evolution when a certain biological complexity was reached. Even the very modest syntactic output claimed for specially trained "talking" gorillas—who make use of sign language, plastic symbols, computer-generated pictures, and the like—is largely attributed by experts to the "Clever Hans effect" already described at the turn of the century, plus the infrahuman primate's use of repetition strategies (subtle imitation of the teacher-interlocutor's prior sequences; cf. Terrace, 1979). As Chomsky (1980) puts it, language confers such enormous selectional advantages that our finding of any such unused capacity in gorillas would be as miraculous as "the discovery, on some unexplored island, of a species of bird that had never thought to fly until instructed to do so through human intervention" (p. 239).

The TG revolution has not been without some relevance as far as dreaming is concerned, thanks to Chomsky's vision that the study of verbal language can lead to broader insights into the nature of mind. Freud's model of dream generation is a two-level system, by which (as we saw in Chapter 2, pp. 18–19) the latent dream thoughts are converted into the manifest dream by what he termed the "dreamwork." As Chomsky (1980) has himself remarked, this system lends itself to comparison with the traditional TG model of sentence generation, by which "deep structures" are mapped onto "surface structures" by the "transformational component." In both models, the conversions can be formally reduced to the processes of insertion, deletion, transposition, and junction of elements. And in both models the operations in question are referred to as *transformations* (this also being the standard translation of Freud's *Verwandlungen* and *Umwandlungen*).

The words of any sentence in a given natural language are, according to traditional TG theory, inserted during the generation process from a fixed (nonidiosyncratic) and finite (though expandable) lexicon of that language. For the manipulation of these elements, Chomsky's transformational component has at its disposal various optional syntactic rules, thus allowing the generation of diverse surface representations with identical underlying meanings (synonymity), such as the active sentence "Kraepelin made no reference to Freud's work" and the passive "No reference to Freud's work was made by Kraepelin." This has parallels in the psychoanalytic dream model. The "lexicon" from which the various pictorial elements of dreams are drawn may, in a sense, also be considered finite, and we saw in Chapter 2 Freud's description of optional dream work mechanisms by which underlying relations between elements in the latent dream thoughts *might* be mapped onto the manifest dream content.

But any attempts to extend these parallels only tends to highlight the differences between the two systems. Freud's dreamwork, unlike Chomsky's system, allows that various pictorial elements (more or less the equivalent of words) may condense into a single element, and that, more importantly, a pictorial element may be arbitrarily displaced by another, which may be a symbolization (a "synonym" of sorts), but is also likely to be an opposite ("antonym"). And whereas, for obvious reasons, there are syntactic mechanisms obligatorily used under appropriate triggering conditions by the traditional TG transformational component, their analogous mechanisms in Freud's dreamwork are optional, and in fact rarely availed of. A case in point, already seen in Chapter 2 (pp. 18–19), is the transformations that could—but by Freud's own account seldom do—map an underlying "either-or" or "since so-and-so, thus such-and-such was bound to happen" relation onto the manifest dream. In other cases, the dreamwork simply has no analogous mechanisms at its disposal, as with the "negative transformation," the rules that in the traditional TG model give to a negatively marked deep structure a negative representation in surface structure. Freud, we recall, stated that " 'No' seems not to exist as far as dreams are concerned."

Ambiguity is, of course, to some extent a feature of natural verbal languages. A surface structure sentence such as "Questioning psychiatrists can be boring" owes its double meaning, according to the TG model, to its possible derivation from two distinct deep structures. But a manifest dream event is far more likely than a surface structure in a natural verbal language to be traceable to two or a multitude of possible underlying meanings. As mentioned in Chapter 2, some of the problem, as Freud well recognized, is inherent in the visual nature of the dream medium. Furthermore, while linguistics has traditionally defined the sentence as the "maximum unit of grammatical analysis," in the study of dreams, its equivalent—roughly, the "event"—is more difficult to delimit. But for Freud there was a theoretical issue transcending mere practicality. Whereas in his own day he could have compared and contrasted the dream events (although he did not do so) to the visual sign-language communications of the deaf, with their extra freedom of sequencing and simultaneous presentation, today Freud could as well compare and contrast the "story grammar" schemata (to use a term from modern research) dealing with the larger narratives (sequences of events) of dreams to the supersentential structures studied by the recently emerging linguistic disciplines of discourse and text analysis. In both cases his conclusion would no doubt be that the "syntactic laws" operating on the lexical "characters" of the dream language, which he said it is "our business to discover," are hardly worthy of the name, since they are haphazardly applied when they exist at all. Constraints that play such an important role in Chomskyan theory and delimit what a story teller, even using visual sign language, cannot do (if he is to be understood) are far looser in the generation of dreams, especially according to the psychoanalytic model.

The most revolutionary feature of the TG model, setting it apart from previous descriptive or prescriptive schools, is its generative nature—"generative" in the formal, mathematical sense.[1] Mechanisms such as recursive rules for any given natural verbal language ensure that, although the number of words and morphemes in the lexicon of that language is finite, the set of different and grammatically correct sentences that can be generated is literally infinite. This "linguistic creativity" inherent in the system of every human verbal language is a central tenet of the TG school. In Chomsky's words:

> [A postinfantile] child will be able to construct and understand utterances which are quite new, and are, at the same time, acceptable sentences in his language. Every time an adult reads a newpaper, he undoubtably comes upon countless new sentences which are not at all similar, in a simple, physical sense, to any that he has seen before, and which he will recognize as sentences and understand.... (1959, p. 42)

Freud, of course, never attempted to formalize his model of dream generation mathematically, but one may safely conclude from the obvious lack of constraints that the number of possible different dream events that his model can generate—and which, in a sense, would be "acceptable" *qua* dream—is likewise infinite. It is, as we have already noted, in the matter of the reverse process, the understanding of the dream through the derivation of its supposed latent thoughts, that the analogy with Chomsky's passage breaks down. A dream is recognized and accepted as a dream (at least after awakening), but its comprehension—assuming, as the psychoanalytic school does, that there indeed is an underlying meaning—requires the techniques of a specialist.

The TG revolution provided an enormous stimulus to the newly emerging discipline of psycholinguistics, which has focused on the *midrange* production processes: what a speaker *can* say and comprehend. This is to be differentiated from a more general "language psychology" encompassing, among many other things, matters of intention: the *whens* and *whys* of a given utterance. (These involve "pragmatic competence," which Chomsky [1980, p. 224] defines, mostly for the purpose of excluding it from further discussion, as the speaker's "knowledge of conditions and manner of appropriate use [of his or her linguistic ability] in conformity with various purposes.") The transformational-generative system is, however, only an abstract model, and does not necessarily claim isomorphism with the psychological processes of the actual speaker-hearer. TG linguists have traditionally contented themselves with rules that are "descriptively adequate" rather than psychologically real. Descriptively adequate rules assign to the parts and segments of generated sentences certain labels ("noun phrase," "verb phrase," and the like) that coincide with linguistic intuitions. The actual psycholinguistic mechanisms that produce such sentences are, of course, no less well internalized in speakers who have never heard the terms "noun phrase" or "verb phrase." It is only in some special pragmatic context— more often in writing than in speaking—that one may *consciously* think of prescriptive school rules and choose one's words (or phrasing) with care.

More important from our point of view is the TG distinction between competence and performance. Due to various psychological limitations, most notably the restrictions inherent in short-term memory, the set of well-formed sentences that the human *can* in fact generate (performance) is a far smaller, probably finite, subset of the infinite set of well-formed sentences capable of being generated by the mechanisms of his internalized grammar (competence). In the same vein, the sentences that speakers actually *do* produce (performance) often deviate from the well-formedness of the sentences generated by the theoretically perfect internalized grammar (competence). Apart from short-term memory restrictions many other factors play a role, such as perceptual limitations, defective feedback, deliberate changes in structure in midsentence, and unconscious interference of the Freudian type. Such loosening of constraints in actual performance makes speech more like dream images and events, by yielding displacements (word substitutions), condensations (word-blends), disjunctions of elements (syntactic ungrammaticality), and the like.

However, it is essential to note (since, as will be discussed in Chapter 8, this may have its parallels in dream imagery) that even the errors in linguistic performance have been shown to display a certain lawfulness. So, referring back to Reverend Spooner's remark that "Patterson . . . reviewed the whole situation and *emanciated* a reasoned scheme," this was at least a "lawful" combination of English-sounding phonemes and syllables. (A permutation such as "tdnmceaaei," by contrast, would not be English-sounding; and while some of its sound combinations might conform to the phonetic rules of other languages, the combination of voiceless and voiced dental stops /t/ and /d/ is likely to be unnatural to any tongue.) Even in the conscious creation of neologisms—as when Spooner's contemporary Lewis Carroll wrote in his fantasy *Through the Looking Glass*, "Twas *brillig* and the *slithy toves* did *gyre* and *gimble* in the wabe;/All *mimsy* were the *borogroves* and the *mome raths outgrabe*"—the words are recognized as being very English-like, albeit largely nonsensical.

Not only phonological and lexical, but also syntactic and morphological errors generally occur with certain restrictions. Whereas, as mentioned in Chapter 3 (pp. 44), such errors were prized by the late–nineteenth-century *Jung-Grammatiker* linguists for offering insights into the mechanisms of language change from one generation to the next, modern psycholinguists analyze performance errors for the window they may provide on the possible psychological reality of the formal, mathematical TG rules. As one example, the performance error "A *boy who I know a boy has hair down to here*" (instead of the intended, "A boy (who(m)) I know has hair down to here") suggests a real psycholinguistic isomorphism with the "relative clause" rule in the traditional TG model, by which a noun phrase ("a boy") within the main clause is copied to the relative clause position and optionally provided with a WH-marker ("who"), while the original noun phrase is normally deleted (Fay, 1980). The fact that the original noun phrase remains in the above type of English performance error—and that its nondeletion is normal in Hebrew and an acceptable option in dialectal French (where it may merely be pronominalized)—indicates that such a relative clause copying rule may be a feature of a so-called universal grammar, in Chomsky's words "the system of principles, conditions and rules that are elements of properties of all human languages" (1976, p. 29).[2] Such a universal grammar is presumed by him to be inherent in the human mind and brain and transmitted by human DNA.

One example of a TG feature generally lacking in psychological isomorphism is the place of lexicalization (word selection), which in the traditional TG model is the final stage of sentence generation; that is, after the complete grammatical structure has been generated. Its possible psychological reality is indicated by the common experience of fishing for the right word for a meaning already in mind when trying to complete a sentence. But, on the other hand, it is also obvious that the entire grammatical structure of a sentence need not be completed before word selection takes place. This is attested to by such performance phenomena as hesitation at a juncture in a compound sentence, or even the shifting to a different construction, as in the following: "Present studies suggest that if the patient picks the right . . . uh . . . if the right problem-solving strategy is picked for the patient, a cold may actually help boost his test score." As we noted in Chapter 3 (p. 46), Kraepelin himself seemed uncertain as to the place of lexicalization in normal sentence production.

Chomsky emphasizes that the innate universal grammar predisposes the child (even with an IQ as low as about 50) to acquire a linguistic competence for his specific native language. This can take place in the absence of any specific teaching. There need only be exposure at an early enough age to a sufficient corpus of that language—a corpus which (as research has shown) is itself in fact typically limited, and degraded by all manner of performance errors. The underlying neurophysiological basis for this lifelong linguistic creativity—the "circuitry or mechanical principles by which this abstract program is realized," in Chomsky's (1980, p. 226) metaphor—is the domain of the expanding field of neurolinguistics, which has attempted to distinguish between the hardware of linguistic competence per se and the auxiliary hardware essential for normal linguistic performance (short-term memory, attention, feedback, and so on; cf. Lesser, 1978). Ethical commandments, of course, restrict any invasive experimentation on humans, but some new data has been forthcoming thanks to techniques unavailable to aphasiologists a hundred years ago: electronic stimulation of the cortex during brain surgery; measurements of event-related potentials; dichotic listening; studies of patients who have undergone commissurotomy (surgical separation) of the hemispheres as the last resort for severe intractable epilepsy; and positron-emission tomographic (PET) scans and magnetic resonance imaging. Apart from this, researchers today, as in the time of Freud and Kraepelin, still rely on observations of victims of cerebrovascular, military, and accidental neuroanatomical trauma.

Of course nontraumatic, usually transient neuropsychological conditions (fugue, drunkeness, psychotic episodes, and so on) variously affect the linguistic ability of a portion of the population. What then of our language production during the peculiar psychological and neurological conditions that all of us experience every night when dreaming?

Speech in Dreams Late in the Twentieth Century ———

In the first place, it seems necessary today to reconfirm that there *is* verbal activity in dreams. A survey of four comparatively recent popular dream psychology books (Gutheil, 1951; Faraday, 1974; Garfield, 1974; Delaney, 1979), containing a total of 177 full reports (presented in more than seven printed lines each), drawn from dream group participants, patients in therapy, and the authors themselves, shows in fact that from fifty to ninety percent of dreams include verbal dialogue or otherwise make reference to conversations. Yet in their theorizing, dream psychologists often exhibit an astonishing deafness to this aspect. Patrick Mahoney and Rajendra Singh (1975), of the Departments of English and Linguistics of the University of Montreal, describe the semiotic transformation of latent dream material into the manifest dream as being "par excellence" analogous to the translating of a "short story into a *silent* movie" (p. 224, italics added).

The philosopher George Steiner (1987), addressing a congress on "The Language of Dreams," stated

> It is a commonplace to suppose that the evolution of mythology and of human speech are concomitant and dialectically interactive. But perhaps we can take a step further. The archetypes, the *ur*-myths which we sense as arising from a no-man's land (because everyman's) just outside daylit consciousness and will, are vestigial, atavistic forms of *dreams before language*. Language is, in a sense, an attempt to interpret, to narrate dreams older than itself. (p. 116)

Perhaps most incredible is the case of the distinguished dream researcher Montague Ullman, formerly director of psychiatry at Brooklyn's Maimonides Medical Center, who presents in his coauthored book *Working With Dreams* his view that the essence of the semiotic language of dreams is "the archaic capacity for *imagery* . . . transformed into a vehicle for expressing feeling in *visual* metaphors" (Ullman & Zimmerman, 1979, p. 73, italics added). The dream specimen he himself offers to illustrate this runs (in part) as follows:

> . . . I left the office together with a woman I knew only slightly. She was *questioning* me as to why I had given unsatisfactory references for "Millie" or "Nellie."

I *explained* my reasons. I then found myself alone on the street and I suddenly realized I didn't have my handbag. . . . I *asked* someone for directions. I tried to follow the directions but found them confusing and frustrating. Finally I *asked* someone for bus fare, thinking I might as well go home. I was given a dime. . . . I then found myself *talking* with my uncle, Walter, perhaps on the phone. He told me *he had found two things from my handbag. One was a picture of my husband, myself, and our sons (taken many years ago) and the other was some form of identification card. He thought maybe I had lost the bag in a taxi rather than in the office.* (p. 55, all italics added)

As in the case of Freud's "Irma" dream, Ullman's "Walter" dream would be quite devoid of its supposed psychological import without its extensive dialogue.

Emil Kraepelin remains today virtually unique for having not only recognized dream speech, but for also having given it extensive treatment. (True, as we have noted, he also drew his specimens from the hypnagogic periods of sleep onset, rather than from dreaming proper. But there has been deafness to the verbal activity of this stage of sleep as well, as evidenced by one modern theorist's description of "the peculiar amalgam of drift, intensity, and symbolism, *all in the absence of words* [italics added], that marks the transition to sleep and dreams" [O'Shaughnessey, 1974, p. 237].) Some of Kraepelin's comments regarding the anomalies of his corpus are all the more worthy of reconsideration in the framework of modern psycho-, neuro- and theoretical linguistics, as well as the more general field of language psychology.

Kraepelin's observation regarding linguistic performance errors—that "in the dream itself, the content of the [deviant] speech utterances is commonly taken to be completely free of mistakes" and that "in dreams we accept them [speech errors] just as unquestioningly as we do all the other contradictions to our usual experience"—clearly refers to the *lack of attention to and feedback on* the execution of our dream actions, comparable, according to Kraepelin, to the situation in "sensory aphasia . . . characterized by the appearance of paraphasic disturbances which are not noticed by the speaker and therefore also not corrected by him." To the extent that there is self-awareness, Kraepelin adds, "the dreamer is, as a rule, completely convinced that he is correctly and intelligibly expressing his thoughts, even when producing the most meaningless combination of syllables."

Yet, in commenting on the comparatively small percentage of morpho-syntactic deviations in his corpus, Kraepelin also points to "drilled-in habits . . . which govern the declension of words and their position in the sentence"; and "general linguistic attitudes . . . which permit us to choose our entire mode of expression in terms of a certain language or dialect, without having to pay particular attention to individual vocabulary words and grammatical rules." This accords with the modern psycholinguistic emphasis on the *automatic nature* of syntactic processes. There may, as mentioned above, be conscious attention to the speech generation process in wakefulness, when, at crucial points, one chooses one's words (or phrasing) with care; but this is conspicuously absent from Kraepelin's descriptions of sleep speech.

As for the *deliberate input* into the speech generation process, preceding the midrange mechanisms, Kraepelin almost totally avoids the words "intend" (*beabsichtigen*), "intended/intentional" (*beabsichtigt*), and "intent" (*Absicht*). Rather he speaks only of the idea or phrase "in mind" (*vorschwebend*), which may be derailed before correct perceptual expression in dreams can be achieved.

Much of the difference between speech output in normal wakefulness and that in dreaming may be viewed as resulting from varying degrees of interaction between these three psychological factors of attention/feedback, automatic mechanisms, and intention.

As for the neurological hardware on which such processes do or do not run their course, we have noted Kraepelin's speculations about conditions such as the deadening of Wernicke's area. Today, however, much more (if still precious little) is known about the neurophysiology of dreaming and, in particular, its cyclical nature.

The Program Schedule of the Dream Theater ─────────

When Kraepelin was a professor at Dorpat in 1891, one of his students, Eduard Michelson, plotted, as part of his doctoral dissertation, several graphs of sleep depth, based on the amount of stimulus needed to wake his subjects in the course of the night. One of these graphs showed a periodicity uncannily resembling a modern hypnogram (see Figure 5.1), and represented a considerable refinement of the work of Ernst Kohlschütter (1862), who had presented a curve merely showing that the depth of sleep is far greater earlier in the night, particularly an hour after sleep onset. (Interestingly, analysis of Kolhschütter's own table values indicates that irregularities were in fact found by him but smoothed out; see Swan, 1929.) Kraepelin included Michelson's article in his *Psychologische Arbeiten*, published in 1899, the year Freud's *Traumdeutung* hit the bookstores. However, only a vague connection was made between dreaming and the regularly oscillating sleep depth.

Around the same time, there were also some indications (reported by G. Trumbell Ladd [1882], a professor of "mental and moral philosophy" at Yale University) that the experience of dreaming is accompanied by movements of the dreamer's eyes. But further advances had to wait several decades for the development of electroencephalographic (EEG) monitoring by the German psychiatrist Hans Berger. Its subsequent systematic application in the fifties, along with electrooculographic measurements, to the study of sleep by Eugene Aserinsky and Nathaniel Kleitman of the University of Chicago, determined human sleep to be of two main types which alternate with clocklike regularity

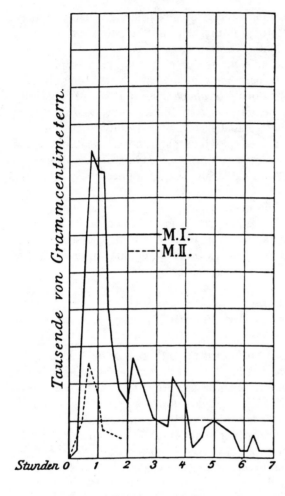

FIGURE 5.1   One of Michelson's (1899) graphs of oscillating sleep depth (in this case using himself as subject), shown above a modern EEG hynogram (27-year-old woman subject) slightly idealized for the purposes of illustration. By convention, the depth of sleep in the hypnogram is downward, whereas in Michelson's graph the depth of sleep (as measured by the amount of auditory stimulus needed to awaken the subject) is upwards. The recurring periods of REM dreaming in the hypnogram are shown by the heavy lines. In Michelson's article only a vague connection was made between dreaming and the oscillating sleep depth.

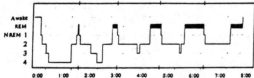

throughout the night: REM (rapid eye movement) periods, which occur four or five times in the course of an average night and take up some twenty percent of our sleep time; and NREM (non rapid eye movement) periods, which, in several variations, make up the rest. Although this division was at first purely physiological (based predominantly on the distinct "signatures" of brain wave patterns and ocular activity for each of the two states), Aserinsky and Kleitman, along with William Dement, soon established that when subjects are awakened from REM periods they are usually able to report a vivid sequential hallucinatory experience—in a word, a dream—and that this is far less often the case with awakenings from NREM periods, which are sooner characterized by more thoughtlike mental activity (Aserinsky & Kleitman, 1953; Dement & Kleitman, 1957). The distinction is so pronounced that REM sleep is now frequently referred to in the scientific literature as D-sleep, simultaneously indicating an almost wakeful-like desynchronization in the EEG pattern on the physiological level and the vivid dreaming experience on the phenomenological level.

This discovery has had profound theoretical implications. Freud, having died in 1939, never knew of the cyclical nature of dream periods. In and of itself, any individual hypnogram (such as in Figure 5.1) need not have presented Freud with a problem, and in fact might have been amenable to a posteriori explanation in terms of mechanisms in his *Project*. (See Figure 2.2) Because the *post coenam et coitum* state (after eating and copulating) is sleep inducing, Freud postulated that, conversely, the absence of such gratification threatens to disrupt sleep, and that the dream, being guardian of sleep, must therefore give temporary hallucinatory gratification. The first discharge of accumulated endogenous stimuli into the perceptual areas of the brain, experienced as a dream and appearing as the first brief REM period in the hypnogram, would allow a period of dreamless (NREM) sleep to follow, during which new endogenous stimuli are stored until there is again pressure for discharge. The later it is in the night, the longer it has been since any actual "coena et coitus," and therefore the more intense must be the stimuli and the shorter and shallower the nondreaming periods between discharges into the perceptual areas of the brain. By the end of the night, saturation threatens, awakening ensues, and satisfaction of biological needs must be sought in the real world by means of motor actions governed by higher ego functions.

A great theoretical problem for Freud would, however, have been posed by the fact that there is little variation in sleep-stage patterns from one person to the next, and in the same person over time; and that the variations that do appear can hardly be viewed as following Freud's basic biological principle. Research has amply shown that the coming and going of REM periods in the course of the night bears no relation to the degree of instinctual gratification obtained prior to falling asleep.

Along the ontogenetic scale, electroencephalographic monitoring has also clearly established that REM periods alternates with NREM periods in human infants and even in the human fetus, taking up, in fact proportionately far more time than in older children and adults (Roffwarg, Munzio, & Dement, 1966). Phylogenetically, cyclic REM sleep patterns in infrahuman mammals have been shown to extend from the ape down to the opossum, with regular REM bursts also being recorded in those other warmblooded animals, the birds (cf. Snyder, 1966; the status of reptiles and amphibians is problematic, with some researchers viewing their whole sleep as basically a form of NREM, while others sooner discern REM characteristics—see Horne, 1988, Ch. 7). While Freud had little to say as to whether dreams in these creatures, too, serve for instinctual gratification (in fact he allowed in *Beyond the Pleasure Principle* that "there was also a time before the purpose of dreams was the fulfilment of wishes" [1920/1955b, p. 33]), he made it clear that dreams in humans after childhood have a far more complex function. Millions of years of cerebral development and the recent rapid evolution of human culture and civilization have brought with them layers of conflicts such as the Oedipal and Electra complexes which interact with the simple need for instinctual gratification to produce—in accordance with the degree of one's repressive mechanisms and the varying success of the sublimation of one's drives—anything from mere perturbations to a veritable stormchart of opposing psychodynamic forces. Theoretically, this, too, should be reflected in the amount of time spent dreaming.

Electroencephalographic monitoring has, however, also clearly shown that the internal biological clock that raises and lowers the curtain on our dream theater is generally as oblivious to the psychodynamic state of the sleeper as it is to the amount of instinctual gratification obtained prior to sleep. (There is, of course, disruption of the usual sleep architecture in conditions such as severe depression or mania, but this cannot be elucidated on a depth-psychology basis.) This obviously means that the one and a half to two hours of nightly *dreaming* in and of itself can no longer be called a symptom, even if the possibility is left open that the content of some dreams may be symptomatic. Whereas the boil on Freud's scrotum was symptomatic and pathological, a more suitable medical analogy for dreaming might be the accelerated heart rhythm that comes from physical exertion. In and of itself this is of course normal, but to the trained ear it may also unmask various pathological conduction defects usually obscured in the resting state. (In his later writings, Freud [cf. 1925/1959a], although unaware of the universal cyclical nature of dreaming, in fact sometimes tended towards a less symptomatic view.)

Another interesting neurophysiological development was the discovery in the sixties, by Michel Jouvet of the University of Lyons, of the activity of ponto-geniculo-occipital (PGO) impulses during REM sleep. As the name implies, these originate in the pontine reticular formation of the brain stem. Some of the impulses go to the geniculate body of the thalamus—which in wakefulness relays signals from the eye to the brain—while other impulses travel directly to the occipital cortex, which is involved with visual perception. As will be discussed in later sections, these PGO impulses are believed to carry commands for the timing and the direction of the eye movements to which REM sleep owes its name; however, such commands are probably devoid of information in the strict sense of the term. On a more global level, some EEG researchers have claimed—although this has recently been strongly disputed—that the transitions from wakefulness to NREM sleep to REM sleep are accompanied by shifts in dominance from the major ("left") cortical hemisphere, known to be responsible for verbal and logical thinking, to the minor ("right") hemisphere, involved in more imagistic and creative thought. (See Gaillard, 1989, for an overview.)

Be this as it may, the states of our neurological hardware during REM sleep may represent physiological concomitants to the varying proportions of automatic mechanisms, attention/feedback, and intention, which may account for many of the differences between everyday human linguistic performance and the "language" (both in the metaphorical and the literal, verbal sense) of human REM dreams. But whereas systematic descriptions of everyday linguistic performance and of the metaphorical language of dreams are abundant, similarly reliable norms for verbal behavior in REM dreaming have been lacking, despite (or in part due to) Kraepelin's pioneering contributions to the field. In the next chapter, experiment results will be reported in which such norms, however provisional, are established. We will then be better able to return to the psychodynamic and neurological theorizing by Freud, Freudians, and neo-Freudians on the dichotomy between the primary and secondary processes previously discussed in Chapter 2 of this book. We will also examine how these relate to Kraepelin's pathological and neuroanatomical considerations and to recent psycholinguistic models, including the quasi-neurological concept of spreading activation, and to the functioning and interplay of the mental factors of automatic mechanisms, attention/feedback, and intention. After the presentation in Chapter 7 of the results of a second experiment dealing with pragmatic linguistic competence, automatic mechanisms, and superordinate and subordinate cognitive systems in sleep, the book will conclude (Chapter 8) with a discussion of the implications for the most recent models of dream generation, the "meaning" of dreams, the use of dreams as an adjunct in psychotherapy, and possible future directions in dream research that may tell us more not only about the nature of dreaming, but of speech and language as well.

Notes

1. For the purposes of explicating the formal, generative nature of the TG revolution in linguistics, references are made to the "*traditional*" TG model of the late 1950s and 1960s. Since the 1970s, however, there has been a shift toward a system consisting of quite simple and general construction-aspecific rules or better rule schemas such as "move alpha" (move any constituent in the syntactic construction anywhere) and "delete alpha" (delete any constituent). A direct consequence of this would be "overgeneration": the output of many syntactic structures that should not be produced (apart from all those that should be), some of which one may even call (in the popular sense) "dreamlike."

In order to prevent overgeneration, a system of universal conditions on the application of rule schemas and their output structures has been formulated. Whether "move alpha" and "delete alpha" apply or not is not an inherent property of the rule schema (as it was with the traditional model), but is now determined by independent triggering principles of grammar, for example, Case Theory (cf. Chomsky, 1986). Whatever the revisions to the theory, however, the revolutionary nature of TG for linguistics still lies in the formalness of the model and the striving for a system of rules that can actually generate (preferably in a way that accords with the intuitions of actual speakers) all and only the grammatical utterances of a given language, and provide insight into underlying relations between various sentences.

2. Nonetheless, on other psycholinguistic grounds, newer variants of the TG model, referred to in the previous note, have "who" already present somewhere in the deep structure, which is then placed by the "move alpha" rule in the appropriate position in the generation of this type of surface structure.

Dreaming Linguistic Performance

In his monograph on dream speech, Kraepelin himself wonders "how far the findings collected by us, and consequently the conclusions drawn from them, will prove to be universally valid when checked against other persons."

This healthy bit of caution was well advised, since Kraepelin's corpus may have been drawn heavily from states other than REM dreaming proper, as well as having been assembled in a very selective manner, with one subject (the researcher himself) providing the vast majority of specimens. Kraepelin obviously makes no pretense that this largely introspectionist study compares to the kinds of rigorous, multipatient research (discussed in Chapter 3, p. 38) on which his enduring place in the annals of medicine deservedly rests. Furthermore, certain powerful concepts and tools were unavailable a century ago. These include not only notions from transformational grammar, such as linguistic creativity, but also stratificational grammar, quasi-neurological spreading activation, tests of significance, new measures of syntactic complexity, and the modern classification of speech errors.

All this motivated the first of our two experiments, drawing inspiration from Kraepelin's study, but with many differences in methodology and analysis, and also addressing certain psychoanalytic issues which Kraepelin studiously ignored.

Partial Replication of Kraepelin's Experiment

In response to articles in several regional Dutch newspapers calling for "good dream recallers" for a home experiment, some two hundred potential subjects requested more information and the appropriate material. These respondents were each sent a detailed instruction sheet and experiment form along with a postpaid reply envelope. Subjects were asked to study the instructions carefully and, if they wished to participate, to return the forms either when they had filled in all ten sections on the forms or by a stated deadline approximately five months after mailing if they had not completed all sections by then. Duly returned forms from 64 female and 14 male subjects, of ages ranging from

13 to 82 years (median 26), comprising a corpus of 580 utterances from as many different dreams, along with concomitant data, supplied the basis of the analysis to be reported below.[1]

Subjects were instructed to fill in the next day's date at night before retiring. Upon awakening by alarm clock at their usual morning hour, they were to write down on the forms the last line of dialogue (or monologue), if there had been any, said in the dream by themselves or another personage if a dream had been in progress. The instructions stressed the importance of not reporting dreams remembered following spontaneous (non–alarm clock) awakening, or dreamlets ensuing from drifting back to sleep. Emphasis was placed on the distinction between REM (or REM-like) dreaming and NREM (or NREM-like) mentation, because verbal material only from the former was to be reported. We impressed upon the subjects the importance of avoiding all selectivity and of reporting each last recalled utterance as nearly verbatim as possible, making no corrections. It was made clear to the subjects that dream utterances could be by wakeful standards either normal or syntactically or semantically deviant.

Along with the last recalled utterances, the subjects were asked to record immediately on the forms by whom and to whom the utterance was said, and in what language or dialect. (If the speaker or hearer was not familiar, the subject was requested to describe him briefly, the term "unknown" thus being restricted to indiscernible characters.) Two additional questions asked whether the dream was in black and white or in color and how long it was thought to have been in progress before awakening. (These questions were intended to help discourage reporting of NREM mentation, and they are not discussed further here.)

The subjects were requested subsequently to judge whether the last recalled utterance was one that they might say, or hear someone else say, in normal waking life in the given language or dialect. If the utterance was deemed to be deviant in any way, the subjects were instructed to reformulate it so that it would be normal. Finally, the subjects were asked to state whether they believed themselves ever actually to have said or heard the utterance previously in waking life with the same or similar words, and, if they had, to write down as accurately as possible the wording of the original and to state when, by whom, and to whom it had been said. (None of these questions had to be answered immediately following awakening, but rather sometime in the course of the morning.)

A specimen dream was provided with an appropriately completed form. This included samples of a nondeviant utterance and of a syntactically and semantically deviant utterance along with a reformulated version.

In tabulating the results, the first and most basic question is the frequency of dream dialogue: whether dreams are in general more like "talkies." or like silent movies. Every 5.1 awakenings on average resulted in the reporting of a "last line" from an ongoing dream. If we assume that in the early morning the probability of the sleeper's awakening during dreaming (a REM "hit") is between one in two and one in three, then roughly half the dream interruptions yielded utterances sufficiently close to the moment of awakening, and in sufficiently clear form, to be consolidated in memory and subsequently reported. Comparisons with Kraepelin are problematical, due to the restricted nature of his data. But our figures are in broad agreement with the ratio of dream dialogue to dream reports found in Freud's *Traumdeutung*, in the previously mentioned recent dream books, and in other research.[2]

Some continuity with verbal behavior in waking life is shown by the fact that 551 (95.0%) of the 580 dream utterances were entirely in the subjects' Standard Dutch or entirely in their own dialect, while only 19 (3.3%) were entirely in a foreign language. The latter, however, were overrepresented among the specimens that the subjects rated as deviant.

For 96 (16.6%) of the 580 corpus specimens, the question of whether the utterance was of the kind one can say oneself or hear someone else say in normal waking life was answered in the negative, or otherwise doubtfully, by the dreamers (see Figure 6.1). The eight of these entirely in a foreign language were excluded from further analysis. The remaining 88 utterances, wholly or mostly in Dutch (or Dutch dialect), were rated for their acceptability by two Dutch applied linguists, working together. For 56 of these 88 utterances there was complete agreement that they were *acceptable* syntactically and semantically. For 22 of the specimens (representing 3.9% of the 561 Dutch utterances), there was agreement between the applied linguist scorers that the utterances were unacceptable in normal waking life. The remaining 10 specimens (1.8% of all the Dutch utterances) were rated intermediately: either deemed by both scorers to be borderline cases (for which, for example, a very far-fetched context would have to be imagined for them to be appropriate), or in a few instances rated as acceptable by one scorer but as unacceptable or borderline by the other.

That almost two-thirds of the "unsayable" Dutch utterances should be deemed acceptable by our scorers was in part due to the subjects' interpretation of the question. Partially with a view toward not making the instructions too complicated for the subjects, we deliberately restricted our analysis to the acceptability by wakeful standards of our corpus specimens in and of themselves, irrespective of the dream context. A slip of the tongue is a deviation from what the speaker had in mind to say; it need not, however, result in an utterance inherently semantically or syntactically deviant. In 21 of the 56 cases in which both scorers found the "unsayable" utterance acceptable, the supposed nature of the slip can be determined from the "corrected" version supplied by the subject. These will be noted in the discussion of the various types of errors in the genuinely deviant specimens (preceded by "*") and borderline specimens (preceded by "?").

The remaining 35 utterances—for which both our scorers disagreed with the subjects as to their "unsayability" in waking life, and for which the nature

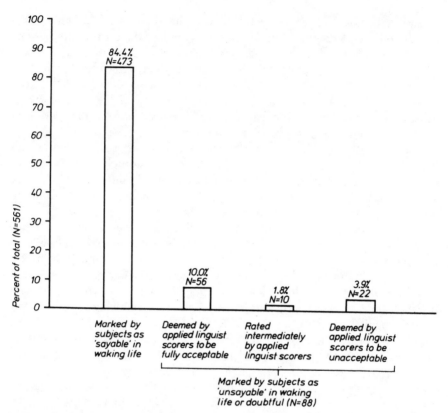

FIGURE 6.1 Acceptable ("sayable/hearable in waking life") versus not acceptable ("not sayable/hearable in waking life") Dutch recalled dream utterances (total 561), as grouped by subjects and applied linguist scorers. The results indicate a high degree of syntactic and semantic grammaticality for recalled dream speech.

of their supposed slips cannot be deduced—are excluded from further analysis. It is, however, worth noting here that two of these (specimens 202 and 275) were considered unsayable due solely to their verbal aggression.[3] (The specimen numbers refer to the original corpus in my dissertation.)

Our classification, though similar to Kraepelin's, is based on more recent studies on errors in linguistic performance. Three of the deviant utterances discussed below are each classified into two categories rather than one.

It should be noted that syntactic errors are exceedingly rare, being limited to just two of the 561 Dutch specimens: (65) *"*Go now, then maybe we can say to it,*" perhaps an interrupted utterance, but not marked as such; (91) *"*I and the world is big enough after all,*" which the subject took to mean "There are so many possibilities (of where to go)."(Cf. Salzarulo and Cipolli [1974], who state that, of the 104 sleep speech specimens they assembled, it was never a question of scattered words, but of verbal sequences correctly organized in one or more sentences.)

Clear–cut semantic anomalies seem to be present in only four specimens; for example, (459) *"What did you say? Spartre's house lives there?" and (311) *"How many flowers must I peck against each other?" There are six borderline specimens; for example, (513) ?"No, that's his usual place. Actually he was sitting at a table," and (561) ?"I didn't think we would come down matured." Fifteen other specimens are of acceptable everyday Dutch, though marked deviant by the respective subjects since they apparently did not express the thought in mind; for example, (280) "My hair is getting all red, darn!" which was intended to mean "My hair is getting less red."(the dye is wearing off), and (30) "I forgot [to do] the mirror with the panes," for "the mirror and the panes."

Lexical substitution due to phonetic similarity (cf. Shattuck–Hufnagel & Klatt, 1980) is found in only one deviant specimen: (408) *"There are enough mill walking around here, Mill," for "There are enough millionaires walking around here, Emile." There is one borderline case: (43) ?"I always put on my slippers and my cardigan," of which the last word, in English in the original, denotes "garbardine." This specimen is also classed as a borderline case of language mixing. One specimen, thought to be perfectly acceptable Dutch, is a clear deviation from the intended communication: (40) "That is an extra cherry tree," for "That is a real [echte] cherry tree."

There are no clear–cut deviant utterances due to lexical substitution on semantic similarity (cf. Hotopf, 1980), and only two borderline specimens, one of which is (47) ?"You thought, no doubt, that it was warmer tomorrow." Three perfectly acceptable though "unsayable" utterances include (161) "Now, a soapbox, for example," where what is meant is a "soap dish."

Two apparent lexical substitutions, both deviant, are untraceable (cf. Dell & Reich, 1980), for example, (189) *"If it is upright it'll be struck by the most flux."

Word–blends (cf. Ellis, 1980) are found in seven deviant specimens; for example, (347) *"I'll pass it [to him] majestialcally;" (198) *"Partly a hoptable;" and (124) *"This is a landpaste, landpaste, landpaste." from "border" ("landpas" in dialect) and "toothpaste" ("tandpaste"). See also (119) below. One word–blend is a borderline case: (491) ? "Come, I'll make a last little rice [rijstje] for you again," from "leftover" ("restje") and "rice"("rijst").

Four utterances owe their deviance to nonexistent proper names derived from existing names: (410) *"Mareyon," from "Marian" or "Marion," (492) *"Recently the Tule Course stopped the course," from "Teleac Course" (the Dutch Public Broadcasting Foundation) or "tai chi course." (See also specimen 459.) Two other specimens contain completely acceptable proper names, though not the intended names.

Language mixing (or dialect mixing) occurs in five deviant utterances. For example, (119) *"Gewoon, reigh-sluddering, gewoon [Simply, reigh-

sluddering, simply]." ("reigh-sluddering" being also classed as an unacceptable word-blend); and (494) *"*Meneer, ik oefen uw vrouw de mogelijkheid. U kunt ook meteen naar Rome, the other night [Sir, I practice your wife the opportunity. You can also go immediately to Rome, the other night].*" (This is also classed as semantically unacceptable due to "oefen" ("practice"), apparently a contamination from the English "offer" or a lexical substitution due to phonetic similarity to the formal Dutch "offreren." There are no borderline instances (but note specimen 43 above).

We remark that syntagmatic phonological errors (the interchange, anticipation, or duplication of phonemes), common in slips of the tongue in normal speech (cf. Söderpalm Talo, 1980) are absent from our corpus, while a few paradigmatic errors (substitution of a phomene), more typical of aphasic speech, are represented. Otherwise, however, our specimens are largely devoid of the severely deviant aphasiclike utterances that are not uncommon in (articulated) somniloquy and are so conspicuous in Kraepelin's corpus.

The Single–Mindedness of Dreams and the Unified Model of Speech Production

The veteran sleep researcher Allan Rechtschaffen of the University of Chicago attributes many of the interesting phenomenological characteristics of REM dreams, including features that Freud termed primary-process manifestations, to "single-mindedness." This refers to the absence of a second, reflective, or evaluative stream of thought that seemingly monitors the first. However, he rejects any "disorganized brain" description of the dreaming process, stating that there is "neither the kaleidoscope of unrelated images, nor the cacophony of isolated thoughts and words one might expect in truly disorganized consciousness." (Rechtschaffen, 1978, p. 106).[4] This description of what dreams, and particularly dream utterances, are *not* is well supported by our data. But it comes close to a description of what hypnagogic and hypnopompic dreamlets *are*—if, that is, we are to consider Kraepelin's corpus as representative.

As mentioned in Chapter 2 (p. 21), Alfred Hoche dismisses his sleep speech specimens as the rattlings of an "idling mill." Even pop psychologist Ann Faraday (1972), who makes a business out of the supposedly life-changing insights revealed by REM dreams, considers hypnagogic dreamlets unlikely to represent much more than "noise" from the brain (pp. 80–81; for classical descriptions of the "kaleidoscopic" visual aspects of hypnagogic dreamlets, as well as their "cacaphonic" verbal characteristics, see Maury, 1847, 1857). Indeed, for want of a better explanation, one is tempted to dismiss most hypnagogic verbal hallucinations as being like the linguistic performance one hears in the movies when some robot—evidently programmed to satisfy the good old Chomskyan condition of being able to generate all and only the sentences of a given natural language—has its hardware squirted randomly with a watergun. However, an analogy having more explicatory power is worth seeking.

In fact, considerations of the hypnagogic state invite comparison with the quasi-neurological Unified Model of sentence generation developed by psychologists Gary Dell and Peter Reich (1980) of the University of Toronto and based, incidentally, not on Chomsky's TG but on another modern, mathematically formalized system, Sidney Lamb's stratificational grammar. The Unified Model (see Figure 6.2) incorporates the biophysical/psychological concept of "spreading activation," which actually shows certain similarities to the notion of the flow of excitations (cathexes) found in Freud's 1895 *Project for a Scientific Psychology* referred to in Chapter 2 (pp. 14–15) of this book.[5]

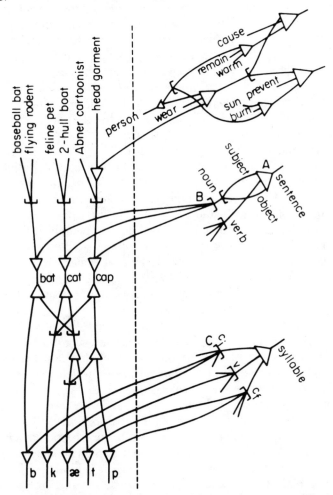

FIGURE 6.2 Fragment of relational network grammar. (From G. S. Dell & P. A. Reich, 1980.)

In brief, the Unified Model relates to the concept of parent schemas activating child schemas. The model allows a certain "leakage" in the signal system, a reverberation between the various levels. On the one hand, this dispenses with the need for an independent "covert monitor" component. "The spreading activation between superordinate and subordinate linguistic units automatically produces editing," write Dell and Reich (1980, pp. 280–281), so that "one need not speak of 'editors' at all, only of the natural process of speech production." This is generalized in the "theory of action" of cognitive scientist Donald A. Norman of the University of California at San Diego. The path from intention to deed consists of the activation of child schemas for the component parts of the action sequence, and then the appropriate triggering of schemas when the conditions match those required for their operations. These child schemas run largely "automatically, without need for intervention except at critical choice points" (Norman, 1981, p. 4; cf. also Kathyrine Bock's [1982] review of the concept of the autonomous syntactic component which should operate outside of awareness, may operate in the absence of intention, and should not interfere with other processes). On the other hand, the Unified Model with its leakage between various levels also allows for the generation of occasional slips of the tongue ("Freudian" and otherwise) such as are observed in the linguistic performance of normal subjects.

Although the developers of the Unified Model nowhere treat dream speech, they consider the principles involved to be applicable to internal actions as well as to external ones. In line with the metamorphosis that the psychic system in Freud's *Project* undergoes in sleep (the unbounded, freely moving cathexes shown in Figure 2.2, p. 17), in the Unified Model one can imagine a similar modification by which, due to neurological conditions, a far greater leakage in the signal system is allowed—a freely flowing spread of activation that generates severely deviant utterances by defeating the covert monitor function and perhaps by reducing the resources to below the threshold for selection of the automatic processes. The output could, conceivably, resemble Kraepelin's corpus in many respects.

However, it should be kept in mind that Freud's description of the neurological system dominated by unbounded, freely-moving cathexes applied in principle to *dreaming in general* and not specifically to the hypnagogic state. The "Autodidasker" dreamlet in the *Traumdeutung*, which was composed almost entirely of this one-word neologism (and to the tracking down of whose supposed disparate roots Freud was able to devote several pages of free-association), is the most Kraepelin-like of his verbal specimens. But such an utterance is, as discussed in Chapter 3 (p. 47), quite the exception that proves the rule in the *Traumdeutung* reports, as it is in our own dream corpus. Although Freud gives no relevant information, it would appear to have been hypnagogic.

In terms of Dell and Reich's Unified Model, it therefore seems that, in view of the infrequency of such deviations, the spreading activation and the leakage in the system during REM dreaming is kept at a level similar to that found in wakefulness, thereby ensuring an adequate degree of covert monitoring and only occasional deviant output.

Pseudo–Overt Monitoring

The delimiting of covert and overt monitoring/editing in the case of dream speech is not, however, without difficulty for the psychologist (not to mention the philosopher). We have seen Kraepelin's observation that in wakefulness, sensory aphasics lack "overt editing" in that, in contrast to normal speakers, they seldom correct their errors. In hallucinated dream speech, whether REM or hypnagogic, there is, of course, no actual articulation prior to reporting (disregarding the rare instances of concomitant somniloquy). Therefore, almost by definition, there can be none of the overt monitoring/editing that in wakefulness takes place after speech is produced.

In waking life, the covert editing process of detecting and correcting errors in inner speech during the planning stages is by nature resistant to empirical study by means other than introspection. (In any case, as has just been discussed, this function has largely been dispensed with in recent psycholinguistic models.) For this very reason, psycholinguists have a potential interest in the occurrence during REM sleep of what might be termed "pseudo-overt" monitoring/editing: reflection upon a hallucinated dream utterance during or just after hallucinated articulation, and even its hallucinated correction—despite the general "single-mindedness" of dream thinking. To the extent we see dream speech as a form of internal speaking (cf. Werner & Kaplan, 1963), investigation of this phenomenon may afford insights into inner speech, which is otherwise refractory to empirical study. More importantly for dream researchers, however, pseudo-overt editing tells something about the extent of our relectiveness in dreams in general, and may therefore indicate the range of functioning that can be allowed the hypothetical "dream monitor" proposed by some theorists (cf. Moser, Pfeifer, Schneider, von Zeppelin, & Schneider, 1983). Furthermore, it has implications for the reliability of recalled dream speech for faithfully representing "actual" dream speech, implications which will be dicusssed in the section.

In the *Traumdeutung*, Freud reports an instance of pseudo-overt editing in one of his own dreams: "I said [in English], referring to one of Schiller's works, '*It is from . . . ,*' but, noticing my mistake, I corrected myself: '*It is by [Schiller]*.'" The latter form was confirmed by Freud's addressee in the dream, who commented to his sister, "*Yes, he said that right*" (1900/1953a, p. 456). In discussing another dream, Freud reports that "I exercised my critical faculties during the dream and noticed my mistake when I said '*Non vixit*' instead of '*Non vivit.*'" (p. 442).[6] This would appear to be inconsistent with his overall dream theory. However, that Freud does not consider such use of critical faculties unusual is shown by his remark that this is merely one of the "many characteristics of dreams," and that "self-correction in dreams, which seems so marvellous to some writers, need not occupy our attention." We have also seen Hacker's self-correction when, in trying on some tight-fitting boots in an English shoe store, he says *"Please, have you these boots smaller?"* and realizes in the dream that (in typical Freudian fashion) this is the opposite of what he meant. Hoche, for his part, notes that, although relatively infrequent, "actual slips of the tongue [may be] recognized as such in the dream itself, and may even be corrected in it," and Kraepelin similarly states that "in three other cases, a word was recognized in the dream itself as being incorrect, and in one case was actually corrected."

In the above examples, choosing one's words with care seems to be as prevalent with foreign languages in dreams as it is with foreign languages in wakefulness. Furthermore, the very existence of foreign language utterances in dreams, even when not accompanied by deliberate reflection or (pseudo-) overt monitoring, lends support to the contention that sentence formation, rather than just conceptualization, takes place in the dream proper. Hacker remarks, "Very many dreams contain no such [linguistic expression] and are clothed in verbal form only in the telling," but doubtlessly he would not count his English shoe store specimen among such cases. (Let it be noted, however, that specimens like Hacker's are at one end of an apparent continuum. Toward the other extreme it is certainly not unheard-of for awakened dreamers, to report in their *native* language the exact content of a dream utterance while maintaining that in the dream itself they "knew" it to be in a specific *foreign language*, perhaps even one of which they have little or no command.)

In our own corpus, we find an interesting instance of pseudo-overt editing: (498) *"Ha, ha, each in turn [ha, ha, om de beurt]."* This was a correction by a non-self actor of the dreamer's previous line of dialogue (written, as an option, on the back of the form), *"En dan om-ste-beurt,"* a Dutch children's expression, which the dreamer's interlocutor apparently considered immature. Another case of the exercise of the critical language faculty is specimen (126) *"A-P-F-E-L? Oh, like in German,"* said by the dreamer to a girlfriend. The lines leading up to this (again written voluntarily on the back of the form) were as follows: Girlfriend: *"We've got a new baby"*; dreamer: *"What's her name?"*; girlfriend: *"Apple"*; dreamer: *"How do you spell that? A-P-P-L-E?"*; girlfriend: *"No, A-P-F-E-L."*

The Factor of Secondary Revision

Not dissimilar to the problem of defining overt and covert editing in the dreaming state is the determination of the extent of the contribution to recalled and reported dream speech of waking processes as opposed to what Freud termed the "dreamwork" proper. Here the word "waking" is intended in both its senses:

"waking up" and "wakeful." Dream speech has the advantages over other dream elements of being easily amenable to direct reporting in the modality (words) in which it was experienced and of being especially quantifiable. But in contrast to daytime speech, this output is by nature inaccessible to direct observation by the experimenter (unless, like Kraepelin, one serves as one's own subject, with all the disadvantages this entails). Thus dream speech presents the problems inherent in all research into cognitive processes in sleep: the unmanipulability of the variables and the intervention of what Freud termed "secondary revision."

A version of the ancient three-component model of sentence generation adopted by Kraepelin (see Chapter 3, p. 45) has also been incorporated into recent psycholinguistic models: *Inventio-dispositio* is called the "conceptualizer"; *elecutio*, the "formulator"; and *pronuntio*, the "articulator" (cf. Kempen & Van Wijk, 1981). One may assume that, since virtually no articulation, but only pseudo-articulation, can occur in dreams, the articulator component can only function in reporting a dream utterance after awakening.[7] The question then remains: Where among the inputs and outputs of the other two components (the conceptualizer and the formulator) should the demarcation be placed between the contribution of dreaming and waking processes to the generation of recalled dream speech?

The above instances of "pseudo-overt editing" in dreams found in anecdotal specimens as well as in our dream corpus strongly indicate that such specimens represent the formulation of dreaming proper. But to what extent should the high degree of syntactic and semantic well-formedness which characterizes most of the other specimens of our corpus, not corrected in the dream, also be seen as representing the output of the "dreamwork" itself? Highly relevant here is Kraepelin's lament at the beginning of his monograph about the trials and tribulations in his attempts to remember precisely his dream speech utterances after awakening. We recall that Freud compares the contribution of secondary revision in the generation of acceptable dream dialogue to the inadvertent process when "in reading, we fill in any letters or syllables that may have been accidently omitted." But Chomsky, approaching this phenomenon from the other side, includes under an adult's linguistic competence that he "be able to determine slight distortions or misprints" in reading new sentences (1959, p. 42). As has been shown by psychologist James Lackner (1980) of Brandeis University and phonetician Anthony Cohen (1980) of the University of Utrecht, there is indeed an unconscious tendency on the part of subjects in (wakeful) experiment situations involving "sentence shadowing" to perceive deviant sentences as correct and (despite instructions to the contrary) to report them in corrected form. But experiments have also indicated that this inadvertent correcting operates only in the case of sentences with a limited degree of deviation (Quirk & Svartvik, 1966). It may therefore be assumed that the sentential output of the formulator in dreams, even if not verifiably perfect, cannot be too deviant. At least this can be said of utterances that are indeed reported: Kraepelin sounds a cautionary note in this regard when he inversely correlates his ability to retain an utterance with the degree of its nonsensical-ness. Hoche reports quite similar difficulties in trying to commit to memory an "insufficiently logical or grammatical structure or . . . a nonsensicality of content which doesn't permit associative connections." Severely deviant utterances may be resistant to reporting, and all the more if, unlike Kraepelin and his colleagues, one is not a practiced introspectionist.[8]

Replay Hypothesis and Mundaneness

In Chapter 2 we examined Freud's "replay hypothesis," by which he maintained that dream dialogue is essentially drawn from utterances that the dreamer has previously heard or said in wakefulness (see pp. 28–31). This represents, in modern terms, a denial that our language faculty in the dreaming state is capable of the "linguistic creativity" highlighted by Chomsky and the TG linguists. (For Freud, even the instances of self-correction in the dream were presumably taken lock, stock, and barrel from thoughts already present in the latent dream material.)

The replay mechanism postulated by Freud can be said to have found at least potential support in the studies of neurologists Wilder Penfield and Karl Lashley and their colleagues in Montreal in the 1950s, in which short, painless cortical stimulation by electrodes during surgery seemed to result in the conscious subject's vividly experiencing of what might be called a video replay of something recorded in the past (cf. Penfield & Jasper, 1954). That recordings may be retrieved even of events long ago corresponds to the "hypermnesic" character Freud attributes to some dreams. The "videotape replay" in the Penfield experiments clearly included auditory (and verbal) as well as visual material. Psychiatrist and sleep researcher Ernest Hartmann (1973) of the Tufts University School of Medicine, although not mentioning verbal conversation specifically, reasonably proposes that during REM periods sporadic ponto-geniculo-occipital (PGO) neural impulses discharged from the brain stem and arriving at the cortex (see Chapter 5, pp. 220–221) may be responsible for introducing into the dream scenario, à la Penfield, certain elements freshly retrieved from memory which the dreaming mind then does its best to assimilate. While the implied haphazardness of such retrieval of stored material threatens to deprive the dream of much of the psychological significance that Freud attributed to it, Hartmann suggests that there is method in the madness: The primary process in dreaming—primitive connections, large discharges of energy, opposites occurring together—can all be seen as characteristic of a "re-connecting" procedure in which daytime residues are linked to large, older, "primitive" brain storage systems.

The still quite undetermined role of PGO spikes and memory consolidation in dreams will come in for greater consideration in Chapter 8. But as for

Freud's replay hypothesis in particular, many cognitive psychologists look at the way Penfield has interpreted his data as rather naive, since it implies that memory is reproductive rather than constructive. Cognitive psychologists are more inclined to view these findings not as elicitation of specific memory tracks but rather as stimulation of mechanisms that generate plausible confabulations of things that might or might not have actually happened in the patients' past.

With a view toward testing Freud's replay hypothesis, we included in our experiment the question of whether the dream utterance was deemed to have been heard or said by the subject previously in waking life with the same, or similar, words. This was answered by the respective subjects for 548 of the specimens. Of these, only 8.0% were thought by their respective dreamers to have been heard or said (and in two cases, read) by them on the *Traumtag* (the day before the dream). For example, the subject who dreamt that she had said to her girfriend (14) "*Yes, but then, if you ask me, we'd better hurry up*" later recollected that on the previous day she had said to her mother,"If we want to catch the train, we'd better hurry up." This percentage is on the same order of magnitude as Hoche's: "The associative genesis of my dream speech-images is recognizable with satisfying certainty in a fifth of the cases, and then the presentation material is of an indifferent content, which usually the day before had been the object of interest, even if only very fleetingly (conversation, reading material, activity, etc.)." This is also as might have been predicted on purely theoretical grounds with reference to the concept of spreading activation. Although Dell and Reich do allow for the storage of whole "memorized texts." and "cliché phrases," no degree of spreading activation or leakage short of causing trauma to the system's hardware would be expected to deprive the system of its normal functioning while allowing the associative activation of these, and only these, memorized texts.

Our modest figure does, however, increase appreciably when we extend the boundaries of when the "recording" may have been made, in line with Freud's less restrictive comment that the replay may be drawn from the previous *days*. A cummulative total of 14.1% of the 548 utterances were deemed by their respective dreamers to have been said or heard previously in waking life on the week leading up to the dream (including the Traumtag). An additional 1.5% of the specimens were deemed to have been said or heard the week prior to this *Traumwoche*. Another 9.1% of the total, mostly of a very commonplace nature, were marked as having been said or heard in waking life, but without any indication as to when. In toto, therefore, 44.5% of the utterances were deemed to have been said or heard (or read) previously in the respective subjects' waking lives. But, unfortunately for Freud's replay hypothesis, fewer than one-tenth of these had been experienced on the Traumtag. That many utterances should have been marked as having been previously said or heard *sometime* in waking life seems therefore sooner to be attributed to their somewhat commonplace nature: a general lack of creativity in the sense of originality, rather than a lack of linguistic creativity in the Chomskyan sense.[9]

Indeed, perhaps the most salient characteristic of our corpus is its very lack of unusualness: the everyday nature of the overwhelming majority of its utterances. A more or less random sampling of the over 90% of the corpus utterances without any syntactic or semantic deviations reveals such mundane specimens as (41) *"One hand was all slimy from the wet pants"*; (76) *"Couldn't some of you gentlemen come sit here up front?"*; (121) *"No, I'd rather have spaghetti"*; (308) *"When you've bought a ticket, you have to let the machine stamp it."*

In short: Freud, as opposed to Kraepelin, may have been supported by our data as to the phenomenology of speech from REM or REM-like dreaming (general syntactic well-formedness, only sporadic neologisms and language mixing, even occasional self-corrections). As for its generation, however, Freud's replay hypothesis appears to be unsubstantiated.

From Linguistic to Literary Creativity

In rather sharp contrast to the commonplace specimens, however, are those dream utterances that may lay some claim to poetic or literary creativity. This gives rise to the question: Even if dream speech (as recalled) is on average not more often deviant than that of wakefulness, do those utterances that *are* deviant manifest a peculiar kind of deviance when compared with errors of everyday speech?

We noted in Chapter 2 (pp. 31–32) that professional poets (most prominently Coleridge) have reported composing whole poems in their dreams. But this should perhaps come as no great surprise, since a certain continuity is to be expected between verbal behavior in wakefulness and in dreaming. However, even among the specimens of non-poet Kraepelin we have seen in his monograph instances of what he calls "jocular contrasts" and even "sneering comedy," as well as some twenty other specimens, meaningful or not, with rhythmical structure, about half of which are clearly verse, albeit with imperfect rhyme. Comparable instances are also found in his newly discovered corpus. Hoche, for his part, labels 3.3% of his collection as being witty, ironical, or satirical, and another 10.7% as rhythmical. Psychiatrist Ian Oswald (1962) of Edinburgh University similarly cites numerous creative hypnagogic specimens of his own and others, selectively assembled. Can literary originality actually *increase* when one crosses the borders into dreamland? And, if so, how might this relate to the matter of types of deviance?

To assess whether dream speech may lay any special claim to poetic value, one of Holland's foremost poets, Rutger Kopland (pseudonym of sleep researcher Prof. R. H. Van den Hoofdakker, whose poems have also appeared in English translation—see Kopland, 1977, 1987, 1991), scored the 561 Dutch utterances of the corpus (including the two Dutch specimens reported with some intrusion of English words). No concomitant data was presented. Sixteen (2.9%) of the utterances were deemed by Kopland to be poetic, while another 18 (3.2%) could not be evaluated since they were difficult or impossible to understand. The remaining 527 (93.9%) were both scorable and deemed to be of no poetic value. A selection of the "poetic" specimens: (524) *"One just didn't see it at first, the sweet feeling which developed in the mother"*; (50) *"What a block of water there is lying on the [river] Waal"*; (259) *"What did you say? Spartre's house lives there?"*

It need not be surprising that for the overwhelming majority of the specimens in the full corpus there seems to be no appreciable novelty in the literary sense, despite the apparent novelty in the Chomskyan sense. In dreams, the *overall* scenarios, though often involving improbable transitions, generally fail to meet the criteria for "narrative creativity" as defined by Robert de Beaugrande (1979) of the English Department of the University of Florida, since the discontinuity within the sequence of events appears to be random rather than motivated. Furthermore, dream scenarios, contrary to popular belief, generally lack novelty in the sense of fantasy (Dorus, Dorus & Rechtschaffen, 1971) (which, however, is of course not to imply that dreams are no more than video replays of wakeful events). Understandably, mundane situational contexts usually call for no more than everyday dialogue.

Nevertheless, approximately one out of every thirty-five utterances was deemed to have poetic value, a proportion perhaps greater than what would have been expected from the utterances of the same subjects in waking life. Some remarks would seem appropriate concerning the genesis of these specimens. It should first be recalled that just over 15 percent of all the Dutch utterances were deemed by their speakers to be unlike utterances they would say or hear someone else say in waking life. For the 16 poetic specimens, however, the figure was 62.5%, a very significant difference (Fisher exact test $p < .0001$). Various language psychologists have viewed poetic creativity as a de-automatization of the everyday process of linguistic performance: the intentional exceeding or modification of the Chomskyan system of rules for linguistic creativity. The poet consciously eschews the usual automatic language-production mechanisms in favor of his own rule-governed devices for lexical inventions, including neologisms. Along with the novel use of productive morphological devices, there is the deliberate transcending of the conventional form classes (nominals, verbs, adjectivals, and so on) by means of processes not usually employed in the formulation of interpersonal communication, which are assembled in working memory and controlled (cf. Bock, 1982). But whether in fact there is any poetic intent on the part of the subjects in the dreaming state is uncertain. Kraepelin points to some of his poetic specimens as resulting from no more than the haphazard surfacing of pure words without accompanying subject-presentations and to the generation of meaningless rhymes. Such processes are analogous to quantum indeterminacy and invite comparison (despite the different modality) to the "random dream state generator" of the activation-synthesis hypothesis to be discussed in Chapter 8.

It may be that the randomness often attributed to the generation of hypnagogic utterances—perhaps due to excess leakage in the spread of activation—to some extent applies to the generation of utterances in the dreaming state proper. That some of these happen to have poetic value may be likened to the adage that enough monkeys with enough typewriters, given enough time, will produce all the works of Shakespeare. But as de Beaugrande (1979) emphasizes, whereas poetry resulting from motivated de-automatization of syntactic processes is often deviant, a given deviant text is not ipso facto "creative," and is all the less likely to be so when the product of random error. As to whether an utterance is perceived as poetic or witty, we have noted, in Chapter 3 (pp. 32–33), that Freud likens dream displacements to certain bad jokes, because they are "connected with the elements they replace by the most external and remote relations, and are therefore unintelligible." As de Beaugrande states, for a witticism to be successful the manipulation performed by the speaker or writer, as well as his or her motivation, must be recoverable or reconstructable by the hearer/reader, although such recovery or reconstruction need not be performed explicitly or consciously. Yet Kraepelin observes that, regardless of their worth by wakeful standards, dream utterances were "regularly conceived as being very successful poems" in the sleeping state itself, while Hoche remarks that only 14 percent of his supposedly witty remarks in sleep did not lose their cleverness upon awakening. Meumann similarly gives several examples of sentences that seemed to be "extraordinarily important and significant or clever" in the dream, but that proved upon awakening to consist of "rather meaninglessly composed words ... sometimes also hav[ing] the character of a pathological phrase." Hacker, for his part, relates a "beautiful poem" in the dream, "which I soon found upon awakening to consist of a constant repetion of the words 'Halli, hallo'" and a "splendid political joke" in rhymed form, which turned out to be "no joke at all" but the apparently meaningless proper-name blend *Lehmanger* and some repetitions of the line "nerves are more and more ajangle." All these may be indications that some manipulations performed during dreaming are recoverable only in that specific state, whether "consciously" or not.

As will be discussed further, neither attention nor intention need be totally absent during dreaming. Even Freud's own dream reports are full of phrases such as "I decided. . . . " "I wondered whether . . . ," "I thought of a plan. . . . " "I was surprised . . . "; and we have seen his instances of apparent self-correction. Freud recognizes this phenomenon, but attributes it to thoughts already present in the latent content. Yet at some points Freud seems to view dreaming as an intermediate phenomenon. He describes the condition of "involuntary ideas" that "emerge owing to the relaxation of a certain deliberate (and no doubt also critical) activity," as being in fact peculiar to the *hypnagogic* state, rather than belonging to dreaming proper (1900/1953a, p. 103).

Perhaps what is most missing in dreams is not so much the second stream of reflective awareness, but rather a sort of third stream that monitors the second—that is, evaluates the appropriateness of the dreamer's decision making, wondering, planning, surprise, and so on, which are often felt as occurring within the dream itself. (Or, equivalently, one might maintain the one- versus two-streams-of-thought distinction between the dream and the wakeful states by treating the dream, as presented to the dreamer, as perception rather than a form of thinking in the first place.) In this light, Kraepelin's and Hoche's statements that the supposedly poetic or witty quality of their utterances proved illusory in the morning may also be seen as relating to the introduction in wakefulness of a third stream that evaluates the product of the second (see Heynick, 1991).

If, however, the third stream of consciousness is introduced into dreaming itself, this results, perhaps by definition, in the lucid state (being "awake" in one's dream and aware of the fact that one is dreaming). LaBerge (1985) cites the dream of the German psychiatrist Harold von Moors-Messmer (1938) in which his verbal behavior is quite premeditated:

> In a large street, with people passing by. I repeatedly feel that I want to address myself to someone, but I always hesitate at the last moment. Finally I gather up the courage and say to a male personage who is passing by, *"You're a monkey."* I choose this particular phrase in order to provoke him into a reply. He remains standing there and looks at me. It is so uncomfortable for me that I would have most liked to have apologized. Then I hear the voice saying, *"I've been waiting for that; you've been weighing it over in your mind for a long time."* . . . He continues speaking with the intonation of a preacher; however, I realize that I will soon have forgotten everything. I therefore grab for my notebook and pull it out of my pocket. Then I realize the absurdity of my intentions, and I throw it aside. (p. 40)

It is obvious from the context that, although in the lucid state the dreamer's own utterance was "weighed over," he did not determine the reply from his dream interlocutor. The lucid dreamer evidently can, however, size up what is said to him or her and evaluate his or her own reaction to it.

Syntactic Elaboration

Irrespective of the presence or absence of any syntactic or semantic deviations or poetic quality, tentative comparisons between dreaming and wakeful verbal behavior can also be made on the basis of syntactic elaboration. Studies by psycholinguists Gerard Kempen, Carel Van Wijk, and Annemieke Luiten of the Department of Experimental Psychology of the University of Nijmegen have shown on the basis of written compositions an increasing ability among school pupils from the age of about nine years onward to use so-called connectivity to express underlying logical relations between sentences. This seems to go hand in hand with the shifting from narrative to expository language use. For example, the narrative sentences "John was very hungry" and "He went to a restaurant" could be expressed expositorially by means of a connective, as in, "Because John was very hungry, he went to a restaurant." This would, however, be rather superfluous since the inference is already clear. By contrast, the logical relation between the sentences "Jam is a sugar product" and "It doesn't spoil" is unclear and calls for explicit marking in the form of an explicatory sentence with a word such as "because." The Nijmegen analysis has furthermore indicated a difference in the manner in which the pupils at the various Dutch secondary schools make these explicit markings: Vocational school pupils have a greater tendency to form coordinations; college-prep pupils are more apt to use so-called subordinations; high school pupils following a general curriculum are intermediate (Van Wijk & Kempen, 1982a,b).

Figure 6.3 presents indices on the formal (written) language use in wakefulness for the three types of secondary school pupils and on the dream speech production of our subjects grouped according to their education and occupational level. The comparative analysis involved declarative speech acts, which constituted about 75 percent of the "T-units" in the total dream speech corpus. (T-units—minimal terminal units—are defined as one main clause plus any subordinate clause or nonclausal structure that is attached to or embedded in it. The subordination index is the number of clauses per T-unit. Words signaling functional or logical-syntactic coordinations are inserts such as "but," "besides," "however," and "nevertheless." Non-functional or enumerative coordinations are words such as "and" and "then.") A certain relative consistency between the formal (written) styles and dream speech styles is quite evident.

As for the absolute values of the dream speech scores, these generally lagged well behind the (formal) comparison scores for each of the three groups. Since under informal conditions scores tend to decrease, the lower values for dream speech are in keeping with expectations. This is especially so in view of the fact that in almost two-thirds of the situations where it can be determined, the dream conversation partner is clearly familiar to the dreamer from waking life, and that in the overall dream speech corpus there is a better than five-to-one predominance of the informal Dutch "jij/jullie" ("thou") second person pronoun over the formal "U" ("you").

In any event, the very presence of such "mature" indicators of underlying sentential relations has consequences for psychoanalytic theory. The "propositional unconscious" in some more recent expoundings on Freud's model of the psyche would allow coding in the unconscious of representational or ideational motive structures in simple or enumerative sentential form (for example, "I want control over *and* pleasure from your body"), but with no marking of logical interrelationships, conditions, or dependencies. Such

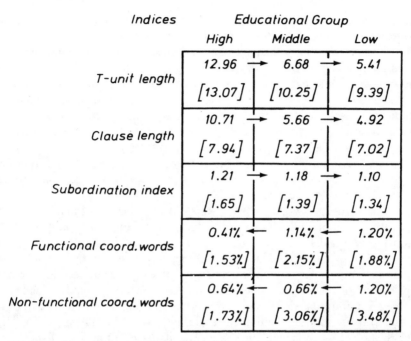

Indices	Educational Group		
	High	Middle	Low
T-unit length	12.96 →	6.68 →	5.41
	[13.07]	[10.25]	[9.39]
Clause length	10.71 →	5.66 →	4.92
	[7.94]	[7.37]	[7.02]
Subordination index	1.21 →	1.18 →	1.10
	[1.65]	[1.39]	[1.34]
Functional coord.words	0.41% ←	1.14% ←	1.20%
	[1.53%]	[2.15%]	[1.88%]
Non-functional coord. words	0.64% ←	0.66% ←	1.20%
	[1.73%]	[3.06%]	[3.48%]

FIGURE 6.3   Pattern in the relation between educational background and several descriptive measures of syntactic elaboration for recalled dream speech and (in brackets) formal language use in wakefulness. (From Heynick, 1983a.)

interrelationships, conditions, and dependencies are, however, all too evident in our dream speech corpus in the form of functional and logical-syntactic coordinations.

By way of summing up this chapter on linguistic performance in dreams, one can imagine a control experiment on wakeful linguistic performance in which our same 78 subjects would be required in daily life, upon hearing a buzzer sounding randomly once a week or so, to write down the last utterance they heard or said if some conversation were, or had just been, in progress. It is far from certain that the buzzer would interrupt or immediately follow a conversation as frequently as once every 5.1 soundings (let alone once every two or three times, the estimated proportion of REM awakenings resulting in recalled speech in our sleep speed experiment). As ubiquitous as verbal language is in the waking life of *Homo loquens*, it seems to be no less, and perhaps even more, prevalent in his dreaming.

Because conversation in everyday life is, by nature, usually "everyday" in the sense of commonplace, it is to be expected that many, perhaps most, of the utterances heard or said in our hypothetical control experiment would be deemed by the respective subjects to have also been said or heard with the same or similar words previously at *some* time in the past. Of course, this is not to imply a lack of "linguistic creativity" in the Chomskyan sense.

Furthermore, the percentage of ungrammatical utterances recorded in this manner in wakefulness could hardly be less than in our corpus of recalled dream speech, and indeed might well be greater. This highlights the fact that Kraepelin's corpora—unlike our own—were never meant to be representative of all dream speech, no more than the specimens of slips of the tongue of normal people in wakefulness assembled by his Jung-Grammatiker contemporaries and more recent authors were meant to be taken as a representative sample of speech in general. Our nonselective corpus, in contrast to Kraepelin's, gives indication that the language faculty functions with wakeful adequacy in generating dream dialogue, at least as recalled.

Finally, there is good reason to suppose that the use of grammatical co-ordination and subordination in everyday spoken language would reflect the norms established for the written language, as indeed they do in our dream speech corpus. In short: Not only is Kraepelin's data unrepresentative, but Freud's attempt to reconcile the occurrence of a supposedly secondary process (speech) within a supposedly primary process (dreaming) appears inadequate as presently formulated. However, the value of a scientific hypothesis lies not so much in its absolute truth as in its ability to stimulate further thought and theorization. So it was with Freud's, as we shall see in the next chapter.

Notes

1. For the general purposes at hand, we did not deem it necessary to have an equal number of male and female subjects. Only when discussing verbal aggression (note 3) is a breakdown according to the sex of the participants relevant. At some more sophisticated stage consideration might be given to recent research into the differences between men and women in hemispheric lateralization and in the development of interhemispheric communication via the corpus callosum. Such considerations become relevant to the extent that dreaming is seen as representing a shift in cortical dominance from the major to the minor hemisphere, factors to be mentioned again below.

2. Frederick Snyder (1970) mentions that 86% to 100% of dream reports of medium and long length contain or make reference to conversation. This invites comparison with the experiments of Piero Salzarulo and Carlo Cipolli (1974) in which 18.2% of 104 awakenings—half from REM periods, half from NREM periods—yielded verbatim recall of hallucinated verbal material as part of the full reports, merely in response to the experimenter's question, "What was passing through your mind before awakening?"

   Our data also confirms Snyder's observation on the pervasiveness of the self, "the all-important 'I' " in dream reports. That dreams are indeed far from being just spectator affairs is shown by the fact that in only 67 (11.6%) of the total of 580 utterances was the self just a bystander, perceiving an utterance said by a non-self actor to a non-self actor. This agrees well with Snyder's figure that in only 6% of the dream reports he collected (all of which were full reports, as opposed to our specimens of only partial reports) did the subjects explicitly state that they were not conscious of taking part in the action of the dream, but rather of simply observing. In 493 (85.0%) of our 580 utterances, the self was a participant in the conversation, confirming that man is a social animal in his dreams. Furthermore, in 327 (66.3%) of these 493 cases, the self was actively engaged as the addresser, speaking to a non-self addressee, while in the other 166 (33.7%) of these 493 utterances, the self was addressed by the non-self. This differs highly significantly ($p < .00001$, sign test) from the 50/50 ratio one would expect in the give-and-take of normal wakeful conversation (but see Chapter 7, note 1). A further 20 (3.4%) of the total of 580 specimens were "monologues," with the self both as addresser and addressee.

3. A fuller treatment of malediction in sleep speech is to be found in Heynick, 1981b. In brief: With reference to Freud's division between the primary and secondary processes, Pinchas Noy (1979) maintains that a necessary condition for the acquisition of language and secondary processes is the ability to isolate verbal signs from their signified meanings. In order to facilitate this isolation, the verbal sign itself must remain as neutral as possible. Obscene words are emotionally contaminated because of their close association with drives and wishes, and therefore have to be continually deleted from the language. Sleep speech may not however be ordinary language, and there are instances in the anecdotal literature on dream speech of malediction that is out of character for the person in waking life.

Yet in the present experiment, only 9 of the 580 specimens (from 2 male subjects and 7 female subjects) contained any verbal aggression or malediction; and of these, only one, containing the expression "wacking off," would have traditionally been considered unprintable. (Only another 7 specimens seem to have overt sexual references, and then, apparently, as often as not involving a prohibition against the sexual drive, thus indicating that dream utterances, though mundane, are not only seldom vulgar, but also seldom licentious.)

Similar results regarding malediction in recalled dreams were obtained in our second experiment, discussed later in this book. The 77 dream (or sleep mentation) reports elicited from 33 volunteer subjects (9 male, 24 female) by telephone awakenings at random nights and at random hours contained 94 immediately recalled lines (reported directly upon awakening, in response to the experimenter's instructions). Of these only one, involving the word "damn," contained any malediction at all.

Such a low frequency of malediction is also found in corpora of somniloquy (the actual articulating aloud in one's sleep) (Arkin, Toth, Baker, & Hastey, 1970).

4. Contrast this to Freud's review in Ch. I(E) of the *Traumdeutung* (1900/1953a) of the opinions of historical authors that mental activity in dreams is the product of "the play of functions left to themselves, and going along uncontrolled and purposelessly" and that "anyone who when he is awake talked in the sort of way that people talk in dreams . . . would give the impression of being muddle-headed or feeble minded" (p. 54).

5. The spreading activation concept is derived from M. R. Quillian (1967) as expanded by A. M. Collins and E. F. Loftus (1975). Dell and Reich trace its earlier antecedents to Wundt, while Collins and Loftus, for their part, cite Pavlov in proposing extensions to the spreading activation model that transform the theory from computer terms to quasi-neurological terms. Yet Dell and Reich's Unified Model, especially as elaborated by John Laver (1980), seems, if anything, most reminiscent of Freud's *Project*.

6. Because in the psychoanalytic interpretation slips of the tongue in dreams, whether caught by the (pseudo-)overt monitor or not, are no less "Freudian" than those of wakefulness, Freud interprets the use of "from" instead of "by" not as simply a too-literal translation into English of the German "von," but as an opportunity to introduce into the manifest dream the concept of "pious" (German "fromm"). Similarly, the element "*Non vixit*" ("He did not live") instead of "Non vivit" ("He is not alive"), with reference to a deceased friend of Freud's appearing in the dream, is interpreted as an overdetermined expression of both affection and hostility.

7. The principle of complementarity, derived from quantum mechanics by the great Danish physicist Niels Bohr (1963), may be operating in research into the cognitive content of dreams. If so, the quantity and clarity of the information we can obtain is directly correlated with the extent to which our observing interferes with the dreaming process we are studying (for example, by provoking awakenings and eliciting reports). The failure of experiments (reported by William Dement, 1972) that, using the techniques of hypnosis and avoidance conditioning, endeavor to induce the dreamer to supply a running narrative of his dream while it is in progress, indicate that we might indeed be dealing with a matter of principle rather than merely practical difficulties. If that be the case, then no technical advances or refinements can alter the situation, and an external dream viewer like that in the 1979 film *Futureworld* will forever remain wishful thinking.

   However, in his book *Lucid Dreaming*, Stephen LaBerg (1985, p. 13) of the Stanford Research Center writes that "for the first time in history, we have been able to receive on-the-scene reports from the dream world as dream events happen (or, should I say, seem to happen)." Although the "reports" in question are limited to a simple "on" signal made with the eyes to signify that lucid dreaming has begun, in theory at least this may still be considered a violation of the complementarity principle. However, some philosophical arguments may be advanced that lucid dreaming (the state, to be discussed again below, of being awake and aware in one's dreams), by the very fact that it allows such signaling, makes itself distinct from dreaming in the strict sense.

8. Our results can, however, be seen as bearing upon a related issue which avoids the problem of secondary revision: whether cognitive functioning directly after awakening is to some extent determined by the preceding sleep state. Some research (cf. Gordon, Frooman, & Lavie, 1982; Bertini, Violani, Zoccolotti, Antonelli, & DiStafano, 1983) points to the performance on verbal ("left" hemispheric) tasks following NREM awakenings as being superior to that following REM awakenings (that is, that the cognitve functioning supposedly characteristic of dreams is temporarily carried over, if not necessarily "phase locked," into the ensuing waking state). Be this as it may, the data from our present experiment and a second one,

reported below, strongly indicates that "grammatical proficiency" as evidenced by syntactic well-formedness and sentential complexity, is functioning in the production of recalled dream speech at about the usual level of daytime wakefulness, regardless of what proportion of the generation process of recalled dream speech one wishes to attribute to dreaming proper or to the ensuing state of waking (up).

9. We have noted in Chapter 4 (p. 55) Freud, Kraepelin, and Hoche's special mention of those utterances that have, in Freud's words, "the sensory quality of speech." Several issues are connected with this.

Kraepelin compares in passing the relatively low frequency of such speech motor-presentations in the small subset of utterances said *to* the dreamer as opposed to those said *by* the dreamer, while Hoche remarks that the speech of non-self characters in dreams seldom takes the form of real auditory hallucinations. However, a supplementary question in our experiment, which asked the subjects whether the dream utterance was perceived as vocalized or nonvocalized, revealed that for the corpus as a whole, the vocalized percentage (disregarding "I-don't-know" responses) was 80 percent, with no significant difference appearing between utterances said by the self or by a personage not the self.

As is also mentioned in Chapter 4, Freud states that, in particular, a dream utterance motor-acoustically said or heard is to be traced to utterances spoken on the Traumtag, and goes on to say that speeches of the nonacoustic "thought" variety often have as their source some material that has been *read* on the Traumtag. Our results are suggestive of support for this assertion but are not statistically significant, perhaps due to the low number of dream speech specimens traceable to read Traumtag material. Similarly, the higher proportion of "vocalized" imperatives in the corpus as compared to nonimperative specimens is suggestive but not statistically significant, again perhaps due to the low numbers involved. (For a theoretical consideration of the role of speech, imperatives, and the Freudian super-ego to the manifest dream content, see Otto Isakower, 1939, 1954. Note also Freud's concept of "cathectic intensity." and Hacker's remark that "in cases of strong inner stimulation, or when the speech would be imparted with a special emotional force, it often came to true speech, that is, distinct acoustic word- and sentence-presentations which frequently tended to be accompanied by clear motoric presentations of the speech organs.")

Dreaming Pragmatic Performance

Up to now we have largely been concerned with the analysis of dream utterances from the narrow psycholinguistic viewpoint, that is, in isolation from their contexts. This is essentially in line with Kraepelin's interest in dream speech *an sich*, and the consequent paucity of data he provided, in his monograph as well as his newly discovered corpus, on its interaction with other aspects of dreaming. However, we have also noted on several occasions (pp. 26 and 55) how very appropriate the title *Theatre of Sleep* is for Almansi and Béguin's dream anthology, and that Freud himself was fond of the theater metaphor. Recent popular books on dream incubation (cf. Delaney, 1979) are heavily based on the metaphor of the dreamer as film director, whose essential functions include the writing of a "screenplay" and the scripting of dialogue. All this invites consideration of the matter of *pragmatic competence* during REM dreaming: the dreamer's knowledge of conditions and manner of appropriate use of his or her grammatical competence in conformity with various purposes (briefly referred to in Chapter 5, p. 212). In terms of the theatrical metaphor, pragmatic competence is the underlying ability of the dreamer-as-scriptwriter to put into his or her own mouth and the mouths of the hallucinated co-stars utterances that, when judged by wakeful standards, are deemed appropriate to the context (regardless of whether the scenario be commonplace or fanciful).

As will be seen, the presence or absence of pragmatic competence during REM sleep has far-reaching implications, not least for the psychoanalytic dream theory.

Automatism as a Primary Process versus the Dreaming Ego as Scriptwriter

We noted in the previous chapter that our continued capacity for Chomskyan linguistic creativity in the REM state means that speech—a supposedly secondary process in the Freudian schema of things—remains an anomaly within the framework of theoretically primary-process dreaming. Freud's formulations have, however, not remained static but have been the object of discussion and revision by later generations of psychoanalysts.

The primary-vs.-secondary-process distinction could conceivably be maintained, despite the occurrence in dreams of substantial syntactic elaboration in the apparent absence of any replay mechanism, by reclassifying speech as somewhat less secondary and somewhat more primary. A potential basis for this could be offered by modern psycholinguistic data on automatic mechanisms in speech production. Consider psychoanalyst Charles Rycroft's (1979, p. 12) definition of the secondary processes as "governed by the laws of grammar and formal logic." Grammar is indeed indisputably linked to the secondary processes in its academic linguistics sense of a formal system of rules by which structural descriptions of sentences are generated. But psycholinguist Gerard Kempen (1981, p. 116), citing the often well-formed utterances of somniloquy (sleeptalking aloud), notes that "syntactic processes can proceed quite unimpeded when the central attention is switched off, as in sleep," and he sees this as emphasizing that (in the daytime as well as at night) "sentence construction largely operates automatically and requires no conscious attention." This modern view is further supported by Dell and Reich's Unified Model, which, as we have seen, largely dispenses with the separate "editing function" incorporated into previous psycholinguistic models. In this way, grammar, in the sense of the syntactic processor by means of which the actual language user converts thought into speech, need not be seen as carrying out exercises in formal logic or (to repeat Freud's term) "intellectual operations" on a par with calculations.

Such a reclassification would still, of course, leave Freud's aforementioned use of his "critical faculties" as in the "Non Vixit" dream as at least an occasional anomaly. But far more important now is the matter of pragmatic competence, and specifically whether the selfsame attention-independent and autonomous nature of our syntactic abilities which is theoretically to thank for the generation of apparently well-formed utterances in dreams may not also lead to an apparent lack of pragmatic competence during dreaming: a *dissociation* during REM sleep of the language faculty from other cognitive faculties which in waking life are usually *superordinate* to it. Evidence of such dissociation should in fact be welcomed by Freudians as a viable alternative for accommodating to the psychoanalytic scheme of things the phenomenon of speech within dreaming.

The search for manifestations of such a dissociation was a focus of our second experiment on verbal behavior during dreaming. But before reporting on the results, we will discuss Freudian, neo-Freudian and neurobiological views on the theoretical place of automatic mechanisms in the hierarchy of superordinate and subordinate control systems that make up the psyche, and (in the following section) to some rethinking of the nature of the primary-vs.-secondary-process dichotomy.

Sleep Speech and the Dissociation of Language
from Other Cognitive Processes

Arthur Arkin's 1981 work *Sleeptalking: Psychology and Psychophysiology* deals primarily with the phenomenon of actually articulating aloud in one's sleep, but it also extends to sleep speech in our sense of hallucinated verbal material in dreams. (There is also an overlap from the other direction, in that more recent researchers report that most hallucinated verbal material during REM sleep is accompanied by subvocal phasic discharges of speech muscles; see Shimizu and Inoue, 1986.) Being the first book since Kraepelin's devoted to the study of the interaction between speech and other cognitive processes during sleep, it calls for special consideration here, particulary in so far as it treats instances in which the interaction in question is characterized by strong dissociation.

Arkin presents results of his own experiments, conducted in the sixties and early seventies, in which instances of sleeptalking recorded in the laboratory were followed by the provoked awakening of the subject and the elicitation of mentation reports by the experimenter. Only approximately half of the mentation reports from REM sleep elicited in this way show an obviously discernible relation (what Arkin terms "first or second order concordance") to the content of the previous articulation, even though both the sleeptalking and the mentation reports are usually quite ample. (Most sleeptalking instances are associated with non-REM sleep, and then the percentage of concordance between the content of the utterance and the mentation report, if there was any, is considerably lower still.)

As an example from REM sleep of a lack of discernible concordance: Subject (sleeptalking): *"Tar(?) smells sort of like Cassius Clay's armpit and old Prein's snatch."* Subject's mentation report (elicited one minute after the sleeptalking episode): "Oh boy—yah—I was going through a turnstile in a subway and put 35 cents in for a hamburger—well, it was kind of silly of me but I didn't realize you couldn't get a hamburger from a turnstile, so I went to the lady in the booth who *I told my problem*; and she said *I'd have to sign a whole bunch of papers and I'd get my 15 or 20 cents back in the mail*—big deal so I watched them come" (Arkin 1981, p. 418). It is interesting that although the report contains verbal dialogue with content specified, it is quite unrelated to the sleeptalking utterance (except, conceivably, as Arkin suggests, at some deeper level of psychoanalytic interpretation).

In discussing this rather anomalous phenomenon, Arkin cites Louis Jolyon West's (1967) clinical review of *psychic dissociation*, said to occur when integration with the normal network of associations is impeded in the case of outgoing information (as in sleeptalking, parapraxes, and automatic writing), stored information (as in dreams and hallucinations), and incoming information (as in daydreaming and reverie). The "neodissociationist theory" of Stanford University's Ernest R. Hilgard (1973, pp. 405–406) is quoted extensively by Arkin as being particularly relevant to sleeptalking. The theory's basic assumption, derived from experimental studies of hypnosis, is that "the unity which exists in personal cognitive functioning is somewhat precarious and unstable." An executive ego is seen as providing "a basis for self-perception and for conceiving the self as an agent." Hilgard writes that "there are many subordinate control systems that represent fractions of total cognitive functioning." He proposes that these structures "have at any one time a hierarchical arrangement, but their hierarchical positions can shift. . . . For example, the cognitive system that produces dreams is more prominent [during sleep periods] than it is in waking." Nevertheless, as daydreams attest, it is present in the daytime as well, if at a lower level. Once activated, a system may, according to Hilgard, "exert its controls automatically, even though it is a subordinate system." Furthermore, each of the subordinate cognitive control structures is "related to a system of inputs and outputs, with feedback arrangements. As a control or monitoring system, the structure can seek or avoid inputs and enhance or inhibit outputs."

Arkin (1981, p. 286) comments that at night "the sleep executive ego acquires ascendency over its wakeful counterpart." Its related subordinate, semi-autonomous cognitive systems include those mediating imagery, hallucinated lines of dialogue/monologue, overt sleeptalking, and memory.

With regard to physiological concomitants, Arkin cites Penfield's cortical stimulation studies (mentioned in Chapter 6, p. 234). He relates this to G. Schaltenbrand's (1975) argument that activation of the thalamus may be involved in the release and termination of practiced speech patterns (as opposed to the actual synthesis of sentences and propositional, abstract expressions), and that sleeptalking may therefore issue from *selective thalamic activation*. As for cortical hemispheric dominance, Arkin cites the literature going back to the nineteenth-century studies by Hughlings Jackson that the major ("left") hemisphere is mainly responsible for verbal, linear, logical, linguistic processes, especially propositional speech; and that the nondominant ("right") hemisphere is essentially without the capacity for significant speech production. Arkin notes, however, that Jackson allowed that the minor hemisphere could produce non-propositional, *automatic, overlearned* phrases, and updates this with evidence, supplied by Alan Searleman (1977) of the State University of New York at Stony Brook, that the right cortical hemisphere is capable of limited speech output. Arkin suggests that the aphasiclike speech characteristic of much sleeptalking, and (so he apparently assumes on the basis of Kraepelin's corpus) of much hallucinated dream dialogue as well, may result from periodic lateral shifts in hemispheric balance during sleep.

More relevantly for the concept of dissociation, Arkin points to the sequelae of *commissurotomy* (surgical separation of the hemispheres), in which complex cognitive activities mediated by the right hemisphere are conducted independently of and outside of the domain of awareness of the left hemisphere and cannot be verbally encoded (Sperry, 1973). Arkin (1981, p. 298) suggests that a comparable "loosening of integration in sleep between intrahemispheric levels of activation and a diminished commissural mediation of intrahemispheric cortical dominance factors" may result from shifting activity in the neural channels of the corpus callosum, which links the two hemispheres. This incoordination may thus manifest itself in overt sleeptalking that is unrelated to mentation reports.

With regard to hallucinated dream dialogue, somewhat similar speculation was advanced by the veteran sleep researcher Michel Jouvet (1978) of the University of Lyons not long before the publication of Arkin's book and not cited by him. Jouvet notes from the observation of over two and a half thousand of his own dreams that in two-thirds of the cases there is a negative correlation between his ability to identify visually (facially) the person speaking to him and the clarity or retainability (though not *ipso facto* the semantic and syntactic well-formedness) of the utterance.

As an example of the 54 percent of the cases in which the content of the hallucinated dialogue was quite clear and retainable but the identity of the speaker obscure, Jouvet offers, "In an unknown place, an unknown girl accompanied by her mother, who is enormous, approaches me. She tells me that *the cats don't tip their berets.*" A specimen of the inverse situation (13 percent of all cases) where the speaker was clearly visualized and identified but the dialogue unclear or unretainable, runs, "At a scientific congress, before taking the floor, I'm looking for some slides in my bag. So M. takes the floor. He seems quite rejuvenated to me and is wearing an electric blue suit. I can't manage to hear him. His voice doesn't carry, since the microphone isn't connected" (pp. 30–31). The remaining cases (33 percent) involve clear/retainable utterances from clearly identified speakers, or unretainable utterances from speakers not identified or not clearly visualized.

Jouvet apparently views this significant negative correlation between what is visually and linguistically retained as more a matter of encoding than of production: "In many cases dream memory uses the activity of only one hemisphere . . . presumably due to the inhibition of information transmission in the corpus callosum" (p. 32).

Returning to Arthur Arkin: He lastly treats the concept of thought *microgenesis* (from the German *Aktualgenese*), which he regards as reconcilable with, and indeed complementary to, the theory of neodissociation. According to John H. Flavell and Juris Draguns (1957) of the University of Rochester: At the early stage of the thought generation process the principles governing the combination of global, diffuse, and undifferentiated fluctuating sets of psychological items are similar to those of Freud's primary process, whereby association is characterized by condensation and displacement based on contiguity and superficial external similarities. Before thought achieves final form, it tends toward dichotomous modes of expression (me–not me, good–bad, and the like) but the primary-process components are then aborted in favor of reality-oriented mentation. Many schizophrenic verbalizations can thus theoretically be viewed as the final product of what would normally be only a transitory phase in thought development—a phase that might also characterize the end product of the speech of normal persons under atypical or abnormal conditions.

Arkin, himself a psychoanalyst, sees many of these basically neurobiological concepts as being in keeping with the spirit of Freudian psychology, in that "the mind is conceptualized as being constructed of descriptively unconscious and conscious interactive components with widely ranging degrees of independence, interrelatedness, and hierarchical organization in which the various components have subordinate and superordinate relations to one another, in themselves subject to change over time" (p. 228).

Other Freudians and neo-Freudians, however, have modified the primary-vs.-secondary-process dichotomy not so much by proposing that supposedly secondary-process speech is automatic and autonomous, but by suggesting that the unconscious as well as its manifestations in dreams is more secondary-process–like than originally formulated. These views now come in for our consideration.

Revision of the Dependency Relationship Between the Freudian Primary and Secondary Processes in Wakefulness and Dreaming

The latter half of the sixties was a period of intense psychoanalytic theorizing. In redefining the operations during dreams of id and ego (the main successors in Freud's tripartite structural model to the systems unconscious and conscious, respectively), Merton M. Gill (1967) of Chicago's Abraham Lincoln School of Medicine highlights the kinship between the Freudian conception of the hierarchy of systems (as Gill interprets it) and Hughlings Jackson's concept of *superordinate inhibition*. The latter hypothesizes a higher system inhibiting the lower one, whereby only the release from inhibition by the superordinate system can permit the subordinate system to come into play. Gill notes on the one hand Freud's (1905/1960a, p. 169) view that the primary-process mechanism of condensation arises "*automatically* [italics added] without any particular intention during thought processes in the unconscious," even if, as we have seen, this automatic mechanism may for creative purposes sometimes be deliberately placed at the disposal of motivated consciousness in wakefulness. As discussed in Chapter 2, Freud sees "the unrecognizability, strangeness and absurdity of the manifest dreams [as] partly the result of the translation of the thought into a different, so to say archaic, method of expression." However, as Gill notes, Freud adds that such dreamwork distortion is also "partly the effect of a restrictive, critically disapproving agency in the mind which does not entirely cease to function during sleep" (Freud, 1923/1961a, pp. 241–242). In other words, the automatic, primary-process mechanisms of the dreamwork serve for the avoidance of censorship and the resultant unpleasure, similarly to the way in which the deliberate primary-process mechanisms of the jokework are motivated for the attainment of pleasure.

Gill (1967) contends on the basis of this that functioning according to primary-process mechanisms is a "theoretical fiction," since "the inhibition imposed by a superordinate structure can never totally disappear." The mechanisms of the underlying structure can, according to Gill, be evidenced "only as they are influenced by some persisting inhibition by the superordinate structure." What one sees is never the primary process as such, but "products of its mechanisms in the context of the dreamwork, jokework, symptom formation, or whatever other compromise function results from the interplay of inhibited and inhibiting forces" (pp. 287–288). In concluding, Gill takes issue with Freud's (1900/1953a) view—which we have heard before in relation to self-correction and mathematical calculations as well as straightforward speech in dreams— that "everything that appears in dreams as the ostensible activity of the function of judgement is to be regarded not as an intellectual achievement of the dreamwork, but as belonging to the material of the dream-thoughts and as having been lifted from them into the content of the dream as a ready-made structure" (p. 445). For Gill such an extreme formulation is the "typical beginning of any major new concept." In order to focus on a new discovery one must "make it unique and radically sever its relations with the more familiar" (p. 293).

Robert Holt (1967), writing at the same time as Gill, also takes note of the traditional view that the sleeping state permits a "change from the relative dominance of the secondary-process . . . the regressive undoing of a developmental progression" (p. 345). He then goes on to argue not so much that dreams and the like represent only a partial lifting of secondary-process inhibition (as maintained by Gill), but that in fact the *primary processes themselves are structured* far more than is generally recognized. Despite Freud's (1933/1964b, p. 73) well-known description of the id as "a chaos, a cauldron full of seething excitations" and, by extension, the primary processes that govern it—or do not govern it—as "without organization [or] logical laws of thought," Holt emphasizes Freud's discovery of meaning where (as we have noted in Chapter 2) the predominant scientific view saw only random error: the elucidation of hidden intelligibility by discerning recurrent regularities and reversible operations of thought. "It is difficult to imagine," Holt contends, "how an inner order can be achieved and maintained without enduring structural means" (p. 351).

Holt cites the assertion of psychoanalyst David Rapaport, similar to Gill's, that both primary and secondary processes play a part in all forms of thought, including dreaming. The difference lies in the kind of synthetic function involved, "the degree of dominance the secondary achieves over the primary" (Rapaport, 1960, p. 241). But Holt then argues that basic units of primary-process functioning may be seen as structured even without the need to assume an admixture of secondary-process functioning. He uses linguistic metaphors to explain how in Freud's determinist outlook, the unconscious (id) has an ancient language and grammar of its own that, however strange and perverse, follow formulatable rules and can be translated with the aid of a dictionary to its symbolic vocabulary.

Psychoanalytic theorist Pinchas Noy's (1969) suggestions for revising the psychoanalytic theory of the primary processes similarly emphasize a continuum between the primary and secondary levels that "results from the inhibition-disinhibition of hierarchic psychic functions" (p. 156). Advocating the abandoning of unconsciousness as a criterion for defining the primary process, Noy would formally distinguish the secondary processes as "all the mental processes that are *monitored and dependent upon constant feedback information* [italics added]" (at least for their development and maintenance, if not always for their actual functioning). Primary processes, by contrast, are "all those . . . that are not dependent on such feedback" (p. 161).

Speech, according to such criteria, remains of course a secondary process. Not that its functioning is necessarily fully conscious as opposed to automatic, but rather in that it is dependent on feedback for its ontogenetic development (consider the difficulties of a deaf child in learning to speak even if he could hear other people's voices) and because its output needs to be monitored. A slip of the tongue immediately comes into awareness (becomes the focus of attention) that it may be corrected, and experiments have shown that when a speaker's own speech is masked from him by noise, his utterances threaten to degenerate into incoherence.

Instead of being strictly identified with the unconscious, the feedback-independent primary processes may, Noy proposes, be subdivided into four categories: (a) both the process and its product are unconscious (as in some neuroses and psychoses); (b) the process is unconscious but the product is conscious; (c) the process and its product are conscious, but the former only *ex post facto*; (d) both the process and the product are conscious and controlled (as in some art forms). To give an example of the second category Noy writes, "We remember that in the dream . . . a strange word or sentence appeared, but we do not discover that this product is a condensation . . . of several familiar words. If it is interpreted to us, we may accept it, but it remains something 'not belonging to me' and we do not feel as if it were our own achievement to distort the . . . words in such a way" (1969, p. 165). This Noy contrasts with wakeful Freudian slips of the third category: mistakes of which we are aware and that we are able to identify—for example as a condensation of two known words or a reversal of a word—and then correct or apologize for.

In an update of a decade later, Noy (1979) rejects as too mechanistic his original strict equating of secondary processes with dependence on feedback for maintenance and development. His new definition links the secondary and primary processes with *reality orientation* and *self-centeredness*, respectively. Noy considers the secondary processes (or, in terms of more recent psychoanalytic ego psychology, the *autonomous ego functions*) to be characterized not so much by dependence on feedback as by "the freedom from the necessity to respond automatically to feedback information": the capacity for a given program to "program itself by itself," or the ability to think about itself. (pp. 203–204; see also Heynick, 1985, where such concepts are traced back to Freud's *Project*).

Such reflection, which is largely absent from dreaming, is closely linked to the ability to use language (both the sign system and the syntax) and the corresponding "propositional logic" developed during the courses of ontogenetic and phylogenetic evolution. Specifically, Noy (1979, p. 205) writes, "The development of language as a socially shared communication system has a reciprocal influence on the development of secondary-process thought," in that the former supplies its "operational patterns and rules of organization" to the latter. (See also Heynick, 1983b.)

These two articles by Noy are exceptional in that they refer, however briefly, to speech in dreams. Unlike Noy (and unlike Freud, Kraepelin, Meumann, Hoche, and Hacker), but very much in keeping with the long tradition of obliviousness to verbal behavior in dreams, the other revisionists ignore this phenomenon, although its very nature represents a peculiar interplay of the theoretically dichotomous primary and secondary processes and would therefore seem of great value in delimiting their functioning. Yet even if most of these authors do not address themselves directly to dream speech, their proposed revisions to the theory of primary and secondary processes and to the structures of the id and ego, respectively, are not without implications as to what dream speech (granting that it exists at all) should be like. Such implications can also be checked against empirical data.

Experiment on Pragmatic Competence in Dreams ——————

Our second experiment is similar to the one reported in the previous chapter in that subjects participated in their home environment and were likewise trained to avoid any selectivity, self-correction, or self-censuring in their reporting. Now, however, the objective was to elicit whole dream "scenarios" along with the verbal dialogue. Furthermore, elicitation was done by *telephone* (connected to a tape recorder). This took place on random nights and at random early-morning hours, with an average of one awakening per week per subject in the course of about three months. (For more details on the elicitation techniques, see Heynick, 1986.)

An analysis was made of 77 dream/mentation reports thus obtained from 24 female and 9 male subjects, ages 18 to 60 (median 27). These 77 scenarios contained a total of 205 instances of monologue or dialogue falling into three categories according to when and how they were reported.

Immediately recalled directly quoted utterances (94 specimens). These were reported immediately upon awakening in accordance with the experiment protocol. The subjects were instructed that, when the phone next to their beds rang, and if a dream/mentation was in progress, they were to attempt to retain word for word the last (and therefore freshest) line or lines of dialogue/monologue, if any had been said or heard by them in the dream. These were then immediately reported to the experimenter, along with information as to who the addressor and addressee were.

Non–immediately recalled directly quoted utterances (78 specimens). These were reported in the telling of the rest of the dream when subsequently, in accordance with the experiment protocol, the subjects were asked to go back to the beginning of the dream/mentation (or as far back as they could) and report in as much detail as possible the entire scenario. This encompasses all the events up to and including the last line or lines of dialogue or monologue originally reported. The directly quoted utterances, whether recalled immediately or not, were reported verbatim; for example, "I told her, '*You'd better chain your bike, otherwise it'll be gone just like that.*'"

Non–immediately recalled indirectly quoted utterances (33 specimens). These, too, were reported as part of the larger dream scenario, but rather than taking a strictly verbatim form, they appeared as nominal clauses, usually introduced by nominal includers (*that, if, whether, how, what, why, when, who,* and so on) embedded in larger sentences; for example, "So I told the children that *they were making too much noise* and that *they should go to bed*," or "The motorcyclists asked *if they could camp there*."

As might have been expected, there were also numerous references to conversation with little or no content being specified, and in any case not taking the form of either direct quotes or nominal clauses; for example, "Then we sat around gossiping," These were not included in the analysis.

Figure 7.1 shows the distribution of the three categories, with each also broken down according to who the addressor and addressee were. In 40.0 percent of the 205 specimens, the self was the addressor, addressing a nonself (except in one instance, when the self spoke "aloud" to himself). In 44.4 percent the self was the addressee, addressed by a nonself. In only 15.6 percent of the specimens did a nonself address a nonself, the dreamer being a passive onlooker. This lends additional weight to Freud's statement that "dreams are completely egoistic . . . the person who plays parts in their scenes is always to be recognized as the dreamer."[1]

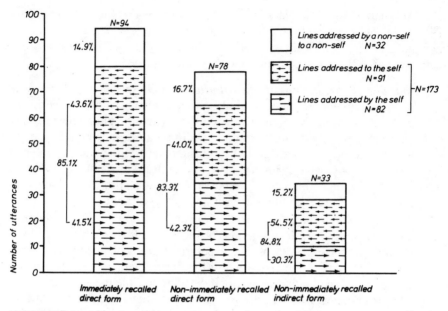

FIGURE 7.1 Addressor-addressee situations, for each of three utterances recall categories. (From F. Heynick, 1986.)

The dream utterances were subsequently scored for their appropriateness to the dream context, that is as indication of the pragmatic competence of the dreamer as scriptwriter. Scoring was carried out by five native Dutch graduate engineering students, who were told, in broad terms, that they would be judging the efficiency of a computer-assisted program in generating utterances compatible with narrative texts, usually recounted in the first person. The scorers were asked to rate each utterance for its appropriateness to the context: the extent to which the lines scripted were lines that, given such situations in real life, one might expect to hear from normal individuals. Each utterance was to be classed into one of four categories of appropriateness.

The agreement between the scorers is quite satisfactory. (Kendall's tau was used as a coefficient of agreement. It ranged from .22 to .49—median .35—for the various pairs of raters; all were significantly different from zero at $p = .0001$). The overall results show a clear skewing toward the "appropriate" end of the scale, with 67.6% of all utterances deemed by the scorers to be fully appropriate to the narrative $(++)$, and 20.5% not entirely $(+)$. Only 7.5% were scored as largely inappropriate $(-)$, and 4.4% entirely inappropriate $(--)$. Figure 7.2 shows the breakdown across the four categories of appropriateness according to utterance type (immediately recalled directly quoted, non–immediately recalled directly quoted, and non–immediately recalled indirectly quoted).[2]

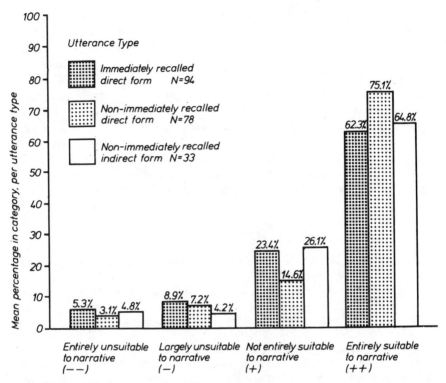

FIGURE 7.2 Average ratings of the appropriateness of utterances to dream context, with each of the three utterance recall categories distinguished. (From F. Heynick, 1986.)

Statistical comparison of this distribution yields the following results. On the one hand, significant difference fails to appear (χ^2 test, df = 3, p = .11) in the distribution of the combined group of 172 directly quoted utterances (some immediately recalled, the others not immediately recalled) and the 33 indirectly quoted utterances (all non–immediately recalled). This argues somewhat against the importance of secondary revision, since it might be assumed that indirectly quoted utterances are potentially more susceptible to greater elaboration, due to their not being reported verbatim. On the other hand, a statistically significant difference is found (χ^2 test, df = 3, $p < .02$) between the distribution of the 94 immediately recalled utterances (all directly quoted) and that of the combined group of the 111 non–immediately recalled utterances (some directly quoted, the others indirectly). The latter tended far more than the former to be scored as entirely suitable to the narrative. This supports the idea that secondary revision after awakening is never entirely discountable. The degree of appropriateness may be seen as partly a function of the amount of time in which secondary elaboration is allowed to take place, with at least some of this revision considered distinct from the dream(work) proper.

Two dream scenarios from one 33-year-old woman subject are presented here as examples, along with the scorers' ratings of the lines of dialogue/monologue. In the first report, each of the utterances received from all five scorers a perfect $(0--,0-,0+,5++)$ or almost-perfect rating for appropriateness to the narrative. In the second report, most of the utterances were variously rated as being less than appropriate. The first utterance of the first report is indirectly quoted and all the rest directly. Immediately recalled utterances, which were reported first upon provoked awakening and then subsequently reported again in the main report, are indicated by (IR). The other utterances were reported for the first time in the telling of the main report.

Report 1

I was sitting in the garden and reading old magazines. Then my son came along. My son was about five years old; now he's already ten. And he took a little girlfriend along, also about five, and she started looking through the magazines. And they were getting wet, since she had such a cold that her nose ran. And I said that *she, your little girlfriend, should rinse her nose with the lotah* $(0--,0-,1+,4++)$, that's a jug used in yoga [instead of a handkerchief]. I use it myself, too. So I let her do it, but because she was so small, it didn't go right, and she started to cry. And then she walked home. So I said to my little boy, "*I'll go to her mother and tell her what happened, otherwise she'll think 'what a strange lady'*" $(0--,0-,0+,5++)$. Then I wanted to take along a few magazines for that girl, but as I was walking in back, through the alley toward her garden, I browsed through the magazine and I came across an article on making dolls, and I tore it out first. And then I thought 'now I can't give her that magazine anymore, since it looks so bad.' And then I entered the garden and everything was dark. . . . At first I didn't know what to do, then my son came again. He went out. Then that girl came out again, and my son had already told her mother that I had tried to help her get rid of her cold with the lotah. I simply knew that he had said that, but I didn't hear him say that literally. Then I said to that girl, "*In the future, when you catch a cold, you should go first to the doctor and have him write out a prescription for medicine*" (IR) $(0--,0-,0+,5++)$.

Report 2

I was at a party; it was my mother's party, in any case, and the house had been entirely cleared out and there were lots of chairs and desks like I had in elementary school—of that light birchwood with steel. And there I was, sitting next to an uncle of mine, and he began a chat, and at a certain point he asked, "*And are you still working?*" (IR) $(0--,0-,0+,5++)$. And I said, "*Yes, I attend a school which rounds everything off*" (IR) $(0--,1-,3+,1++)$ . . . Everyone at the party had lightly colored clothes on, white and yellow, soft, gay colors . . . I was suddenly walking in a park. . . . There was a bench to the right of the path where I was walking, and three girls, about fourteen years old, were sitting there.

They were calling out and laughing, and then I noticed that one of my shoes wasn't on right. The strap was around my ankle, but I was walking on the heel of the shoe; it was folded over a bit. And the girls called out, *"That lady is walking on her shoe" (IR)* $(0--,0-,4+,1++)$. And then I had to laugh myself. To the right it was a bit higher, a sort of ball. I put my foot up on it and undid my shoe, and put it on again. And meanwhile, I said to my foot or shoe, *"Walk away, my little shoe, sweep the ash from my feet" (IR)* $(2--,2-,1+,0++)$ [the first two words of this utterance are in English in the original].[3]

Implications of Dream Speech for Neo-Freudian Models of the Dreaming Psyche ⎯⎯⎯⎯

We return to the main question posed earlier. Granting that sentence production is generally largely automatic and attention-independent, and that this might theoretically make grammatical proficiency compatible with primary-process dreaming (according to the redefinition of Freud's primary processes), the issue is whether our data lends any support to the psychodynamically inspired prediction that the selfsame autonomy of grammatical proficiency in dreams should also result in an apparent lack of pragmatic competence: a divorcing of the dialogue from the context of the scenario.

Obviously, there is psychic dissociation in dreaming in the sense of Louis J. West's description of the dissociative reaction. Stored information that is hallucinatorily activated is treated by the dreamer as incoming information from the real world. But it would also appear that the *pseudo-outgoing* information, which takes the form of hallucinated dialogue spoken *by* the dreamer, is well integrated into, and in conformity with, the hallucinated scenario. (Furthermore, one should be cautioned against overemphasizing the "stored" quality of the information in dreams that is hallucinated as incoming. Utterances perceived as spoken *to* the dreamer show, along with a general well-formedness and appropriateness to the context, strong indication of being novel, rather than replayed, just like those spoken by the dreamer.) In terms of Ernest Hilgard's neodissociationist theory, it would seem that the executive ego in the dream continues to be aware of the self and to conceive of the self as an actor in the dream scenario. We recall in this regard the overall figures provided above, showing the strong participation of the self as addressor or addressee rather than onlooker. Whatever changes may take place during the shifting in the hierarchical arrangements from wakefulness to sleep, it appears from the appropriateness scores that language capacity remains largely subordinate rather than independent as far as hallucinated dream speech is concerned. In contrast to what often seems to occur in the case of overt sleeptalking, hallucinated speaking in dreams does not acquire a semi-autonomous status. What Arkin calls the "sleep executive ego" (as opposed to the wakeful executive ego) retains a large degree of control over the cognitive system of verbal language, at least during REM periods. "The master of the school is gone and the boys are in an uproar," was Tom Paine's metaphor, in his 1795 "Essay on Dreams," for the nocturnal release from inhibition (quoted in Hobson, 1988, p. 203). Yet, the dialogues of dream reports hardly show any such undisciplined commotion.

In neurophysiological terms, it would appear that the disruption in the normal (wakeful) cerebral processes cited by Arkin to explain the anomaly of overt sleeptalking need not generally be invoked in the case of hallucinated dream speech. Our dream dialogue seems far removed from the "nonpropositional, automatic, overlearned phrases" that Jackson allowed that the right hemisphere may produce when released from domination by the left. Not only does dream speech display the grammatical well-formedness and complexity usually credited to the left hemisphere, there is furthermore little to suggest a strong loosening of integration between the two hemispheres either à la Jouvet or otherwise. Dream dialogue, presumably generated by the left hemisphere, seems (again in contrast to many a case of overt sleeptalking) closely linked to the visual scenario, which is correctly or incorrectly assumed to be generated by the right hemisphere. Furthermore, over half of the dream characters addressing to the dreamer recallable utterances are in fact identifiable (usually as relatives, friends or colleagues), while even those who are not identifiable are not necessarily indiscernible (insufficiently facially visualized).

As far as John Flavell and Juris Dragun's concept of microgenesis is concerned, there seem to be only sporadic examples in our corpus of recalled dream speech that would represent earlier ("premature") stages in the normal thought-generation process. One cannot, of course, totally disregard the possible influence of secondary revision. As we have noted, the final stage in the generation of *reported* dream speech—as opposed to the generation of hallucinated dream speech—is the overtly articulated (if not written) rendering after awakening; just as the final stage in the generation of speech in waking life is overt articulation. The aborting of primary-process components, which according the the microgenesis concept takes place (automatically and unconsciously) in wakeful speech, may no doubt be occurring in the reporting of dream speech as well, despite all deliberate attempts to avoid it. Nevertheless, it remains very noteworthy that our looking through the potential "window" onto a supposedly earlier stage in the normal speech generation process—a unique opportunity provided by the recalling of hallucinated dream speech—should yield specimens that are generally well formed and appropriate by wakeful standards. All this does not in itself necessarily argue against the validity of the microgenesis concept of thought production, be it in sleeping or wakefulness. It does, however, indicate that even dream speech as originally presented to the dreaming psyche may represent a stage in the speech generation process more advanced than has hitherto been generally acknowledged.

Our results can only lend support to Merton Gill's contention that Freud's exclusion of all intellectual achievement from the dreamwork proper represents too radical a formulation—and certainly insofar as the scriptwriting (a combination of grammatical proficiency and pragmatic competence) is considered to be a product of the intellect. The inhibition that in psychoanalytic theory is exercised in wakefulness by the secondary process upon the primary process is only partially relaxed during dreaming, and in fact, as far as speech is concerned, even less so than Gill himself seems to have recognized. Indeed, dream speech seems by no means to be the product of fundamentally primary processes, but rather of secondary processes that by perhaps relaxing some of their inhibitions may have compromised themselves with the inhibited forces thus released.

Alternatively, one may argue along the lines of Robert Holt that Freud's more extreme comments likening the id to a "chaos" and "seething cauldron" are indeed overly bold metaphors, a hypothetical limit, and that the unconscious retains a high degree of structure. But if one takes the dreamwork to be by definition a manifestation of processes of the unconscious, then inevitably one is forced to recognize a higher level of structural development in the id (as indicated by dream speech) than would seem reasonably tenable. In the absence of any significant evidence in favor of Freud's replay hypothesis for the generation of dream speech, one is better off viewing the dreamwork as representing regression in the developmental process, and a relatively modest regression at that. While the hypothetical id may have its own ancient language, grammar, and vocabulary, these are unlikely to be the linguistic tools capable of generating complex, propositional lines of dialogue that are furthermore largely appropriate to their contexts.

Regarding Pinchas Noy's original subdivision of the primary processes across four categories: His second subdivision, which allows that the primary process itself may be unconscious, but the product conscious—as in the case of a strange word or sentence in a dream that is a condensation of several familiar words—seems to be an accurate phenomenological description. But the product thus described is far more the exception than the rule in dream speech. If one wishes to maintain, as Noy does, that normal speech is indeed a secondary process in that it is dependent upon feedback for its ontogenetic development, then one must recognize that speech in dreams is largely the product of a secondary process, with only modest disturbances apparently due to primary-process contamination. Furthermore, instances of Noy's third subdivision (the primary process and its products are conscious, but the former only *ex post facto*), as exemplified by Freudian slips in wakefulness, are not totally unknown in dreaming, as attested to by the specimens of self-correction found in Freud's own dream reports as well as in our experiment corpus.

This has implications as well for Noy's more recent article with its self-centered versus reality-oriented distinction between the primary and secondary processes, respectively. Dialogue reported from dreams shows few characteristics that might be associated with self-centered autistic speech, since it adheres to the communal syntax of reality-oriented wakefulness and usually shows an appropriateness to context that one would expect of objective interpersonal communication.

In concluding, we may quote from Ernest Jones (1953), Freud's definitive biographer:

> Freud's revolutionary contribution to psychology was not so much his demonstrating the existence of an unconscious, and perhaps not even his exploration of its content, as his proposition that there are two fundamentally different kinds of mental processes, which he termed primary and secondary. (p. 436)

From the present and the previous chapter, however, we have seen that many of the psychoanalytic (neo-Freudian as well as classical) notions about dreaming are challenged when it comes to the matter of speech in dreams. This is not to say that the conception of the primary and secondary processes as characterizing the workings of the unconscious and conscious is necessarily invalid, but only that the matter of the respective contributions to dream formation of these processes and components of the mind is far from resolved. Alternatively: To the extent which dreams are viewed as *par excellence* manifestations of the unconscious, notions as to its structure are due for yet more revision.

Notes

1. See also note 2 of Chapter 6. It may be mentioned that the relative frequencies in the categories "by self," "nonself to self" and "nonself to nonself" (82, 91, and 32, respectively) differ highly significantly (χ^2 test, df $= 2$, $p < .0001$) from those in the previous experiment (also when the previous figures are compared to those for each of the three present utterance recall types separately). This reflects in particular the lesser participation of the self, especially active participation. (There is in fact significantly more "take" than "give"; sign test, $p < .01$.) The difference may be partly a consequence of difference in elicitation technique and the ubiquitous effect of secondary revision. Conceivably there is a tendency when recalling and telling a full dream scenario to include more nonself participation than when recalling only the single last line of dialogue, which may be more selectively retrieved. This is supported by Kraepelin's figures: Only nine of the almost three hundred dream speech specimens in his monograph issued from other persons.

2. Fewer than three percent of all directly quoted Dutch utterances showed apparent syntactic or morphological irregularities, a scarcity that can only contribute to the general acceptability. Dialect appears in fewer than two percent of these directly quoted Dutch utterances, and fewer than four percent of all the direct-form specimens involve a foreign language, including the last specimen in the second dream report given below. (Compare with the similar percentages of the first experiment.)

    As for the Freud's replay hypothesis, only for fewer than four percent of the immediately recalled directly quoted utterances for which the question of replay was asked did the respective subjects make a distinct connection with conversation of the day before the dream.

3. The unique nature of the telephone elicitation technique also motivated a comparative analysis of our dream corpus with laboratory-elicited dream reports and home diaries of dreams along various scales of social interaction (aggression, friendliness, and sex) and achievement (failure, success, misfortune, and good fortune) of Calvin Hall and Robert Van de Castle (1966). There appears a generally closer proximity of the telephone scores to the lab scores than to the home diary scores, and this is taken as indicating that in dream (report) production any conscious or unconscious inhibition is more operative in the dream retention and reporting process than in the formation process. In other words, factors such as interpersonal, oral communication with the experimenter—as opposed to indirect, anonymous, written communication—seem to have a greater influence on the final report than does the presence or absence of an experimental setting during the dreaming itself. The results are also broadly consistent with a presumed selectional bias operating in the retaining and written reporting of home dreams. This lends support to the contention that for normative dream studies the lab EEG-monitoring method is preferable to the home diary method. (See Heynick & De Jong, 1985.)

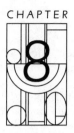

The Mind
and the Cognitive Capacities
of "Homo Somniloquens"

Of all the stuff of which dreams are made, only the verbal element can easily be reported in the same modality in which it was experienced, and subsequently be subjected to rigorous quantification and comparative analysis. This remains the major legacy of Kraepelin's study. In our own research we have endeavored to carry on from where Kraepelin left off, by providing corpora and concomitant data that are far more systematically elicited and far less biased than his and analyzing them in the light of recent knowledge from the cognitive and other sciences.

While our observations do not represent the final word on the matter (replications with EEG monitoring are strongly to be encouraged), it now seems reasonable to require that the characteristics of dream speech presented in the previous chapters—not least of all its ubiquity—be accounted for in a non–ad hoc way by any dream theory that pretends to completeness. Thus the phenomenon of dream speech becomes a crucial factor for discriminating between the value of one model of dream generation and that of the next.

Whereas Freud's theory exerted a profound influence on our view of dreams for most of the twentieth century, the past fifteen years or so have seen the introduction of several newer models of dream generation. These are generally non-Freudian—but sometimes aggressively anti-Freudian, thereby showing that Freud remains influential today, even if as an object of refutation. Be this as it may, the new models sometimes, like Freud's, have implications for the nature and functioning of the human mind in general. The question now is: Are they any better than the (neo-)psychoanalytic models in accommodating the experiment data presented in the previous chapters?

Dream Speech and Recent Theories
of the Function of Dreaming

The neurologically based *activation-synthesis hypothesis* was proposed by Harvard psychiatrists J. Allan Hobson and Robert McCarley. In their 1977 review of the influence of Freud's *Project* upon the psychodynamic model of dream generation presented in the *Traumdeutung*, these authors (McCarley & Hobson, 1977) criticize Freud for having based his dream theory upon inadequate (now largely out of date) neurological knowledge, and for consequently incorporating several principles that are gratuitous, if not blatantly false. These include Freud's assumption that neural energy cannot be canceled and must consequently be discharged at night in dream form. In a companion article, Hobson and McCarley (1977), while declaring their support for Freud's original mind-body isomorphism, present a model of dream generation that otherwise strongly differs from the psychoanalytic one. The present-day state of the art in neurobiology leads the two researchers to propose a hypothesis by which the dreamlike features of dreams are the product of largely random stimuli originating from the pontine brain stem (activation). Such inputs would have "little or no primary ideational, volitional, or emotional content" (p. 1347). This is a clear reversion, on a far more sophisticated physiological level, to the views of the nineteenth-century scientific establishment on the random nature of dream production. Something akin to Freud's "secondary revision" accounts for the reaction of the dreaming brain as these incoming pontogeniculo-occipital stimuli are integrated in the forebrain (synthesis). It is only here that any "psychological" significance may be acquired.

The psychoanalytic and the activation-synthesis models thus differ greatly as to the initial input to the dreaming process. Although Freud's sometimes varied formulations have understandably led to certain problems among psychoanalytic theorists, the most consistent interpretation of the psychoanalytic model is that the initial input includes some sort of real information, and that this is subsequently degraded by the entropy of the primary processes, which can so readily serve the requirements of the censor. The secondary revision, which later imposes a semblance of order and coherence (but no restoration of the original information) might not, according to one of Freud's formulations, even be part of the dreamwork proper. As we have noted, a main function of dreaming is, in Freud's view, the protection of sleep by the hallucinatory gratification of potentially disturbing wishes. This underlying "optative" content, which is transformed into the "present indicative" while also undergoing various primary-process degradations, theoretically stems, like the primary processes themselves, from early childhood. A side benefit—one that, in principle, achieved optimization with the advent of psychoanalysis—is the diagnostic and therapeutic use of the dream as symptom, through the recovery of the original information by means of free association, a kind of reversal of the primary processes. By contrast, Hobson and McCarley's activation-synthesis model—although allowing that, as in a Rorschach test, some psychological insight might be gained by the analysis of the way a given dreamer happens to synthesize the incoming stimuli—maintains that there is no original information to be retrieved or restored.

Be this as it may, Hobson and McCarley's strong emphasis on the *visual* areas of the cortex, and their consequent ignoring of the role played by verbal dialogue in the overall dream scenario, is in its own way reminiscent of Freud's degrading of the language faculty in dreams.

Dr. Hobson's recent book *The Dreaming Brain* elaborates the principles of activation-synthesis. With regard to one's lack of critical attention in dreams and subsequent general amnesia for what was dreamt—topics treated by Freud, Kraepelin, and others—Hobson suggests that there is a sort of shunting out for repairs of certain neurological systems during REM sleep. (This general proposition has roots going back some time. As one mid-nineteenth century scientist noted, "Sleep appears to be that particular state of cerebral inactivity which is essentially associated with the nutrition and repair of the brain substance" [Durham, 1860, p. 151]; and Kraepelin writes that "the highest and most difficult performances of our mental life are the ones which most urgently require the interpolation of recovery periods.") More specifically, the action potentials of the (evolutionarily more advanced) small neurons crucially necessary for attention and for the registering of events in memory are, according to Hobson, given a rest while their nuclei continue to manufacture vital synthetic enzymes.

Most relevant for explaining Freud's "primary process" features is Hobson's proposition that, furthermore, an array of repertories is exercised at night in the safe setting of general muscular paralysis. Although Hobson gives no historical references here, this concept, too, can be traced back many years—at least as far as a 1912 publication by the German psychoanalyst A. Maeder (cited by Freud in one of the revised editions of the *Traumdeutung*), who drew parallels between dreams and the play of animals and children, viewing both as the operation of innate instincts. This view draws support from studies of cats by Michel Jouvet and François Delorme (1965), which show that when the locus of the brain that normally inhibits the excitation of motor neurons during REM periods has been surgically destroyed, body movements involving pursuit, rage, or fear occur.

In his book, Hobson (1988) largely, if no longer totally, disregards the verbal element of dreams. One of his own dreams, here quoted in full, is highly illustrative:

I am in Williamstown, Massachusetts, talking to a colleague, Van, who is wearing a white shirt (he usually wears blue) open at the neck (he is normally neck-

tied, and even collar-clipped) and khakis (he usually sports flannels). Casual. Van says, as if by the way, that *he attended the committee meeting that has yesterday considered my candidacy for an invited lecture series.* (I know from his tone that he is going to deliver bad news.) The committee has decided against it because *"They don't feel that psychoanalysis should be confronted with laboratory data."*
I allowed as to how bad this idea was. *"It's the wrong reason,"* I said. *"And their timing is off, because Adolf Grünbaum is just about to publish his important new book in which he insists that this is precisely what psychoanalysis must do."* Van ignores this statement, appearing never to have heard of A. G.
Van then begins a gentle pirouette and tosses me a piece of hardware, something like the lock of a door or perhaps a pair of paint-frozen hinges. It is as if to say, "Here, take this as recompense." Despite my scavenger nature, I think I should refuse this "gift," and so I toss it back to Van on his next choreographic spin. He insists that *it is meant for me,* and the scene changes without clear resolution of whether or not I will keep it.
We go out a door (which is on the corner of the building) to behold the beautiful Williams campus. A red-brick walk extends down a green lawn to the classic white Puritan buildings.
Van says, *"They chose Mary"* (or seems to say that) *"reflecting their priorities, to attract a speaker who might help them with their fundraising efforts."*
"That is why you have such beautiful buildings," I note, *"and why there is nothing in them."* (pp. 232–233)

Hobson views Freud's primary-process manifestations (the incongruous dress, the pirouette, the uncertain object, and the abrupt change of scene) as being motivated by real physiological motor commands or eye movements of the auto-activated dreaming brain and lacking inherent symbolic or underlying meaning. This particular dream, however, does have psychological significance, according to Hobson himself: his anti-Freudian concerns and how these relate to various academic squabbles with his colleagues. This is clear from the *non*-primary process elements in the dream. Specifically (and also ironically, since it is just as in the case of Freud's "Irma" dream), Hobson's "Van" dream would be devoid of its anti-Freudian meaning if it were not for the abundant dialogue. And (again, just like Freud) Hobson seems to have difficulty incorporating within his overall dream model this all-important "secondary-process" dialogue, whose well-formedness and general appropriateness to the context would indicate a particular invulnerability to disruption from brain-stem impulses.
The problem of the place of dream speech in the activation-synthesis model is highlighted by a rather peculiar review of Hobson's book in the *New York Times*, which begins thus:

Years ago when I was a student, one of my friends went to West Germany to study for a few years. Before long, he found himself thinking and even dreaming in German. But something puzzled him about his dreams. Did the Germans in his dreams speak with the clumsy grammar and American accent that plagued my friend, or did they talk like native speakers? (Kolata, 1988, p. 36)

The reviewer states that "reading between the lines" in Hobson's book, she seems to have found the answers. She then goes on to give a simple summary of the activation-synthesis hypothesis (in essence not dissimilar to the one I have presented above), which in fact tells nothing of how speech even in one's native language is generated in dreams, let alone how to resolve the philosophically loaded matter of whether a foreign language spoken by foreigners in dreams may be more grammatical and accent-free than the dreamer's wakeful production in that language. Hobson himself (1988, p. 232), while acknowledging a general contribution of the "linguistic faculty of our brain-minds" to the overall dream narrative, readily concedes that we still know far too little about our brain in any of its functional states to hope to account for this contribution.

As noted in Chapter 1 (pp. 10–11), John Hughlings Jackson in England and Robert in Germany proposed a memory waste-disposal function of dreams, which was subsequently rejected by Freud. Eclipsed by the psychoanalytic view for most of the twentieth century, this housecleaning approach has, however, recently been dusted off, thanks to the renewed influence of physiology on sleep and dream research and, simultaneously, the general impact of the computer sciences on the cognitive sciences.

The late computer scientist and experimental psychologist Christopher Evans, of Britain's National Physics Laboratory, coauthored in the sixties a series of articles pointing to possible parallels between dreaming undergone by the brain during the relative isolation of nighttime and the cleaning-off of out-dated instructions and routines to which computers are regularly subjected during safe, offline periods. Evans' hypothesis was that dreams serve primarily as a memory filter, "a nightly examination of the vast mass of material collected in the course of the day, with a subsequent 'rejection' of redundant or inappropriate memories and responses" (Evans & Newman, 1964/1973, p. 372). In neither the biological nor the electronic brain is this process intended to erase old routines or memories, since, according to Evans, storage space is not the problem. Furthermore, there may be advantages in retaining old routines which could come in handy some day. Penfield's experiments by which short painless stimulation of the cortex during surgery seems to result in the patient's vivid reexperiencing of old memories, are interpreted by Evans as indicating that superfluous memories are sooner sealed off from normal access rather than erased.

The computer analogy approach is elaborated in Evans's (1983) recent book *Landscapes Of The Night*, which was edited, updated, and published posthumously by his colleague Peter Evans. Due account is taken of phylogenetic considerations (that sleep is more urgently required by the evolutionarily more advanced animals), and ontogenetic data (that the animal at a younger stage of development sleeps the most). Also considered are various anecdotal pieces of data on participants in stay-awake marathons, which Evans and Evans have distilled as follows: Hallucinations (cobwebs, animals, fire) appearing after several days of continual wakefulness are at first recognized as such by some overriding stream of consciousness (analogous, one might say, to the lucid state during dreaming). But as the sleepless days accumulate, the hallucinations can no longer be discriminated from reality. At the same time, paranoid delusions appear. (Let it be noted in this regard that, although manifestations of decreased cerebral cortex functioning, including speech difficulties, are well demonstrated, James Horne [1988, Ch. 2] of Loughborough University's Department of Human Sciences, in evaluating several series of sleep-deprivation studies, strongly doubts whether in otherwise normal subjects hallucinations typically do progress, even after more than a week of deprivation, to the point where they are indeed accepted by the subjects as probably or definitely real.)[1]

The prevention of such pathological phenomena is supposedly accomplished by the running of "keyword" programs during offline periods. Evans (1983) maintains that with a certain effort such thematic patterns can regularly be discerned in dreams:

> Let us imagine that the program being inspected is concerned with "metal": keys; furnaces; knife-grinder; motor cars. The conscious brain, coming to, could in a flash impose on this assemblage of images a coherent (if quaintly logical) story about losing car keys, vainly *asking* a passing knife-grinder *if he can cut some more*, returning forlornly to the locked automobile to see it being towed away by the police to a local furnace for melting down. (p. 200)

Quite clearly, the running of such programs would call for (to stick to Freud's term) secondary revision contributed by the waking (up) mind to the keywords, in this case the four things involved with metal. This secondary revision would apparently also be responsible for the addition of appropriate dialogue such as the question asked of the knife-grinder, which even in this merely hypothetical dream would most probably have gone on to include various conversations with the parking police if the authors had cared to invent some more details. How could such an incredibly large amount of secondary revision be accounted for?

That Evans and Evans also allow that certain dreams may be involved in more than thematic housecleaning is not very helpful in answering the above question. In a way not dissimilar to that of Hobson's "repertories," the authors permit the testing of various primitive programs. They in fact speculate that Jung's archetypes of the collective unconscious are indications of these and as such require no recourse to mystic explanations. In apparent contrast to Hobson, however, Evans and Evans also allow for the running of evolutionarily far more advanced programs, clearly on what Freud would call the secondary-process level. These are concerned with, among other things, situations such as "meeting people at social gatherings or sitting examinations" (p. 199). But the authors expressly state that the overwhelming majority of programs run are *not* of this nature but of the keyword type. The abundant dialogue therefore remains largely unaccounted for in any unforced way.

A similar approach, dubbed "reverse learning," has been taken by Francis Crick (the Nobel laureat codiscoverer of the structure of DNA) of California's Salk Institute and mathematician Graeme Mitchison of Cambridge's Kenneth Craik Laboratory. Rather than being based on analogies to digital computers, in which information is specifically addressed in specific locations, the reverse learning hypothesis draws upon studies of small-scale computer *modeling* of the types of neural nets presumed to underlie some of the actual functioning of the human and animal brains.

As such, Crick and Mitchison's (1983) approach recalls Freud's pre- and proto-psychoanalytic work in neurology of the early 1890s—a similar effort, likewise using neurons and synapses as the basic building blocks for the modeling of certain functions of the human mind. As we noted in Chapter 4 (p. 59), among the characteristics detailed in Freud's *On Aphasia* is the overdetermination of a given function. "The safeguards... against breakdown" are such, he writes, that "it can easily stand the loss of one or the other element" (1891/1953b, p. 74). In the *Project*, Freud (1895/1966) described the "defects" in the process of judgment arising from the tendency to substitute for the correct thing-complex of neurons a different complex that shares its "object" characteristics, but varies as to its "predicate" (attribute) component. This vulnerability is "necessitated precisely by the immense complexity" of the process (p. 384).

The modern computer-simulation model chosen by Crick and Mitchison is the so-called Hopfield net. Among its properties are that memories are distributed (that is, not stored exclusively in one or a few connections, but in the larger network), robust (resistant to destruction if a few synapses are altered), and superimposed (a single synapse can be involved in the storage of several overlapping but different memories). This last property is most relevant for the reverse-learning dream theory. If too many different memory patterns are superimposed, or the associations between the memories is so great that too much overlap results, there is overloading. The consequent outputs are the equivalents of fantasy (farfetched or bizarre associations), obsessions (any input produces the same state or small set of states), and hallucinations (those nets that feed back on themselves are inappropriately activated by an input signal that should normally produce no activation). Such phenomena would be severely detrimental to the survival of the organism if they occurred in wakefulness.

The underlying mechanism of Crick and Mitchison's reverse-learning theory are the same random ponto-geniculo-occipital (PGO) spikes that play such a prominent role in Hobson and McCarley's activation-synthesis hypothesis. Theoretically, these serve to trigger the aforementioned parasitic modes during the safety (isolation and paralysis) of REM sleep. The results appear in dream reports as Freud's primary-process features of condensation and displacement— if they happen to be recalled. Under the conditions of amnesia that accompany the great majority of dream experiences, the parasitic connections are successively dampened by the weakening of their synapses, and thus forgotten ("unlearned") and not reported.

The reverse-learning hypothesis further distinguishes itself from Evans and Evans's (digital) computer-cleaning analogy by drawing on certain specific ontogenic and phylogenetic data. The amount of REM sleep in the human foetus (as in the newborn) is vast both percentagewise and in absolute time, even though there are in the womb no events being recorded in memory to be subsequently unlearned. Crick and Mitchison believe its function to be the dampening of the parasitic synaptic modes that are the presumed consequence of the semirandom nature of early cortical growth. As for comparative phylogeny, recent studies of the Australian spiny anteater (*Echidna*) and the bottlenosed dolphin—whose enormous neocortexes rival in size those of man but whose cognitive abilities (presumably) are very much inferior to ours—show these mammals to be without REM sleep or PGO spikes. Crick and Mitchison interpret this as at least an indication that (in contrast to Evans) storage space is a factor, and that an alternative to the superimposition of memories is increased cortical mass, which would also eliminate the need for REM sleep and unlearning.

In contrast to Hobson and McCarley and to Evans and Evans, Crick and Mitchison reject the idea that routines or programs may also be practiced and reinforced during REM sleep. (Their reverse-learning hypothesis considers play during wakefulness to be sufficient for this purpose, and also allows that NREM sleep, which has no PGO spikes, may somehow be involved with memory consolidation.) What the dampening during REM sleep does accomplish is the reduction of confusion by sufficiently separating from one another those memories that are distinct but have features in common.

Noteworthy from the point of view of the present book is that, when it comes to accounting for dream dialogue, the reverse-learning approach seems to incorporate the most disadvantageous features of both Hobson and McCarley's activation-synthesis hypothesis and Evans and Evans's computer analogy. In at least one of their articles, Crick and Mitchison (1983) permit bizarre intrusions (mixings) to occur as often as every second or so. This presumed frequency might be expected to have all the more disruptive an influence on any attempt at the generation of appropriate dialogue. The authors furthermore quite frankly concede that their theory "has nothing useful to say about the narrative" (p. 113) of dreams—and by extension nothing useful to say about their verbal dialogue, which is presumably based on similar human cognitive capacities. Such explanations would have to be on a vastly more sophisticated level than the modeling of associative neural nets of the Hopfield type.

As for the psychological interpretation of dreams and their potential use in psychotherapy, the reverse-learning theory also happens to be the least hospitable. Crick and Mitchison, maintaining that dreams contain patterns of thought that are meant by nature to be forgotten, do not encourage their recall. This would not exclude the occasional use of dreams if the psychotherapeutic benefits were to outweigh the theoretical disadvantages. But such is unlikely to be the case, especially since the existing dream interpretation techniques are supposedly based on fundamental misconceptions about the nature and function of dreaming.

Not involving reverse learning, the activation-synthesis approach is less hostile to the concept of the psychological significance of some dreams and their analysis, even while strongly opposing the Freudian views of reductionism or camouflage. For Hobson (1988), the random errors involved in dream activation produce imagination, which may provide self-understanding when synthesized, and in any event may be likely to reflect our inner concerns.

Evans and Evans's computer-analogy approach might be expected, on the basis of the presumed housecleaning function of dreaming, to be as ill-disposed to the remembering of dreams as is the reverse-learning view. But the authors see some psychological significance possibly deriving from the supposed memory-consolidation function. They point to the speculation of Ernest Hartmann, who views condensation in dreams as nodal points between multiple brain pathways. New pieces of information left unconnected from the previous day link with old brain pathways to which they are somehow related, and achieve sufficient prominence to come to the awareness of the dreaming brain. Day's residues that are meaningful in terms of the dreamer's psychodynamics are especially likely to require the dreaming process for their incorporation into long-term memory. All this is broadly compatible with Freud's conception of the day's residues stimulating ancient wishes. But Hartmann (1973) modifies the psychoanalytic view. While allowing that old wishes and fears may indeed be among the main and most primitive channels for forming such connections, he maintains that they need not be the only ones.

A somewhat similar, but far more elaborate, memory consolidation approach has been proposed by Stanley Palombo of the Washington Psychoanalytic Institute. In his book *Dreaming and Memory: A New Information-Processing Model*, Palombo (1978) sees dreaming as being both adaptive and maladaptive (defensive). The Freudian primary-process feature of condensation is supposedly a manifestation of the former, while displacement indicates the latter.

Condensation (adaptive) in dreams supposedly indicates a matching process involving superimposition, by which specific locations in the permanent memory structure are determined for certain sensory impressions and experiences of the day before. These experiences are presumed to have already been flagged as novel and noteworthy by a filtering process during the previous NREM sleep period. For each transfer of such a day residue from short-term memory, a closely related long-term memory in the labyrinth of the memory structure has to be recovered. When, during REM sleep, superimposed images are deemed coherent, the day residue can be introduced into the permanent memory structure. According to Palombo, the process is consciously experienced as an hallucinatoid dream because, when the memories are in the sensory (visual, auditory, and so on) modes, they are as close as possible to the form in which they were originally experienced in wakefulness and can elicit corresponding emotions. This would, in a way similar to that proposed by Hartmann, aid in determining the pathways to the appropriate ancient memory, which may be similarly affect-laden.

In keeping with other dream theorists, such as Jung, Crick, and Foulkes, Palombo points to the importance of the investigation of *series* of dreams on consecutive nights. This aspect was basically de-emphasized by Freud, who did, however, make some passing references to "confirmation" or "corroboration dreams" occurring on the night following the dream he originally analysed. The value of dream series follows from Palombo's theorization that an anxiety dream that leads to awakening is not usually a wish whose insufficiently disguised fulfillment causes the dream to defeat what Freud presumed to be its purpose as protector of sleep. Rather, according to the information-processing model, such awakenings during REM sleep result when the matching mechanism fails to find a reasonably close fit between a day residue and the contents of the permanent memory structure, especially when the older memory being tested carries an affective charge that indicates a danger situation apparently overlooked the previous day. The memory of the failed dream then becomes part of the following day's residue, and the integrative mechanisms of the ego go to work, sorting new information that may be relevant to the problem posed by the dream. The "correction dream" on the following night will, hopefully, succeed in integrating into the permanent memory structure the short-term memory that resisted incorporation the previous night, and this time consequently there will be no heightened anxiety or awakening.

A matching failure in the original dream is theoretically caused by a censor, quite similar in nature to the one Freud described. This is manifested in the dream by the maladaptive-defensive primary process mechanism of displacement: the substitution in the matching process of a closely associated memory representation for the original one, due to the latter's overly strong affective charge. Whereas for Freud such censorship was in keeping with the natural function of dreams, for Palombo this runs contrary to it. However, the skillful interpretation of those dreams that cause awakening and are offered by analysands may, in Palombo's theory just as in Freud's, afford insight into the psychic structure of the dreamer. In Palombo's view, this may also subsequently enhance and accelerate the presumed information-processing function of dreams.

Palombo's divergence from Freud as to the function of dreams also leads him to suggest a revision of the traditional psychoanalytic model of the psyche, along lines quite similar to Robert Holt's, discussed above.

Palombo allows a certain structure to what he terms the "archaic adaptive ego," which he considers to be part of the unconscious id (and, as such, distinct from Freud's ego). The archaic adaptive ego develops under the influence of feedback from the environment. The primitive mechanism of comparison in dreaming—as opposed to the reflective problem-solving characteristic of the mature adaptive ego—is typical of the structure designed for the rapid processing of large amounts of information. In the archaic ego, Palombo (1978) states, "decisions are computed rather than willed, automatic rather than thought through." Subsequent evolutionary development leading to Freud's secondary processes involve, Palombo writes, "the voluntary aspects of conscious thought, the sense of 'making up one's mind' or 'making a conscious choice.' Only at this later stage of evolution would consciousness have been shaped and organized by *narrative, grammatical, and logical* [italics added] conventions of the output program which now dominates our awareness" (pp. 191–192).

The question now is the extent to which the secondary processes, thus defined, contribute to dream formation, if they do at all. Palombo ignores the verbal aspect of dreams, even though dreams that he himself presents contain dialogue. ("I asked him *how he met her,* and he said *his cousin fixed him up in Iceland*"; "Finally the guy gave me some correct change and took the two Richmond bills and said *he would get change of some sort.*") Palombo does, however, directly address the question, "Is the mechanism of superimposition sufficient to account for the *narrative* [italics added] complexity of a dream? . . ." He answers this by saying that "until more direct evidence of . . . higher-level integrative processes appears, . . . I would prefer to assume that the matching process, together with the censorship, accounts for *all* [italics added] the observable features of the manifest dream" (pp. 129–130). In Palombo's information-processing approach, the narrative sequence of the dream may itself be derived from memory representation (a sort of video tape playback comparable to the audio tape in Freud's replay hypothesis). Alternatively, a "relatively simple . . . quasi-linguistic mechanism" may be responsible for arranging the dream elements into a sequence with narrative continuity. Palombo refers to digital computers having a simple program capable of generating syntactically correct sentences when provided with words whose parts of speech (noun, verb, adjective, and so on) have been marked. The frequent semantic meaninglessness of such output (Palombo cites Chomsky's classic example, "Colorless green ideas sleep furiously") are described by Palombo as "dreamlike."

But these simple generative mechanisms, being not linguistic but "quasi-linguistic," are put forward (whether sufficiently convincingly or not) in order to explain the generation of the dream *narrative* and not the dream speech within it. We have repeatedly seen how, in its general appropriateness and importance to the overall dream scenario, dream dialogue is typically not dreamlike in Palombo's sense, and is in fact far more meaningful than constructions of the "Colorless green ideas sleep furiously" variety.

In summary: None of the approaches considered in this and the previous chapters—neither Freud's (and the Freudians'), Hobson and McCarley's, Crick and Mitchison's, Evans and Evans's, nor Palombo's—are capable of accounting satisfactorily for the abundant verbal dialogue in dreams and its well-documented characteristics.

What else do these theories have in common? Two of the five—Hobson and McCarley's and Crick and Mitchison's—are basically physiological, and Freud's is at least partly derived from his semineurological *Project*. Only Freud's and Palombo's have as a prime purpose the use of dreams in psychotherapy (dreams being presumed to contain messages), and only their theories go on to encompass general models of the structure of the normal and the deviant psyche. What all five approaches do have in common, however, is an attempt to explain the biological *function* of dreaming, even if their respective explanations are often radically at odds with one another.

It is perhaps this constructing of a model around some function of dreaming that (especially when that model is fundamentally physiological in nature) results in the greatest inadequacies when it comes to accounting for the verbal aspects of dreams, given the present state of the art. Interestingly, Freud (1900/1953a, p. 75) himself declares that "it need not necessarily be possible to infer a *function* of dreaming (whether utilitarian or otherwise) from [a] theory." What "deserves to be called a theory of dreams," according to Freud, is "any disquisition upon dreams which seeks to explain as many as possible of their characteristics from a particular point of view, and which at the same time defines the position occupied by dreams in a wide sphere of phenomena."

Psycholinguistics and Psychoneirics

The psychoneirics approach, proposed by David Foulkes of Emory University's Department of Psychiatry and the Georgia Institute of Mental Health, is patterned on the discipline of psycholinguistics that resulted from the transformation-generative revolution in linguistics. As we discussed in Chapter 5 (p. 212), psycholinguistics concentrates on the *midrange* stages of speech production: what speakers *can* say and comprehend and *how* they do so, given the grammar of the language they have internalized and the capacities and limitations of the auxiliary psychological mechanisms at their disposal, such as short-term memory. This focus, we recall, is distinct from that of a more general language psychology, concerned with such matters as pragmatic competence: the situations in which speakers produce a given utterance and their purpose for doing so. Of course, psycholinguistics in no way denies that (at least in wakefulness) speech-acts usually have a purpose and that verbal language has a function. Indeed, an often restated theme in the present book is the undeniably enormous selectional advantage of the development of verbal language in the course of human evolution. But this is not the primary focus of modern psycholinguistics.

For its part, the psychoneirics approach allows that dreaming *may* likewise have a function. Perhaps, à la Hobson and McCarley, REM sleep has something to do with programming our minds to deal with novel situations adaptively; or it might contribute, à la Evans and Evans, to our ability to retrieve recent experiences in evocative memory and to integrate recent evocative memories with older evocative memories (Foulkes, 1985). But such speculation is quite peripheral. Furthermore, it should be noted that, unlike the case with verbal languages, the development of dreaming, or of a grammar of dreams, of course requires no exposure to a corpus of dreams of other people, although it may be dependant in other respects upon social and linguistic development.)

Similarly, although psychoneirics, like psycholinguistics, may take some neurophysiological findings into consideration, one of its major contentions (Foulkes, 1981) is that the rather fruitful collaboration between dream research and neurophysiology since the discovery of REM sleep (notably the methodology of laboratory awakenings to elicit dream reports), has reached a point of diminishing returns. In the foreseeable future there will remain, just as in the case of psycholinguistics, far too large a gap between the level at which neurophysiologists work and the complex cerebral and cognitive integration that must be involved in what should be viewed as the skillful act of human dream generation.

As our experiment results have clearly demonstrated, the shifts from left to right cortical hemispheric dominance detected by some researchers when their subjects cross the border into dreamland are, at most, relative changes rather than signs of verbal disengagement, a point emphasized by Foulkes (1982). This fact allows the possibility on the psychological level that the *midrange stages of dream production* may to a large extent be identical to those of speech production. Dreaming processes involve "schematic selection" and "element activation," which are the analogues of syntactic frame (sentence structure) selection and word selection, and may draw upon the same uniquely human capacities. The narrative aspects of the dream, about which other theories admit that they have so little to say, can be readily accounted for with such an approach. Among the anecdotal evidence for a common linguistic and dream-narrative competence are reports that aphasics lose their capacity to dream, and not just their capacity to verbally report their dreams.

The psychoneiric emphasis is on the "lawfulness" of dream generation, which is seen as inviting comparison to the normal rule-governed production of speech. This is not to deny that many, perhaps most, dreams, contain Freud's primary-process features, such as condensations. Rather, psychoneirics views such anomalies as residual flux of a dream production mechanism that has otherwise done a reasonably good job of adapting to the diffuse activation of mneumonic elements certain syntactic plans that conform to the formal principles of narrative development (Foulkes, 1985). Furthermore, psychoneirics emphasizes that such anomalies, while atypical by wakeful standards, are "lawfully atypical" in that they obey certain constraints in combining, by which, for example, overdetermined faces in dreams are far more likely to be segmented horizontally than vertically (an indication of the nature of human memory organization). This is analogous to the "lawful" errors in linguistic performance referred to in Chapter 5 (p. 213).

But if Foulkes's psychoneirics model stands in opposition to Freud's and to Hobson and McCarley's (and to Crick and Mitchison's variant) in that its origins are psychological rather than neurobiological, it seems to be lined up with Hobson and McCarley's against Freud's on the matter of randomness, at least as this applies to the degree of informational content of the original input. Foulkes's initial diffuse activation of cortical knowledge and mnemonic systems is (like the initial brainstem input to the cortex in the activation-synthesis model) inherently devoid of information before being acted upon and sustained by a process similar to Freud's secondary revision. On this theoretical difference hinges much of the age-old question of whether dreams contain what may be considered messages, as well as much of their ultimate value as an adjunct in psychotherapy. Although Foulkes believes that the Freudian technique of free association may be of scientific value for tracking down the mnemonic elements in question, he sees this as serving no diagnostic or therapeutic purpose. In this sense, the anti-Freudianism of the psychoneirics model is even more extreme than that of the activation-synthesis approach.

Yet, one wonders whether the psychoneirics processes Foulkes proposes may nevertheless be biased toward producing a greater amount of dream content with psychodynamic significance than he himself would allow. Here, certain of Freud's comparisons and contrasts between dream language and verbal language (treated in Chapter 2, pp. 12–21) become particularly relevant. The theoretical concept that dreams have as their underlying *input* childhood wishes whose information is degraded by primary-process interference, may now indeed be outdated. But Freud's views on language have, as we have seen, a wide scope. These may be more viable today than is generally recognized, and may—in so far as our dreams and verbal language are presumed to make use of the same uniquely human cognitive capacities—be worthy of renewed consideration.

We can return to the matter of overdetermination as a case in point. Foulkes refers on the one hand to a certain regularity in dream production in that a pattern of mnemonic activation, once initiated, is constrained by the structure of the dreamer's memory network; on the other hand, radical discontinuity in the theme of the dream would indicate a shift to a new site in symbolic memory "without obvious connections to the sites previously activated" (Foulkes, 1985, p. 151). Regarding the Freudian concept that multiple meanings may be condensed into a single dream image, Foulkes states that "the analogy to speech and ordinary waking thought totally breaks down, since semantic intent typically is unitary (you mean one thing and that is what you say and think)" (p. 165). But in fact the analogy does not totally break down, at least not in the psychoanalytic scheme of things. Freud maintained that even everyday verbal language is far from always unitary, and he particularly pointed to condensations and displacements in parapraxes (as well as in jokes and poetry). In such cases, the initial input into the language generation process is not infantile; rather, theoretically retrogressive primary-processes are exerting influence on secondary-process speech.

The psychoneirics model does not ignore the fact that slips of the tongue occur in normal waking life. But Foulkes dismisses such puzzling outputs of symbolic processing as simply "lawful occurrences in a standard cognitive system." Since the product obeys the rules of permissible phonological and morphological combinations, there is supposedly no need to "conjure up hidden motives to explain errors of speech" (p. 162). Yet, in the *Psychopathology of Everyday Life* and other writings, Freud, for his part, gives no indication that for a slip of the tongue (Spooner's "emanciated") or a joke word ("famillionairely" in the Heine story) to be "Freudian," it has to violate such combinatory rules—any more than a psychodynamically signficant composite image in the *Traumdeutung* needs to violate the lawful combinatory rules involving the nature of human memory organization and segmentation (typified, again, by the fact that dreams are far more likely to present a face composed of different lower and upper halves—as in the composite of Freud's brother and Freud's colleague M.—than of different left and right halves). Furthermore, "Freudian" slips have been evoked in the laboratory, and indications are that these are enhanced by diversion of attention and the relaxation of inhibitory mechanisms (Motley, 1980). Referring back to the quasi-neurological concepts of Chapter 6 (pp. 229–230), it would seem plausible that the spreading activation operating within the freedom and constraints of the hierarchical network under the peculiar circumstances of dreaming may—at certain times and with certain people—yield dream elements whose links to one another have psychodynamic significance. This may even be the case when the elements are (to repeat Foulkes's phrase) "without obvious connection."

Here, instances of speech, that uniquely human and quantifiable activity, *within* dreaming may serve to index the extent to which our nightly life may be *either more or less prone* to psychodynamically significant disruption and interruption than our everyday life.

Apparent word-blends characterize less than two percent of all the directly quoted utterances retrieved in our second experiment. One utterance consists of the single compound word *"Surf-wound-powers,"* which the subject had in mind upon awakening from a reverie over a beach. Another example concerns a kryptogram and a nonexistent word: *"Hey, it comes out 'senerarisol.' "* A third specimen likewise involves recreation: *"Yes, you've got keent,"* said in the dream by one cardplayer to another in explaining an unusual game. The fourth instance, *"Did you know the pin-areas?"* (or *"pin-mountains,"* the subject was not sure), was said to the dreamer by a classmate, in reference to homework.

The 11 of the scored utterances (just over five percent) whose ratings fall predominantly on the "inappropriate" side of the scale are likewise relevant here. These include the half-English, half-Dutch specimen that the dreamer addressed to her shoe in report 2, (p. 259). Or consider the following excerpt:

> And then a black carriage came by and a man was sitting in it with black clothes on. . . . And we began to ride, and then I got terribly ill and had to vomit. And then it appeared that I had swallowed a little bird. And then the man sang *"You ate the household garbage up, and left the tasty things over."*

The last line was recognized by the awakened subject as a distortion of the well-known Dutch children's song in which a parrot says, "I ate my food up and left my drink over." This variation seems to have been composed in the dream itself.

An excerpt from another dream may also be illustrative:

> And then I'm with some people . . . in a café or bar. And, yeah, I was doing some looking around and I was surprised by the fact that so many people made contact so quickly with one another. And, yeah, someone said with regard to this, *"It's just as if they were walking around with their headlights on."*

In most of these instances it seemed in fact quite unclear to the subject what was meant. Any attempt to establish whether the errors were indeed Freudian in the psychodynamic sense would, of course, have been beyond the immediate scope of the experiment. It is, however, worth noting, anecdotally, that the respective subjects seemed quite ready to speculate on the latent meanings of the word-blends, along lines similar to Freud's analysis of his "Here comes the breakfastship" utterance and his "Autodidasker" dream.

This brings to mind the widely recognized principle that dreams are especially suitable for use in therapy, since analysands are more apt to consider the dream as products of their unconscious or repressed mental life than they are (wakeful) slips of the tongue or acting out (Eisenstein, 1980). But admittedly this does not in and of itself provide evidence that psychodynamic processes in fact contributed to the dream generation. Just as Foulkes (1985, p. 207) quite reasonably points out, "life is meaningful and interconnected," so one can always, in the manner of a Rorschach test, "start with a dream and end off with all sorts of more-or-less valid statements about the dreamer."

From the viewpoint of psychoneirics, the secondary benefit from the study of dreaming is not for the psychotherapist but rather for the cognitive and developmental psychologist. For example, the typically thematic as opposed to pictorial link between various dream images—the image, for example, of a spoked wheel is more likely (in a way similar to the running of Evans's hypothetical keyword programs) to be followed by some transportation theme than by an image of a daisy or a bullethole in glass—may indicate that human memory is not pictorial but involves abstract representations of symbolic knowledge. Similarly, features found in the systematic study of events in children's dreams indicate that human recollection is reconstructive rather than a matter of reproductive visual replays. Furthermore, dreams can, as we have seen, help discriminate between automatic and self-controlled mental processes and index their ontogenetic development. And manifest errors in dreams offer clues to the inner workings that generate them, just as language performance errors in wakefulness do.

The phenomenon of reversals, something supposedly standing for its opposite, is a case in point. We have seen (Chapter 2, p. 18) that in the "Market" dream in the *Traumdeutung*, a *closed* meat shop supposedly represented an open meat shop, and how such reversals are paralleled by slips of the tongue in Freud's *Psychopathology of Everyday Life*, such as the Austrian president's opening the parliament by declaring the sitting closed. While Freud treated both instances as psychodynamically determined, psychoneirics, like psycholinguistics, sooner sees such "primary-process" phenomena merely as indications that some concepts may be encoded in a negative form in memory (an hypothesis supported by many word-association experiments) and hence be particularly susceptible to switching.

So it may also be that the study of specifically verbal aspects of nighttime mental activity is rewarding even in the absence of psychodynamic implications. Comparisons with sleeptalking (the actual articulation of words in sleep) may be instructive, even though this phenomenon is usually not directly related to REM periods. Although the evidence is still largely anecdotal, Arthur Arkin indicates in his book that the sleeptalker is unlikely to reveal, either in a manifest or traceable latent way, his indiscretions to his bedmate—or in fact to communicate any message particularly worth losing sleep over. If this anecdotal data is someday confirmed by systematic studies, it may deprive not only novelists and playwrights (going back at least as far as Shakespeare) of a favorite dramatic device, but also depth pyschologists of a window on (in the words of the Italian psychiatrist G. Andriani, 1892, a forerunner of Freud) "the mind freed of restraints stemming from reality, conscience, education and consciousness [which] reveals itself 'in the nude' " (quoted in Arkin 1981, p. 277). Nevertheless, staying up at night and studying this phenomenon has proven worthwhile for cognitive and language psychologists. As we saw in Chapter 7 (p. 247), the data obtained has lent support to a general (wakeful) psycholinguistic model in which syntactic processes are assumed capable of operating in the absence of central attention. Similar rewards may come from the study of our hallucinated verbal behavior in REM dreaming and hypnagogic dreaming.

Kraepelin's approach was, as we noted in the Introduction, in line with John Hughlings Jackson's dictum, "Find out about dreams and you will find out about insanity." Similarly, Hobson (1988) makes several references to dreaming as a "model of psychopathology, a normal functional psychosis whose understanding could provide a key to major psychiatric dysfunctions" (p. 229). As far as speech in REM dreams is concerned, these seem to be overly optimistic expectations. Even two millenia ago Plato (1987, p. 129) quoted Theaetetus and Socrates (two quite sane men) as agreeing: "There is no difficulty in supposing that during all this discussion we have been talking to one another in a dream; and when we are actually dreaming and talk in our dreams, the resemblance of the two states in quite astonishing." As for hypnagogic and hypnopompic verbal phenomena, only future research may determine whether Kraepelin was indeed on the right track in comparing them to various forms of psychotic and aphasic speech.

The further establishment of indices for verbal behavior in, on the one hand, REM dreams, hypnagogic dreamlets, and overt sleeptalking, and, on the other hand, normal speech, natural and laboratory-induced parapraxes, and various pathological conditions—as these relate to such factors as automatic mechanisms, feedback/attention, intention, and entropy, and, to the extent possible, to their underlying neurophysiological substrata—would not only be fully in keeping with the most modern cognitive approach to dream research. It would also be very much in the spirit of Kraepelin's study of more than three-quarters of a century ago.

Whatever such future research may reveal, we seem already to have a reasonably certain answer to the question posed at the beginning of this book: Can the label *Homo somniens* serve as well as *Homo sapiens* and *Homo loquens* to distinguish species?

Animals think and communicate, and it is also quite possible that they have dreams of sorts. But the gap between animal and human dreams would most likely be on the same order of magnitude as the gulf between animal and human cognition, and between animal communication and human verbal language. Our REM dreams, for all their aberrations, generally show adherence to a story grammar unique to the cognitive abilities of *Homo sapiens*. And included in the dream scenarios thus generated is abundant verbal material, the product of the unique linguistic capacities of *Homo loquens*.

Note

1. With regard to sleep rebound (extra sleep taken by the laboratory subject during the first few nights after deprivation), Horne (1988) notes that this usually amounts in toto to less than 25 percent of the total amount of deprived sleep time. Of this, the

regain of stages 1 and 2 NREM is minimal, while the regain of stage 4 NREM is over two thirds, with stage 3 NREM scoring intermediately. The amount of REM sleep regained is about half the total of the lost REM sleep. Horne interprets this as showing that at least half our REM sleep is dispensible, while the other half (along with most of the stage 4 NREM sleep, which is evidently all the more essential) may indeed be involved in cerebral restitution. These and other considerations lead Horne to postulate the following distinction: "Core sleep," which occupies the first five or six hours of the night and contains much stage 4 NREM, some stage 3 NREM, little stage 1 and 2 NREM, and about half the night's REM sleep, probably has a restitution function. "Optional sleep," occurring in the last two or so hours of the night, containing mostly stages 1 and 2 NREM and the other half of a normal night's REM sleep, may have evolved simply to keep the organism safe and quiet until daylight, without serving any restorative purpose.

References

Alexander, F. G. & Selesnick, S. T. (1968). *The history of psychiatry*. New York: Mentor.

Almansi G. & Béguin, C. (Eds.). (1987). *Theatre of sleep: An anthology of literary dreams*. London: Picador.

Anderson, E. W. (1962). Foreword. In M. Hamilton (Ed.), *Fish's schizophrenia* (pp. xiii–xiv). Bristol, England: John Wright & Sons.

Andriani, G. (1892). Fisiologia psicologica del somniloquio [Psychological physiology of somniloquy]. *Annali di Neurologia* (Torino), *10*, 299–308.

Aristotle. (1987). Are dreams prophetic? [excerpt from De divinatione per somnum]. In G. Almansi & C. Béguin (Eds.), *Theatre of sleep: An anthology of literary dreams* (pp. 129–131). London: Picador.

Arkin, A. M. (1981). *Sleeptalking: Psychology and psychophysiology*. Hillsdale, NJ: Lawrence Erlbaum.

Arkin, A. M., Toth, M. F., Baker, J., & Hastey, J. M. (1970). The degree of concordance between the content of sleeptalking and mentation recalled in wakefulness. *Journal of Nervous and Mental Disease, 151*, 375–393.

Aserinsky, E., & Kleitman, N. (1953). Regularly occurring periods of eye motility, and concomitant phenomena, during sleep. *Science, 118*, 273–274.

Baudry, F. (1974). Remarks on the spoken word in dreams. *Psychoanalytic Quarterly, 43*, 581–605.

Beaugrande, R. de. (1979). Towards a general theory of creativity. *Poetics, 8*, 269–306.

Berrios, G. E., & Hauser, R. (1988). The early development of Kraepelin's ideas on classification: A conceptual history. *Psychological Medicine, 18*, 813–821.

Bertini, M., Violani, C., Zoccolotti, P., Antonelli, A., & DiStafano, L. (1983). Performance on a unilateral tactile test during waking and upon awakenings from REM and NREM. In W. P. Koella (Ed.), *Sleep 1982* (pp. 383–385). Basel: Karger.

Bock, J. K. (1982). Towards a cognitive psychology of syntax: Information processing contributions to sentence formulation. *Psychological Review, 89*, 1–47.

Bohr, N. (1963). *Essays (1958–1962) on atomic physics and human knowledge.* New York: International Universities Press.

Brill, A. A. (1946). *Psychoanalytic Psychiatry.* New York: Vintage Books.

Campbell, J. (1982). *Grammatical man: Information, entropy, language and life.* New York: Simon and Schuster.

Charcot, J.-M. (1883). Des variétés de l'aphasie [On varieties of aphasia]. *Progrès Medical, 11,* 487–488.

Chomsky, N. (1957). *Syntactic Structures.* The Hague: Mouton.

Chomsky, N. (1959). [Review of B.F. Skinner's *Verbal Behavior*]. *Language, 35,* 26–58.

Chomsky, N. (1976). *Reflections on language.* London: Temple Smith.

Chomsky, N, (1980). *Rules and representations.* Oxford: Basil Blackwell.

Chomsky, N. (1986). *Knowledge of language, its nature, origin and use.* New York: Praeger.

Cicero. (1987). Dreams and diet [excerpt from De divinatione]. In G. Almansi & C. Béguin (Eds.), *Theatre of sleep: An anthology of literary dreams* (pp. 135–136). London: Picador.

Cohen, A. (1980). Correcting of speech errors in a shadowing task. In V. A. Fromkin (Ed.), *Errors in linguistic performance: Slips of the tongue, ear, pen, and hand* (pp. 157–163). New York: Academic Press.

Collins, A. M., & Loftus, E. F. (1975). A spreading-activation theory of semantic processing. *Psychological Review, 82,* 407–428.

Comb, G. (1841). *The constitution of man: Considered in relation to external objects.* Boston: William Ticknor.

Crick, F., & Mitchison, G. (1983). The function of dream sleep. *Nature, 304,* 111–114.

Cudworth, R. (1731). *A treatise concerning eternal and immutable mortality.* London.

Darwin, C. (1981). *The descent of man.* Princeton: Princeton University Press. (Original work published 1871).

Dawood, N. J. (1968). Introduction. In *The Koran* (pp. 9–12). Harmondsworth, England: Penguin.

Delaney, G. (1979). *Living your dreams.* New York: Harper & Row.

Delboef, J. R. L. (1885). *Le sommeil et les rêves* [Sleep and dreams]. Paris.

Dell, G. S., & Reich, P. A. (1980). Toward a unified model of slips of the tongue. In V. A. Fromkin (Ed.), *Errors in linguistic performance: Slips of the tongue, ear, pen, and hand* (pp. 273–286). New York: Academic Press.

Dement, W. C. (1972). *Some must watch, while some must sleep.* San Francisco: W. H. Freeman.

Dement, W. C., & Kleitman, N. (1957). The relation of eye movements during sleep to dream activity: An objective method for the study of dreaming. *Journal of Experimental Psychology, 53,* 339–346.

Dorus, E., Dorus, W., & Rechtschaffen, A. (1971). The incidence of novelty in dreams. *Archives of General Psychiatry, 25,* 364–368.

Dunne, J. W. (1927). *An experiment with time.* London: Faber & Faber.

Durham, A. E. (1860). Physiology of sleep. *Guy's Hospital Reports, 6,* 149–173.

Eisenstein, S. (1980). The dream in psychoanalysis. In J.M. Natterson (Ed.), *The Dream in Clinical Practice* (pp. 319–331). New York: Harper & Row.

Ellis, A. W. (1980). On the Freudian theory of speech errors. In V. A. Fromkin (Ed.), *Errors in linguistic performance: Slips of the tongue, ear, pen, and hand* (pp. 81–86). New York: Academic Press.

Emerson, R. W. (1884). *Lectures and biographical sketches.* Boston: Houghton Mifflin.

Emrich, H. M., & Wiegand, M. (Eds.) (1991). *Integrative biological psychiatry.* Berlin: Springer Verlag.

Evans, C. (1983). *Landscapes of the night.* New York: Washington Square.

Evans, C. R., & Newman, E. A. (1973). Dreaming: an analogy from computers. In S. G. M. Lee & A. R. Mayes (Eds.), *Dreams and dreaming: Selected readings* (pp. 371–377). Harmondsworth, England: Penguin. (Original work published in 1964).

Faraday, A. (1974). *The dream game.* Harmondsworth, England: Penguin.

Fay, D. (1980). Transformational errors. In V. A. Fromkin (Ed.), *Errors in linguistic performance: Slips of the tongue, ear, pen and hand* (pp. 111–122). New York: Academic Press.

Fischer-Homberger, E. (1975). Germany and Austria. In J. G. Howells (Ed.), *World history of psychiatry* (pp. 256–290). London: Baillière Tindall.

Fisher, C. (1976). Spoken words in dreams: A critique of the views of Otto Isakower. *Psychoanalytic Quarterly, 45,* 100–109.

Flavell, J. H., & Draguns, J. (1957). A microgenetic approach to perception and thought. *Psychological Bulletin, 54,* 197–215.

Fliess, R. (1953). On the "spoken word" in the dream. In R. Fliess (Ed.), *The revival of interest in the dream: A critical study of post-Freudian psychoanalytic contributions.* New York: International Universities Press.

Foulkes, D. (1981). Dreams and dream research. In W. P. Koella (Ed.), *Sleep 1980* (pp. 168–169). Basel: Karger.

Foulkes, D. (1982). A cognitive-psychological model of REM dream production. *Sleep*, 5, 169–187.

Foulkes, D. (1985). *Dreaming: A cognitive-psychological approach*. Hillsdale, NJ: Lawrence Erlbaum.

Freud, S. (1953a). The interpretation of dreams. In J. Strachey (Ed. and Trans.), *The standard edition of the complete psychological works of Sigmund Freud* (Vols. 4–5) London: Hogarth Press. (Original work published 1900)

Freud, S. (1953b). *On aphasia* (E. Stengel, Trans.). New York: International Universities Press. (Original work published 1891)

Freud, S. (1954). *The origins of psychoanalysis: Letters to Wilhelm Fliess*. New York: Basic Books.

Freud, S. (1955a). Analysis of a phobia in a five-year-old boy. In J. Strachey (Ed. and Trans.), *The standard edition of the complete psychological works of Sigmund Freud* (Vol. 10, pp. 1–150). London: Hogarth Press. (Original work published 1909)

Freud, S. (1955b). Beyond the pleasure principle. In J. Strachey (Ed. and Trans.), *The standard edition of the complete psychological works of Sigmund Freud* (Vol. 18, pp. 1–64). London: Hogarth Press. (Original work published 1920)

Freud, S. (1955c). Two encyclopedic articles. In J. Strachey (Ed. and Trans.), *The standard edition of the complete psychological works of Sigmund Freud* (Vol. 18, pp. 241–242). London: Hogarth Press. (Original work published 1923)

Freud, S. (1957a). The antithetical meaning of primal words. In J. Strachey (Ed. and Trans.), *The standard edition of the complete psychological works of Sigmund Freud* (Vol. 11, pp. 153–162). London: Hogarth Press. (Original work published 1910)

Freud, S. (1957b). A metapsychological supplement to the theory of dreams. In J. Strachey (Ed. and Trans.), *The standard edition of the complete psychological works of Sigmund Freud* (Vol. 14, pp. 217–236). London: Hogarth Press. (Original work published 1915)

Freud, S. (1957c). The unconscious. In J. Strachey (Ed. and Trans.), *The standard edition of the complete psychological works of Sigmund Freud* (Vol. 14, pp. 159–204). London: Hogarth Press. (Original work published 1915)

Freud, S. (1958a). An evidential dream. In J. Strachey (Ed. and Trans.), *The standard edition of the complete psychological works of Sigmund Freud* (Vol. 12, pp. 267–278). London: Hogarth Press. (Original work published 1913)

Freud, S. (1958b). Psychoanalytic notes on an autobiographical account of a case of paranoia (dementia paranoides). In J. Strachey (Ed. and Trans.), *The standard edition of the complete psychological works of Sigmund Freud* (Vol. 12, pp. 1–84). London: Hogarth Press. (Original work published 1911)

Freud, S. (1959a). An autobiographical study. In J. Strachey (Ed. and Trans.), *The standard edition of the complete psychological works of Sigmund Freud* (Vol. 20, pp. 1–70). London: Hogarth Press. (Original work published 1925)

Freud, S. (1959b). Inhibitions, symptoms and anxiety. In J. Strachey (Ed. and Trans.), *The standard edition of the complete psychological works of Sigmund Freud* (Vol. 20, pp. 75–172). London: Hogarth Press. (Original work published 1926)

Freud, S. (1960a). Jokes and their relation to the unconscious. In J. Strachey (Ed. and Trans.), *The standard edition of the complete psychological works of Sigmund Freud* (Vol. 8). London: Hogarth Press. (Original work published 1905)

Freud, S. (1960b). The psychopathology of everyday life. In J. Strachey (Ed. and Trans.), *The standard edition of the complete psychological works of Sigmund Freud* (Vol. 6). London: Hogarth Press. (Original work published 1901)

Freud, S. (1961a). The ego and the id. In J. Strachey (Ed. and Trans.), *The standard edition of the complete psychological works of Sigmund Freud* (Vol. 19, pp. 1–59). London: Hogarth Press. (Original work published 1923)

Freud, S. (1961b). Introductory lectures on psychoanalysis. In J. Strachey (Ed. and Trans.), *The standard edition of the complete psychological works of Sigmund Freud* (Vols. 15–16). London: Hogarth Press. (Original work published 1916–17)

Freud, S. (1964a). Moses and monotheism: Three essays. In J. Strachey (Ed. and Trans.), *The standard edition of the complete psychological works of Sigmund Freud* (Vol. 23, pp. 1–17). London: Hogarth Press. (Original work published 1939)

Freud, S. (1964b). New introductory lectures on psychoanalysis. In J. Strachey (Ed. and Trans.), *The standard edition of the complete psychological works of Sigmund Freud* (Vol. 22, pp. 1–182). London: Hogarth Press. (Original work published 1933)

Freud, S. (1964c). An outline of psychoanalysis. In J. Strachey (Ed. and Trans.), *The standard edition of the complete psychological works of Sigmund Freud* (Vol. 23, pp. 139–208). London: Hogarth Press. (Original work published 1940)

Freud, S. (1966). Project for a scientific psychology. In J. Strachey (Ed. and Trans.), *The standard edition of the complete psychological works of Sigmund Freud* (Vol. 1, pp. 281–387). London: Hogarth Press. (Original work written 1895)

Freud, S., & Abraham, K. (1965). *A psychoanalytic dialogue: The letters of Sigmund Freud and Karl Abraham*. New York: Basic Books.

Freud, S., & Jung, C. (1974). *The Freud-Jung letters*. Princeton: Bollingen/Princeton University Press.

Gaillard, J.-M. (1989). Brain lateralization during sleep and dreaming. In J. Horne (Ed.), *Sleep '88*. (pp. 177–181). Stuttgart/New York: Fischer Verlag.

Garfield, P. L. (1974). *Creative dreaming*. New York: Ballantine.

Gill, M. M. (1967). The primary process. *Psychological Issues*, 5(2/3), Monograph 18/19, R. R. Holt (ed.), *Motives and thought: Psychoanalytic essays in honor of David Rapaport*, 260–298.

Gordon, H. W., Frooman, B., & Lavie, P. (1982). Shifts in cognitive asymmetries between wakings from REM and NREM sleep. *Neuropsychologia, 20,* 99–105.

Gutheil, E. A. (1951). *The handbook of dream analysis.* New York: Liveright.

Hall, C., & Van de Castle, R. (1966). *The content analysis of dreams.* New York: Appleton-Century-Crofts.

Hartmann, E. (1973). *The functions of sleep.* New Haven: Yale University Press.

Haskell, R. E. (1985). Dreaming cognition and physical illness. *Journal of Medical Humanities and Bio-Ethics, 6,* 109–122.

Herodotus (1988). Xeres and Artabanus [excerpt from Histories]. In G. Almansi & C. Béguin (Eds.), *Theatre of sleep: An anthology of literary dreams* (pp. 126–128). London: Picador.

Heynick, F. (1981a). Linguistic aspects of Freud's dream model. *International Review of Psycho-Analysis, 8,* 299–314.

Heynick, F. (1981b). Verbal aggression in Dutch sleeptalking. *Maledicta, 5,* 285–297.

Heynick, F. (1983a). Dream speech and neurobiological dream models. *Sleep Research, 12,* 179.

Heynick, F. (1983b). From Einstein to Whorf: Space, time, matter, and reference frames in physical and linguistic relativity. *Semiotica, 45*(1/2), 35–64.

Heynick, F. (1984). Verbal behavior in dreams: Neurolinguistic implications for LSP reading? In A. K. Pugh & J. M. Ulijn (Eds.), *Reading for professional purposes: Studies in native and foreign languages* (pp. 48–56). London: Heinemann Educational.

Heynick, F. (1985). Dream dialogue and retrogression: Neurolinguistic origins of Freud's "replay hypothesis." *Journal of the History of the Behavioral Sciences, 21,* 321–341.

Heynick, F. (1986). The dream scriptor and the Freudian ego: "Pragmatic competence" and superordinate and subordinate cognitive systems in sleep. *Journal of Mind and Behavior, 7,* 169–201.

Heynick, F. (1991). Linguistic and literary creativity in dreams: A psychoanalytic and an experimental approach. In J. Gackenbach (Ed.), *Dream Images* (pp. 79–96). Amityville NY: Baywood.

Heynick, F., & De Jong, M. A. (1985). Dreams elicited by telephone: A comparative content analysis. In W. P. Koella, E. Rüther, and H. Schulz (Eds.), *Sleep '84* (pp. 341–343). Stuttgart/New York: Fischer Verlag.

Hilgard, E. R. (1973). A neodissociation interpretation of pain reduction in hypnosis. *Psychological Review, 80,* 396–411.

Hobson, J. A. (1988). *The dreaming brain.* New York: Basic Books.

Hobson, J. A. & McCarley, R. (1977). The brain as dream-state generator: An activation-synthesis hypothesis. *American Journal of Psychiatry, 134,* 1335–1348.

Hoche, A. E. (1920). Mögliche Ziele der Traumforschung [The possible goals of dream research]. *Archiv für Psychiatrie, 61,* 451–454.

Hoche, A. E. (1922). Über Sprachbildung in Traume [On language production in dreams]. *Archiv für Psychiatrie, 64,* 618–622.

Hoche, A. E. (1923). Haben unsere Traumbilder halluzinatorischen Charakter? [Do our dream images have hallucinatory character?]. *Archiv für Psychiatrie, 67,* 110–113.

Hoche, A. E. (1927). *Das träumende Ich* [The dreaming ego]. Jena: Fischer Verlag.

Hoche, A. E. (1928). *Schlaf und Traum* [Sleep and dreams]. Berlin: Ullstein.

Hoff, P. (1991). Alzheimer and his time. In G. E. Berrios & H. L. Freeman (Eds.), *Eponymists in medicine: Alzheimer and the dementias* (pp. 29–55). London: Royal Society of Medicine Services.

Holt, R. R. (1967). The development of the primary process: A structural view. *Psychological Issues, 5,* 345.

Horne, J. (1988). *Why we sleep: The function of sleep in humans and other mammals.* Oxford: Oxford University Press.

Hotopf, W. H. N. (1980). Semantic similarity as a factor in whole-word slips of the tongue. In V. A. Fromkin (Ed.), *Errors in linguistic performance: Slips of the tongue, ear, pen, and hand* (pp. 97–110). New York: Academic Press.

Hunter R., & Macalpine, I. (1963). *Three hundred years of psychiatry.* London: Oxford University Press.

Isakower, O. (1939). The exceptional position of the auditory sphere. *International Journal of Psycho-Analysis, 20,* 340–348.

Isakower, O. (1954). Spoken words in dreams: A preliminary communication. *Psychoanalytic Quarterly, 23,* 1–6.

Jackson, J. H. (1958). *Selected writings of John Hughlings Jackson,* (J. Taylor, G. Holmes, & F. Wolse, Eds.). New York: Basic Books. (Original work published 1911)

Jones, E. (1951). *On the nightmare.* New York: Liveright.

Jones, E. (1953). *The life and work of Sigmund Freud* (Vol. 1). London: Hogarth Press.

Jouvet, M. (1978). Mémoires et "cerveau dédoublé" au cours du rêves: À propos de 2525 souvenirs de rêve [Memories and "split brain" during dreaming: Based on 2525 dream recalls]. *L'Année du Practicien, 29,* 30–31.

Jouvet, M., & Delorme, F. (1965). Locus coeruleus et sommeil paradoxal [Locus coeruleus and paradoxal sleep]. *C.R. Société Biologique, 159,* 895–899.

Jung, C. G. (1919). *Studies in word association* (M. D. Eder, Ed. and Trans.). New York: Moffat.

Jung, C. G. (1967). *Memories, dreams, reflections* (R. Winston & C. Winston, Trans.). London: Collins/Fontana. (Original work published 1961)

Jung, C. G. (1974). *Dreams* (R. F. C. Hull, Trans.). Princeton: Bollinger/Princeton University Press.

Kempen, G. (1981). De architektuur van het spreken [The architecture of speaking]. *Tijdschrift voor Taal- en Tekstwetenschap, 2*, 110–123.

Kempen, G., & Van Wijk, C. (1981). Leren formuleren [Learning to formulate]. *Tijdschrift voor Taalbeheering, 3*, 32–44.

Kohlschütter, E. (1862). Messungen der Festigkeit des Schlafes [Measurements on the soundness of sleep], *Zeitschrift für rationelle Medicin (3R), 17*, 210–253.

Kohlschütter, E. (1869). Mechanik des Schlafes [Mechanism of sleep], *Zeitschrift für rationelle Medicin, 34*, 46.

Kolata, G. (1988, March 27). The good clean fun of dreaming [review of J. Alan Hobson's *The Dreaming Brain*]. *New York Times*, Book Review Section, p. 36.

Kolb, L. C. (1977). *Modern Clinical Psychiatry*. Philadelphia: W.B. Saunders.

Kopland, R. (1977). *An empty place to stay* (R. Leigh-Loohuizen, Trans.). San Francisco: Twin Peaks Press.

Kopland, R. (1987). *The prospect and the river* (J. Brockway, Trans.). London: Jackson's Arm.

Kopland, R. (1991). *A world beyond myself* (J. Brockway, Trans.). London: Enitharmon Press.

Kraepelin, E. (1920). Die Erscheinungsformen des Irreseins [The manifestations of insanity]. *Zeitschrift für die gesamte Neurologie und Psychiatrie (Orig.), 62*, 1–29.

Kraepelin, E. (1962). *One hundred years of psychiatry* (W. Baskin, Trans.). London: Peter Owen. (Original work published 1918)

Kraepelin, E. (1987). *Memoirs* (C. Wooding-Deane, Trans.). Berlin: Springer Verlag. (Original work completed 1919 and published 1983)

LaBerg, S. (1985). *Lucid dreaming*. New York: Ballantine Books.

Lackner, J. R. (1980). Speech production: Correction of semantic and grammatical errors during speech shadowing. In V. A. Fromkin (Ed.), *Errors in linguistic performance: Slips of the tongue, ear, pen and hand* (pp. 157–164). New York: Academic Press.

Ladd, G. T. (1882). Contribution to the psychology of visual dreams. *Mind* (New Series), *1*, 299.

Laver, J. (1980). Monitoring systems in the neurolinguistic control of speech production. In V. A. Fromkin (Ed.), *Errors in linguistic performance: Slips of the tongue, ear, pen, and hand* (pp. 287–306). New York: Academic Press.

Leibniz, G. W. (1967). *Philosophical papers and letters* (Vol. 1) (L. E. Loemker, Trans. and Ed.). Chicago: University of Chicago Press. (Original work published 1666–1667)

Lemattre, G. (1870). Transfusion du sang [Blood transfusion]. *Revue des Deux Mondes, XL* (sec. période), 387–406.

Lesser, R. (1978). *Linguistic investigation of aphasia*. London: Edward Arnold.

Lucretius (1987). On dreams [excerpt from De natura rerum]. In G. Almansi & C. Béguin (Eds.), *Theatre of sleep: An anthology of literary dreams* (pp. 133–134). London: Picador.

Maeder, A. (1912). Über die Function des Traumes [On the function of dreams]. *Jahrbuch für psychoanalytische und psychopatholgische Forschungen, 4,* 692.

Mahoney P., & Singh, R. (1975). *The interpretation of dreams,* semiology and Chomskian linguistics: A radical critique. *Psychoanalytic Study of the Child, 30,* 222–241.

Malcolm, N. (1959). *Dreaming.* London: Routledge & Kegan Paul.

Marshall, J. C. (1974). Freud's psychology of language. In R. Wollheim (Ed.), *Freud: A collection of critical essays* (pp. 349–365). New York: Anchor/Doubleday.

Maury, A. (1848). Des hallucinations hypnagogiques ou des erreurs des sens dans l'état intermediaire entre le sommeil et la veille [On hypnagogic hallucinations or sensory errors in the intermediate state between sleep and wakefulness]. *Annales Médico-Psychologiques, tôme 11.*

Maury, A. (1857). De certains faits observés dans les rêves et dans l'état intermediaire entre le sommeil et la veille [On certain data observed in dreams and in the intermediate state between sleep and wakefulness]. *Annales Médico-Psychologiques, sev. 3, tôme 3,* 157–176.

Maury, A. (1861). *Le sommeil et les rêves* [Sleep and dreams]. Paris.

McCarley, R., & Hobson, J. A. (1977). The neurobiological origins of the psychoanalytic dream theory. *American Journal of Psychiatry, 134,* 1211–1221.

Meringer, R., & Mayer, K. (1895). *Versprechen und Verlesen: Eine psychologisch-linguistische Studie* [Slips of the tongue and in reading: a psychological-linguistic study]. Stuttgart: Göschensche Verlagbuchhandlung.

Meumann, E. (1907). Über Organempfindungsträume und eine merkwürdige Traumerinnerung [On dreams with organic sensations and a curious dream recollection]. *Archiv für die gesamte Psychologie, 9,* 26–62.

Michelson, E. (1899). Untersuchungen über die Tiefe des Schlafes [Investigations into the depth of sleep]. In E. Kraepelin (Ed.), *Psychologische Arbeiten* (zweiter Band, pp. 84–117). Leipzig: Engelmann.

Moors-Messmer, H. von. (1938). Traume mit gleichzeitigen Erkenntis des Traumzustandes [Dreams with simultaneous recognition of the dream state]. *Archiv für Psychologie, 102,* 291–318.

Moser, U., Pfeifer, R., Schneider, W., von Zeppelin, I., & Schneider, H. (1983). Experiences with computer simulation of dream processes. In W. P. Koella (Ed.), *Sleep 1982* (pp. 30–44). Basel: Karger.

Motley, M. T. (1980). "Freudian slips" and semantic prearticulatory editing. In V. A. Fromkin (Ed.), *Errors in linguistic performance: Slips of the tongue, ear, pen, and hand* (pp. 133–147). New York: Academic Press.

Newcombe, F., & Marshall, J. C. (1980). Transcoding and lexical stabilization in deep dyslexia. In M. Coltheart, K. Patterson, and J. C. Marshall (Eds.), *Deep dyslexia* (pp. 176–188). London: Routledge & Kegan Paul.

Norman, D. A. (1981). Categorization of action slips. *Psychological Review, 5,* 1–5.

Noy, P. (1969). A revision of the psychoanalytic theory of the primary process. *International Journal of Psycho-Analysis, 50,* 155–178.

Noy, P. (1979). The psychoanalytic theory of cognitive development. *Psychoanalytic Study of the Child, 34,* 169–216.

O'Shaughnessey, B. (1974). The id and the thinking process. In R. Wollheim (Ed.), *Freud: A collection of critical essays* (pp. 222–241). New York: Anchor/Doubleday.

Oswald, I. (1962). *Sleeping and waking: Physiology and psychology.* New York: Elsevier.

Palombo, S. (1978). *Dreaming and memory: A new information-processing model.* New York: Basic Books.

Penfield, W., & Jasper, H. (1954). *Epilepsy and functional anatomy of the human brain.* Boston: Little Brown.

Piaget, J. (1937). *The construction of reality in the child.* New York: Basic Books.

Piaget, J. (1962). *Play, dreams and imitation in childhood.* London: Routledge & Keagan Paul. (Original work published 1951)

Plato (1987). The illusion of the senses [excerpt from Theaetetus or of the soul]. In G. Almansi & C. Béguin (Eds.), *Theatre of sleep: An anthology of literary dreams* (pp. 128–129). London: Picador.

Porter, R. (1987). *A social history of madness: Stories of the insane.* London: Weidenfeld & Nicholson.

Potter, J. M. (1980). What was the matter with Dr. Spooner?. In V. A. Fromkin (Ed.), *Errors in linguistic performance: Slips of the tongue, ear, pen and hand* (pp. 13–34). New York: Academic Press.

Preyer, W. (1876). Über die Ursachen des Schlafes [On the causes of sleep], *Tagblatt* der 49. Versammlung Deutscher Naturforscher und Ärzte, Beilage september, 16–20. Hamburg: Friederichsen.

Proctor, R. N. (1988). *Racial hygiene: Medicine under the Nazis*. Cambridge: Harvard.

Proust, M. (1987). Swann's dream [excerpt from Swann's way]. In G. Almansi & C. Béguin (Eds.), *Theatre of sleep: An anthology of literary dreams* (pp. 82–84). London: Picador. (Original work published 1913)

Quillian, M. R. (1967). Word concepts: A theory and simulation of some basic semantic capabilities. *Behavioral Science, 12*, 410–430.

Quirk, R., & Svartvik, P. (1966). *Investigating linguistic acceptibility*. The Hague: Mouton.

Rapaport, D. (1960). The structure of psychoanalytic theory: A systematizing attempt. *Psychological Issues, 6*, 1–158.

Rechtschaffen, A. (1978). The single-mindedness and isolation of dreams. *Sleep, 1*, 97–109.

Robert, W. (1886). *Der Traum als Naturnotwendigkeit erklärt* [Dreams explained as natural necessity]. Hamburg.

Roffwarg, H., Muzio, J., & Dement, W. (1966). Ontogenetic development of human sleep-dream cycle. *Science, 152*, 604–618.

Russell, B. (1948). *Human Knowledge*. London: Allen & Unwin.

Rycroft, C. (1979). *The innocence of dreams*. New York: Pantheon.

Salzarulo, P., & Cipolli, C. (1974). Spontaneously recalled verbal material and its linguistic organization in relation to different stages of sleep. *Biological Psychology, 2*, 47–57.

Sasanuma, S. (1980). Acquired dyslexia in Japanese: Clinical features and underlying mechanisms. In M. Coltheart, K. Patterson, and J. C. Marshall (Eds.), *Deep dyslexia* (pp. 160–188). London: Routledge & Kegan Paul.

Schaltenbrand, G. (1975). The effects on speech and language of stereotactical stimulation in thalmus and corpus callosum. *Brain and Language, 2*, 70–80.

Scherner, K. A. (1861). *Das Leben des Traumes* [The life of the dream]. Berlin.

Searleman, A. (1977). A review of right hemisphere linguistic capabilities. *Psychological Bulletin, 84*, 503–528.

Sebeok, T. A., & Umiker-Sebeok, J. (1979). Performing animals: Secrets of the trade. *Psychology Today, 13*(11), 78–91.

Shattuck-Hufnagel, S., & Klatt, D. H. (1980). How single phoneme error data rule out two models of error generation. In V. A. Fromkin (Ed.), *Errors in linguistic performance: Slips of the tongue, ear, pen, and hand* (pp. 35–46). New York: Academic Press.

Shimizu, A. & Inoue, T. (1986). Dreamed speech and muscle activity. *Psychophysiology, 23,* 210–213.

Snyder, F. (1966). Towards an evolutionary theory of dreaming. *American Journal of Psychiatry, 123,* 121–142.

Snyder, F. (1970). The phenomenology of dreaming. In L. Madow and L. H. Snow (Eds.), *The psycho-dynamic implications of the physiological studies on dreams* (pp. 124–151). Springfield, IL: Charles C. Thomas.

Söderpalm Talo, E. (1980). Slips of the tongue in normal and pathological speech. In V. A. Fromkin (Ed.), *Errors in linguistic performance: Slips of the tongue, ear, pen, and hand* (pp. 81–86). New York: Academic Press.

Sperry, R. W. (1973). Lateral specialization of cerebral function in the surgically separated hemispheres. In F. J. McGuigan and R. A. Schoonover (Eds.), *The psychophysiology of thinking: Studies of covert processes.* New York: Academic Press.

Spinoza, B. (1951). *A theologico-political treatise* (R. H. M. Elwes, Trans.). New York: Dover. (Original work published 1677)

Spinoza, B. (1955). *On the improvement of the understanding; The ethics; Correspondence* (R. H. M. Elwes, Trans.). New York: Dover. (Original work published 1677)

Steiner, G. (1987). Before language. In G. Almansi & C. Béguin (Eds.), *Theatre of sleep: An anthology of literary dreams* (p. 116). London: Picador.

Sully, J. (1893). The dream as revelation. *Fortnightly Review, 53,* 354.

Swan, T. H. (1929). A note on Kohlschütter's curve on the 'depth of sleep.' *Psychological Bulletin, 26,* 607–610.

Terrace, H. S. (1979). How Nim Chimsky changed my mind. *Psychology Today, 13*(6), 65–76.

Ullman, M., & Zimmerman, N. (1979). *Working with dreams.* New York: Laurel/Dell.

Van de Castle, R. L. (1973). The psychology of dreaming. In S. G. M. Lee & A. R. Mayes (Eds.), *Dreams and dreaming* (pp. 17–32). Harmondsworth, England: Penguin Educational.

Van Praag, H. (1974). Sleep research: Its impact on biological psychiatry. In H. M. Van Praag and M. Meinardi (Eds.), *Brain and sleep* (pp. 3–6). Amsterdam: De Erven Bohn.

Van Wijk, C., & Kempen, G. (1982a). De ontwikkeling van syntactische formuleerbaarheid bij kinderen van 9 tot 16 jaar [The development of syntactic formulability in 9- to 16-year-olds]. *Nederlands Tijdschrift voor de Psychologie, 37,* 491–509.

Van Wijk, C., & Kempen, G. (1982b). Syntactische formuleervaardigheid en het schrijven van opstellen [Syntactic formulation skills and the writing of compositions]. *Pedagogische Studieen, 59,* 126–136.

Werner, H., & Kaplan, B. (1963). *Symbol formation: An organismic and developmental approach to language and the expression of thought.* New York: Wiley.

West, L. J. (1967). The dissociative reaction. In A. M. Freedman and H. J. Kaplan (Eds.). *Comprehensive Textbook of Psychiatry* (pp. 885–899). Baltimore: Williams & Wilkins.

Wolheim, R. (1971). *Freud.* Glasgow: Fontana/Collins.

Wundt, W. (1896). *Lectures on human and animal psychology* (J. E. Creighton & E. B. Titchener, Trans.). New York: Macmillian. (Original work published 1892)

Wundt, W. (1900). *Völkerpsychologie: Teil I. Die Sprache* [Ethnopsychology Vol. I. Language]. Leipzig.

Wundt, W. (1906). *Völkerpsychologie: Teil II. Mythus und Religion* [Ethnopsychology: Vol. II. Myth and religion]. Leipzig.

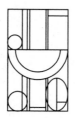

Author Index

References in **bold type** refer to the translated works
of Kraepelin, Meumann, Hacker, and Hoche.

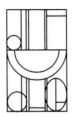

Subject Index

References in **bold type** refer to the translated works
of Kraepelin, Meumann, Hacker, and Hoche.